THE ARTHUR

OF THE GERMANS

Statue of King Arthur at the monumental tomb of Emperor Maximilian I in the Hofkirche, Innsbruck. Photograph by kind permission of the Tiroler Volkskunstmuseum, Innsbruck.

ARTHURIAN LITERATURE IN THE MIDDLE AGES

III

THE
ARTHUR
OF THE
GERMANS

THE ARTHURIAN LEGEND IN MEDIEVAL GERMAN AND DUTCH LITERATURE

edited by

W. H. Jackson and S. A. Ranawake

CARDIFF
UNIVERSITY OF WALES PRESS
2000

British Library Cataloguing-in-Publication Data.
A catalogue record for this book is available from the British Library.

ISBN 0–7083–1595–X

Typeset at University of Wales Press
Printed in Great Britain by Cambrian Printers, Aberystwyth

ARTHURIAN LITERATURE IN THE MIDDLE AGES

Series Editor

W. R. J. Barron

I   The Arthur of the Welsh
Edited by Rachel Bromwich, A. O. H. Jarman, Brynley F. Roberts
(Cardiff, 1991)

II   The Arthur of the English
Edited by W. R. J. Barron   (Cardiff, 1999)

III   The Arthur of the Germans
Edited by W. H. Jackson and S. A. Ranawake   (Cardiff, 2000)

IV   The Arthur of the French
Edited by G. S. Burgess and Karen Pratt   (in preparation)

V   The Arthur of the Iberians
Edited by David Hook   (in preparation)

Further volumes in preparation

The *ALMA* series is a co-operation between
the University of Wales Press and the Vinaver Trust

CONTENTS

PREFACE

When, some years ago, the Vinaver Trust considered revising the standard history of its academic field, *Arthurian Literature in the Middle Ages* (ed. R. S. Loomis, Oxford, 1959), the authors of the opening chapters on Celtic texts were the first to be approached. Their feeling was that the passage of time and the advance of scholarship made necessary a more fundamental revision than was possible within the original single-volume format. The book had served several generations of students well, but the Trustees were persuaded that the time had come for a more fundamental approach to Arthurian literary history.

ALMA, as it appeared in the Abbreviations to a hundred volumes, had reflected its editor's professional interest closely and, even within the limitations of a single volume, given a rather narrow picture of Arthurian studies. Changing perspectives, the accumulation of scholarship and the more flexible technology of publishing now make possible a fuller record. The basis of the volumes listed on p. vi is cultural rather than purely linguistic, as more appropriate to a period when modern nationalism, and in many cases modern nation states, had not yet evolved. Each takes into account extraneous influences and includes some texts which the influence of the mother culture carried into the wider world.

Each volume in the series is primarily addressed to students of the individual culture in question, but also to those of other cultures who, for the appreciation of their own Arthurian literature, need to be aware of the various expressions of the legend. With this dual readership in mind, the volumes aim to present the present state of knowledge as individual contributors see it, concisely expressed and structured in a way which, it is hoped, will help readers to appreciate the development of Arthurian themes within the particular culture. The contributors also address the needs of specialist scholars by discussing current academic controversies, and themselves treating open questions of research.

Within this remit, the editors have had complete control over their individual volumes. They themselves would admit that they have not ensnared that rare bird, the Whole Truth of the Arthurian legend, and that in time a new survey will be needed, perhaps on a different basis. But if, for the moment, they have allowed others to catch a glimpse of that universal phoenix, the Arthurian myth, through the thickets of academic speculation, they will feel that they have done what was presently necessary.

W. R. J. Barron

ACKNOWLEDGEMENTS

The production of this volume has been made possible by financial support from the Vinaver Trust. Individual contributions have been supported by research grants from the British Academy, the Trinity College Cambridge Research Fund and the Research Funds of the Schools of Modern Languages of Queen Mary and Westfield College and the University of St Andrews. Translations into English of some chapters received subsidies from the Royal Netherlands Academy of Arts and Sciences and the Vinaver Trust respectively. We are grateful to the translators Stewart Spencer and Ans Bulles for their painstaking work, to Fiona Campbell for her work on the index, to Karen Pratt for expert advice on the chapter on the Western Background and to Ray Barron for his generous help with editorial matters. Emma Wagstaff provided practical assistance with the preparation of the *Tristan* chapter. The project benefited greatly from the secretarial support provided by the Queen Mary and Westfield School of Modern Languages, and we are particularly grateful to Nicola McGee for secretarial help and her unfailing patience and commitment. We further wish to acknowledge the assistance of the Queen Mary and Westfield College Arts Computing Centre. Finally, we acknowledge our gratitude to the staff of the University of Wales Press for their helpful efficiency in producing the volume.

THE CONTRIBUTORS

DR ELIZABETH ANDERSEN, University of Newcastle upon Tyne, UK

DR BERND BASTERT, Universität zu Köln, Germany

PROFESSOR DR BART BESAMUSCA, Universiteit Utrecht, The Netherlands

DR MARK CHINCA, University of Cambridge, UK

PROFESSOR JOHN L. FLOOD, Institute of Germanic Studies, University of London, UK

DR MARION GIBBS, Royal Holloway and Bedford New College, University of London, UK

PROFESSOR DR VOLKER HONEMANN, Westfälische Wilhelms-Universität Münster, Germany

DR W. H. JACKSON, University of St Andrews, UK

PROFESSOR DR INGRID KASTEN, Freie Universität Berlin, Germany

TIMOTHY MCFARLAND, University College London, University of London, UK

PROFESSOR DR VOLKER MERTENS, Freie Universität Berlin, Germany

DR MATTHIAS MEYER, Freie Universität Berlin, Germany

PROFESSOR DR ULRICH MÜLLER, Universität Salzburg, Austria

PROFESSOR SILVIA RANAWAKE, Queen Mary and Westfield College, University of London, UK

PROFESSOR JAMES RUSHING, Rutgers University, Camden College of Arts and Sciences, USA

JOHN E. TAILBY, University of Leeds, UK

PROFESSOR ALFRED THOMAS, Barker Center, Cambridge, Mass., USA

DR ROSEMARY WALLBANK, formerly University of Manchester, UK

PROFESSOR DR WERNER WUNDERLICH, HSG Hochschule St Gallen, Switzerland

ABBREVIATIONS

ABäG	*Amsterdamer Beiträge zur älteren Germanistik*, Amsterdam
AfdA	*Anzeiger für deutsches Altertum*, Wiesbaden
AfK	*Archiv für Kulturgeschichte*, Cologne
AL	*Arthurian Literature*, Woodbridge, Suffolk
AStnSpr	*Archiv für das Studium der neueren Sprachen*, Braunschweig
ATB	Altdeutsche Textbibliothek, Tübingen
BBIAS	*Bibliographical Bulletin of the International Arthurian Society*, Madison
BLV	Bibliothek des Literarischen Vereins, Stuttgart and Tübingen
CFMA	Classiques français du moyen âge, Paris
ColG	*Colloquia Germanica*, Berne
DVj	*Deutsche Vierteljahrsschrift für Literaturwissenschaft und Geistesgeschichte*, Stuttgart
Euph	*Euphorion*, Heidelberg
FCS	*Fifteenth-Century Studies*, Marygrove College, Detroit
FMLS	*Forum for Modern Language Studies*, St Andrews
GAG	Göppinger Arbeiten zur Germanistik, Göppingen
GLL	*German Life and Letters*, Oxford
GR	*Germanic Review*, Columbia University, New York
GRM	*Germanisch-romanische Monatsschrift*, Heidelberg
HJb	*Heidelberger Jahrbücher*, Berlin
IASL	*Internationales Archiv für Sozialgeschichte der deutschen Literatur*, Tübingen
JEGP	*Journal of English and Germanic Philology*, University of Illinois, Urbana
KTRM	Klassische Texte des romanischen Mittelalters, Munich
LiLi	*Zeitschrift für Literaturwissenschaft und Linguistik*, Göttingen
MA	*Le Moyen Age*, Brussels

Med. Aev.	*Medium Aevum*, Oxford
MHRA	Modern Humanities Research Association
MLA	Modern Language Association
MLQ	*Modern Language Quarterly*, University of Wisconsin, Madison
MLR	*Modern Language Review*, London
MTU	Münchener Texte und Untersuchungen zur deutschen Literatur des Mittelalters
NdW	*Niederdeutsches Wort*, Münster
Neophil	*Neophilologus*, Groningen
NM	*Neuphilologische Mitteilungen*, Helsinki
NTg	*De nieuwe taalgids*, Groningen
OGS	*Oxford German Studies*
PBB	*Pauls und Braunes Beiträge zur Geschichte der deutschen Sprache und Literatur*
PMLA	*Publications of the Modern Language Association of America*, New York
RhVjbl	*Rheinische Vierteljahrsblätter*, Bonn
Rom	*Romania*, Paris
RUB	Reclams Universal-Bibliothek, Stuttgart
Spec	*Speculum*, Medieval Academy of America, Cambridge, Mass.
St Med	*Studies in Medievalism*, Oxford, Ohio
TLF	Textes Littéraires Français, Geneva
TNTL	*Tijdschrift voor Nederlandse Taal- en Letterkunde*, Leiden
VL	*Die deutsche Literatur des Mittelalters. Verfasserlexikon*, 2nd edn, ed. by K. Ruh *et al.*, 1978–, Berlin and New York
WB	*Weimarer Beiträge*, Vienna
WdF	Wege der Forschung
WSt	Wolfram-Studien
ZfdA	*Zeitschrift für deutsches Altertum*, Wiesbaden
ZfdPh	*Zeitschrift für deutsche Philologie*, Berlin
ZfrPh	*Zeitschrift für romanische Philologie*, Tübingen

INTRODUCTION

W. H. Jackson and Silvia Ranawake

As part of the Vinaver Trust project to survey afresh the spectrum of Arthurian literature in the Middle Ages, the present volume is devoted to the German and Dutch fields. The two terms are in the first instance linguistic descriptors, indicating literature that was produced and transmitted in Dutch and in German as languages. Moreover, 'German' and 'Dutch' do not have the same meanings when applied to the medieval period as they do today, for, whereas the terms now refer to two different (though clearly related) languages, in the Middle Ages Dutch and German were only just beginning to separate out as distinct languages, and both were still part of the Continental West Germanic language continuum that was known as *tiutsch* in Middle High German and *dietsch* in Middle Dutch (Beckers 1995, 147). Whilst the modern terms 'Dutch' and 'German' are used throughout this volume, the term 'German' in the main title of the volume should be understood in the medieval, integrative sense of the word *dietsch* or *tiutsch*.

These linguistic categories point to communities of speakers from areas of northern and central continental Europe that were geographically linked, but differed in size and cultural complexity, and within and between which there were varying degrees of social, political and cultural exchange. Overall, the areas concerned stretch from the South Tirol to the North Sea and Baltic coasts, and from the borders of France in the west to the kingdom of Bohemia in the east. During the period when Arthurian literature spread in the Middle Ages, the speakers of Dutch lived in principalities which owed titular allegiance to the French or German rulers but were in fact more like 'independent "mini-states"' (Prevenier 1994, 12). The kingdom of Germany itself was a conglomeration of lordships which combined considerable independence with a degree of cohesion that derived from shared social and cultural traditions.

The historical and geographical scope of the volume marks a key stage in the diffusion of the Arthurian legend, when it spread outward from France; and the interplay of common features and variables in the treatment of Arthurian themes throws light on the cultural history of the areas under consideration and on the transmission of Arthurian material in Europe as a whole. In the Dutch and German areas, Arthurian literature was first adopted from French sources, and then indigenous works were also produced. Almost all the sizeable corpus of medieval Dutch Arthurian works seems to have been produced in the thirteenth century. The corpus of texts and their chronological spread is larger yet in medieval German literature, with major Arthurian works arising as early as the late twelfth century and as late as the last quarter of the fifteenth century.

The kingdom of Bohemia formed part of the Holy Roman Empire. Here German-speakers interacted with speakers of Czech in the upper levels of society, and towards the end of the fourteenth century two Arthurian works were adapted from German into Czech. The Czech romances will also be discussed briefly in this volume. Their reception is important in showing a further eastward spread of Arthurian literature into the Slav world through the medium of German, and they also have features which are characteristic of late medieval adaptations of chivalric romances in other parts of Europe: a certain medial-style realism, and some reduction and simplification of the courtly ideology of the high medieval romance (see the contribution by Alfred Thomas in this volume).

The main focus of the present volume is on Arthurian literature. However, literature had a strong social dimension in the Middle Ages, which is expressed for instance in the relation of author and patron, in didactic narration, in the articulation of group values and in the performance situation of oral delivery. The chapters on literary works contain much information about their wider role, and the volume also considers Arthurian material in other fields of social life so as to build up a broader picture of its cultural impact. The thematic range of the volume expresses the wealth and complexity of the Arthurian contribution from this large and varied part of Europe. At the same time it is useful to plot pathways through the material, and the remainder of the Introduction will draw some of the main strands of the individual chapters together and add further connecting links so as to provide a brief overview of the emergence, spread and range of the Arthurian subjects treated in the volume, highlighting some major trends and acting as a framework for the individual contributions. An introductory survey is particularly appropriate for the German field, which is complex in itself and is spread over many different contributors. Information about research on specific texts or topics is provided in the individual contributions, and the reader is also directed to the useful discussions of recent scholarship on medieval Arthurian literature in the Low Countries by Bart Besamusca (1996) and in Germany by William C. McDonald (1996).

There was a considerable expansion of literary activity in the German empire from the twelfth century onwards. Arthurian literature played a major part in this process, and German works are established in the canon of European Arthurian literature. Arthur, his court and the knights of the Round Table first appear in German literature in the late twelfth century. However, there are important unanswered questions about the beginnings of Arthurian literature in German and in Dutch which arise largely from two pieces of evidence. First, Arthurian names are recorded in the Low Countries already in the early twelfth century, while the earliest Middle Dutch Arthurian texts date from the thirteenth century. Consequently, some knowledge of the Arthurian subject matter is postulated for this north-western area before the extant texts. And second, the earliest Arthurian romances produced in southern Germany, by Hartmann von Aue, Ulrich von Zatzikhoven and Wolfram von Eschenbach, in the years around 1200, were adaptations from French sources, but these works also contain linguistic features of north-western origin. These findings have sparked heated debate about the early history of Arthurian literature in the German and Dutch areas, as the questions pose themselves: what knowledge of Arthurian matters underlies the use of names in the north-west, and by what route did words of north-western origin find their way into Arthurian works produced much further south?

In answer to these questions some scholars have postulated the existence of a lost corpus of Arthurian literature that was produced somewhere along the Lower Rhine before the earliest existing texts, and of which no manuscript traces have been preserved, but which has left its mark on the southern German texts. Pentti Tilvis (1959) went so far as to hypothesize that the earliest German Arthurian romances, by Hartmann von Aue, were not, as is commonly held, adapted directly from the French works of Chrétien de Troyes, but were based on lost Arthurian works from the area of the Lower Rhine which reflected a pre-Chrétien stage of the stories. Tilvis does not produce firm evidence to support his hypothesis in its extreme form, but the matters he addresses cannot be said to be settled yet. It has also been argued that Wolfram von Eschenbach drew on the Middle Dutch Arthurian romance *Moriaen* in composing his *Parzival*, which would involve dating a *Moriaen* text around 1200. However, David Wells (1971/3) has shown that the parallels between *Moriaen* and *Parzival* are too general to indicate direct dependence, and he dates the Dutch text after 1250, thus eliminating it as a piece of evidence in support of a corpus of twelfth-century Arthurian literature. Similarly, Beckers convincingly rejects the view that Wolfram may have taken his *Parzival* from a Middle Franconian *Parcheval* which was itself a version of the Middle Dutch *Perchevael* (1989a, 214).

Beckers brings a balanced and open-minded view of the old question of a lost Rhenish German Arthurian literature. Whilst rejecting some of the more extreme claims, he points out that manuscript fragments of the *Parcheval*, the *Prosa-Lancelot* and a Merlin poem show that there were, in the thirteenth and early fourteenth centuries, Arthurian interests in the Rhenish border area linking Dutch- and German-speakers, and this, together with the onomastic evidence, suggests that the possibility of some literary treatment of Arthurian matter here in the twelfth century should not be dismissed out of hand (Becker 1989a; 1989b, 29–31). There is little reason to doubt that the German authors who introduced Arthurian romance in south Germany in the years around 1200 were indeed working from French sources. However, they may also have had access to Arthurian traditions that were cultivated in the north-west and that provided name forms and other elements of vocabulary. How extensive this lost repertoire might have been, and whether it was transmitted orally or in written stories, or both, escapes our knowledge. But it seems clear that, already in the twelfth century, there was a degree of Arthurian interest that went beyond the extant texts.

If we turn to German (as opposed to Dutch) literature, the main types of narrative in which the Arthurian world figures, Arthurian romances proper, Grail romances and Tristan romances (though the relation of the Tristan theme and the Arthurian world was an uneasy and shifting one), were all established here by the first decade of the thirteenth century and in the hands of leading poets whose work transformed the German literary scene and rapidly acquired canonical status: Hartmann von Aue, Wolfram von Eschenbach and Gottfried von Strassburg. A lively production particularly of Arthurian romances continued throughout the thirteenth century; Hans-Jochen Schiewer (1988, 224) calculates that evidence exists of twenty-four post-classical German 'Artus-romane' (and this number does not include treatments of the Tristan theme, or the Titurel and Lohengrin works).

Even the first generation of German Arthurian, Grail and Tristan romances were never straight translations in a modern sense, but adaptations which often showed much independence of style and attitude; and during the thirteenth century works were produced that were no longer based on individual French sources, so that the German Arthurian world, whilst preserving a connection to the French matrix that generated the international themes and concepts of Arthurian chivalry, developed its own distinctive profile.

The thirteenth century also saw the introduction of prose Arthurian literature in Germany, with at least part of the German *Prosa-Lancelot* dating back to around 1250. However, it is a feature of the German cultural scene that prose, with its historiographical associations, remained a minor strand in Arthurian literature. In England, Geoffrey of Monmouth presented Arthur in a historio-graphical manner, and Geoffrey's portrayal of the Arthurian world was used in historically real constitutional documents (Ullmann 1965). In its reception in France the Arthurian subject matter initially preserved some connection with the Plantagenet dynasty (Schmolke-Hasselmann 1980, 232–44), but it also acquired greater fictional independence, whilst in Germany Arthurian literature arose quite separately from historiography. Here the Arthurian romances were further removed from specific dynastic interests and had (even) more of a fictional status than was the case in England and France. In Germany, the influential Arthurian genealogy of Wolfram von Eschenbach hindered the link-up of the Arthurian world with Troy and the Roman empire that was familiar in the Anglo-French cultural area, and it seems to have been only with the reception of Latin historiography from the fourteenth century onwards that Arthur gradually found his place as a historical figure in German writings (Kornrumpf 1984, 180f.).

The late twelfth to the end of the thirteenth century is the period of greatest productivity in medieval German Arthurian narratives. Further Arthurian subject matter was introduced into Germany from France in the *Rappoltsteiner Parzifal* in the first half of the fourteenth century; and in the late fifteenth century Ulrich Füetrer adapted older German Arthurian romances and linked the Arthurian world with the story of Troy in the massive Arthurian cycle of his *Buch der Abenteuer*. These two works are characteristic of a late medieval tendency to gather material into large summations. Continuing interest in Arthurian subject matter is further evidenced in the manuscript transmission of earlier works during the fourteenth and fifteenth centuries. Finally, a few works made their way into printed editions, so that the history of medieval German Arthurian narratives covers the shifts from oral presentation (which still strongly informs the style of early romances) to written literature, and then from manuscript to printed book.

The rise of Arthurian romance in Germany had as its essential social context the lordly households, the courts, which formed the main centres of cultural activity and large-scale sociability for the aristocracy, and which provided the material resources necessary for a spread of literary activity into the sphere of the vernacular and of secular culture (Bumke 1986, Fleckenstein 1990). Far from being static and homogeneous institutions, these courts were characterized by cultural complexity, even tension, which sprang from the interaction of groups and individuals whose value-systems did not always smoothly harmonize: noble and knightly males who cultivated a dynastic and military ethos; aristocratic women who were objects of poetic veneration, but who had a far more restricted legal condition than their male counterparts; clerically trained men who had the literary skills needed for the production of romances; and individuals who combined characteristics of more than one group, such as the educated knight Hartmann von Aue.

Arthurian literature arose from this cultural mingling, and constructs a fictional world which was closely geared to the upper levels of society. Arthurian romance is an important expression of the cultural self-understanding of the

German aristocracy in the figure of the knight as warrior and lover, a figure that provided the aristocracies of Europe with a supranational cultural identity. The spread of Arthurian interests is closely connected with the rise and spread of other supranational chivalric forms in German society (knighting ceremonies, tournaments); and the recurrent descriptions of noble *realia*, which are a stylistic feature of courtly romance, testify both to the authors' drawing on Latin poetics and to the sociologically normative function of romance in aristocratic life.

German Arthurian literature was cultivated chiefly at non-royal courts, but it does not show a particular anti-royal tendency (though there is criticism of royal tyranny); rather it springs from a large-scale political situation of the twelfth and thirteenth centuries in Germany, when, in spite of frequent conflicts between kings and disaffected princes, as there were conflicts between the magnates themselves, there was also 'an extraordinary degree of interdependence and cooperation between king and princes' (Arnold 1991, 11). In the thirteenth century in particular, when the Capetian kings of France were gaining ground at the expense of the great nobles, the current was if anything running in the opposite direction in Germany, where the magnates who, so far as we can see, were the chief sponsors of romance had less reason to fear the power of the crown. Within the nobility, Arthurian literature met the interests of great lords and lesser nobles, for instance by propagating the image of the knight as defender of justice, which gave ethical legitimacy to the nobles' bearing of arms (and helped to draw a line of social demarcation between the nobility and other groups), and which also matched the state-building efforts of rulers who aimed to stabilize peace and justice. Violence and the control of violence were ever-present problems amongst the sword-bearing aristocracy of medieval Germany, and they are recurrent themes in Arthurian romance.

There is no record of a medieval German narrative involving King Arthur having been written by a woman. However, ample evidence, including comments drawn from Arthurian literature, shows that women formed an influential part of the literary public in the formative period of the twelfth and thirteenth centuries (Bumke 1986, 704–6). The recurrent portrayal of violence against women in Arthurian romances is a reminder of the strength of patriarchal forces in society at this time. At the same time important thematic and stylistic features of the romances, not least the elaboration of love scenes and scenes of aristocratic socializing, point to an influence of women's tastes and suggest some mitigation of these forces at least at the ideological level. The ability to read seems to have been more common amongst noblewomen than noblemen in lay society in the central Middle Ages; the education open to such women led generally to the vernacular rather than to Latin, and the spread of vernacular literature is due partly to their encouragement (Green 1994, 290, with further literature). The well-known vignette of a noble girl reading from a French book to her parents in Chrétien's *Yvain* ('un romanz', v. 5366) and in Hartmann von Aue's adaptation (*Iwein* vv. 6455–70) typically indicates a community of interest between author and female reader of courtly romance. Similarly, the many instances of scenes from the Tristan story on textiles worked by women suggest that the topic of Tristan and Isolde's love was popular amongst noble and burgher women (Becker 1977, 230).

Preachers and educators testify to the influence of Arthurian literature in Germany from the early thirteenth century onwards. Caesarius, monk in the monastery of Heisterbach, tells in his *Dialogus miraculorum* (written 1219–23) how Abbot Gevardus (died 1208) roused the dozing monks in his congregation by suddenly bringing King Arthur into a sermon (IV, 36), and he refers to the deceased King Arthur holding court in the afterlife (XI, 12). Heisterbach was in the archdiocese of Cologne, and Caesarius's anecdote is thus another indication of early Arthurian interests along the Lower Rhine (Beckers 1989a, 219). Thomasin von Zirklaere sees secular literature as inferior in its truth content to religious works, but he nevertheless ascribes an educational function to vernacular romances and advocates Arthurian stories as morally useful reading for young nobles, male and female (*Der wälsche Gast* vv. 1023–62; Düwel 1991), while Hugo von Trimberg, schoolmaster in Bamberg, writing at the close of the thirteenth century, comments that books about Erec, Iwein, Tristan, Parzival and Wigalois are better known than religious works treating God and the saints, and that these books are dangerous to the souls and bodies of youths who risk their lives in trying to emulate the jousting deeds of Round Table knights (*Der Renner* vv. 21637–66). Thomasin and Hugo refer to the figures of romance almost as if they were persons in real life. Indeed, the medieval German reception of Arthurian literature seems to have been highly personalized in that the interest lay as much with the Arthurian characters as with authors, works or themes; and the impact of the romances is seen in terms less of abstract ideas than of persons acting as role models. Moreover, Hugo and Thomasin both speak of young people as recipients of romance, and this focus on youth is an important strand in the thematic and social history of Arthurian literature in the areas considered in this volume, and elsewhere in Europe.

The vitality of Arthurian material and its importance for the self-under-standing of the German aristocracy are shown also in the way that Arthurian figures and motifs spread out widely into other types of literature and other aspects of social life in the German empire. King Arthur is praised for the lavishness of his hospitality in Rudolf von Ems's *Der guote Gêrhart* (vv. 5908–16), and as a model of courtesy to whom Ottokar von Steiermark, at the beginning of the fourteenth century, compares the contemporary Duke Albrecht of Austria in his *Österreichische Reimchronik* (vv. 22945–65); and at the end of the thirteenth century Heinrich von Freiberg, in an encomiastic poem, places the Bohemian noble Johann von Michelsberg in a line with Arthurian heroes and describes him as 'the new Parzival' (*Die Ritterfahrt des Johann von Michelsberg* v. 178). The Arthurian world also forms a point of orientation in fictitious treatments of the German past in historicizing romances of the late thirteenth and early fourteenth centuries: Round Table knights are referred to as exemplars of chivalric prowess in *Reinfried von Braunschweig* (e.g. vv. 20158–73) and in *Friedrich von Schwaben* (vv. 4811ff.), while in Johann von Würzburg's *Wilhelm von Österreich* the hero Wilhelm is a fictional member of the historical Babenberg dynasty and also linked, on his mother's side, with the Arthurian family (Dietl 1993, 174f.).

These instances indicate that during the thirteenth century figures from Arthurian literature gained such a firm place in the minds of authors and public in the German empire that they could be deployed as a framework of reference in works of widely varying genre and in the treatment of contemporary historical figures. The centuries-long cross-fertilization of Arthurian romance and German heroic poetry, and the reception of Arthurian motifs and figures (albeit in an extremely reduced form) in drama and *Meisterlieder* at the end of the Middle Ages will be treated in separate contributions in this volume (chapters 13 and 14) and they testify further to the literary influence of Arthur and his court.

The outward spread of Arthurian motifs from literature into pictorial representations and into various aspects of noble life such as name-giving, military sports and other forms of socializing will be discussed in chapters 16 and 17. Here it is important to note three general points about these developments because of the light they throw on the German reception of Arthurian material. First, in terms of chronology, evidence of the impact of Arthurian and Grail motifs on 'real life' beyond literature starts in the thirteenth century in Germany and is still strong in the fifteenth century; indeed, the second half of the fifteenth century saw a resurgence of Arthurian interest as part of the broader 'chivalric renaissance' of this period. Second, with regard to social levels, Arthurian motifs appear first in the life of the feudal aristocracy and then show some percolation into the urban patriciate. Third, with regard to regional distribution, Arthurian interests are particularly widely documented in southern areas, and this matches the regional spread of other forms of aristocratic culture to indicate a certain two-part division of Germany along an axis running northwest to south-east, but at the same time there was more cultivation of matters chivalric and Arthurian in towns in north-east Germany than has perhaps generally been recognized (Paravicini 1994, 102).

The contributions in the present volume show important shifts of emphasis in research on German Arthurian literature since the appearance of Loomis's

Arthurian Literature in the Middle Ages. Socio-historical interpretations have enhanced our understanding of Arthurian romance in an ongoing debate that is discussed by McDonald (1996, 360–70). Advances have also been made in narratological studies, and Arthurian romance (including the Grail and Tristan themes) appears in current work as more self-conscious and complex in its poetics than was the case forty years ago. The reflecting narrator has emerged as a key component in romance and irony as an important feature alongside idealization (Green 1979). The concept of the dialogic has sharpened readers' awareness of the variety of standpoints within romance (Groos 1995). Walter Haug's controversial claim that it was the genre of Arthurian romance that introduced truly fictional narration into medieval vernacular literature (Haug 1985, chapter 5) has provoked a lively and ongoing debate about fictionality and aesthetic autonomy in romance (Mertens and Wolfzettel 1993, Grünkorn 1994). The concept of intertextuality illuminates the way in which romances feed off each other (Draesner 1993). German Arthurian literature is characterized by frequent direct and indirect allusions to other texts and other authors, which give this literature a particularly strong self-referential and intertextual quality. Indeed, the interaction between the self-consciously literary and intertextual quality of romance on the one hand, and on the other hand its social function as a focus of aristocratic values, gives the genre a complexity of texture that can lead to widely different interpretations of individual works.

The past twenty years have, in particular, brought a considerable increase of interest in and a better understanding of 'post-classical' romances (see also McDonald 1996, 355–60). The treatment of German Arthurian literature in Loomis's volume of 1959 was shaped by the view that, from *c.* 1220 onwards, German literature was in a process of decay after the flowering, the *Blütezeit* or classical period, of the decades around 1200. This view, which grew up in the nineteenth century and which often associated the poetic flowering with Hohenstaufen rule, has been widely challenged in recent decades. Hartmann von Aue, Wolfram von Eschenbach and Gottfried von Strassburg, the only German authors named in chapter headings in Loomis's volume, are still seen as major figures, and the critical developments sketched in the previous paragraph throw new light on their works. However, recent studies also see far more literary interest and value in later works, especially works of the thirteenth century, than was the case forty years ago.

The dominance of less problematizing, more open-textured romances in the later thirteenth century, by contrast with the double structure of Arthurian romance in the works of Chrétien, Hartmann and Wolfram and the theme of the hero's personal crisis that is associated with this structure, is seen in recent work not so much as a sign of cultural decline, but rather as the development of a valid – and flexible – alternative type of Arthurian narrative. Later authors' expressed admiration for and adoption of stylistic features of the 'classical' masters emerge in recent scholarship less as a naive imitation and more as the self-conscious building of a literary canon so that the later authors can project their own works, at times with some critical or playful distancing from the great predecessors. Interpretative studies of individual 'post-classical' works show not a uniform and bland imitative manner, but a variety of styles, attitudes and responses in later romances to the challenge of the masters, considerable intertextual playing with Arthurian motifs and much cross-fertilization between Arthurian romance and other genres. In order to do justice to these new insights, later Arthurian literature (including fragments of romances) is given far more space in the present volume than it received in Loomis.

The decades since Loomis's volume have also seen advances in research into the manuscript transmission of medieval German literature, which throws valuable light on the reception of Arthurian works from the thirteenth to the sixteenth century. Some information on manuscripts will be found in the individual contributions in this volume. Here it may be useful to point to some general features and patterns of transmission.

The earliest surviving manuscripts of German Arthurian romances date from the first third of the thirteenth century, with two manuscripts of Wirnt's *Wigalois* in the period *c.* 1220–*c.* 1230 (Schneider 1987, 84f.; Bertelsmeier-Kirst 1992, 282). The earliest surviving fragment of Eilhart's *Tristrant* is now thought to date from the early thirteenth rather than the end of the twelfth century, and the earliest *Iwein* manuscript from the second rather than the first quarter of the thirteenth century (Schneider 1987, 52 n. 198, 148). There was then a remarkable continuity of manuscript production of courtly narrative literature for almost three hundred years, with considerable activity in the thirteenth century, some decline in the second half of the fourteenth century (which may be explicable partly by the spread of the plague), and still a lively production in the fifteenth century (Becker 1977, 233). The history of manuscript production thus shows that, whilst few new works were produced in the fourteenth and fifteenth centuries, the romances of Arthur's knights were still very much alive from the point of view of reception, since patrons were willing to commision expensive manuscripts. Nor was it merely a few canonical works that were still transmitted at this time, for many manuscripts of the post-classical romances stem from the fifteenth century. On this chronological point Schiewer draws attention to an interesting difference between the German and French areas for, whereas fifteenth-century manuscripts exist for all the German Arthurian romances that are known as complete works, there are hardly any fifteenth-century manuscripts of the French post-classical verse romances (1988, 241 n. 82). Recent work on variance (Bumke 1996) and on shortened versions (Strohschneider 1991) provides further evidence of the living reception of courtly romances, since they were not merely copied out slavishly for antiquarian purposes, but scribes made stylistic alterations and even produced shorter versions to meet the taste of patrons.

With regard to the circumstances of transmission there are very many single-work manuscripts from the early thirteenth century onwards, and single-manuscript transmission seems to dominate especially with the post-classical Arthurian romances (Schiewer 1988, 241). In collected manuscripts (*Sammelhandschriften*) it is a general feature of the German tradition that courtly narratives are gathered together almost exclusively with other German vernacular works, which indicates that these manuscripts were designed for a lay audience that was not versed in Latin (Becker 1977, 171). With regard specifically to German Arthurian romances, Gisela Kornrumpf observes (1984, 180) that, so far as the often fragmentary record of the thirteenth and fourteenth centuries allows a view, these romances are transmitted singly, or with their own kind, or with non-historical literature, unlike the position in France, which again suggests that the Arthurian subject matter had more of a free-floating fictional status in Germany than further west.

The main sponsors of manuscript production stemmed from the nobility, though there is evidence of interest in urban patrician circles in the fifteenth century (Becker 1977, 218). Regionally, manuscripts of Arthurian literature tend to show more of a southern than a northern spread, but recent work has also shown manuscripts of Hartmann's *Iwein* and Wolfram's *Parzival* being transmitted along a track from the south-east to the north-east (Klein 1988, 122f.; Beckers 1992, 91). This is a further reminder that the interest in courtly and Arthurian matters in the north-eastern parts of Germany should not be overlooked. Wolfram's *Parzival* is regionally the most widely transmitted Arthurian work, often together with the *Jüngerer Titurel* (Becker 1977, 226f.). Gottfried's *Tristan* shows a distinctive geographical distribution based in the south-west (Klein 1988, 124f.), and many of the post-classical romances seem not to have spread beyond their local dialect area (Schiewer 1988, 234f.). These are only some of the geographical findings of recent manuscript research that is shedding more specific light on the diffusion of German Arthurian literature in the Middle Ages.

As to the number of known manuscripts, Wolfram's *Parzival* heads the list, with a total of 82 (16 complete + 66 fragments), followed by Albrecht's *Jüngerer Titurel* (which was transmitted under Wolfram's name in the late Middle Ages) with 56 (11+45), Wirnt's *Wigalois* with 41 (13+28), Hartmann's *Iwein* with 32 (15+17) and Gottfried's *Tristan* with 31 (14 complete – including three that have been lost – and fragments from 17 others). The figures are taken from the relevant sections in the present volume. Estimates of the ratio of the known manuscripts to the total medieval production vary widely, between *c.* 1:150 and (probably more realistic) *c.* 1:10–1:20 (Schirok 1982, 59f.). Given the vagaries of manuscript survival, the number of extant manuscripts should not be taken on its own as a evidence of the degree of popularity in the Middle Ages, especially where only a small number of manuscripts has survived, but these larger figures agree with other evidence such as references by other medieval authors, name-giving in real life and pictorial representations to suggest what were the most widely known works in the Middle Ages.

A special feature of the German Arthurian scene was indeed the massive influence of Wolfram von Eschenbach. His *Parzival* is the most widely transmitted work of medieval German narrative literature, and far from exercising an enervating influence on later authors by the weight of his achievement, it may be that the energy of Wolfram's narration, especially his sharp profiling of the commenting narrator, had a stimulating effect. Connected with Wolfram's authority is the importance of the Grail as a quasi-religious guarantee of secular order in later literature. Moreover, the German Wolfram tradition developed the special feature that the Grail was located here on earth, in India, as an optimistic utopia which could also include King Arthur and his court (Blank 1993, 134f.). While the manuscript record agrees with twentieth-century critical opinion in giving high rank to Wolfram's *Parzival*, Hartmann's *Iwein* and Gottfried's *Tristan*, the medieval popularity of *Wigalois* probably stems in part from qualities of unproblematical and colourful narration which have, until recently, perhaps been undervalued by modern scholars in comparison with romances of personal crisis, but which form an estimable feature of medieval German Arthurian literature. The popularity of *Wigalois* was such that a printed version was appearing as late as the seventeenth century, and the work was also adapted into Yiddish (see chapter 8).

Dutch Arthurian literature shows similarities and differences in comparison with German. In the Low Countries as in Germany, Arthurian works express and reflect on the concerns and values of aristocratic society and also show a new literary self-consciousness: both areas are part of a common tradition that originated in France and spread out to other parts of Europe, adjusting to the different cultural circumstances.

The county of Flanders was a key area for the transmission of French aristocratic culture into the Germanic world in the Middle Ages. The county was French-speaking in its southern parts and mainly Flemish (as a form of Dutch) in the north, so that the linguistic circumstances were propitious here for the passage of Arthurian subject matter from the Romance into the Germanic world. Chrétien de Troyes himself was closely associated with Philip of Alsace, count of Flanders, when he worked on *Perceval*, and interest in Arthurian literature seems to have been greater in Flanders than in other parts of the Low Countries.

Dutch Arthurian literature shows a stronger connection with French prose romances and with historiographical traditions of King Arthur than is the case with German. The Lancelot subject matter is also far more prominent in Dutch than in German. No single Dutch author gained the status and influence of Wolfram in the field of Arthurian literature. Indeed, the influential Flemish poet Jacob van Maerlant cultivated what he saw as the historical truth of King Arthur but rejected the many invented stories. Nevertheless, as Bart Besamusca's contribution in this volume shows, fictional Arthurian romances flourished in Dutch literature in the thirteenth century, and like their German counterparts they show a variety of attitudes that testify to the vitality and the diversity of the Arthurian tradition in this period.

The manuscript transmission of Dutch Arthurian literature also has a different profile from that of German since most of the Dutch Arthurian romances are contained in only two manuscripts: ten in the *Lancelot* Compilation (written *c.* 1320), and three in a codex of *c.* 1425 that is written in Low German. The manuscript transmission of Arthurian romances in Dutch peaks in the early fourteenth century and fades out earlier than is the case in German. The absence of fifteenth-century manuscripts of Arthurian romances in Dutch contrasts sharply with the position in German: Middle Dutch literature seems not to have experienced the late burst of Arthurian interest that was a feature of fifteenth-century Germany. The socio-cultural dimensions of this contrast merit further study and may prove to be connected with varying degrees of urbanization. The Low Countries were, together with northern Italy, the most urbanized region in medieval Europe: in the fifteenth century 'more people lived together in cities in the Low Countries than anywhere else in the world: up to 36 per cent in Flanders and 45 per cent in Holland' (Prevenier 1994, 12). Whilst it would be historically inaccurate to see Arthurian interests as incompatible with urban life, it may be that, in the long run, the advanced development of urban structures at the expense of feudal ones in the Low Countries created a climate that was less propitious for the continuing reception of the old Arthurian verse romance than was the case in southern Germany in the fifteenth century.

We have already mentioned the controversy about a possible lost corpus of Arthurian narratives along the Lower Rhine. So far as the extant texts are concerned, Dutch and German Arthurian literature seem to have developed largely independently of each other. However, it is now generally accepted that the early part of the German *Prosa-Lancelot* rests on a Middle Dutch version (see chapter 9), and the fragments of manuscripts of *Parcheval* and a Merlin poem, to which reference has already been made, suggest that there may have been more cultural contact involving Arthurian literature in the border regions linking the Low Countries and Germany than has yet been documented. There are also generic similarities between Middle Dutch Arthurian works and German post-classical romances that merit further comparative study (Besamusca 1996, 226).

Like the rise and spread of Arthurian subject matter, its fading and its subsequent modern revival are supranational processes which receive particular form in the German-speaking areas. The lively, continuing manuscript transmission of Arthurian romances in the fifteenth century is a striking characteristic of the German scene. Equally striking is the sudden ending of this three-hundred-year tradition in the years around *c.* 1480–*c.* 1490, for the few manuscripts produced after that time, even though they include the magnificent 'Ambraser Heldenbuch' commissioned by Emperor Maximilian I, were isolated cases (Becker 1977, 239f.). Nor was it a case of the printing press taking up where scribes left off, for only four German Arthurian works made it into print: *Parzival* and the *Jüngerer Titurel* (1477), and prose redactions of Eilhart's *Tristrant* (1484) and Wirnt's *Wigalois* (1493). Of these four it was only the abbreviated, prose versions treating adulterous love (*Tristrant*) and the un-problematical biography of the knight who enjoyed good fortune and God's favour (*Wigoleis*) that went into further editions during the sixteenth century and beyond (see chapter 18). These were narratives that were not bound into a medieval aristocratic ideology and could make the transition into adventure stories for a wider public.

This development in literary history matches other evidence to indicate a fading of Arthurian interest in German society after the end of the fifteenth century. To some extent this retreat was due to the sheer availability of new forms of cultural expression in Renaissance Europe, but here again the history of Arthurian matter also reflects broader trends in the history of the German aristocracy. Recent research has questioned the view that the German nobility experienced a general decline, or even crisis, in the fourteenth and fifteenth centuries (see the contribution by Bernd Bastert in this volume). However, the decades around 1500 did bring a sharpening in the concentration of power in the hands of territorial rulers and a decline in the independence of the lesser nobility, who were tending increasingly to withdraw from military activity and to become more dependent on the patronage of rulers and on the economic strength of towns. Becker rightly suggests a connection between growing central authority, the nobility's loss of the right of feud and the fading of manuscript transmission of medieval epics and romances at the end of the fifteenth century (1977, 240), and to this list could be added the ending of the series of supraregional aristocratic tournaments of the Four Lands in 1487 (Ranft 1994, 176–9): all mark an important stage in the long process whereby the military aristocracy of the Middle Ages, on whose existence the rise and spread of Arthurian literature was predicated, gave way to changed forms of nobility in the early modern state.

Only vestigial traces of Arthurian subject matter remained in seventeenth-century Germany; for instance *Tristrant* and *Wigoleis* continued to appear until just after the middle of the century. But in Germany as elsewhere in Europe there was an increase of antiquarian interest in medieval literature from the middle of the eighteenth century onwards which also brought Arthurian themes back into view (see chapter 19). The interest gathered strength in the Romantic movement and, with shifts of focus and intensity, has remained to the present day, though the Arthurian legends have not gained such widespread popularity in the German- as in the English-speaking world.

The social framework for the revival of Arthurian themes in the nineteenth century was no longer an aristocratic society, but more a matter of the educated middle class, the *Bildungsbürgertum*; and the Arthurian world was no longer intimately connected with the ethos of a military aristocracy but was free to express quite different imaginative and philosophical concerns. In Germany it was chiefly the epic *Nibelungenlied*, based on early German legend, that captured the nationalist imagination in the medieval revival. In the field of Arthurian legends Richard Wagner's music dramas have been the most dominant cultural force, with a consequent privileging of the (reinterpreted) figures of Parzival, Tristan and Isolde and the themes of the Grail quest and love that leads to nirvana in death. The socially cohesive image of King Arthur and the Round Table has impinged less on the modern German public consciousness than these Wagnerian themes. However, in recent decades new works produced in the German-speaking world (not least Tankred Dorst's *Merlin*) have gone hand in hand with Arthurian films and translations of American and British Arthurian novels to broaden the spectrum of Arthurian themes and their treatment in the contemporary German cultural scene. It seems that postmodernism, with its problematizing approach to history and to the concept of individual authorial creation, its suspicion of grand ideologies and its interest in pastiche (Connor 1989), provides fertile soil for yet another revival of the protean matter of Arthur.

A brief account of the selection and arrangement of material in this volume is called for. An opening chapter will sketch the origins and early development of Arthurian material in Britain and France so as to place the following contributions in a historical perspective. These contributions will then discuss the medieval German, Dutch, and Czech works that come into the category of Arthurian literature. Like the other volumes in the present series, we follow

Loomis's collaborative volume in treating the Tristan theme together with Arthurian literature. This inclusion needs little justification, since Arthur and his knights figure already in the earliest German Tristan romance in the late twelfth century (that of Eilhart von Oberg) and, although Arthur's court plays no part in the *Tristan* of Gottfried von Strassburg, it was more often the case that Tristan was in the medieval German view closely associated with the Round Table. We have adopted a broader rather than a narrower approach by including discussions not only of Arthurian romances in a strict sense, but also works in which Arthur and his court play only a minor role (for example *Lohengrin* and *Lorengel*). We do not wish, by including these works, to define them as 'Arthurian' romances, but they are texts in which Arthur and his court enter into interesting relations with other types of literature. We include Wolfram's *Titurel* fragment on the grounds that, although Arthur does not figure in the work, its characters are drawn from Wolfram's own Arthurian and Grail romance *Parzival* and are related by family to the Grail and Arthurian dynasties, and later Albrecht, in expanding and 'completing' *Titurel*, did give Arthur's court a prominent role. We include chapters on Arthurian themes and motifs in heroic poetry, in drama and *Meisterlieder*, in pictorial representations and in German social life in the Middle Ages, so as to show the wider impact of Arthurian culture in literature and in life. Finally, chapters on early printed editions of Arthurian romances and on the modern reception of the Arthurian legend trace the fading and revival of interest in Arthurian subjects in the German-speaking world.

The contributions to the volume are arranged partly according to chronology, and partly according to theme or genre, and most contributions treat a group of texts or a subject that stretches over considerable time. We hope by this arrangement to convey some idea of the complex lines of influence and reception that run in various directions through the Arthurian corpus.

Bibliography

Primary Sources

Caesarius of Heisterbach, *Dialogus miraculorum*. Ed. by J. Strange, 1851. Cologne.
Friedrich von Schwaben. Ed. by H. Jellinek, 1904 (Deutsche Texte des Mittelalters, 1). Berlin.
Heinrich von Freiberg, *Die Ritterfahrt des Johann von Michelsberg*, in *Heinrich von Freiberg*. Ed. by A. Bernt, 1906. Halle, 239–48.
Hugo von Trimberg, *Der Renner*. 4 vols. Ed. by G. Ehrismann and G. Schweikle, 1970. Berlin.
Ottokar von Steiermark, *Österreichische Reimchronik*. Ed. by J. Seemüller, 1892 (Monumenta Germaniae Historica. Deutsche Chroniken, V, 1–2). Hanover.
Reinfried von Braunschweig. Ed. by K. Bartsch, 1871 (BLV, 109). Tübingen.
Rudolf von Ems, *Der guote Gêrhart*. Ed. by J. A. Asher, 1971 (ATB, 56), 2nd edn. Tübingen.

Thomasin von Zirklaere, *Der Wälsche Gast*. Ed. by H. Rückert, 1852. Quedlinburg and Leipzig (repr. Berlin, 1965).

Other Literature

Arnold, B. 1991. *Princes and Territories in Medieval Germany*, Cambridge.

Becker, P. J. 1977. *Handschriften und Frühdrucke mittelhochdeutscher Epen. 'Eneide', 'Tristrant', 'Erec', 'Iwein', 'Parzival', 'Willehalm', 'Jüngerer Titurel', 'Nibelungenlied' und ihre Reproduktion und Rezeption im späteren Mittelalter und in der frühen Neuzeit*, Wiesbaden.

Beckers, H. 1989a. 'Wolframs *Parzival* und der Nordwesten. Neue Ansätze zur Lösung einer alten Streitfrage', in Gärtner, K. and Heinzle, J., eds, *Studien zu Wolfram von Eschenbach: Festschrift für Werner Schröder zum 75. Geburtstag*, Tübingen, 211–23.

Beckers, H. 1989b. 'Die mittelfränkischen Rheinlande als literarische Landschaft von 1150 bis 1450', *ZfdPh*, 108, Sonderheft, 19–49.

Beckers, H. 1992. 'Sprachliche Beobachtungen zu einigen *Parzival*-Bruchstücken niederdeutscher Schreiber', WSt, 12, 67–92.

Beckers, H. 1995. 'Die volkssprachige Literatur des Mittelalters am Niederrhein', *Queeste*, 2, 146–62.

Bertelsmeier-Kirst, C. 1992. 'Zur ältesten Überlieferung des *Wigalois*. I. Die Handschrift E', *ZfdA*, 121, 274–90.

Besamusca, B. 1996. 'The Low Countries', in Lacy 1996, 211–37.

Blank, W. 1993. 'Zu den Schwierigkeiten der Lancelot-Rezeption in Deutschland', in Jones and Wisbey 1993 (see Gen. Bibl.), 121–36.

Bumke, J. 1986. *Höfische Kultur. Literatur und Gesellschaft im hohen Mittelalter*, 2 vols., Munich 1986.

Bumke, J. 1996. *Die Vier Fassungen der 'Nibelungenklage'. Untersuchungen zur Überlieferungs-geschichte und Textkritik der höfischen Epik im 13. Jahrhundert*, Quellen und Forschungen zur Literatur- und Kulturgeschichte, 8 [242], Berlin and New York.

Connor, S. 1989. *Postmodernist Culture: An Introduction to Theories of the Contemporary*, Oxford and Cambridge, Mass.

Dietl, C. 1993. '"Du bist der aventure fruht". Fiktionalität im *Wilhelm von Österreich* Johanns von Würzburg', in Mertens and Wolfzettel 1993, 171–84.

Draesner, U. 1993. *Wege durch erzählte Welten. Intertextuelle Verweise als Mittel der Bedeutungskonstitution in Wolfram's 'Parzival'*, Mikrokosmos, 36, Frankfurt.

Düwel, K. 1991. 'Lesestoff für junge Adlige. Lektüreempfehlungen in einer Tugendlehre des 12. Jahrhunderts', *Fabula*, 32, 67–93.

Fleckenstein. J., ed. 1990. *Curialitas. Studien zu Grundfragen der höfisch-ritterlichen Kultur*, Veröffentlichungen des Max-Planck-Instituts für Geschichte, 100, Göttingen.

Green, D. H. 1979. *Irony in the Medieval Romance*, Cambridge.

Green, D. H. 1994. *Medieval Listening and Reading: The Primary Reception of German Literature 800–1300*, Cambridge.

Groos, A. 1995. *Romancing the Grail: Genre, Science and Quest in Wolfram's 'Parzival'*, Ithaca and London.

Grünkorn, G. 1994. *Die Fiktionalität des höfischen Romans um 1200*, Philologische Studien und Quellen, 129, Berlin.

Haug, W. 1985. *Literaturtheorie im deutschen Mittlelalter*, 2nd revised edn, 1992, Darmstadt.

Klein, T. 1988. 'Ermittlung, Darstellung und Deutung von Verbreitungstypen in der Handschriftenüberlieferung mittelhochdeutscher Epik', in Honemann and Palmer 1988 (see Gen. Bibl.), 110–67.

Kooper, E., ed. 1994. *Medieval Dutch Literature in its European Context*, Cambridge Studies in Medieval Literature, 21, Cambridge.

Kornrumpf, G. 1984. 'König Artus und das Gralsgeschlecht in der Weltchronik Heinrichs von München', WSt, 8, 178–98.

Lacy, N. J., ed. 1996. *Medieval Arthurian Literature: A Guide to Recent Research*, Garland Reference Library of the Humanities, 1955, New York and London.

Loomis, R. S., ed. 1959. *Arthurian Literature in the Middle Ages: A Collaborative History*, Oxford.

McDonald, W. C. 1996. 'Germany', in Lacy 1996, 349–99.

Mertens, V. and Wolfzettel, F., eds. 1993. *Fiktionalität im Artusroman. Dritte Tagung der Deutschen Sektion der Internationalen Artusgesellschaft*, Tübingen.

Paravicini, W. 1994. *Die ritterlich-höfische Kultur des Mittelalters*, Enzyklopädie deutscher Geschichte, 32, Munich.

Prevenier, W. 1994. 'Court and city culture in the Low Countries from 1100 to 1530', in Kooper 1994, 11–29.

Ranft, A. 1994. *Adelsgesellschaften. Gruppenbildung und Genossenschaft im spätmittelalterlichen Reich*, Kieler Historische Studien, 38, Sigmaringen.

Schiewer, H.-J. 1988. ' "Ein ris ich dar vmbe brach / Von sinem wunder boume". Beobachtungen zur Überlieferung des nachklassischen Artusromans im 13. und 14. Jahrhundert', in Honemann and Palmer 1988 (see Gen. Bibl.), 222–78.

Schirok. B. 1982. *Parzivalrezeption im Mittelalter*, Erträge der Forschung, 174, Darmstadt.

Schmolke-Hasselmann, B. 1980. *Der arthurische Versroman von Chrétien bis Froissart*, Beihefte zur *ZfrPh*, 177, Tübingen.

Schneider, K. 1987. *Gotische Schriften in deutscher Sprache. Band 1. Vom späten 12. Jahrhundert bis um 1300*. Textband, Wiesbaden.

Strohschneider, P. 1991. 'Höfische Romane in Kurzfassungen. Stichworte zu einem unbeachteten Aufgabenfeld', *ZfdA*, 120, 419–39.

Tilvis, P. 1959. 'Über die unmittelbaren Vorlagen von Hartmanns *Erec* und *Iwein*, Ulrichs *Lanzelet* und Wolframs *Parzival*', *NM*, 60, 29–65, 129–44 (repr. in Wais, K., ed., *Der arthurische Roman*, WdF, 157, Darmstadt 1970).

Ullmann, W. 1965. 'On the Influence of Geoffrey of Monmouth in English History', in Bauer, C. et al., eds., *Speculum Historiale. Geschichte im Spiegel von Geschichtsschreibung und Geschichtsdeutung. Festschrift J. Spörl*, Freiburg and Munich, 257–76.

Wells, D. A. 1971/3. 'The Middle Dutch *Moriaen*, Wolfram von Eschenbach's *Parzival*, and medieval tradition', *Studia Neerlandica*, 7, 243–81.

Part One

Reception and Appropriation: The German Verse Romances, Twelfth Century to 1300

1

THE WESTERN BACKGROUND

Ingrid Kasten

Stories about the legendary King Arthur circulated not only in the British Isles but also in many parts of continental Europe in the Middle Ages. In Germany, as in other areas, these stories enjoyed great popularity, for they provided high-class entertainment and also acted as a framework for the presentation and discussion of new patterns of chivalric and courtly behaviour. The Arthurian material acquired its own history in Germany, but it also has a prehistory that is important both in its own right and for an understanding of the German developments. The stories of Arthur and his knights were transmitted north-wards and eastwards through French or Anglo-Norman mediation. The great German Arthurian romances of Hartmann von Aue and Wolfram von Eschenbach arose as free adaptations of the works of the French poet Chrétien de Troyes, who himself had drawn on various written and oral sources. The aim of this opening chapter is to sketch the early history of the Arthurian legend, which preceded its reception in German literature.

Geoffrey of Monmouth and the Earliest References to Arthur

Although the figure of King Arthur was not, strictly speaking, invented by the British cleric Geoffrey of Monmouth, Geoffrey is none the less generally credited with having created the Arthurian myth and raised Arthur to the status of national hero among the Britons in his *Historia Regum Britanniae*, a legendary history of the kings of Britain probably completed at the end of 1138.

Earlier historians knew of only one Arthur, a military leader said to have distinguished himself in the fighting between the Britons and Saxons in the early sixth century: as *dux bellorum*, he first figures in Nennius' early ninth-century *Historia Brittonum*. Nennius claims that this Arthur carried on his shoulders the image of the Virgin Mary in one of the twelve battles that he fought against the Saxons and that in his last battle alone, on the Mons Badonicus, he killed no fewer than 960 men in a single day. By contrast, Arthur is not mentioned either by Gildas, a contemporary chronicler of the Saxon wars, whose *De excidio et conquestu Britanniae* (*c.* 545) contains an account of the same battle, or by Bede in his *Historia ecclesiastica gentis Anglorum* (*c.* 730). One piece of evidence that does, however, appear to confirm Arthur's early legendary fame is the Welsh elegy *Gododdin* ascribed to a bard by the name of Aneirin and believed to date from the late sixth century. (It survives only in a later linguistic form.) Here a hero's valour is praised, 'though he was not Arthur'.

It is clear from Nennius' *Historia Brittonum* and the *Mirabilia* appended to that work that by the early ninth century a nexus of legends had already grown up around the figure of Arthur. Evidence of the increasing number of legends on the subject, which taken together paint an ambivalent picture of the king, is afforded not only by the anonymous *Annales Cambriae* of the second half of the tenth century but also by various saints' lives dating from the years between 1070 and 1120. Following on from Nennius, the *Annales Cambriae* report that in the Battle of Badon in 516 Arthur carried Christ's Cross on his shoulders for three days and three nights and that the Britons were finally victorious. Whereas Arthur appears here as a hero fired by religious zeal, he figures in the lives of the saints (texts in Faral 1929, I, 237–44 and Chambers 1927, 241–7; 262–4) as an overweening tyrant. In the *Vita Cadoci* (*c.* 1090) by Lifris of Llancarfan he is tempted to assault a young woman, and in the *Vita Sancti Gildae* (*c.* 1120/30) by Caradoc of Llancarfan, he is described as *rex rebellis et tyrannus*, a negative counterpart to the saintly Gildas. It is the *Vita Sancti Gildae*, finally, that first proposes a link between the Arthurian tradition and an older abduction myth, a link that was to have considerable repercussions for the later history of the legend: here St Gildas helps Arthur to win back his wife Guennuvar following her abduction by a foreign king (Chambers 1927, 263).

Even before embarking on his *Historia Regum Britanniae*, Geoffrey had already completed a *Vita Merlini*, telling of the life of the legendary magician Merlin (1135), and it is clear that in his later work he drew not only on the few written sources that were available to him but also on oral Celtic narrative tradition, a tradition which, precisely because of its oral nature, is virtually impossible to reconstruct with any degree of certainty. In its basic outline, his *Historia* is clearly influenced by traditional models of medieval soteriological historiography, and the suggestion that Geoffrey was not only influenced by Virgil's *Aeneid* but that, in creating the figure of King Arthur, he sought to give the Britons a ruler who, like Charlemagne, would help to create a sense of national identity is entirely plausible, given the newly awakened interest in classical subjects in the twelfth century and the literary significance of the Continental legends surrounding the figure of Charlemagne.

Geoffrey took up the idea of the *translatio imperii* and combined it with the legend of Trojan ancestry, retelling the story of the Britons from the mythical foundation of their kingdom by Aeneas' great-grandson, Brutus, to its downfall as the result of moral decline and, finally, to the rise of the Saxons. It is against this background that Arthur's role must be seen. The victorious king is bold enough to challenge even the hegemony of the Roman empire, and he would have succeeded in achieving his aim of world dominion if he had not been prevented by treachery from within his own ranks in the person of his nephew, Mordred. His failure notwithstanding, Arthur appears not only as the representative of a glorious British past but as the embodiment of hope for the present.

It is the political aspect of the story which, in keeping with the work's historiographic structure, is emphasized in the form of a series of power struggles, endless battles and intrigues among rival clans and tribes. There are, however, a number of fantastical episodes that depart from this pattern. One such episode is the account of Arthur's conception, which results from an act of adultery arranged by the magician Merlin (the Amphitryon motif). Another is Arthur's battle with a rapist giant on the Mont-Saint-Michel. Finally, there is the scene in which the king is spirited away to the faery isle of Avalon following his fatal wounding at the hands of the adulterous usurper Mordred. Thematically speaking, the work comes full circle, with Arthur's birth and death both taking place against a background of adultery. In this way, two ideas that were to be of major importance in the later Arthurian tradition are already prefigured in Geoffrey's *Historia*, namely, the image of Arthur as a courtly figure and the disintegration of his kingdom as the result of treachery and adultery.

It is clear from his various dedications to highly placed political figures at the English court that, in writing his *Historia Regum Britanniae*, Geoffrey was anxious to ingratiate himself with the Anglo-Norman rulers and, at the same time, to predispose them in favour of the Britons by depicting the latter as heirs to a glorious historical tradition reaching back to classical antiquity. Although contemporary scholars such as Giraldus Cambrensis were disinclined to regard Geoffrey's historical distortions as serious historiography, it is evident from the *Historia*'s huge success (more than 200 manuscripts have survived) that it satisfied a sudden upsurge of interest in the mythical and aesthetic elaboration of history on the part of cultivated audiences.

Arthur in Vernacular Poetry: Wace and the Breton *Lais*

In the course of the twelfth century, the English court for which Geoffrey wrote his *Historia* developed into an important centre of political power and at the same time became a focus of the new courtly literature (Bezzola 1944–63, part III). It was here that the *matière de Bretagne* first found written expression. Geoffrey had already mediated between oral and written poetic traditions, but his *Historia*, written in Latin prose, inevitably reached only the *litterati*.

However, the courtly society that was emerging at this time comprised not only clerics versed in Latin, but also the illiterate secular aristocracy, whose claims to cultural standing and a stake in literary discourse could be satisfied only by means of the vernacular. It was to the Jersey-born cleric Wace (*c.* 1110–after 1170) that this mediating role now fell: completed around 1155, his *Roman de Brut* is an Anglo-Norman reworking in verse of Geoffrey's *Historia* and marks the decisive transition of the Arthurian tradition from Latin to the vernacular. Wace was for a long time connected to the English court and is known to have been active there as a *clerc lisant* (i.e. reader) between 1135 and 1170; between 1165 and 1169 he held a benefice at Bayeux, which he received from Henry II. His *Roman de Brut* was, in turn, the principal source of a rambling retelling of the material (*c.* 1200) by the English priest Layamon, according to whom Wace's account was dedicated to Henry's wife, Eleanor of Aquitaine, one of the leading patrons of courtly literature in the twelfth century.

Wace follows the basic outlines of his source, but stresses Arthur's courtly characteristics, not only emphasizing the king's open-handedness, his readiness to show pity, his courtly manners and his eloquence but also expatiating on the lengthy period of peace under Arthur and, in general, treating him as the paragon of a 'good king'. Wace is also the first writer to describe the legendary Round Table ('la Roünde Table', v. 9751), which Arthur is said to have set up in order to prevent his knights from arguing over where they should sit. The Round Table thus figures as a symbol of equality, the prototype of an exclusive, feudal male society (though this symbol of equality was not fully realized in later romances, and did not completely eliminate hierarchical attitudes in the portrayal of Arthur's court, see Schmolke-Hasselmann 1998, 59f.). And it is Wace, too, who is the first to mention the Britons' belief that Arthur will one day return from Avalon (vv. 13275ff.).

Wace's *Roman de Brut* marks the first stage in the great success story of the *matière de Bretagne* in the vernacular literatures of Europe. At about the same time as Wace's work a number of *lais* arose, also in the environs of the English court. These *lais* were not written with any historiographical aim, but concentrate on individual episodes. Here the king of the Britons appears as a somewhat problematical or at least ambivalent figure. The earliest evidence of this tradition is the Anglo-Norman *Lai du Cor* by Robert Biket (or Bicket), which dates from the second third or third quarter of the twelfth century. Central to the narrative is a fantastical motif that takes the form of an ivory drinking horn hung with tiny bells. Given to Arthur as a present, it produces a whole series of unexpected consequences when used as a test of chastity. (This motif was to be taken up in a number of later Arthurian texts, including the First Continuation of *Perceval* and the Prose *Tristan*, with variants in *Le manteau mautaillié* and in Heinrich von dem Türlin's *Diu Crône*.) Even the queen fails the test, and only a single knight succeeds in drinking from the horn without spilling any of its contents. Arthur is so enraged that he first thinks of killing the queen, but he finally regains his regal composure.

The figure of Arthur is also seen as problematical in Marie de France's *Lai de Lanval*. Here, too, we find the motif of adultery, but on this occasion it is set in the new context of a faery background, thereby acquiring a new perspective. In this way, the theme of love acquires independent importance for the first time in the written Arthurian tradition. A Whitsun festival offers Arthur an opportunity to lavish lands and womenfolk on his knights. But one of them – a king's son, Lanval – is undeservedly passed over. Saddened, he wanders away from the court and finds himself in a faery realm. Here a woman showers love and wealth on him, but on condition that he says nothing about their relationship. He returns to Arthur's court, where the queen tries to seduce him. In an attempt to resist her, he reveals his secret and loses his lover. The queen for her part falsely accuses him of making improper advances, and he is haled before his judges. At the very last moment, his faery mistress appears and attests to his innocence. Lanval thereupon returns with her forever to the realm from which she has come – to Avalon.

In this work Arthur's court presents a picture of troubled order: the king fails to distribute his gifts fairly, while the queen is anything but a faithful wife. The hero, too, is either unwilling or unable to assert himself, with the result that he sees his only solution in flight into an 'other world' the world of faery. The world of Arthur and the faery world are thus shown to be irreconcilable opposites.

Chrétien de Troyes and his Continuators

It is, however, Chrétien de Troyes who is undoubtedly the most important writer to have reshaped the Arthurian legends and introduced them to the Continent. We know little about the circumstances of his life. He clearly had a clerical training; and commentators are generally agreed that he was active as a writer between 1160 and 1191. It was during this period that he produced his five great Arthurian romances (not all of which were completed): *Erec et Enide*, *Cligès*, *Yvain ou Le Chevalier au lion*, *Lancelot ou Le Chevalier de la charrette* and *Perceval ou Le Conte du Graal*. It remains unclear whether Chrétien had any links with the English court and, if so, what form they may have taken. *Lancelot*, he states, was written at the behest of Marie of Champagne, the daughter of Eleanor of Aquitaine; and he was closely associated with Philip of Alsace, Count of Flanders, while he was working on *Perceval*.

Chrétien was surely familiar with Geoffrey's *Historia* and Wace's *Roman de Brut*, as well as with vernacular reworkings of classical themes. And it would appear from his polemical outburst at the ineptitude of professional storytellers

(*Erec et Enide* vv. 20–26) that he also used other, oral sources: presumably he is alluding here to multilingual bards who, as representatives of the old oral poetic tradition, were spreading their tales about Arthur on the Continent. At all events, there are many parallels of motifs and other links between Chrétien's romances and the Celtic tradition. Here, particular significance may be attached to the names that Chrétien uses (especially in *Erec et Enide*) and that can be traced back to Celtic origin.

The question of the relationship between Chrétien's romances and the *Mabinogion* is a further bone of scholarly contention. The Celtic *Mabinogion* poems likewise tell of Erec (= Gereint), Yvain (= Owein) and Perceval (= Peredur) but survive, essentially, in only two late manuscripts, the late thirteenth-century White Book of Rhydderch and The Red Book of Hergest of *c*. 1400. In recent years a scholarly consensus seems to have emerged to the effect that *Gereint, Owein* and *Peredur* do not derive from original Welsh tradition but that, in comparison to Chrétien's versions, they must be regarded as secondary, owing their existence to the oral reception of the French romances and to cross-fertilization with autochthonous traditions. It has nevertheless been suggested that the *Mabinogion* stories ultimately derive, at least on the level of motif, from early Celtic or early European religion (Birkhan 1989).

Chrétien consciously distances himself from the narrative stance of the historiographer, while at the same time going well beyond the episodic structure of the *lais*. Battles and political power struggles are no longer central to his romances; Arthur no longer features as a great warrior and, although he still functions as a 'good king', there is now an ironic element to that portrayal; and he has ceased to be the main hero. As in Marie de France's *Lai de Lanval*, it is individual knights who now figure as the protagonists. In contrast to the older narrative tradition, with its 'monologic' structures (Gaunt 1995), in which social relationships were conceived for the most part as involving only men, women now play a role in the way in which society and masculine identity are conceived, a development that reflects the cultural synthesis of *amour* and *chevalerie* already anticipated by the *romans d'antiquité*. At the same time, the importance of family structures is – at least initially – overshadowed by a chivalric ideal that transcends differences of rank within the nobility and incorporates elements of the Christian code of chivalry that arose in the context of the Crusades. But Chrétien also adopts a critical approach to the new, conceptualized attitude to love both as a form of service, such as we find in the lyric poetry of the *trouvères*, and as an example of the sort of passion found in the *Tristan* romances. Although the Tristan legend forms part of the *matière de Bretagne* it represents a different strand from the Arthurian tradition, and it is above all the Tristan story (perhaps in the version of Thomas) that provides the background for a complex series of often ironic intertextual references in Chrétien's romances.

In Arthurian romance, as the genre was defined by Chrétien, the hero is torn between knighthood, love and marriage, and is bound to find himself wanting in consequence of his inability to meet the expectations of either society or of a woman, or to satisfy religious norms. As a result, he suffers a crisis, which he then has to overcome. These romances have a courtly setting – generally Arthur's court – but also involve an 'other world', the world of *aventure*, where all seems alien, dangerous and evil, but it is also an imaginary world where marvels routinely occur. In this complex, Arthur's court represents a normative model of feudal, courtly society, albeit one that is by no means beyond criticism. The hero achieves his goal not simply by confirming Arthurian norms: rather, there is a changing relationship between the hero and Arthur's court, a relationship, moreover, that involves creative tension. The hero brings stability to Arthur's court by successfully warding off the dangers that threaten it, but in the course of his adventures he also transcends the norms that obtain there.

In terms of their narrative technique, Chrétien's romances are based on binary structures that find expression in the doubling of motifs, in recapitulations along an ascending line and in elaborate ways of linking episodes ('conjointure', see *Erec et Enide* v. 14). The meaning of the romance is conveyed by the network of (figural) relationships linking the separate episodes (Warning 1979). Moreover, a central role in the organization of the narrative is played by systems of rules ('costume', see Köhler 1960, Maddox 1991), on the basis of which models of social order, of power and dominion and of relations between the sexes are played out in the course of the narrative.

It would appear from the catalogue of his works included in the prologue to *Cligès* that it was with *Erec et Enide* that Chrétien made his début as a writer of romances. *Erec et Enide* is commonly dated *c.* 1165–70, though Luttrell (1974, 26–46) argues for a date as late as 1184–86. The work has a paradigmatic value representing the 'classical' Arthurian romance. In the first part, the hero successfully defends the honour of the Arthurian court and in the process wins a woman, whom he then proceeds to marry. But this apparently happy ending is by no means the end of the story. Rather, it ushers in a crisis that unfolds in narrative form in the second half of the romance, before finally being resolved. In the specific case of *Erec et Enide*, the crisis takes the form of the hero's abandoning himself to the joys of love and taking no further part in knightly activities (the motif of *recréantise*). The court's criticisms lead to a crisis in the lives of the married couple: Erec orders his wife to accompany him on a series of perilous adventures and forbids her to speak to him or share bed and board with him. Later he explains that he wanted to test her and see whether she really loved him; but since her love was never explicitly questioned, Erec's behaviour remains puzzling (the *Gereint* poet offers a belated excuse for the hero's actions by having him suspect his wife of infidelity, while Hartmann von Aue stresses her innocence). Nevertheless, it is clear that the second part of the narrative constitutes a test, with Enide proving herself a loyal wife and Erec demonstrating his bravery and chivalry by defending himself and the rights of others. The couple's reconciliation is followed by a final episode, the *joie de la cour*, in which Erec 'liberates' two lovers who have cut themselves off from society. (Here and elsewhere there are obvious parallels with *Tristan*.) As such, the episode provides a concluding reflection on the crisis suffered by Erec and Enide and, at the same time, mirrors its resolution. The romance culminates in Erec's coronation, with the hero now representing the ideal prototype of a cultivated ruler who combines within himself both *clergie* and *chevalerie*.

This same underlying structure (the rise of the hero, his fall or peripeteia and his renewed rise) is also found, with certain variations, in Chrétien's other works (Bezzola 1947, Frappier 1957, Maddox 1981). Only in the case of *Cligès* (*c.* 1176) does Chrétien depart noticeably from this model, which may be seen as bipartite or tripartite, depending on the structural function of Arthur's court. Moreover, there is no evidence to suggest that the subject matter of *Cligès* is Celtic in origin; indeed, Chrétien specifically claims that he found the story in the library of the bishop of Beauvais, although the romance in fact shows him in consummate command of the most disparate narrative material. Particularly striking are the ironic references to *Tristan*. At the same time, however, Chrétien locates the action in a topographically recognizable world, thereby setting up equally ironic resonances with older historiographical patterns of storytelling and with the romances of love and travel in classical antiquity. In the prologue to *Cligès* Chrétien cites the *translatio* motif, a topos of medieval historiography, but he redefines the motif by supplementing the concept of a shift in political power with that of a shift in cultural supremacy (*translatio studii*) and by claiming contemporary cultural hegemony for France. It is hard to imagine a clearer expression of a programme of narrativization and aestheticization of the 'historical' and, with it, an attempt on the poet's part to distance himself from the factuality of the 'merely' political.

Even in its basic outline, *Cligès* emerges as a highly original work. Like *Tristan*, it is divided into two parts, with the main part of the narrative preceded by a subsidiary narrative or *Vorgeschichte*. In this it follows a conceptual model determined by genealogical structures. The action is set in Britain, Germany and, above all, Greece. Although Arthur's court is portrayed as an exclusive preserve of *courtoisie* and, as such, the goal of all young noblemen with aspirations to self-improvement, it is of only peripheral significance, and Arthur himself once again assumes the (older) features of a potential world ruler and military commander whose power is threatened by an act of treachery within his own ranks. Central to the romance, however, is courtly discourse on the subject of love.

On the strength of its wealth of allusions to *Tristan*, scholars have concluded that, with *Cligès*, Chrétien was keen to propose an alternative to the adulterous love of *Tristan*, in other words, to create an anti-*Tristan* (Foerster 1910, XXXIX). And it does indeed seem as though Chrétien is making a point when the heroine of his main story, the German princess Fenice, who has been married against her will to her lover's uncle, refuses – unlike Isolde – to share her body between two men, an aim she achieves by using a magic potion to evade her husband's demands. *Cligès* thus explicitly calls into question the concept of the feudal marriage of convenience and in many ways is even more radical than *Tristan* in its championship of the emotions, with the result that it has also been described as a 'neo-*Tristan*' (Gaston Paris 1912, 292f.) and as a 'hyper-*Tristan*'.

Chrétien's subsequent romances all constitute more or less radical variants of the 'classical' structure first realized in *Erec et Enide*. Closest to this structural model is *Yvain* (*c.* 1180), a matchless example of Chrétien's sovereign artistry in his handling of comedy and irony. Here, too, the hero wins a wife in the first part of the narrative – on this occasion, she is a ruler in her own right, Laudine, whose dowry is a whole country. Following their wedding, Yvain asks her for her permission to leave for a while, permission that she readily grants him. But he stays away longer than the time agreed, and so she repudiates him. This rejection precipitates a crisis in Yvain, when he goes out of his mind as a result of his pain at the loss of Laudine. He wanders around naked in the wilderness before being found and cured by women, who take pity on him. He helps a lion in its fight with a dragon, and the royal beast now becomes his constant companion. It is as the 'Knight of the Lion' that he champions the rights of others and finally wins back Laudine.

The centre of gravity shifts from Arthur's court to Laudine's in *Yvain*, and *Lancelot* (*c.* 1180) departs even further from the structure of Chrétien's first romance. The plot of *Lancelot* is believed to be based on a Celtic abduction myth: a mysterious stranger, generally of otherworldly or faery origin, demands a married woman as his own. He wins her by means of a ruse (the motif of the *don contraignant* or 'rash boon') and carries her off to his otherworld kingdom. The husband pursues the abductor, triumphing over apparently insuperable obstacles, and finally wins back his abducted wife. This abduction myth had been transferred to Arthur and his wife already in the *Vita Sancti Gildae* but, whereas the king himself still plays the part of the pursuer in the *Vita* (as he does in the *Lanzelet* of Ulrich von Zatzikhoven, albeit here with the assistance of his knights), this role later passes to one of his knights: in *Yvain*, it is taken over by Gauvain and in *Lancelot* by the eponymous hero. Chrétien seems to have been the first writer to combine the abduction myth with the love story between Lancelot and Guinevere, a story that has thematic parallels with the queen's adultery with Mordred.

Lancelot seems to be the only one of Chrétien's romances not to have been adapted into German; perhaps this lack of reception was due to the prior existence of the version by Ulrich von Zatzikhoven. The structure of Chrétien's *Lancelot* is determined by the abduction and recapture of the queen. Even at the beginning of the narrative, where the king is too impotent and weak to protect his wife and subjects from attack, it is clear that Arthur's world is no longer a place of order. This impression is strengthened by the narrative's apparent lack of coherence, its numerous uncertainties and the baffling events with which it is strewn: we are not told anything about the origins and identity of the knight who, following Gauvain, rushes after the abductor; it remains unclear what sort of a relationship Lancelot has with Arthur and Guinevere; and it is not explained how Lancelot knows about the queen's abduction, or what happened previously, or why he recognizes Gauvain when the latter does not recognize him. Possibly Chrétien could reckon on his audience's familiarity with the story, but since he adopts a different narrative approach in his other romances, this is not a satisfactory explanation. Rather, the element of uncertainty seems to imply a specific poetological programme.

In *Lancelot*, the contrast between Arthur's world – Logres – and the world of adventure receives particular expression. The abductor's otherworld home is called Gorre and is described as 'the land from which no one returns' (v. 1918). The two countries are governed by differing rules (the *coutume de Logres* and the *coutume de Gorre*, see Maddox 1991), and each has its own ambivalent attitude to love, desire, brute force and order. At the same time, however, it is implied that there are links between these two worlds on both a superficial and a deeper level. This also applies to the two antagonists, both of whom desire the queen, namely, her abductor, Meleagant, and her rescuer, Lancelot. Further links emerge in the form of parallels between significant motifs and the relationships between the characters, as well as in the names of the two countries, with Logres proving a (partial) anagram of Gorre.

As with *Tristan*, the central theme is love, which is treated in both works as an absolute, an erotic passion made yet more intense by the use of religious terminology. It is therefore all the more striking that adultery is portrayed in *Lancelot* but without being explicitly thematized as a problem. Lancelot appears in a paradoxical dual role: as a result of his love for the queen, the existing social order is thrown into disarray, but he alone is capable of restoring that order by freeing Guinevere and Arthur's people from their imprisonment. But Lancelot himself has no place in their order, hence his mysterious disappearance following the queen's release.

With *Perceval*, Chrétien once again struck out in a new direction, linking the world of Arthurian legend with the story of the Grail in a way that was to prove immensely influential. At the same time, the central problem within the field of tension created by love, marriage and society acquires a different emphasis and gains a new religious dimension. Structurally, too, the romance undergoes an important change inasmuch as Chrétien begins with the hero's childhood (*enfance*), thereby adopting a biographical approach and introducing a new perspective. The story of Perceval, who grows up with his mother far from the courtly world, is the story of a search, the hero's search, first for his place in society, for knighthood, and then for his mother, a search that is eventually replaced by his quest for the Grail. As a result of his meetings with various kinsfolk (all of them on his mother's side), the hero progressively discovers his identity and his vocation. A further innovation consists in the doubling of the protagonists in the second part of the (unfinished) romance, with Gauvain emerging as a second hero alongside Perceval. This doubling has at times been regarded as so puzzling that doubts have been raised about the whole relevance of Gauvain's worldly adventures to the story of Perceval, which acquires elements of a quest for religious meaning (Pollmann 1965), but the numerous contrastive and complementary links between the two plots suggest that the narrative concept was fully thought through from the outset.

A central role in the narrative structure is played by the mysterious Grail: Perceval abandons his mother, becomes a knight and wins an *amie* (vv. 2912, 2922) for himself before stumbling upon the Grail Castle, whose lord offers him his hospitality. Here Perceval witnesses a strange procession, in the course of which a lance dripping with blood and a golden vessel – a *graal* – are carried past him. He is perplexed by what he sees but dares not ask the significance of the lance or who is fed by the *graal*. When he attempts to make good his omission the following morning, he finds the castle deserted. From now on he is repeatedly reproached for this failing and gradually made aware of what he has done. In Chrétien's case (but not in Wolfram's), Perceval's silence at the Grail Castle is the result of a sin that he has committed ('pechiez la langue te trancha', v. 6409): he has caused his mother's death.

The quest for the Grail is also central to the *Roman du graal* by Robert de Boron, who equates the Grail with the chalice or dish used at the Last Supper. Chrétien is far more ambiguous in his own interpretation of the Grail. Although the Grail is a dish for him, too, it proves to embody a whole series of different levels of meaning: the quest for the Grail becomes a substitute for the hero's search for his mother and leads to his discovery of fragmentary details of a family history overlaid by ideas of Christian redemption that ultimately suggest a mythical dimension.

The fact that Perceval regains his faith in God while staying with a hermit suggests that all will turn out for the best: the terrible picture of disorder that is painted at the beginning of the romance was perhaps to have given way to a conciliatory ending. The lines of suspense that remain unresolved in *Perceval* (they include not only the quest for the Grail but also Gauvain's search for the lance that drips blood and that will one day destroy Arthur's kingdom, a motif not taken over by Wolfram) are a challenge to the imagination, so it is hardly surprising that various writers quickly emerged on the scene with the aim of continuing Chrétien's unfinished narrative.

Of the total of six continuations of *Perceval*, two – the *Elucidation* and the *Bliocadran* – are really only prologues. Of these, by far the more interesting is the *Bliocadran*, since it contains information which goes beyond anything given by Chrétien but agrees with what Wolfram narrates in the first two books of *Parzival*.

For Chrétien's true continuators, the unfinished quest for the Grail was naturally the central concern. In its original form, the First Continuation (also known as the Pseudo-Wauchier) dates from around 1200. Here it is Gauvain who is cast in the role of the knight who searches in vain for the Grail, whereas in the Second Continuation, the Grail hero is once again Perceval, with Gauvain's adventures being reported only to the extent that they impinge on Perceval's quest. Perceval reaches the Castle of the Grail but is unable to provide any definite answer to the mysteries surrounding the Grail. The Third Continuation is by Manessier and dates from the early thirteenth century. It is the first continuation to provide the story with an ending: Perceval succeeds the Fisher King and, following his death, the Grail, lance and silver dish are carried up to heaven. A further continuation beginning and ending with Perceval's visit to the Castle of the Grail was written by Gerbert de Montreuil in 1126/30, evidently in ignorance of Manessier and apparently with the aim of bringing the Second Continuation to a satisfactory conclusion. An attempt to press the Grail story into the service of a foundation myth for the dynasty of the counts of Flanders, it, too, remained incomplete.

Later, the theme of the Grail quest became increasingly bound up with an ideal of piety that proved militant and spiritual by turns, while at the same time the courtly debate about love lost much of its former urgency. Written between 1190 and 1215, the *Didot Perceval* takes up the theme of the disintegration of Arthur's kingdom as a result of Mordred's act of treachery, while also linking the story of Perceval with the originally independent Grail narrative of Robert de Boron. One innovation on a purely formal level that was to have important consequences for later writers was the use of prose. The ascetic features of the tale were further emphasized in *Perlesvaus*, another text written under the influence of the *Didot Perceval* that draws not only on *Perceval*, its various Continuations and Robert de Boron, but also on Chrétien's *Lancelot*.

The Lancelot–Grail Cycle (Vulgate Cycle)

Dating from between 1215 and 1235, the great Vulgate Cycle has something of the character of a summation about it. It takes up the whole Arthurian tradition and subjects it to a new idea; and presumably several writers were involved in the project. At the heart of the five-part cycle is the story of Lancelot (*Lancelot propre*), which is based on Chrétien's romance and on a source close to the *Lanzelet* of Ulrich von Zatzikhoven. At the same time, the story of Lancelot is combined with the Grail quest (*Queste del Saint Graal*) and with the disintegration of Arthur's empire (*La mort le roi Artu*). The collapse of his kingdom is sealed by Mordred's treachery but can be traced back to the intrigues that result from the illicit love between Lancelot and Guinevere.

The introductory section consists, first, of a later addition, the *Estoire del Saint Graal* (after Robert de Boron), the action of which begins with the disappearance of the Grail (here the chalice used at the Last Supper that Joseph of Arimathea is said to have received from Christ), and, second, the *Estoire de Merlin* (also based on Robert de Boron, who in turn drew on Geoffrey of Monmouth's *Vita Merlini*). The narrative is thus set within a soteriological framework. In spite of its use of *entrelacement* as a narrative device (a device already essayed by Chrétien but now far more subtly elaborated), the narrative style is closely modelled on that of a chronicle, while the conceptualization of the subject matter is inspired by a new chivalric ideal influenced by Cistercian spirituality that marks the moral downgrading of secular knighthood. Deception, betrayal, treachery and intrigue thus attend the beginning, development and end of the Arthurian world.

This increasingly negative stance is also clear from the changing picture of Arthur himself. In keeping with tradition, he is fathered with the help of Merlin, but his birth is not legitimated by marriage. Consequently, he first has to assert his rights as his father's successor following the latter's death, which he does by drawing the sword Escalibur from a stone – the only hero able to achieve this feat. Nevertheless, a number of vassals refuse to accept his rule. One of these rebels is King Loth, on whose wife an unrecognized Arthur had earlier fathered a son, Mordred. (This feature, too, is new to the tradition.)

In contrast to Arthur, Lancelot appears as a model knight whose watchword is love and who is not interested in power. With his unconditional love and devotion to the queen, he is committed to the ideal of a lofty passion that does not baulk at total self-denial. But this love is not only glorified, it is also overshadowed by the reproach of adultery and, as a result, is ultimately stigmatized as sinful and secular. Although Lancelot once renounces his love of Guinevere, he is incapable of sticking to his resolve, with the result that the disintegration of Arthur's kingdom is inevitable. 'Courtly love' as a cultural model that gives meaning to life is emphatically dismissed, albeit apparently with a certain regret; alongside it, Galehaut's devoted love for Lancelot emerges as a relationship that is both new and old, and that is emotionally committing in a different way: friendship between men. On his death, Lancelot's soul is claimed by angels, but his body is laid to rest in the grave beside Galehaut.

In the *Queste del Saint Graal* Arthur's knights are no longer guided by an ideal of courtly sociablity, but by the religiously motivated quest for the Grail. To only a few is it given, however, to approach the Grail, and the extent to which they succeed is determined by their own degree of perfection. Lancelot is one of the few. But it is his son, Galahad, who is alone destined to succeed in the quest for the Grail. The fact that Galahad can trace his ancestry back to both David and Joseph of Arimathea emphatically underscores the religious dimension of the cycle.

The end of the Arthurian world is prefigured by the history of its subject matter. However, as was the case already in Chrétien, adultery and treachery are no longer linked in the prose *Lancelot*; instead, they are divided between two protagonists, namely, Lancelot and Mordred. Arthur breaks off a campaign of vengeance against Lancelot to take up arms against his treacherous son Mordred, whom he kills. But he is mortally wounded himself and taken to Avalon. Girflet, the last surviving knight of the Round Table, throws Arthur's famous sword, Escalibur, into a lake, where it is seized by a hand that then disappears. For the survivors, the only way forward is the way that leads to monastic seclusion.

The great Vulgate Cycle marks a high point and in some ways also an end point in the development of Arthurian themes in France. The reception of the cycle also forms a caesura in the literary relations between France and Germany, for whereas earlier German versions of French works – for instance the Arthurian romances of Hartmann and Wolfram – had been more or less free adaptations, the parts of the Vulgate Cycle that were transmitted into German show hardly any significant deviations; rather, the adaptors remained close to their source texts, so that the German texts appear far more as translations than as independent works of literature (see the contribution of Elizabeth Andersen in this volume). Moreover, the German *Prosa-Lancelot* enjoyed far less success than its French source, and this was perhaps because the great themes that it treated had already received authoritative expression east of the Rhine: the Grail theme in Wolfram's *Parzival* and the theme of love as unconditional passion in Gottfried von Strassburg's *Tristan*.

Bibliography

Literature

For more detailed bibliographies and discussion of the literature treated in this survey see Bromwich et al. 1991 (Welsh literature), Echard 1998 (Latin narratives) and Keith Busby's Foreword on recent scholarship in Old French Arthurian literature in Schmolke-Hasselmann 1998, xi–xlvi.

Primary Sources

(Works arranged in the sequence in which they are treated in the text)

Nennius, *Historia Brittonum*. Ed. and transl. by J. Morris under the title *British History and the Welsh Annals*, 1980 (Arthurian Period Sources, 8). London and Chichester.

Nennius, *The Historia Brittonum: The 'Vatican Recension'*. Ed. by D. N. Dumville, 1985. Cambridge.

Gildas, *De excidio et conquestu Britanniae*. Ed. and transl. by Michael Winterbottom under the title *The Ruin of Britain*, 1978 (Arthurian Period Sources, 7). London and Chichester.

Annales Cambriae. Ed. by E. Phillimore, 1888. In *Y Cymmrodor* 9, 141–83.

William of Malmesbury, *Gesta Regum Anglorum*. 2 vols. Ed. by W. Stubbs, 1887–9 (Rolls Series, 90). London.

Mabinogion, in *The Text of the Mabinogion from the Red Book of Hergest*. Ed. by J. Rhys and J. G. Evans, 1887. Oxford; and *The White Book Mabinogion*. Ed. by J. G. Evans, 1907. Cardiff.

The Mabinogion. Transl. G. Jones and T. Jones, 1949. London. German translations of the *Mabinogion* by Birkhan 1989 (see Other Literature).

Geoffrey of Monmouth, *Historia Regum Britanniae*. Ed. by A. Griscom, 1929. London.

Geoffrey of Monmouth, *Historia Regum Britanniae*. Ed. and transl. by N. Wright, 1991. Cambridge.

Geoffrey of Monmouth, *Vita Merlini*. Ed. and transl. by J. J. Parry, 1925, in *University of Illinois Studies in Language and Literature*, X, 3, Urbana, 251–380.

Wace, *Le Roman de Brut*. 2 vols. Ed. by I. Arnold, 1938–40 (Société des Anciens Textes Français). Paris.

Wace, *Roman de Brut. A History of the British*. Ed. and transl. by J. Weiss, 1997. Exeter.

Layamon, *Brut*. Ed. and transl. by W. R. J. Barron and S. C. Weinberg, 1995. Harlow.

Wace and Lawman, *The Life of King Arthur*. Transl. by J. Weiss and R. Allen, 1997 (Everyman). London and Rutland, Vermont.

Robert Bicket, *Lai du Cor*. Ed. by C. T. Erickson, 1973 (Anglo-Norman Text Society, 24). Oxford.

Mantel et Cor: deux lais du XIIe siècle. Ed. by P. Bennet, 1975. Exeter.

Marie de France, *Les Lais*. Ed. by E. Hoepfner, 1921. Strasbourg; ed. by A. Ewert, 1960. Oxford.

The Lais of Marie de France. Transl. by G. Burgess and K. Busby, 1986. Harmondsworth.

Chrétien de Troyes, *Œuvres complètes*. Under direction of D. Poiron, ed. and transl. by A. Berthelot et al., 1994 (Bibliothèque de la Pléiade, 408). Paris.

Chrétien de Troyes, *Romans*. Under direction of M. Zink, ed. and transl. by O. Collet et al., 1994. Paris.

Chrétien de Troyes, *Erec et Enide*. Ed. by W. Foerster, 1934 (Romanische Bibliothek, 13), 3rd edn. Halle. Transl. into German by I. Kasten, 1979 (KTRM, 17). Munich.

Chrétien de Troyes, *Cligès*. Ed. by W. Foerster, 1910 (Romanische Bibliothek, 1), 3rd edn. Halle.

Chrétien de Troyes, *Lancelot (Der Karrenritter)*. Ed. by W. Foerster, 1899 (*Christian von Troyes.*

Sämtliche Werke, vol. 4). Halle. Transl. into German by H. Jauss-Meyer, 1974 (KTRM, 13). Munich.

Chrétien de Troyes, *Yvain* (*Der Löwenritter*). Ed. by W. Foerster, 1912 (Romanische Bibliothek, 5), 4th edn. Halle. Transl. into German by I. Nolting-Hauff, 1962 (KTRM, 2). Munich.

Chrétien de Troyes, *Le Roman de Perceval ou Le Conte du Graal*. Ed by W. Roach, 1959 (TLF, 71), 2nd edn. Geneva and Paris. Transl. into German by F. Olef-Krafft, 1991 (RUB, 8649). Stuttgart.

Chrétien de Troyes, *Arthurian Romances*. Transl. by D. D. R. Owen, 1987. London.

Robert de Boron, *Roman de l'estoire dou Graal*. Ed. by W. A. Nitze, 1927 (CFMA, 57). Paris.

The Continuations of the Old French 'Perceval' of Chrétien de Troyes. 3 vols. Ed. by W. Roach, 1949–55. Philadelphia.

The Didot Perceval. Ed. according to the manuscripts of Modena and Paris by W. Roach, 1941. Philadelphia (repr. Geneva 1977). Manuscript E of the *Didot Perceval* transl. by D. Skeels, 1961. Seattle.

Perlesvaus. Li Haut Livre du Graal. 2 vols. Ed. by W. A. Nitze and T. Jenkins, 1932–7. Chicago (repr. New York 1972). Transl. by N. Bryant, 1978. London.

The Vulgate Version of the Arthurian Romances. 8 vols. Ed. by H. O. Sommer, 1909–16. Washington (repr. New York 1969).

Lancelot. Roman en prose du XIIIe siècle. 9 vols. Ed. by A. Micha, 1978–83 (Textes littéraires français, 247, 249, 262, 278, 283, 286, 288, 307, 315). Geneva and Paris.

La Queste del Saint Graal. Ed. by A. Pauphilet, 1949. Paris. Transl. by P. Matarasso, 1969 (Penguin Classics). Harmondsworth.

La Mort le roi Artu. Ed. by J. Frappier, 1964 (TLF, 58), 3rd edn. Geneva and Paris. Transl. by J. Cable, 1971 (Penguin Classics). Harmondsworth.

Other Literature

Bezzola, R. R. 1944–63. *Les Origines et la formation de la littérature courtoise en occident (500–1200)*, 3 parts in 5 vols., Paris.

Bezzola, R.R. 1947. *Le Sens de l'aventure et de l'amour*, Paris.

Birkhan, H. 1989. *Keltische Erzählungen von Kaiser Arthur*, 2 vols., Kettwig.

Bromwich, R., Jarman, A. O. H., Roberts, B. F., eds. 1991. *The Arthur of the Welsh: The Arthurian Legend in Medieval Welsh Literature*, Cardiff.

Bruckner, M. T. 1993. *Shaping Romance: Interpretation, Truth, and Closure in Twelfth-Century French Fictions*, Philadelphia.

Burns, E. J. 1985. *Arthurian Fictions: Rereading the Vulgate Cycle*, Columbus, Ohio.

Busby, K., Kelly, D., Lacy, N. J., eds. 1987–8. *The Legacy of Chrétien de Troyes*, 2 vols., Faux Titre, 31 and 37, Amsterdam.

Chambers, E. K. 1927. *Arthur of Britain*, London (repr. Cambridge and New York 1964).

Echard, S. 1998. *Arthurian Narrative in the Latin Tradition*, Cambridge Studies in Medieval Literature, 36, Cambridge.

Faral, E. 1929. *La Légende arthurienne. Etudes et documents*, 3 vols., Paris (repr. Paris 1969).

Foerster, W. 1910. See Primary Sources, Chrétien de Troyes, *Cligès*.

Frappier, J. 1957. *Chrétien de Troyes. L'homme et l'œuvre*, Connaissance des Lettres, 50, 1957.

Frappier, J. 1972. *Chrétien de Troyes et le mythe du Graal*, Paris.

Gaunt, S. 1995. *Gender and Genre in Medieval French Literature*, Cambridge.

Haidu, P. 1968. *Aesthetic Distance in Chrétien de Troyes: Irony and Comedy in 'Cligès' and 'Perceval'*, Geneva.

Jones, M. H. and Wisbey, R., eds., 1993. *Chrétien de Troyes and the German Middle Ages. Papers from an International Symposium*, Arthurian Studies, 26, Cambridge and London.

Kelly, D. 1993. *Medieval French Romance*, New York.

Kennedy. E. 1986. *Lancelot and the Grail: A Study of the Prose 'Lancelot'*, Oxford.

Köhler, E. 1956. *Ideal und Wirklichkeit in der höfischen Epik. Studien zur Form der frühen Artus-und Graldichtung*, Beihefte zur *ZfrPh*, 97, Tübingen (French translation Paris 1974).

Köhler, E. 1960. 'Le rôle de al "coutume" dans les romans de Chrétien de Troyes', *Rom* 81, 386–97.

Loomis, R. S. 1949. *Arthurian Tradition and Chrétien de Troyes*, New York.

Lot, F. 1918. *Etude sur le Lancelot en prose*, 2nd edn, Paris.

Luttrell, C. 1974. *The Creation of the First Arthurian Romance*, London.

Maddox, D. 1981. 'Trois sur deux. Théories de bipartition et de tripartition des œuvres de Chrétien de Troyes', *œuvres et critiques*, 5, 91–102.

Maddox, D. 1991. *The Arthurian Romances of Chrétien de Troyes: Once and Future Fictions*, Cambridge Studies in Medieval Literature, 12, Cambridge.

Méla, C. 1984. *La Reine et le Graal. La Conjointure dans les romans du Graal de Chrétien de Troyes au livre de Lancelot*, Paris.

Micha, A. 1987. *Essais sur le cycle du Lancelot-Graal*, Geneva.

Paris, G. 1912. 'Cligès', in Roques, M., ed., *Mélanges de littérature française du Moyen Age*, Paris, 229–327.

Pollmann, L. 1965. *Chrétien de Troyes und der Conte del Graal*, Tübingen.

Schmolke-Hasselmann, B. 1998. *The Evolution of Arthurian Romance: The Verse Tradition from Chrétien to Froissart*, transl. by M. and R. Middleton, Cambridge Studies in Medieval Literature, 35, Cambridge.

Stanesco, M. and Zink, M. 1992. *Histoire européenne du roman médiéval*, Paris.

Topsfield, L. T. 1981. *Chrétien de Troyes: A Study of the Arthurian Romances*, Cambridge.

Warning, R. 1979. 'Formen narrativer Identitätskonstitution im höfischen Roman', in Marquard, O. and Stierle, K, eds., *Identität*, Poetik and Hermeneutik, 8, Munich, 553–89.

Zaddy, Z. P. 1973. *Chrétien Studies: Problems of Form and Meaning in 'Erec', 'Yvain', 'Cligès' and the 'Charrette'*, Glasgow.

2

THE EMERGENCE OF GERMAN ARTHURIAN ROMANCE: HARTMANN VON AUE AND ULRICH VON ZATZIKHOVEN

Silvia Ranawake

Hartmann von Aue, *Erec* and *Iwein*

I

Hartmann von Aue's *Erec* is the first German adaptation of Chrétien's Arthurian romances, and a key work in the opening phase of Arthurian literature in Germany. The German *Erec* introduces an important period lasting from *c.* 1180 to *c.* 1220 in which a number of outstanding works based on French narratives of the *matière de Bretagne* genre were composed. Designed to entertain and instruct noble and princely patrons and their households they reflect the interests and aspirations of their audiences. They elaborate the literary theme of love, and they promote the status and values of knighthood based on shared knightly functions and way of life, both as part of the reception of their French models and as a reflection of the German reality (Jackson 1994). In their endeavour to imitate French romances, they also set new standards for both the form and content of secular literature in the vernacular. Hartmann in particular, with his Arthurian romances, was influential in determining the presentation of knighthood and the formal requirements which future courtly narratives were to follow. He was well equipped for this task, since he combined knightly status with clerical training. He describes himself as a *ministerialis* (*dienstman*, see *Der arme Heinrich*[1] v. 5), a member of the class of unfree military and administrative functionaries at the princely courts whose status began to approximate that of the *nobiles* by the end of the twelfth century (Jackson 1994, 63–71). At the same time he refers to himself as 'a knight who was so learned, that he (could) read in books whatever he found written there' (*Der arme Heinrich* vv. 1f.), and was as such an example of the emerging lay literacy. His works do indeed portray his familiarity with the pedagogic and rhetorical tradition of the schools and a thorough grounding in basic philosophical and theological knowledge (Hruby 1979). Linguistic evidence suggests that, like other adaptors of French literary works, Hartmann came from the south-west of Germany, where contact with French culture was easiest, an assumption confirmed by Heinrich von dem Türlin (*Crône* v. 2353). Hartmann's well-informed adaptations make a knowledge of French on his part virtually certain.

Hartmann was a prolific, innovative and versatile author. He wrote a versified disputation between the body and heart of a young man, the *Klage* ('Complaint'), which discusses the meaning of love service. His narrative work comprises the two Arthurian romances *Erec* and *Iwein*, both modelled on narratives by Chrétien de Troyes, a hagiographical legend *Gregorius*, also an adaptation of a French work (*La Vie du Pape Saint Grégoire*), and a courtly miracle story *Der arme Heinrich* (*Poor Henry*). Eighteen songs on the themes of courtly love and the crusade are ascribed to him. The dating and chronology of all his works has to rely on internal stylistic and metrical evidence and links to contemporary literature. The *Klage* and *Erec* are assumed to have been composed first, probably in the (early?) 1180s, and to have been followed by *Gregorius*, *Der arme Heinrich* and *Iwein*, in this sequence. Judging from a reference in Wolfram's *Parzival* (253, 10–14; 436, 4–10), *Iwein* was known in the first decade of the thirteenth century. Hartmann's three crusading songs may have been occasioned by the crusades of 1189/90 or 1197, whilst no specific dates can be assigned to his love songs. In his literary excursus (*c.* 1210) Gottfried von Strassburg refers to Hartmann as being alive (*Tristan*, ed. Ranke, vv. 4621–35). That Hartmann did not survive beyond 1220 can be inferred from Heinrich von dem Türlin's obituary (*Crône* v. 1220).

Although Hartmann makes no mention of patronage, it is likely that he relied for the provision of his source materials and additional support on one or more of the dynasties of the region, such as the Dukes of Zähringen (Berthold IV and Berthold V) who had close links with the aristocratic circles that sponsored Chrétien (Mertens 1986, 124, 131).[2] The Zähringen dynasty might well have aspired to equal their French relations as patrons of literature and supporters of chivalric ideology as a public manifestation of their political ambitions (Thomas 1989). The survival of *Iwein* manuscripts within the Welf domain (Upper Swabia), on the other hand, might suggest Welf patronage (Klein 1998, 122f.).

II

Erec has survived (in almost complete form, but with the beginning missing) only in the 'Ambraser Heldenbuch' (Vienna, cod. ser. nov. 2663), a manuscript compilation of texts written between 1504 and 1515/16 by Hans Ried for the Emperor Maximilian I (Edrich-Ponzberg 1994). In addition, there are some thirteenth-century fragments: K=Coblenz Landeshauptarchiv Best. 701, no. 759,14, V=Vienna, Nordösterreichisches Landesarchiv no. 881. A third set of fragments, Wolfenbüttel, Herzog-August-Bibliothek, cod. 19.26.9 Aug. 4°, contains two episodes of a version of the story that is closer to Chrétien's. Their precise relationship to Hartmann's adaptation is still under discussion.

Hartmann's *Erec* is a free adaptation of Chrétien's romance *Erec et Enide,* which in turn was composed between 1170 and 1185. The story is also the subject of the Cymric Mabinogi *Geraint ab Erbin* and the *Erexsaga*, a thirteenth-century(?) Old Norse prose version, based on Chrétien. Although Hartmann's version shares details with both against Chrétien, these do not amount to evidence that Hartmann used another written source besides Chrétien's romance. Some north-western German name forms may indicate that Hartmann had knowledge of oral Arthurian traditions of the Lower Rhenish region. Despite the fact that the German author both condenses and expands his source material, his version is considerably longer (10,192 against 6,958 lines in the standard editions). The transfer of Chrétien's work from one socio-cultural environment to another required commentaries and added detail which would help introduce his German audience to the customs and norms of Chrétien's courtly world. Attempts to clarify lead to shifts in emphasis, to a reinterpretation and recasting of the material. This rationalization results in a more 'logical' rearrangement of the material and closer attention to motivation, often in the form of interior monologues. The heightening of negative and positive characteristics provides additional guidance for moral orientation, and reiteration of key terms brings to the fore the system of courtly values in the light of which the action was to be assessed, and which itself was under discussion. Eager to apply his rhetorical expertise, Hartmann excels in amplification or *dilatatio*, e.g. in the description of Enite's horse and saddle (Worstbrock 1985). In general the immediacy of Chrétien's account with its large proportion of direct speech is replaced by a more reflective narrative style.

As an integral part of his model Hartmann adopted and further refined the bipartite structure devised by Chrétien for his romances. It is a format that relies on the use of repetition, variation and opposition in order to establish relationships between adventures and thus organize their seemingly random sequence into a meaningful whole (Kuhn 1948). The two main segments follow a similar pattern. In both parts the hero's loss of honour makes him decide to leave court. The following adventures test and prove his worth and enable him finally to return to court for reinstatement and advancement. Typically for the Arthurian romance, the action begins at Arthur's court, when Erec, a young knight and future king of Destrigales, is publicly shamed by the servant of an unknown knight. As he follows the knight unarmed and unaccompanied in order to vindicate his honour, his loss of status is reflected in his state of deprivation that appears to render his mission impossible. However, a chance encounter with an impoverished count and his beautiful daughter Enite turns his humiliation into a triumph, which surpasses mere rehabilitation. Father and daughter are able to provide Erec with the means to defeat his opponent, and Erec's quasi-miraculous rise from shame to fame is mirrored in the restitution of the count's and Enite's fortunes. Erec asks for Enite's hand in marriage, thus raising her and her family from a life of shameful poverty. On Erec and Enite's return to Arthur's court they are accorded the highest social acclaim. Enite is declared the most beautiful lady at court, while Erec, who distinguishes himself in a tournament arranged by Arthur in his honour, is acknowledged as the best knight.

In the second part, Erec, now married to Enite and ruler in his own country, loses everything he has won. Since his life is taken up with making love to his wife, he neglects his duties as head of his court, and consequently his chivalric renown and the reputation of his court suffer. So does his marital relationship; a distressed Enite reveals to him unwittingly that in the eyes of his followers marriage to her has turned him into a lie-abed. Shamed for a second time, Erec leaves court with his wife, withdrawing her marital status, and forbidding her to speak to him. In two parallel sequences of adventures, Enite paradoxically proves her loyalty by disobeying her husband's strict instructions and warning him of imminent danger, despite being punished for such disobedience. With Enite's support, the protagonist fends off his attackers in the first sequence of three adventures (highway criminals, a count who covets Enite, a dwarf king), but he nearly succumbs in the following second sequence, when only Enite's unswerving devotion averts a catastrophe. It becomes clear that survival and success depend on the couple's reciprocal commitment, a fact Erec seems to acknowledge when he recognizes his wife's faithfulness and asks her to forgive his harsh treatment of her.

His marriage thus restored, Erec is ready to redeem his reputation. The final adventure of *Joie de la curt*, which is distinguished by its mythical features, brings together several thematic strands. The isolated existence of Erec's opponent Mabonagrin, who lives in a magic garden together with his lady love, has been taken to mirror in quasi-allegorical fashion (Rider 1991) the earlier withdrawal of Erec and Enite from court. Erec's victory therefore constitutes victory over their old selves. At least of equal importance, however, are the contrasting features of both couples as a commentary on the courtly value system. Mabonagrin, compelled by his adherence to the demands of his jealous lady, mercilessly kills eighty knights. He may have increased his reputation thereby, but not without causing great sorrow and destroying the 'joy' of the court. In contrast Erec, supported by Enite's 'good' love, whose prowess is tempered by humility, mercy and the 'right' fear of God, is able to restore such joy, the *raison d'être* of courtly society.

The theme of chivalry performed in the service of others, with its Christian undertones, is already present in the previous cycle of adventures when, moved by compassion, Erec frees a captive knight from law-breaking giants. Hartmann has, independently of Chrétien, reinforced the religious dimension of the work: Erec, stirred by pity for Mabonagrin's victims, secures their Christian burial and a happier future for their widows – both Christian 'good works' (Tax 1963, 301), before returning with Enite to an exemplary life as the independent ruler of Distrengales.

Much of the interpretation of the work revolves around the question of the hero's 'development'. It is possible to focus on his initial immaturity, on flaws that are responsible for his fall and which have to be corrected in subsequent adventures. Such deficiencies can be of a personal and social nature, e.g. inability to integrate sexual and marital love (Schulze 1983). Alternatively, their ethico-religious aspects may be regarded as paramount: Erec's failings are manifestations of sins, such as concupiscence (Tax 1963, 43f.), pride (Fisher 1986) or sloth (Ranawake 1988), to be overcome by Christian virtues such as humility and charity (Tax 1963). Erec's marriage in particular is viewed as being in need of reorientation, in order to reflect the divine order (Firestone 1988).

However, such a personal development of the hero has been called into question on the grounds that the gradual formation of individual identity is a modern notion, foreign to medieval authors and audiences who conceived of man as part of an objectively ordered universe (Voß 1983, 14). According to this view, Erec fulfils the norms of knightly ideology in the first part, and his crisis does not originate in deficiencies of character. It is, rather, a manifestation of man's fallibility, part of the human condition. The subsequent adventures take on a quasi-penitential quality, and Erec's full restitution to his original state does not rest solely on the hero's own achievements, but on the workings of God's grace. Such an interpretation does not necessarily preclude progression by stages, an 'ethical dynamism' (Jackson 1994), because Erec's fall can be conceived as a test followed by heightened moral awareness, perceptible for example in Erec's admission to his own misplaced chivalric pride (vv. 7007–23) and his concern for the well-being of others and for the restoration of peace and harmony.

Chrétien's figure of Enite has been substantially modified by Hartmann. Whereas in the French version Enite asks for and is granted forgiveness for having presumed to voice criticism of her husband's conduct, it is Erec who, in the adaptation, asks his wife's forgiveness for his harsh treatment of her, which, in retrospect, appears as an unwarranted testing of her faithfulness. By removing Enite's guilt by association, Hartmann turns her into a model wife (Hahn 1986). Enite nevertheless recognizes her objective 'guilt' in having been, albeit unwittingly, the cause of Erec's downfall (Voß 1983, 94). The question of whether her initial silence in respect of Erec's reprehensible conduct constitutes failure or guilt (Pérennec 1984, McConeghy 1987), later to be corrected or atoned for by her warnings, has been investigated in the context of the role and expected conduct of married women within a patriarchal society (Smits 1981).[3] Guidance as to Enite's role is provided by the symbolism of Enite's horses and her dominion over them (Hurst 1994). The complexity of the figure can be said to originate, at least partially, in the coming together of different traditions. She shows features of the seductress, the obedient and submissive wife, the courtly lady, the loyal partner and the saint. Amidst conflicting interpretations most scholars would agree that a central issue is Hartmann's advocacy of a reciprocal marital relationship to which both partners actively contribute in equal measure (Quast 1993).

III

Hartmann's *Iwein* is an adaptation of Chrétien's *Yvain* (*Le Chevalier au lion*), as is the Old Norse *Ivens-Saga* and the Mabinogi *Owen*. The popularity of Hartmann's work is attested by the large number of manuscripts (thirty-two, including fragments, see Schirok 1982, 57) in which it has survived, dating from the period close to its completion in the first decade of the thirteenth century to the beginning of the sixteenth century. Superb handling of rhyme and metre, the clarity and fluency of the language and the sophisticated use of stylistic and narrative techniques have ensured the work's reputation from the very beginning as the epitome of the 'classical' Middle High German romance.

In contrast to *Erec*, Hartmann here follows his model fairly closely, but not without imposing his own interpretation and narrative style. In line with Chrétien's bipartite composition, Iwein, an Arthurian knight of royal blood, sets out from court to avenge the shameful defeat of his cousin Kalogrenant at the hands of King Askalon. Having killed Askalon, Iwein wins Askalon's widow as his wife together with her land, and receives the acclaim of the Arthurian community. During the crisis following on from this first cycle, he loses everything. Engrossed in tournaments, he misses the deadline for his return set by his wife Laudine; he is rejected by her and lapses into insanity. After a second cycle of adventures, the hero regains his former status, is fêted by Arthur's court and accepted back by his wife.

The adventure of the first cycle betrays its origins in Celtic legends that provided Chrétien and his predecessors with their material (O'Riaen Raedel 1978). Askalon, lord of the spring, is reminiscent of the guardian of the otherworld, whilst his widow, who is closely associated with the spring and sets conditions that remain unfulfilled, shows features of the waterfairies of Celtic folktales. Integration of such material into the courtly romance with its different value-system posed some difficulties (Simon 1990, 47–56). Both Chrétien and Hartmann tried to overcome these by distancing themselves from Laudine's remarriage to her husband's killer by means of irony and humour (Ranawake

1982). At the same time, the Laudine figure was rationalized to fit the courtly context: whilst Chrétien turned her into a *dame sans merci* to explain her severe punishment of Iwein's tardiness, Hartmann emphasizes her concern for her country's safety as a motivating factor (Mertens 1978), and for the couple's final reconciliation he transforms her into a contrite and docile wife. Iwein's failure to observe Laudine's deadline has been regarded by some critics as too slight to carry the ethical weight of the action, and the merciless killing of Askalon, rooted in the Celtic fable, has been held to constitute the main transgression that had to be expiated (Wapnewski 1979). However, Hartmann never refers to this killing as constituting the hero's guilt, and, furthermore, the missed deadline of one year has serious legal and political implications. Hence Iwein's failure represents a temporary lack of loyalty (*triuwe*, see Kraft 1979), which in turn is symptomatic of the hero's failure to grasp his personal and socio-political responsibilities as Laudine's husband, and as ruler and defender of her country (Mertens 1978).

Iwein's response to the challenges of the adventures in the second cycle corrects this failure. The carefully executed encapsulation technique of the adventure sequence highlights the hero's ability to observe deadlines and keep his promises, despite potentially fatal delays. Iwein demonstrates his loyalty, acting in response to personal obligations and remaining faithful to his estranged wife throughout. As he champions the just causes of his friends and of deserving strangers, all of these women in need of protection, he shows his commitment to fighting for peace and justice, and with it his ability to take on the responsibilities of the ruler. He is accompanied and assisted by a faithful lion whom he has rescued from a serpent, the symbol of evil. The lion mirrors not only Iwein's qualities of gratitude and loyalty, but also indicates divine support for the 'knight with the lion', since the lion can be symbolically associated with Christ and His justice.

The fundamental change that Iwein undergoes between his adventures in the first and second part of the work finds expression in the motif of his insanity, which is the loss of his individual and social identity in response to Laudine's rejection (Ragotzky and Weinmayer 1979; Fischer 1983, 4–18). Brought about by his sense of failure and self-recrimination, his madness is not merely the psycho-medical condition known as *melancholia* (Schmitz 1986). In fact, Iwein's recovery of identity takes place in a succession of different states of self-awareness (McFarland 1988). It is here that it may be most appropriate to talk about the development of the hero, marked by changes in recognition of his failure and in the perception others have of his intentions (Schnell 1991).

In *Iwein*, as in *Erec*, Arthur's court provides the forum for the hero's humiliation and success. However, in *Iwein* the hero is more clearly shown as transcending the expectations and achievement of other Arthurian knights

(Lewis 1975). This is emphasized by the frequently humorous and ironic portrayal of Arthur's companions, who seem to suffer defeat throughout and are unable to provide protection for those in need. Their failure to do so is emphasized by the account of Ginover's abduction, a new episode that Hartmann developed from a mere mention by Chrétien (Christoph 1989).

IV

In both works the irony and humour that balance Hartmann's undoubted didactic tendencies are particularly noticeable in the commentaries and asides of the narrator, who takes on a life of his own even more in the German adaptations than in the French works. Of particular interest are the narrator's reflections on the relationship between reality and fiction which betray a new authorial self-awareness, a main focus of recent scholarly debate (Singer 1990, Kellermann 1992, Strasser 1993 on *Erec*, Grünkorn 1994). This is particularly prominent in the prologues to *Iwein* and to Hartmann's non-Arthurian works (Ragotzky 1992). Hartmann's development of the narrative voice, his rationalizing tendencies, and his emphasis on the moral and religious dimension and its associated symbolism (Combridge 1988) exerted a significant influence on Wolfram's adaptation of Chrétien's *Conte del Graal*.

Borrowings from and allusions to Hartmann's *Erec* testify to the continuing interest in this work during the thirteenth century (Edrich-Ponzberg 1994). The popularity of *Iwein* can be gleaned from thirteenth-century frescos, and the use of Iwein-motifs for the fourteenth-century Malterer Embroidery (see Rushing in this volume). In his *Book of Adventures* (c. 1480), Ulrich Füetrer based *Iban* on Hartmann's work. There even exists an eighteenth-century adaptation: *Ritter Twein* by Gerhard Anton von Halems (Beutin 1994). Both *Erec* and *Iwein* have been central works in the critical study of medieval German literature since the first half of the nineteenth century.

Ulrich von Zatzikhoven, *Lanzelet*

Ulrich von Zatzikhoven's *Lanzelet*, a poem of over 9,400 lines in rhymed couplets, is preserved in its entirety in two manuscripts, W (no. 2698 at Vienna) belonging to the second quarter of the fourteenth century, and P (CPG 371 at Heidelberg), dating from 1420 (Combridge 1993).[4] Nothing is known about the author, who names himself in MS W as *von zatzichoven* (MS P *zezichoven*) *Volrich* (v. 9344). Identification with the *capellanus Volricus de Cecinchovin plebanus Loumeissae*, parish priest (?) of Lommis near Zezikon in the Swiss canton of Thurgau, who is mentioned in a St Gallen document of 1214, remains at best doubtful. *Cecinchovin* has also been linked to Zizingen near Neuenburg on the Rhine (Bärmann 1989). There is some linguistic evidence for the author's having come from either the Alemannic or the Rhine region. Ulrich claims that his work is a faithful rendering of the 'French' – probably Anglo-Norman – 'book of Lanzelet' (v. 9341), which was brought to Germany by its owner Hugh de Morville (v. 9338), one of Richard Cœur de Lion's hostages to the Emperor Henry VI in 1194. Historical documents fail to mention Hugh of Morville amongst the hostages. Of the three English nobles of this name living at the time two have been considered: the *archidiaconus Hugo* who in 1207 became bishop of Coutances (Norman 1965, 286), and Hugh of Morville, who was attached to Henry II's court and appears as witness to some royal charters up to 1170, in which year he is named as one of the murderers of Thomas Beckett. This Hugh de Morville is attested as living on his Cumberland estates from 1194 until his death in 1202. He is considered the most likely owner of Ulrich's 'French' book, of which no trace remains. It is not identical with Chrétien de Troyes's *Chevalier de la charrette*, despite some motifs common to Ulrich's and Chrétien's romances. Traces of north-western German have been taken as an indication that Ulrich used an intermediary Rhenish source, either alongside or in place of a French original (Kantola 1982).

Ulrich traces the adventures of Lanzelet, the future king of Genewis, from his infancy in exile, through knightly and amorous exploits to the hero's eventual accesssion to the throne, and concludes with the establishment of a line of succession and his death. As a fully biographical variant of the narrative pattern of exile and return it is an example of a literary trend, discernible since the twelfth century, to commence narratives with an account of the education and youthful exploits of their hero (Pérennec 1979), and differs from the model created by Chrétien for his Erec and Yvain romances which portray only an important period in the hero's life.

The first and last episodes constitute a political framework distinguished by its relative 'realism'. At the beginning, Lanzelet's tyrannical father offends against the bond of obligation between king and vassals and is overthrown and killed; at the end his son gains the respect and loyalty of the aristocracy through his capacity to show generosity, *milte,* a virtue of rulers, in addition to wielding authority firmly. Lanzelet's youthful career is therefore concerned in no small measure with his education and qualification for kingship (Jackson 1974/5). Furthermore, his quest for his royal identity and the search for a suitable consort, which are important themes in the sequence of adventures, also form the precondition of his accession. Once his rule is secured, he ensures the position of his dynasty, passing on four kingdoms, his own and his wife's, to their four offspring. Ulrich's *Lanzelet* is thus firmly in favour of dynastic continuity, as promoted not only by the Hohenstaufen emperors, but also increasingly by the

German princes themselves. It is therefore possible that either the imperial court or one of the prominent German dynasties may have acted as Ulrich's patron.

The romance's biographical pattern can be linked to medieval ideas on the ages of man (Zellmann 1996). The infant, exposed to a world of strife, loses home and identity. His abduction by the fairy Queen of the Island of Maidens signals a new stage and brings into play supernatural forces which will influence his career; the boy 'without a name' receives a physical, moral and social education (but not a military one!) in a female environment. On reaching adolescence, Lanzelet departs in search of his identity and enters the world of chivalric adventure. Three times Lanzelet wins a bride and a land, killing either the father or uncle of the young woman, the increasing danger of his adventures matching the enhanced qualities of the respective lady. Upon defeating his third opponent, Iweret, father of Iblis, his future wife, Lanzelet learns that his own father was King Pant of Genewis, and that his mother Clarine is King Arthur's sister.

Having discovered his identity and won personal fame and a bride, Lanzelet leaves adolescence behind, now fully qualified to become a member of Arthur's Round Table, the epitome of chivalric society, and to prove his knightly excellence in the service of the courtly community. He successfully champions Queen Ginover when King Valerin claims her as his erstwhile bride, and he leads an army of knights to free his cousins Erec and Walewein. A fairy-tale adventure – Lanzelet breaks the enchantment of a princess turned dragon, by agreeing to kiss the monster – marks the threshold that leads from early youth to an age of *gravitas*, as Lanzelet leaves Arthur's court to take on the responsibilities of kingship.

Besides the biographical pattern, a two-part structure on the lines of the Chrétien's Erec and Iwein romances has been suggested for *Lanzelet*: Part One, the quest for selfhood, is followed in Part Two by the hero's integration into the community (Ruh 1980, 47; McConeghy, 1982, 68). Such bipartite division is, however, overridden by closely interwoven thematic strands: Lanzelet's erotic conquests continue in Part Two with his marriage, albeit an enforced one, to the lady of Pluris which also brings about a final vindication of his personal honour (Combridge 1973, 45). Furthermore, the theme of social integration is by no means restricted to the second part: from the very beginning of his knightly career, Lanzelet is increasingly drawn into Arthur's orbit.

There is also no central crisis separating the two parts. Lanzelet remains a flawless hero throughout. His inherited qualities of bravery, loyalty, liberality and charisma (*sælde*) are never in doubt (Schultz 1980). The demands of love and chivalry are not in conflict with each other, and neither factor interferes with the functioning of the social order. The hero's unproblematic nature has earned the work the reputation of being superficial, even amoral, compared to the romances of Chrétien, Hartmann and Wolfram. Yet, despite the ease with which

Lanzelet who is 'lucky with women' (*wîpsælic*, v. 5529) appears to acquire and lose several brides, great emphasis is placed on the exemplary union of Lanzelet and Iblis as a basis of dynastic monogamy, a union sealed by the gift of the magic tent of love. Iblis's virtue is proven by a magic cloak that only fits the perfectly faithful woman (a recurrent motif of French origin which continues to figure in Arthurian literature up to the sixteenth century) and the couple embark on a model marriage which also ends without their being divided, when both die on the same day (Combridge 1973, 58–60).

The portrayal of the hero's chivalric deeds is not without its moral aspects. It is true that in accordance with the conventions of myth and fairy tale, the guardians of Lanzelet's brides are killed without being offered the chance to surrender. Similarly, neither the lives of Valerin and the sorcerer nor those of their subjects are spared (Borck 1984, 348f.). Yet this is amply justified by the enemies' evil intentions. Lanzelet is in fact expressly cleared of the accusation of being bloodthirsty (v. 5342). Absence of compassion for a defeated opponent does not imply callousness in *Lanzelet*. There is no lack of human sympathy, however such sympathy is reserved for liege, family, and friends, i.e. it is an expression of loyalty. Lanzelet, for example, although normally protected from sadness, is inconsolable at the prospect of his cousins' death in captivity, and thus impelled to embark on his rescue operation. Such concern is, of course, not identical with Yvain's compassion (*pitié*) for victims of oppression and injustice in his later adventures. It lacks the Christian overtones to be found in Erec's *Joie de la curt* adventure. Yet whether Lanzelet's aristocratic ethos based on personal loyalty should therefore be designated 'archaic' (Grubmüller 1993) remains questionable.

For Loomis the romance's significance lay in the light it shed on the mythological prehistory of the Arthurian romance (Loomis 1951, 10). The Land of the Maidens, Iweret's Forest Beautiful, Valerin's castle in which captives succumb to a deathlike sleep, all recall the 'otherworld' scenarios of Celtic myth. Ulrich's version of Ginover's abduction appears to predate other versions, and could be considered a reworking of the myth of the 'otherworld' woman married to a mortal (O'Riain-Raedel 1978, 75; Haug 1978, 6–10). The killing of the bride's father, too, may have its roots in mythology (Pérennec 1979, 41f.). These mythical elements are frequently associated with the strong magical dimension of the romance. In contrast to the restraint in the use of fairy-tale motifs practised by Chrétien and Hartmann in the Erec romance, a pronounced fascination with the fabulous comes to the fore in the inclusion of *mirabilia* such as the Shrieking Marsh or the Growing Lookout (Loomis 1951, 7f.). This may be a characteristic of Ulrich's Anglo-Norman source material, but it also foreshadows the penchant for the supernatural prominent in the later romances, and by itself it offers little guidance to the date of the work. Indeed, the mixture of mythical or fairy-tale elements with courtly sophistication in Ulrich's work (expressed for instance when the princess who is released from a dragon's form becomes arbiter in amorous disputes at court, vv. 8033–40) is characteristic of an important strand in Arthurian romance in general.

A good grasp of the role of the principal Arthurian personages and the work's sophisticated structure, together with shared motifs and names, suggests that the author of the source may have had knowledge of Chrétien's *Erec*, and Ulrich himself seems to have been familiar with the work of Eilhart and Veldeke, as well as with Hartmann's *Erec* (Richter 1934, 102, 144, 260). Although his style lacks the elegance of Hartmann's and Wolfram's language – 'filler' lines are frequent and his transitions are often abrupt – he is not without stylistic ambitions. His vocabulary is wide-ranging, he takes care to use only pure rhymes (Kantola 1982, 23, 161), and his writing shares unusual stylistic features with Wolfram's work. This opens up the possibility that the romance has been composed much later than generally assumed, perhaps as late as the second decade of the thirteenth century (Pastré 1984).

The narrator's asides betray an author highly conscious of the fictional nature of his material. His humorous account of young Lanzelet's exploits (Pérennec 1979, 33) recalls the humour and irony found in the canonical romances, without reaching the same level of sophistication. Whether the pronounced 'normality' of his well-adjusted hero should be seen as a deliberate send-up of the problem-ridden 'classical' Arthurian knight (Feistner 1995) must remain doubtful, since the potential allusions seem neither numerous nor specific enough for a sustained literary parody.

Ulrich's colourful romance is told with zest and humour and with the clear objective of presenting a model knight firmly rooted in a conventional aristocratic value-system. It appears to have been well received. Rudolf von Ems praises Ulrich (*Alexander* vv. 3199–3204, *Willehalm von Orlens* v. 2198), as do Heinrich von Freiberg and Jacob Püterich von Reichertshausen. The popularity of the work can be gleaned from a miniature in the Codex Manesse which portrays a minnesinger and his lady reading *Lanzelet* (Salowski 1975, 40–52).

Notes

[1] Ed. by H. Paul, 16th edn, rev. K. Gärtner, 1996 (Altdeutsche Textbibliothek, 3). Tübingen.

[2] These dukes were lords of a family of *ministeriales* of Aue near Freiburg (attested since 1112).

[3] The difficulties with verbal communication may also extend to Hartmann's male protagonists, Erec as well as Iwein; see Hasty 1996, 45.

[4] Closest in time to the poem's composition is the oldest of the three sets of fragments, B, MS German b. 3.3, f. 9–10 in the Bodleian Library in Oxford (Combridge 1963). A Strasbourg fragment S from *c.* 1300 was destroyed. Two further fragments from one manuscript Gk (Klagenfurt, UB, Perg.-Hs 47) and G (Goldhahn's Fragment, Cambridge, Mass., Harvard University, Houghton Library Ger 80) belong to the first half of the fourteenth century.

Bibliography

Hartmann von Aue, *Erec* and *Iwein*

For guidance to the voluminous secondary literature on Hartmann's Arthurian romances see Neubuhr 1977, Haase 1988, Cormeau/Störmer 1993, Hasty 1996.

Primary Sources and Translations

Hartmann von Aue, *Erec*. Ed. by A. Leitzmann, rev. L. Wolff, 6th edn, prepared by Ch. Cormeau and K. Gärtner, 1985 (Altdeutsche Textbibliothek, 39). Tübingen.

Hartmann von Aue, *Erec*. Transl. by Th. Keller, 1987. New York.

Hartmann von Aue, *Iwein*. Ed. by G. F. Benecke and K. Lachmann, 7th edn, rev. Ludwig Wolff, 1968. Berlin.

Hartmann von Aue, *Iwein*. Ed. and transl. by P. McConeghy, 1984. New York.

The Narrative Works of Hartmann von Aue. Transl. by R. W. Fisher, 1983 (GAG, 370). Göppingen.

Other Literature

Beutin, H. and Beutin W. 1994. *Der Löwenritter in den Zeiten der Aufklärung. Gerhard Anton von Halems Iwein-Version 'Ritter Twein', ein Beitrag zur dichterischen Mittelalter-Rezeption des 18. Jahrhunderts*, GAG, 595, Göppingen.

Christoph, S. 1989. 'Guenevere's abduction and Arthur's fame in Hartmann's *Iwein*', *ZfdA*, 118, 17–33.

Combridge, R. 1988. 'The uses of biblical and other symbolism in the narrative works of Hartmann von Aue', in McFarland and Ranawake 1988, 271–84.

Cormeau, Ch. and Störmer, W. 1993. *Hartmann von Aue. Epoche, Werk, Wirkung*, 2nd edn, Munich.

Edrich-Ponzberg, B. 1994. *Studien zur Überlieferung und Rezeption von Hartmanns 'Erec'*, GAG, 557, Göppingen.

Firestone, R. 1988. 'Boethian order in Hartmann's *Erec* and *Iwein*', *ABäG*, 26, 117–30.

Fischer, H. 1983. *Ehre, Hof und Abenteuer in Hartmanns 'Iwein': Vorarbeiten zu einer historischen Poetik des höfischen Epos*, Munich.

Fisher, R. 1986. 'Räuber, Riesen und die Stimme der Vernunft in Hartmanns und Chrétiens *Erec*', *DVj*, 60, 353–74.

Grünkorn, G. 1994. *Die Fiktionalität des höfischen Romans um 1200*, Philologische Studien und Quellen, 129, Berlin.

Haase, G. 1988. *Die germanistische Forschung zum 'Erec' Hartmanns von Aue*, Europäische Hochschulschriften, ser. I, 1103, Frankfurt.

Hahn, I. 1986. 'Die Frauenrolle in Hartmanns *Erec*', in Hauck, K. et al., eds., *Sprache und Recht: Beiträge zur Kulturgeschichte des Mittelalters. Festschrift für R. Schmidt-Wiegand zum 60. Geburtstag*, vol. 1, Berlin and New York, 172–90.

Hasty, W. 1996. *Adventures in Interpretation: The Works of Hartmann and their Critical Reception*, Literary Criticism in Perspective, Columbia, SC.

Hruby, A. 1979. 'Hartmann als *artifex*, *philosophus* und *praeceptor* der Gesellschaft', in Ch. Cormeau, ed., *Deutsche Literatur im Mittelalter. Kontakte und Perspektiven. Gedenkschrift H. Kuhn*, Stuttgart, 254–75.

Hurst, P. 1994. 'Enîte's dominion over the horses: notes on the coalescence of Platonic and hagiographic elements in an episode from Hartmann's *Erec*', *Med. Aev.*, 63, 211–21.

Jackson, W. H. 1994. *Chivalry in Twelfth-Century Germany: The Works of Hartmann von Aue*, Arthurian Studies, 34, Cambridge.

Kellermann, K. 1992. '*Exemplum* und *historia*. Zu poetologischen Traditionen in Hartmanns *Iwein*', *GRM*, 42, 1–27.

Klein, Th. 1998. 'Ermittlung, Darstellung und Deutung von Verbreitungstypen in der Handschriftenüberlieferung mittelhochdeutscher Epik', in Honemann and Palmer 1988 (see Gen. Bibl.), 110–67.

Kraft, K.-F. O. 1979. *Iweins Triuwe. Zu Ethos und Form der Aventiurenfolge in Hartmanns 'Iwein': Eine Interpretation*, Amsterdam.

Kuhn, H. 1948. 'Erec', in *Festschrift für Paul Kluckhohn und Hermann Schneider* (repr. in Kuhn and Cormeau 1973), 17–48.

Kuhn, H. and Cormeau, Ch., eds., 1973. *Hartmann von Aue*, WdF, 359, Darmstadt.

Lewis, R. E. 1975. *Symbolism in Hartmann's 'Iwein'*, GAG, 154, Göppingen.

McConeghy, P. M. 1987. 'Women's speech and silence in Hartmann von Aue's *Erec*', *PMLA*, 102, 771–83.

McFarland, T. 1988. 'Narrative structure and the renewal of the hero's identity in *Iwein*', in McFarland and Ranawake 1988, 129–57.

McFarland, T. and Ranawake, S., eds., 1988. *Hartmann von Aue: Changing Perspectives: London Hartmann Symposium, 1985*, GAG, 486, Göppingen.

Mertens, V. 1978. *Laudine: Soziale Problematik im 'Iwein' Hartmanns von Aue*, Beihefte zur ZfdPh, 3, Berlin.

Mertens, V. 1986. 'Das literarische Mäzenatentum der Zähringer', in Schmid, K., ed. *Die Zähringer*, Sigmaringen, 118–34.

Neubuhr, E. 1977. *Bibliographie zu Hartmann von Aue*, Berlin.

O'Riain-Raedel, D. 1978. *Untersuchungen zur mythischen Struktur der mittelhochdeutschen Artusepen: Ulrich von Zatzikhoven, 'Lanzelet' – Hartmann von Aue, 'Erec' und 'Iwein'*, Berlin.

Pérennec, R. 1984. *Recherches sur le roman arthurien en vers en Allemagne aux XIIe et XIIIe siècles*, GAG, 393, 2 vols., Göppingen.

Quast, B. 1993. '*Getriuwiu wandelunge*: Ehe und Minne in Hartmanns *Erec*', *ZfdA*, 122, 162–80.

Ragotzky, H. 1992. '*sælde und êre* und *der sêle heil*. Das Verhältnis von Autor und Publikum anhand der Prologe zu Hartmanns *Iwein* und zum *Armen Heinrich*', in Hahn, G. and Ragotzky, H., eds., *Grundlagen des Verstehens mittelalterlicher Literatur*, Kröners Studienbibliothek, 663, Stuttgart.

Ragotzky, H. and Weinmayer, B. 1979. 'Höfischer Roman und soziale Identitätsbildung. Zur soziologischen Deutung des Doppelwegs im *Iwein* Hartmanns von Aue', in Cormeau, Ch., ed., *Deutsche Literatur im Mittelalter. Kontakte und Perspektiven. Hugo Kuhn zum Gedenken*, Stuttgart, 211–53.

Ranawake, S. 1982. 'Zur Form und Funktion der Ironie bei Hartmann von Aue', in WSt, 7, Berlin, 75–116.

Ranawake, S. 1988. 'Erec's *verligen* and the sin of sloth', in McFarland and Ranawake 1988, 93–116.

Rider, J. 1991. 'De l'énigme à l'allégorie. L'Adaptation du "merveilleux" de Chrétien de Troyes par Hartmann von Aue', *Rom*, 120, 100–28.

Schirok, B. 1982. *Parzivalrezeption im Mittelalter*, Darmstadt.

Schmitz, H.-G. 1986. 'Iweins *zorn* und *tobesuht*. Psychologie und Physiologie in mittelhochdeutscher Literatur', in Debus, F. and Dittmer. E., eds., *Sandbjerg 85. Dem Andenken von H. Bach gewidmet*, Kieler Beiträge zur deutschen Sprachgeschichte, 10, Neumünster, 87–111.

Schnell, R. 1991. 'Abaelards Gesinnungsethik und die Rechtsthematik in Hartmanns *Iwein*,' *DVj*, 65, 15–69.

Schulze, U. 1983, '*âmîs unde man*. Die zentrale Problematik in Hartmanns *Erec*', *PBB* (Tübingen), 105, 14–47.

Simon, R. 1990. *Einführung in die strukturalistische Poetik des mittelalterlichen Romans. Analysen zu deutschen Romanen der matière de Bretagne*, Epistemata, Reihe Literaturwissenschaft, 66, Würzburg.

Singer, J. 1990. ' "*nû swîc, lieber Hartman: ob ich ez errâte?*" Beobachtungen zum fingierten Dialog und zum Gebrauch der Fiktion in Hartmanns *Erec*-Roman (7493–7766)', in Rickheit, G. and Wichter, S., eds., *Dialog. Festschrift für Siegfried Grosse*, Tübingen, 59–74.

Smits, K. 1981. 'Enite als christliche Ehefrau', in Smits, K., Besch, W. and Lange, V., eds., *Interpretation und Edition deutscher Texte des Mittelalters. Festschrift für J. A. Asher*, Berlin, 13–25.

Strasser, I. 1993. 'Fiktion und ihre Vermittlung in Hartmanns *Erec*-Roman', in Mertens and Wolfzettel 1993 (see Gen. Bibl.), 63–83.

Tax, P. 1963. 'Studien zum Symbolischen in Hartmanns *Erec*: Erec's ritterliche Erhöhung', *Wirkendes Wort*, 13, 277–88; repr. in Kuhn and Cormeau 1973, 287–310.

Thomas, H. 1989. '*Matière de Rome – matière de Bretagne*. Zu den politischen Implikationen von Veldekes *Eneide* und Hartmanns *Erec*', *ZfdPh*, 108, Sonderheft, 65–104.

Voß, R. 1983. *Die Artusepik Hartmanns von Aue: Untersuchungen zum Wirklichkeitsbegriff und zur Ästhetik eines literarischen Genres im Kräftefeld von soziokulturellen Normen und christlicher Anthropologie*, Cologne.

Worstbrock, F. J. 1985. '*Dilatatio materiae*. Zur Poetik des *Erec* Hartmanns von Aue', *Frühmittelalterliche Studien*, 19, 1–30.

Wapnewski, P. 1979. *Hartmann von Aue*, 7th edn, Sammlung Metzler, 17, Stuttgart.

Ulrich von Zatzikhoven, *Lanzelet*

Primary Source and Translation

Ulrich von Zatzikhoven, *Lanzelet. Eine Erzählung*. Ed. by K. A. Hahn, 1845. Frankfurt. Repr. with 'Nachwort' by F. Norman, 1965. Berlin.

Ulrich von Zatzikhoven: *Lanzelet: A Romance of Lancelot*. Transl. by K. G. Webster, rev. with introduction and notes by R. S. Loomis, 1951. New York.

Other Literature

Bärmann, M. 1989. 'Ulrich von Zatzikhoven und die Entstehung des mittelhochdeutschen *Lanzelet*-Romans. Überlegungen zur Herkunft des Dichters und zur Gönnerschaft', *Das Markgräflerland*, 2, 62–84.

Borck, K. H. 1984. 'Lanzelets *adel*', in Besch, W. et al., eds., *Festschrift für Siegfried Grosse zum siebzigsten Geburtstag*, GAG, 423, Göppingen, 337–53.

Combridge, R. 1963. 'Das Fragment B des *Lanzelet* Ulrichs von Zatzikhoven', *Euph*, 57, 200–9.

Combridge, R. 1973. 'Lanzelet and the queens', in Robson-Scott, W. D., ed., *Essays in German and Dutch Literature*, London, 42–64.

Combridge, R. 1993. 'Der *Lanzelet* Ulrichs von Zatzikhoven im Kreuzfeuer der Editionsprinzipien', in Bergmann, R. and Gärtner, K., eds., *Methoden und Probleme der Edition mittelalterlicher Texte. Bamberger Fachtagung 26.–29. Juni 1991. Plenumsreferate*, Tübingen.

Feistner, E. 1995. '*er nimpt ez allez zeime spil*. Der *Lanzelet* Ulrichs von Zatzikhoven als ironische Replik auf den Problemhelden des klassischen Artusromans', *AStnSpr*, 232, 241–51.

Grubmüller, K. 1993. 'Die Konzeption der Artusfigur bei Chrestien und in Ulrichs *Lanzelet*. Mißverständnis, Kritik oder Selbständigkeit? Ein Diskussionsbeitrag', in Jones and Wisbey 1993 (see Gen. Bibl.), 137–49.

Haug, W. 1978. *Das Land, von welchem niemand wiederkehrt. Mythos, Fiktion und Wahrheit in Chrétiens 'Chevalier de la Charrete', im 'Lanzelet' Ulrichs von Zatzikhoven und im 'Lancelot'–Prosaroman*, Tübingen.

Jackson, W. H. 1974/5. 'Ulrich von Zatzikhoven's *Lanzelet* and the theme of resistance to royal power', *GLL*, NS 28, 285–97.

Kantola, M. 1982. *Studien zur Reimsprache des 'Lanzelet' Ulrichs von Zazikhoven. Ein Beitrag zur Vorlagenfrage*, Turku.

Loomis, R. S. 1951. 'Introduction', in Ulrich von Zatzikhoven, *Lanzelet*. See Primary Source and Translation.

McConeghy, P. M. 1982. '"Aventiure" and Anti-"aventiure" in Ulrich von Zatzikhoven's *Lanzelet*', *GR*, 57, 60–9.

Norman, F. 1965. 'Nachwort', in Ulrich von Zatzikhoven, *Lanzelet*. See Primary Source and Translation.

O'Riain-Raedel, D. 1978. *Untersuchungen zur mythischen Struktur der mittelhochdeutschen Artusepen. Ulrich von Zatzikhoven, 'Lanzelet' – Hartmann von Aue, 'Erec' und 'Iwein'*, Berlin.

Pastré, J.-M. 1984. '"L'Ornement difficile" et la datation du *Lanzelet* d'Ulrich von Zatzikhoven', in Buschinger, D., ed., *Lancelot. Actes du colloque des 14 et 15 janvier 1984*, GAG, 415, Göppingen, 149–62.

Pérennec, R. 1979. 'Artusroman und Familie. "*Daz welsche buoch von Lanzelete*"', *Acta Germanica*, 11, 1–51.

Pérennec, R. 1993. 'Ulrich von Zatzikhoven: *Lanzelet*', in Brunner, H., ed., *Interpretationen. Mittelhochdeutsche Romane und Heldenepen*, Stuttgart, 129–45.

Richter, W. 1934. *Der 'Lanzelet' des Ulrich von Zatzikhoven*, Deutsche Forschungen, 27, Frankfurt.

Ruh, K. 1980. *Höfische Epik des deutschen Mittelalters. II. 'Reinhart Fuchs', 'Lanzelet', Wolfram von Eschenbach, Gottfried von Straßburg*, Grundlagen der Germanistik, 25, Berlin.

Salowsky, H. 1975. 'Ein Hinweis auf das *Lanzelet*-Epos Ulrichs von Zazikhoven in der Manessischen Liederhandschrift. Zum Bilde Alrams von Gresten', *HJb*, 19, 40–52.

Schultz, J. A. 1980. 'Lanzelet: a flawless hero in a symmetrical world', *PBB*, 102, 160–88.

Thoran, B. 1984. 'Zur Struktur des *Lanzelet* Ulrichs von Zatzikhoven', *ZfdPh*, 103, 52–77.

Zellmann, U. 1996. *'Lanzelet'. Der biographische Artusroman als Auslegungsschema dynastischer Wissensbildung*, Studia humaniora, 28, Düsseldorf.

3

THE EMERGENCE OF THE GERMAN GRAIL ROMANCE: WOLFRAM VON ESCHENBACH, *PARZIVAL*

Timothy McFarland

I

Wolfram's *Parzival* was almost certainly composed in the first decade of the thirteenth century, at least for the greater part, and alongside Hartmann von Aue's *Erec* and *Iwein* it constitutes the latest of the three outstanding adaptations of romances by Chrétien de Troyes. *Parzival* is much the most radical reworking and at 24,810 lines by far the longest of the three, and it is generally held to be one of the three or four greatest works in German literature before the eighteenth century. From the beginning, modern Wolfram criticism has praised the distinctive originality and power of Wolfram's poetic language, his depiction of the main hero's spiritual crisis and the manner of its resolution, and the juxtaposition of the Arthurian court and the community of the Grail as models of chivalric society. In recent years increasing attention has been paid to the remarkable persona of the narrator inscribed in the text, and to the related questions of narrative structure and technique.

For our knowledge of the author we are largely dependent upon what the narrator in the text tells us about himself, although we do not know how much of this is biographically reliable. He names himself three times (*Pz.* 114, 12; 185, 7; 827, 13) as Wolfram from Eschenbach, almost certainly the Franconian town south-west of Nuremberg now called Wolframs-Eschenbach, where a noble family of that name is attested from 1268 on. This may have been the poet's family, but it is not proven, and neither is it certain that his family was of noble or *ministerialis* status. He only refers to himself as a knight indirectly, and not unambiguously as Hartmann does. On the other hand, his texts reveal an ability to depict the details of the world of lived knighthood equalled by no other poet of his time. The statement that it is his station in life to bear a shield (115, 11) means in its context that he wishes to be seen as a soldier by profession, and not as a bookish scholar. Similarly his claim to be illiterate, made in the same context (115, 27), is to be seen as a means of dissociating himself from the learned and rhetorical tradition of the clerical schools, as it is displayed with pride in the work of his contemporaries Heinrich von Veldeke, Hartmann and Gottfried von Strassburg. On the other hand he was knowledgeable in many areas such as medicine, astronomy and natural history and clearly had access to learned, i.e. Latin material (see e.g. Groos 1995). He knew French, but perhaps not well enough to avoid occasional misunderstandings of his sources.

In addition to *Parzival*, Wolfram is the author of the thematically related *Titurel* fragments (see Gibbs in this volume), of seven songs, five of which are in the *alba* or dawn-song tradition, and of the major epic *Willehalm*, an incomplete adaptation of the Old French *chanson de geste Aliscans*. The general view that *Parzival* was composed in the first decade of the thirteenth century rests primarily on a reference in book VII (379, 18) to the still visible, and therefore recent, devastation of the vineyards at Erfurt in Thuringia during the siege of 1203. There is also a reference (563, 8–11) to the sack of Constantinople in 1204. *Willehalm* has a reference in the prologue (4, 19–24) to audience response to *Parzival*, and later in the text (393, 30–394, 5) to the imperial coronation of Otto IV, which took place in 1209. It is therefore the later work.

The only explicit reference to a patron in Wolfram's work is in the prologue to *Willehalm*, where he tells us (3, 8–9) that Landgrave Hermann of Thuringia (1190–1217) had provided him with his source text for that work. The landgrave and the life at his court are also mentioned in *Parzival* (297, 16–27) and it is generally accepted that Wolfram spent some time at this, the most literary of the German courts of the period. There are also a number of significant allusions to castles and members of the nobility of Wolfram's home region in Books IV and V of *Parzival*, including Count Poppo of Wertheim (184, 4–6) and the castles of Abenberg (227, 13) and of Wildenberg, the home of the lords of Durne (230, 12–13). These families had had close and well-documented connections to the Hohenstaufen court before the crisis of 1197 (Meves 1984), and it is likely that Wolfram's literary career began under the protection of members of this circle. The original mode of reception probably consisted both of people listening to a public recitation of portions of the work, and of a smaller group of interested private readers (Green 1989, 271–88). The role of the storyteller performing for an audience and interacting with it is an important dimension of the narrator-figure in *Parzival*, but the literacy of the poet and the written nature of the text are not in doubt.

The practice and cultural values of chivalry, imported from the French-speaking world, had taken root in the German lands in the latter half of the twelfth century. Here, as there, the vernacular narrative texts which provided a historical mythology of chivalry are an integral, essential element in the whole complex phenomenon. Wolfram is familiar with the early German adaptations of French narratives in this tradition, and also with heroic epic and with older, Latin-based clerical works in German. The two major German literary models available to him as he began his work were Heinrich von Veldeke's *Eneit,* an adaptation of the French romance of Aeneas, and Hartmann von Aue's *Erec.* Veldeke introduced the literary elaboration of courtly chivalry, including the Ovidian conventions, into German poetry. Hartmann was the more immediate model because of his achievement in adapting Chrétien's innovations, including his manipulation of intricate narrative structures, into the German version of Arthurian romance.

II

Chivalry and lordship, love, marriage and the values of courtly society were the main themes of these works and of Hartmann's later Chrétien adaptation, *Iwein.* Christian values in relation to chivalry had been implicitly (and occasionally explicitly) present, but not central. In his final romance, the unfinished *Perceval* or *Le Conte du Graal,* Chrétien had enlarged the scope of the romance by making religion into a major theme. The hero's quest embraces the experience of sin, repentance and forgiveness (see Kasten in this volume); the central episode in this narrative is his failure to ask the questions expected of him at the Grail Castle, where his host is the maimed and suffering Fisher King, and where he is confronted with the mysterious procession of the bleeding lance and the golden dish called a grail. This is generally regarded as the first ocurrence of the Grail in Western literature and as Chrétien's invention (Ruh 1980, 58–69), and the motifs of the suffering king and the unasked question have remained central to the Grail story in its various reworkings through the centuries. As the questions which Perceval failed to ask remain unanswered in Chrétien's fragment, the interpretation of this enigmatic episode assumes central significance in subsequent treatments of the subject (Johnson 1982).

Whether the sources of the Grail are to be sought in the horn or cauldron of plenty of Celtic myth, related to myths of fertility and regeneration, or in Christian legend and liturgy, or in a blending of some of these strands (Loomis 1963), is still uncertain and the problem is perhaps insoluble. Also controversial is the relationship between Chrétien's romance and Robert de Boron's *Roman de l'Estoire dou Graal* which linked the Grail directly to Christ's Last Supper and Passion through the figure of Joseph of Arimathea. Later French texts (including the continuations of Chrétien's fragment, the prose romances *Perlesvaus* and the so-called *Didot-Perceval,* and the *Queste dou saint graal* contained in the Lancelot-Grail cycle) were to blend motifs from Chrétien and Robert.

It is generally believed that Wolfram did not draw directly on Robert, but based his work on Chrétien's *Perceval,* and may have known some of its continuations. In Chrétien's text a major series of episodes devoted to the early history of Perceval is followed by another sequence devoted to the history of Gauvain, which is interrupted by a short section depicting Perceval's visit to his hermit uncle. Wolfram's *Parzival* adheres to the sequence of episodes (with some important additions), but so many details are altered, expanded and differently motivated, that an entirely original narrative is the result. Wolfram's adaptation expanded Chrétien's 9,234 lines to about 16,000. To this he added extended opening and closing sections of nearly 9,000 lines.

The Grail in *Parzival* is neither the chalice nor the dish of the French texts. The hermit Trevrizent tells Parzival (469, 1–470, 20) that it is a stone with the enigmatic Latin name 'lapsit exillis' and with mysterious powers: it provides food and drink for its guardians, it burns the phoenix and gives it rebirth, and those who see it are preserved from ageing or death for a week. Every Good Friday a dove brings a wafer from heaven which renews its powers. Upon the Grail appear inscriptions revealing the names of the maidens called to tend the Grail and the young men called to protect it; the latter, called *templeise*, form a celibate order of knights. The Grail had at first been guarded on earth by angels who had remained neutral during the revolt of Lucifer, and was later entrusted to Titurel and his descendants, the dynasty of Grail kings who reside at Munsalvæsche.

This conception of the Grail is specific to Wolfram. There has been much speculation but little agreement about literary or legendary and esoteric, possibly Oriental, sources for it (Bumke 1970, 198–268). Wolfram had told his readers a little earlier that his source was the Provençal Kyot (416, 20–30; 453, 1–10) who had reconstructed the true story of Parzival in French on the basis of information contained in a heathen (i.e. Arabic) astrological treatise about the Grail by Flegetanis, and in a dynastic chronicle discovered in Anjou (453, 11–455, 22). It is not clear whether Kyot (or Guiot, Guido) is to be considered a writer or an oral informant, and while some scholars continue to believe that he may have existed (Kolb 1963; Ruh 1980, 94–9) the more widely held view is that Kyot, the 'famous master' (453, 11) and his Arabic and Latin sources are an elaborate fictional construct devised by Wolfram (Nellmann 1988).

The narrator's information about himself and his sources are to be seen as materials in the highly innovative discourse on authorship and work-awareness contained within the text (Ridder 1998). The narrator-figure and the related topic of the self-consciously employed narrative technique and style have been central topics in recent *Parzival* studies (especially Curschmann 1971, Nellmann 1973, Green 1982, Stein 1993; see also Bumke 1997, 128–51). Important aspects of this field are the distinctive brand of humour (Wehrli 1950; Bertau 1983, 60–109), the complexity of the intertextual relationships (Draesner 1993) and the pluralistic narrative voices and generic models within the text (Groos 1995).

Detailed comparisons with Chrétien's *Conte du Graal* (e.g. Bertau 1983, 24–59; Haug 1971) have shown how Chrétien's enigmatic and allusive style has given way to a dense network of cross-references and hidden but significant explanations and allusions.

The narrator speaks to his public most directly in a number of prologues, epilogues and digressions within the text. The most important of these, the introductory prologue (1, 1–4, 26) opens with a *sententia*-like passage (1, 1–14) invoking a man who is both black and white, like the magpie, in that both heaven and hell are possibilities for him, and whose salvation may be in danger because of the lurking presence near his heart of *zwîvel* (1, 1: 'doubt', 'despair' or 'vacillation'). These lines indicate that a discourse in religious terms is to follow, but whether they refer to the protagonist of the work or not is controversial (see Brall 1984, 21–61; Haug 1992, 159–67). The prologue emphasizes the difficulty of the following text and the demands it makes upon the reader's powers of discernment, but commends it in a final passage (3, 28–4, 26) as a tale about great love and fidelity (*triuwe*, 4, 10), greeting the as yet unborn hero in a significant phrase as 'brave, but slow to gain wisdom' (*küene, træclîche wîs*, 4, 18).

III

Chrétien's brief mention of Perceval's father and brothers is replaced in Wolfram's *Parzival* by an extended parental history (Books I and II).[1] Gahmuret is a younger son of the house of Anjou left disinherited by primogeniture. A glamorous incarnation of knight-errantry, he journeys to the Orient in pursuit of glory in combat, and there he wins honour and riches, two kingdoms and a wife. Ever restless, he abandons his black, heathen wife Belakane and her unborn child and returns to the West, where his prowess in a tournament leads to his marriage with Herzeloyde. He leaves this white Christian wife in her turn and returns to the Orient, where he dies fighting. His story ranges across a worldwide stage, juxtaposing Christian and heathen societies, and dealing with issues of kinship and marriage. As it shares some features with the *chanson de geste*, some with pre-Arthurian German texts of aristocratic adventure and some with the dynastic chronicle (see Brall 1984, 107–96), it arouses non-Arthurian generic expectations which remain implicit in *Parzival* before returning in Book XV to help shape the conclusion.

A unique shift in the narrative perspective after Gahmuret's death gives us a female protagonist for a brief but significant episode. Herzeloyde presents herself in monologues framing the birth of her son Parzival (110, 11–114, 4) as the embodiment of the mourning mother, prepared to embrace poverty and suffering (*riuwe*) as the expression of her faithful love (*triuwe*). Her Christian virtues are thereby firmly established as female-determined in the text. After Herzeloyde's death they continue to be embodied forcefully in the figure of her niece Sigune, whose undiminished mourning for her slain lover continues throughout the four episodes in which she appears, moving from uncontrolled grief through a life as enclosed anchoress to a saintly death. Although Gahmuret continues to be praised as an exemplary knight, he leaves behind him stricken women to mourn and die, paying the price exacted by the violent profession of arms. This recurrent pattern determines the initial construction of male and female identity in *Parzival* and casts its distinctive shadow over the adaptation of Chretien's romance which follows.

The section of the text (Books III to VI, *c.* 6,700 lines) devoted to the early history of Parzival follows the broad narrative outline of the first Perceval section of Chrétien's romance in tracing the hero's progress from infancy to the achievement of knighthood (III), to the winning of a wife and kingdom (IV), and then on further, after the first troubling, enigmatic visit to the Grail Castle Munsalvæsche (V), to the conferment of high honour and membership of the Round Table at King Arthur's court (VI). But then, in accordance with the narrative model established by Chrétien (see Kasten, above p. 27f.) and Hartmann (see Ranawake, above pp. 40f., 43f.), this success is followed by crisis. Parzival is denounced before Arthur and the court for his failure to ask the question expected of him at the Grail Castle. In reaction to this public shaming he leaves the court.

Wolfram's shaping of this narrative confirms the continuing importance of the chivalric and the religious strands as established in the histories of the protagonist's parents. On the one hand, it is a seemingly exemplary history of chivalric success. The boy raised in total ignorance of chivalry by his grieving mother encounters knights in the forest and resolves to become a knight. Notwithstanding his ignorance (*tumpheit*) of society and chivalry (a source of comedy and pathos in the initial episodes), he achieves this goal rapidly. At the court of Arthur he kills Ither to gain possession of his horse and armour. By Gurnemanz he is instructed in the skills of knighthood and in the code of chivalry. He offers his service to the beleaguered queen Condwiramurs, defeats her enemies and wins her love and her hand in marriage, thus emulating his father's success with Belakane in the Orient. Although his ignorance in matters of love is comically revealed in earlier episodes, the encounter with Condwiramurs demonstrates how initial inhibitions soon yield to a full and model partnership of love in marriage, to which, unlike his father, he remains constant through years of separation. After more than a year as a just ruler he leaves, intending to return. Instead the next three days bring him first to the Grail Castle and then to the court of Arthur. Here, with his chivalric status proven by notable victories in single combat, he is acclaimed and awarded membership of the Round Table.

Intertwined with this secular narrative of love and chivalry, however, there is a second, more maternally oriented, strand which traces the hero's path into religious crisis. Less explicit than the first, the significance of events becomes apparent to the reader with hindsight. Herzeloyde's enigmatic religious instruction to her son leads Parzival to mistake the knights in the forest for gods, a mistake soon corrected but retaining its paradigmatic importance for what is to follow. In his ignorance (*tumpheit*) and haste to become a knight he unwittingly causes his mother's death by leaving her, and he does not know that in Ither he has killed a kinsman – two mortal sins marking his entry into chivalry, as we learn later. At Munsalvæsche he observes what he considers proper decorum and refrains from asking questions; he fails thereby to bring about the expected healing of the Grail King Anfortas whom he (like the reader) does not yet know to be his mother's brother. It is the women associated with Munsalvæsche, his cousin Sigune and the Grail messenger Cundrie, who denounce him for this omission, accusing him of lacking his mother's qualities of love, loyalty (*triuwe*) and compassion, and declare him to have forfeited his honour and hope of salvation (255, 1–30; 314, 23–318, 4).

Parzival's response demonstrates that the religious and chivalric elements of his dual parental inheritance are confused. He employs the terminology of contractual service to renounce his obligation to God, abandoning a lord who has been too weak to help him (332, 1–8), and declaring himself willing to bear his hatred: 'hat er haz, den wil ich tragn' (332, 8). At the same time, in order to rectify his failure towards Anfortas, he undertakes the arduous quest for the Grail which will occupy him until the end of the narrated action. Unaware of the implicit contradiction in these two decisions, he embarks upon a fruitless course of action which makes him profoundly unhappy. In the ensuing gap of over four years in the narrated time, Parzival, shunning both God and courtly society in which he believes his chivalric identity to have been destroyed, is temporarily displaced as protagonist by Gawan (Books VII and VIII).

His return introduces Book IX, the centre of the work. The figures whom he encounters – Sigune, now an anchoress, the pilgrim knight Kahenis, and the lay hermit Trevrizent – embody the modes of life of lay piety characteristic of the period around 1200 (see Wynn 1984, 211–300). The long Good Friday conversation with Trevrizent informs both Parzival and the reader of many things previously unknown and brings the decisive turning point. Parzival's hatred of God is addressed by Trevrizent in an account of the history of salvation which expounds the nature of God and emphasizes the importance of original sin (461, 28–467, 10). He then explains the history and function of the Grail (468, 10–471, 29; see above). The ground is now prepared for Parzival to understand that the service required by God is not chivalric activity but humility and repentance, and that by rebelling against God he has been aligning himself with Lucifer. He can now accept his guilt in killing his kinsman Ither and in causing the death of his mother, and confess that it was he who failed to ask the question at Munsalvæsche. Trevrizent regards the two deaths caused by the young, ignorant Parzival as constituting his two great sins (499, 20), thereby appearing to attach less importance to the rejection of God in itself and also to the unasked question, which is the mainspring of the action. There is now a general consensus (following Wapnewski 1955) that Wolfram's theology was orthodox, and that he was less concerned with systematic definitions than with representing the personal, existential experience of sinfulness. The important contributions made by Wolfram scholars in the middle decades of the twentieth century, debating the relative gravity of Parzival's sins (especially from Mockenhaupt 1940 via Schwietering 1944/6, Maurer 1950 and Mohr 1952 to Wapnewski 1955), remain valuable for their demonstration of the nature and seriousness of Wolfram's religious thinking.

However, the achievement of Book IX resides not in the theology itself but in the skill with which it is integrated into the process of Parzival's self-discovery, whereby the strands of his parental heritage come together in a restored wholeness. Gahmuret's Angevin lineage is known to the reader from Book I (56, 1–24) and to Parzival from Sigune (140, 25–141, 1). But that his mother Herzeloyde was a member of the Grail dynasty is made clear to the reader (455, 17–22) only shortly before Parzival learns it himself, in the central moment of recognition after he has identified himself to Trevrizent as the son of Gahmuret and the killer of Ither (474, 27–475, 20). He learns from Trevrizent, now revealed as his mother's brother, the measure of his responsibility for the death of his mother and for the sufferings of his mother's other brother Anfortas (476, 12–484, 30). His awareness of himself as a member of both the Grail and the Arthurian families and his consciousness of personal guilt are thus developed together; in this new frame of mind he does penance and leaves Trevrizent with his sins forgiven.

Wolfram follows Chrétien in placing Parzival's adventure of spiritual self-discovery between two extended sections of the text, amounting to almost 10,000 lines, which deal with the more secular chivalric adventures of Gawan. Two self-contained episodes occupy Books VII and VIII, and a single complex narrative forms Books X to XIV. Wolfram is thus adapting the bipartite pattern of Hartmann's romances by constructing a second cycle shared by two heroes, whose histories are oriented towards the Grail Community and the Round Table respectively. At the moment of Parzival's greatest crisis and isolation, the narrator significantly shifts his primary attention to Gawan, traditionally a paradigmatic representative of Arthurian *courtoisie*: sociable, responsive, reluctant to fight unnecessarily, and for whom the relationship of chivalry and religion is not problematic. The audience is thereby being invited to read Gawan's history as a contrasting commentary on the story of Parzival. In major episodes such as those of the castles Munsalvæsche and Schastel Marveile, where each hero is confronted with the task of releasing his own closest maternal relatives from great suffering, and in many other allusions and cross-references, the meaningful juxtaposition of the two protagonists enhances the understanding of the whole text (see especially Mohr 1958 and other essays in Mohr 1979).

The central theme of the Gawan books is the power of love, seen both negatively, in the capacity of injured or misdirected passion to cause unhappiness and conflict, and also positively, in its role as reconciler and healer. As a series of case studies of erotic behaviour, these episodes, alongside those elsewhere in *Parzival*, make of it a text which explores this theme with an unrivalled variety of both comic and serious writing. Gawan's own encounters with women take place in a disordered world where personal and political relations are in disarray. Confronted with war at Bearosche (Book VII), he is able to enter the fray only because he has assumed the formal role of knight-servitor to the precocious ten-year-old Obilot, without any serious emotional involvement on his part. Here, his ability to exploit the social convention of chivalric love-service intelligently empowers him to act as the 'catalyst of the humane' (Mohr 1957 and 1958, 14). At Schampfanzun (Book VIII), on the other hand, it is Gawan himself, sexually easily aroused, who loses control of the situation and gets into trouble when he responds to the attractions of Antikonie, but the narrator refrains from explicit criticism in a piece of masterly and allusive comic storytelling (see Schnell 1974 and Draesner 1993, 311–35). In the main action (Books X to XIV), when Gawan is in love with Orgeluse, he is simultaneously both intelligent healer and helpless victim. In response to his devoted service Orgeluse relinquishes her mistrustful and vengeful behaviour and is transformed, but the extreme suffering which Gawan undergoes in her service is described at length. The narrator's two polemical commentaries (532, 1–534, 8; 585, 5–587, 14), together with the earlier one on Parzival (291, 1–293, 16), are Wolfram's main discussion of the power of love and its literary representation (Schnell 1985, 187–224; Draesner 1993, 342–54).

Some of the major figures in these books are rulers, whose aggressive actions, mostly in connection with erotic passion, have consequences for the well-being of society. Melianz and Vergulaht (Books VII and VIII) are inexperienced kings who neglect the code of reciprocal loyalty on which the relationship of princes and crown depends, and are themselves a threat to political stability. Vergulaht prefers counsels of cynical expediency to the traditional code of princely honour in a debate which may reflect topical political concerns (Mohr 1965). Melianz attacks his vassal Lippaut, the father of his bride Obie, because of her reluctance to yield to his impatient demands. Lasting war between Orgeluse and King Gramoflanz (Books X to XIV) has resulted from his passion for her, which led him to kill her husband and hold her prisoner for a year. The enchanted castle of Schastel Marveile is the work of the sorcerer Clinschor, who after suffering castration as a punishment for adultery had turned to necromancy in his Lucifer-like hatred of mankind (McFarland 1993). The hundreds of prisoners held there, including the closest female relatives of Gawan and King Arthur, are liberated when Gawan, the champion of good against evil, surmounts the challenge of the castle with courage and faith in God. The many prisoners held in isolation by Clinschor may re-enter society and experience human love anew. For them, as for Orgeluse, long years of grief end in restored happiness as a consequence of Gawan's achievements. In spite of the presence of great suffering, the Gawan narrative presents us with a more optimistic social model and with happier outcomes for women than do the earlier books, where the sombre images of suffering and bereavement dominate the depiction of female experience.

In the concluding Gawan books (XIII and XIV) Wolfram, now no longer adapting Chrétien's text, develops this more optimistic view in a celebration of the civilizing power of courtly society to end the long-established state of enmity, fear and violence operating in these lands before Gawan's arrival. Gawan has challenged Gramoflanz on Orgeluse's behalf and, as an actor in the feud, cannot himself bring about peace. Gramoflanz and Gawan's sister Itonje are now lovers, although they have never met – an instance of *amor de lonh* unique in Wolfram's work. The demands of chivalric honour, which will lead to blood-shed, make a tragic outcome for Gawan inevitable, no matter who wins. It is significant that the alternative of a political solution arises at this point and that it is King Arthur who assumes the role of peacemaker. Wolfram depicts the diplomatic skill with which he develops a plan to end the blood feuds by mutual compromise, and negotiates it with the hostile parties. The marriage of the lovers, and further marriages to cement the peace, are agreed. The settlement of disputes by such non-violent means is clearly seen to be superior to chivalric combat and gives substance to Arthur's role as *rex pacificus*, engaged in spreading an enlightened Arthurian conception of knighthood to regions over which he exercises no political control (see Brunner 1983). This is Wolfram's most original contribution to the concept of Arthurian kingship.

The last books (XV and XVI) reveal how Wolfram chose to conclude the history of Parzival without Chrétien's text as source to adapt. Previous phases of the work are successively recalled and reintegrated into the narrative (see Bumke 1991). In the figure of Parzival's brother and alter ego (740, 29; 752, 15–16) Feirefiz, whose piebald black-and-white appearance invokes the imagery of the prologue, the Angevin dynastic theme of the first book returns and with it the framework of a wider chivalric culture embracing the heathen Orient. When they fight, only divine intervention prevents Parzival from killing a kinsman once more and re-enacting the death of Ither. Again the Grail messenger appears before the Round Table, this time to summon Parzival. Now no longer ignorant of what is required, he returns to Munsalvæsche, asks the prescribed question which leads to the miraculous healing of Anfortas, and becomes Grail king. Condwiramurs, Trevrizent and Sigune, the latter now released in death, are all assigned their places in the concluding tableau.

The order of Grail knights or *templeise*, whose leadership Parzival now assumes, is described by Trevrizent as a celibate community with a divinely appointed task. It evidently reflects the twelfth-century military orders to some extent and has traditionally been seen as representing a higher form of knighthood than the secular Arthurian community. The prophecies of Sigune (252, 5) and Cundrie (782, 18–21) appear to foretell a form of Messianic world rulership and a restored prelapsarian paradise under Parzival's Grail kingship (Wisbey 1973; Ruh 1980, 133–6; Groos 1995, 184–7); but the ultimate status of these visions of a spiritual utopia is unclear, and some recent critics have seen the depicted reality of the Grail community as that of a dysfunctional institution in crisis, and have detected inhumane features in the order's rule which make Arthurian chivalry seem superior in some respects (Bumke 1982; Brunner 1983, 70–2; Pratelidis 1994). The hierarchical or gradualistic model which subordinates Arthurian chivalry to the higher religious vocation of the Grail knights may therefore seem less appropriate than a view of the two communities as complementary case studies of contrasting types of chivalric organization, in each of which the narrative is concerned with the study of success and failure in realising the ideals of a code or rule. In this sense, the celebrated *sententia* of the narrator's epilogue, praising the attempt to retain the favour of both God and the world (837, 9–14), is seen to be general in its application and not restricted to the figure of the main protagonist.

The comic narration of Feirefiz's falling in love, conversion, baptism and marriage links the dynasties of Anjou and the Grail once more and leads into the brief accounts of Prester John and Loherangrin, the sons of Feirefiz and Parzival, with which the work ends. These narratives raise new unanswered questions of their own, enhancing the sense of an open ending (Bumke 1991) and implicitly addressing twelfth-century preoccupations with the recovery of Jerusalem and the Christianization of the Orient. They also allow the narrative to end as it had begun, as a family history of the fictional dynasty of Anjou.

Wolfram's version of Arthurian romance is innovative by comparison with Chrétien and Hartmann in its incorporation of substantial elements derived from non-Arthurian narrative forms, and in the copious variety of his narrative.

Common to all parts of the work is the pervasive employment of the concepts and terminology of kinship. In many episodes the principal issues and the identity of the figures are presented in terms of family relationships. A web of kinship-based ties of loyalty and obligation embraces Orient and Occident; former enemies are drawn into the network by marriage. The themes of inheritance and kinship are central to all medieval Grail romances (Schmid 1986), but Wolfram employs a more extensive kinship vocabulary and constructs more complex genealogical networks than any other medieval poet (Jones 1990, 15–44), and exploits their narrative significance to greater effect (Bertau 1983, 190–240; Delabar 1990). In doing so, he was appealing to the values of his lay aristocratic audience and providing them with the means of grasping an underlying unity in his wide-ranging treatment of the human condition.

IV

The evidently canonical status of *Parzival* from its first appearance is attested by the exceptional evidence for its medieval popularity (see Schirok 1982). With sixteen complete manuscripts, at least sixty-six securely attested fragments and an incunable print of 1477, it is by far the best-transmitted German courtly romance. The text we read today, still based upon Karl Lachmann's edition of 1833, is essentially that of the mid-thirteenth-century St Gallen manuscript no. 857. Wolfram's contemporaries Gottfried von Strassburg and Wirnt von Grafenberg and many later poets refer to *Parzival*; the didactic *Wartburgkrieg* (*c.* 1250) confronts the Christian layman Wolfram, a role clearly derived from the narrator-figure in *Parzival* (Ragotzky 1971), with his own creation, the heathen magician Klingsor; two major narrative texts, *Der jüngere Titurel* and *Lohengrin* are directly based upon *Parzival*; the text was extended by Claus Wisse and Philipp Colin (the *Rappoltsteiner Parzifal*) in the fourteenth century, and adapted by Ulrich Füetrer in his *Buch der Abenteuer* in the fifteenth century.

The modern reception begins with J. J. Bodmer's publication of excerpts of 1753, since which time the central position of *Parzival* in medieval literature has been uncontested in the German-speaking world. Of the many modern versions of the material, by far the most important in terms of its worldwide influence is Richard Wagner's *Parsifal* (1882), in which the greater part of Wolfram's work is ignored or distorted, but where the motif of the guileless fool who fails to ask the expected question of the suffering Grail king receives a potent nineteenth-century interpretation (Wapnewski 1978). The Grail theme, drawing on both Wagner and Wolfram in its German variants, remained popular into the twentieth century, and through Jessie L. Weston's *From Ritual to Romance*

(1920) it found its way indirectly into T. S. Eliot's *The Waste Land*. From 1980 on, a new wave of works by German writers including Tankred Dorst, Peter Handke, Christoph Hein and Adolf Muschg, and based more closely on Wolfram (Wasielewski-Knecht 1993, 231–305), bears witness to the continuing vitality of the subject.

Note

[1] It is usual to refer to the different sections of Parzival by means of the sixteen books into which Karl Lachmann divided the text in his edition of 1833. There is no evidence that Wolfram intended any such division, but the book numbers are retained for the sake of convenience and ease of reference.

Bibliography

For further bibliography on *Parzival* see Bumke 1997. Publications since 1984 are listed in the Wolfram-Studien from vol. 10 (1988). For older literature see Pretzel/Bachofer 1968 and Bumke 1970.

Primary Sources, Translations and Commentary

Pz. = Wolfram von Eschenbach, *Parzival*, in *Wolfram von Eschenbach*. Ed. by K. Lachmann, 1926. 6th edn. Berlin and Leipzig.
Wolfram von Eschenbach, *Parzival*. 2 vols. Ed. by K. Lachmann, revised with a commentary by E. Nellmann, transl. by D. Kühn, 1994 (Bibliothek des Mittelalters, 8/1 and 8/2). Frankfurt.
Wolfram von Eschenbach, *Parzival*. Transl. by A. T. Hatto, 1980 (Penguin Classics). Harmondsworth.

Other Literature

Bertau, K. 1973. *Deutsche Literatur im europäischen Mittelalter*, vol. II, Munich.
Bertau, K. 1983. *Wolfram von Eschenbach. Neun Versuche über Subjektivität und Ursprünglichkeit in der Geschichte*, Munich.
Brall, H. 1984. *Gralsuche und Adelsheil. Studien zu Wolframs Parzival*, Heidelberg.
Brunner, H. 1983. ' "Artus der wise höfsche man". Zur immanenten Historizität der Ritterwelt im *Parzival* Wolframs von Eschenbach', in Peschel, D., ed., *Germanistik in Erlangen. Hundert Jahre nach der Gründung des Deutschen Seminars*, Erlangen.
Bumke, J. 1970. *Die Wolfram von Eschenbach Forschung seit 1945*, Munich.
Bumke, J. 1979. *Mäzene im Mittelalter. Die Gönner und Auftraggeber der höfischen Literatur in Deutschland 1150–1300*, Munich.
Bumke, J. 1982. 'Die Utopie des Grals. Eine Gesellschaft ohne Liebe?' in Gnüg, H., ed., *Literarische Utopie-Entwürfe*, Frankfurt, 70–9.
Bumke, J. 1991. 'Parzival und Feirefiz – Priester Johannes – Loherangrin. Der offene Schluß des *Parzival* von Wolfram von Eschenbach', *DVj*, 65, 236–64.
Bumke, J. 1997. *Wolfram von Eschenbach*, Sammlung Metzler, 36, 7th edn, Stuttgart.

Curschmann, M. 1971. 'Das Abenteuer des Erzählens. Über den Erzähler in Wolframs *Parzival*', *DVj*, 45, 627–67.

Delabar, W. 1990. *'Erkantiu sippe unt hôch geselleschaft'. Studien zur Funktion des Verwandt-schaftsverbandes in Wolframs von Eschenbach 'Parzival'*, GAG, 518, Göppingen.

Draesner, U. 1993. *Wege durch erzählte Welten. Intertextuelle Verweise als Mittel der Bedeutungskonstitution in Wolframs 'Parzival'*, Mikrokosmos, 36, Frankfurt.

Green, D. H. 1978. 'Homicide and *Parzival*', in Green, D. H. and Johnson, L. P., *Approaches to Wolfram von Eschenbach: Five Essays*, Mikrokosmos, 5, Berne, 11–82.

Green, D. H. 1982. *The Art of Recognition in Wolfram's 'Parzival'*, Cambridge.

Green, D. H. 1989. 'Zur primären Rezeption von Wolframs Parzival', in Gärtner and Heinzle 1989 (see Gen. Bibl.), 271–88.

Groos, A. 1995. *Romancing the Grail: Genre, Science and Quest in Wolfram's 'Parzival'*, Ithaca.

Haferland, H. 1994. 'Parzivals Pfingsten. Heilsgeschichte im *Parzival* Wolframs von Eschenbach', *Euph*, 88, 263–301.

Hasty, W., ed. 1999. *A Companion to Wolfram's 'Parzival'*, Columbia, SC.

Haug, W. 1971. 'Die Symbolstruktur des höfischen Epos und ihre Auflösung bei Wolfram von Eschenbach', *DVj*, 45, 668–705.

Haug, W. 1992. *Literaturtheorie im deutschen Mittelalter. Von den Anfängen bis zum Ende des 13. Jahrhunderts*, 2nd edn, Darmstadt.

Johnson, L. P. 1982. 'The Grail Question in Wolfram and Elsewhere', in Green, D. H., Johnson, L. P. and Wuttke, D., eds., *From Wolfram and Petrarch to Goethe and Grass: Studies in Literature in Honour of Leonard Forster,* Baden-Baden, 83–102.

Jones, W. J. 1990. *German Kinship Terms (750–1500): Documentation and Analysis*, Berlin.

Kolb, H. 1963. *Munsalvaesche. Studien zum Kyotproblem*, Munich.

Kugler, H. 1990. 'Zur literarischen Geographie des fernen Ostens im *Parzival* und im *Jüngeren Titurel*', in Dinkelacker, W. et al., eds., *Ja muz ich sunder riuwe sin. Festschrift für Karl Stackmann*, Göttingen, 107–47.

Kuhn, H. 1956. '*Parzival*. Ein Versuch über Mythos, Glaube und Dichtung im Mittelalter', *DVj*, 30, 151–80.

Loomis, R. S. 1963. *The Grail: From Celtic Myth to Christian Symbol*, Cardiff.

Maurer, F. 1950. 'Parzivals Sünden', *DVj*, 24, 304–46 (repr. in Rupp 1966, 49–103).

McFarland, T. 1993. 'Clinschor. Wolfram's adaptation of the *Conte du Graal*: the Chastel Marveile episode', in Jones and Wisbey 1993 (see Gen. Bibl.), 277–94.

Meves, U. 1984. 'Die Herren von Durne und die höfische Literatur zur Zeit ihrer Amorbacher Vogteiherrschaft', in Oswald, F. and Störmer, W., eds., *Die Abtei Amorbach im Odenwald,* Sigmaringen, 113–43.

Mockenhaupt, B. 1942. *Die Frömmigkeit im Parzival Wolframs von Eschenbach*, Bonn (repr. Darmstadt 1968).

Mohr, W. 1952. 'Parzivals ritterliche Schuld', *Wirkendes Wort*, 2, 148–60 (repr. in Mohr 1979, 14–36).

Mohr, W. 1957. 'Obie und Melianz. Zum 7. Buch von Wolframs *Parzival*', in *Gestaltprobleme der Dichtung. Günther Müller zu seinem 65. Geburtstag am 15. Dezember 1955*, Bonn (repr. in Rupp 1966, 261–86 and in Mohr 1979, 94–119).

Mohr, W. 1958. 'Parzival und Gawan', *Euph* 52, 1–22 (repr. in Rupp 1966, 287–318 and in Mohr 1979, 62–93).

Mohr, W. 1965. 'Landgraf Kingrimursel. Zum VIII. Buch von Wolframs *Parzival*', in *Philologia deutsch: Festschrift für Walter Henzen*, 21–38 (repr. in Mohr 1979, 120–37).

Mohr, W. 1979. *Wolfram von Eschenbach. Aufsätze*, GAG, 275, Göppingen.

Nellmann, E. 1973. *Wolframs Erzähltechnik: Untersuchungen zur Funktion des Erzählers*, Wiesbaden.

Nellmann, E. 1988. 'Wolfram und Kyot als "vindaere wilder maere"', *ZfdA*, 117, 31–67.

Ohly, F. 1985. 'Die Pferde im Parzival Wolframs von Eschenbach', in *L'uomo di fronte al mondo animale nell'alto medioevo*, II, Spoleto, 849–933 (repr. in Ohly, *Ausgewählte und neue Schriften zur Literaturgeschichte und zur Bedeutungsforschung*, ed. by U. Ruberg and D. Peil, Stuttgart and Leipzig, 1995, 323–64).

Pérennec, R. 1984. *Recherches sur le roman arthurien en vers en Allemagne aux XIIe et XIIIe siècles*, 2 vols., GAG, 393 I and 393 II, Göppingen.

Pratelidis, K. 1994. *Tafelrunde und Gral. Die Artuswelt und ihr Verhältnis zur Gralswelt im 'Parzival' Wolframs von Eschenbach*, Würzburg.

Pretzel, U. and Bachofer, W. 1968. *Bibliographie zu Wolfram von Eschenbach*, 2nd edn, Berlin.

Ragotzky, H. 1971. *Studien zur Wolfram-Rezeption. Die Entstehung und Verwandlung der Wolfram-Rolle in der deutschen Literatur des 13. Jahrhunderts*, Stuttgart.

Ridder, K. 1998. 'Autorbilder und Werkbewußtsein im *Parzival* Wolframs von Eschenbach', WSt, 15, 168–94.

Ruh, K. 1980. *Höfische Epik des deutschen Mittelalters*, vol. 2, Berlin.

Rupp, H., ed. 1966. *Wolfram von Eschenbach*, WdF, 57, Darmstadt.

Sacker, H. 1963. *An Introduction to Wolfram's 'Parzival'*, Cambridge.

Schirok, B. 1982. *Parzivalrezeption im Mittelalter*, Erträge der Forschung, 1974, Darmstadt.

Schmid, E. 1986. *Familiengeschichten und Heilsmythologie: Die Verwandtschaftsstrukturen in den französischen und deutschen Gralromanen des 12. und 13. Jahrhunderts*, Tübingen.

Schnell, R. 1974. 'Vogeljagd und Liebe im 8. Buch von Wolframs Parzival', *PBB*, 96, 246–69.

Schnell, R. 1985. *Causa Amoris. Liebeskonzeption und Liebesdarstellung in der mittelalterlichen Literatur*, Berne.

Schwietering, J. 1944/6. 'Parzivals Schuld', *ZfdA*, 81, 44–68.

Stein, A. 1993. *'wort unde werc'. Studien zum narrativen Diskurs im Parzival Wolframs von Eschenbach*, Mikrokosmos, 31, Frankfurt.

Wapnewski, P. 1955. *Wolframs Parzival. Studien zur Religiosität und Form*. Heidelberg.

Wapnewski, P. 1978. 'Parzival und Parsifal oder Wolframs Held und Wagners Erlöser', in Kunze, S., ed., *Richard Wagner. Von der Oper zum Musikdrama*, Berne and Munich, 47–60.

Wasielewski-Knecht, C. 1993. *Studien zur deutschen Parzival-Rezeption in Epos und Drama des 18. bis 20. Jahrhunderts*, Frankfurt.

Wehrli, M. 1950. 'Wolframs Humor', in *Überlieferung und Gestaltung. Festgabe für Theophil Spoerri*, Zurich, 9–31 (repr. in Rupp 1966, 104–24).

Wisbey, R. 1973. 'Marvels of the East in the *Wiener Genesis* and in Wolfram's *Parzival*', in W. D. Robson-Scott, ed., *Essays in German and Dutch Literature*, Publications of the Institute of Germanic Studies, 15, London, 1–41.

Wynn, M. 1984. *Wolfram's 'Parzival': On the Genesis of its Poetry*, Mikrokosmos, 9, Frankfurt.

4

FRAGMENT AND EXPANSION: WOLFRAM VON ESCHENBACH, *TITUREL* AND ALBRECHT, *JÜNGERER TITUREL*

Marion Gibbs

In the present context there is much to be said for considering these two works together, although they could hardly be more different in many important respects. The massive work by Albrecht (6,327 strophes of four long lines each) is an incongruous partner for the fragile, enigmatic two fragments which constitute the work by Wolfram von Eschenbach usually known as *Titurel*. Yet literary history has thrown them together, and rightly so, given that those who first received them side by side appear to have done so without question. The situation might be described as one of the most extraordinary literary hoaxes ever, were it not for the fact that deliberate deception can hardly have been in the mind of Albrecht, composing some decades after Wolfram's death and unmasking himself, albeit late in the poem. Rather does his huge offering constitute one of a number of attempts by post-classical writers of the German Middle Ages to complete a work left unfinished by a great predecessor.

Medieval listeners may well have been sure that Wolfram's story was in need of completion, and it may be an indication that they placed more importance on the story than on the finer points of its telling that Albrecht's masquerade passed unchallenged for so long. Modern critics are not so unanimously convinced that the fragment needed anything to perfect it, though most would agree that Albrecht's method was inappropriate. Equally, assessments of Albrecht's work vary, often depending upon whether it is seen from the perspective of Wolfram's fragments or (the view which prevails in the relatively abundant research of the past twenty years) as an independent work which occupies a unique position in the development of medieval German narrative poetry.

Wolfram's *Titurel* already raises some difficult questions. The two which dominate critical discussion emerge on a fairly superficial acquaintance with the work, and they can hardly be separated from one another. Closer investigation reveals that the fragmentary nature of the work and its relationship with *Parzival* are indeed inseparable issues which together lead to some of the more complex questions which the work raises, about its genre, Wolfram's intention in writing it, and its relationship to the evolution of the medieval romance in

Germany in the thirteenth century. It is probably this last matter which has taxed scholars most in recent decades, and which has also bound the study of *Titurel* to that of the *Jüngerer Titurel.*

Most critics agree that *Titurel* is a late composition, written certainly after *Parzival* and possibly during a pause in the writing of *Willehalm.* That suggests a date of about 1217–20, and a date post-1217 is supported by the only reference to a historical event, the death of Hermann von Thüringen, in strophe 82a, now widely accepted as authentic. We know that Hermann prompted the composition of *Willehalm* (3, 8–9), and his death is usually assumed to have been a major factor in Wolfram's failure to complete it. That does not necessarily mean that Hermann commissioned the writing of *Titurel*, but no other suggestion presents itself. For Wolfram's source, one need look no further than his own *Parzival*: the story of Sigune is told somewhat impressionistically in the course of four episodes based on the single scene in Chrétien's poem which tells of the encounter between the hero and his first cousin. The transformation of Sigune from the distraught young woman cradling her recently slain lover to the saintly recluse who can find ultimate peace through her love of God is seen to be made possible only by the passage through bitterness and self-accusation, and it is sealed only in her own death. The parallelism between her progress and that of Parzival means that they both achieve what appears to be individual fulfilment, and her story is in a sense completed when the elected King of the Grail reunites her with her lover in his coffin. The one piece of her story which remains unplaced concerns the death of Schionatulander, and more tantalizing than mere uncertainty is the 'information' which Wolfram supplies when he allows her to refer so puzzlingly to the hound's leash which brought him his death (*Parzival* 141, 16). A work in other respects so complete thus has a single frustrating question mark hanging over it, and the simplest explanation of the existence of *Titurel* is that Wolfram sought to supply an answer to that question.

On the face of it, that is precisely what he does not do in the two densely packed, exquisite fragments which are traditionally called *Titurel*, after the old King of the Grail who dominates the opening part of the first fragment with his abdication speech, his eulogy of his descendants, and his explanation of the sacred office which his family fulfils as the selected custodians of the Grail. Along with these more factual strands, largely familiar from *Parzival*, are his moving evocation of a youth spent in the service of chivalry and his elevation of love as the motivating force of his whole family. Thus this prelude to what is clearly to be the story of Sigune and Schionatulander raises issues which may be expected to dominate it. Yet *Titurel* does not tell this story, and the audience is left to piece together the two disconnected fragments and supplement them with the knowledge available from *Parzival.*

The longer first fragment (131 strophes) recapitulates events already known – the marriage of Herzeloyde and Gahmuret, and his departure in response to a call from his master and friend, the Baruch – but the focus is on two younger members of the family, Herzeloyde's dead sister's child, Sigune, and Gahmuret's young cousin, the orphan Schionatulander. Wolfram evokes the burgeoning love of this pair who have been brought together by death, and he describes their uncertainty in the face of a new experience, yet also the accompanying optimism. Although the shadow of the doomed love of their parents hangs over them, they both take encouragement from their present guardians, and only the audience is aware that the love of Herzeloyde and Gahmuret will soon come to sorrow. Products as they all are of the court, they submit unquestioningly to the code of chivalry which equates love with service. Schionatulander's departure with Gahmuret may come as a disappointment at the point when their love is beginning to grow, but it will afford him the chance to prove himself. Sigune is shown as a young woman fully aware of her power, a strange mixture as she teases him with her coy analysis of the nature of love (64) in the course of the conversation between the pair of them about love's strength and its universal impact. Characteristically, Wolfram strikes a balance in his presentation of youth and inexperience, and precocity in the face of a future which, as we know, will bring tragedy.

What lies between the end of the first fragment and the beginning of the second, much shorter one (thirty-nine strophes) remains untold in *Titurel*, though it is known to some extent from *Parzival*. Presumably some time has elapsed, and Gahmuret has died in the East; presumably Parzival has been born to the grieving Herzeloyde. Once more the action is focused on Sigune and Schionatulander, but the fragment begins in the middle of this new stage of Wolfram's narrative, with its opening half-line 'sus lâgen si unlange' ('they had not been lying like this for very long'). Where precisely they are, how they come to be encamped in the forest, does not really matter, for it is the next event which will prove to be the turning point in their relationship. When they hear the hound pursuing its prey, Schionatulander jumps up, catches it and brings it back to Sigune. Now all attention is on the bejewelled leash, for this exotic object enthrals her and becomes the impetus to future events. Wolfram's audience cannot have failed to react to this echo from *Parzival* and to presume that some kind of elucidation was at hand. Not so, however, and what we have not known from *Parzival* is that this is no ordinary dog's lead. Not only is it very costly, but it contains a lengthy inscription in precious stones, only part of which Sigune manages to read before the dog escapes again. What she has read is the beginning of a love story, concerning the young queen Clauditte who sent the dog to her beloved Duke Ehkunat, from whom it escaped that morning. Encapsulated in that story is another, the tragic history of the love of Clauditte's sister Florie for Ilinot, known from *Parzival* (585, 29f.) as the son of King Arthur.

The superficial explanation of Sigune's obsession with the leash, and her demand that Schionatulander retrieve it, is that she wishes to finish reading the story. Her declaration that nothing, not even her kingdom itself, will have any meaning for her if she does not do so, and that the future for herself and Schionatulander depends on it, may be construed as the extravagant response of a young girl used to getting her own way. It constitutes ammunition for those who attribute guilt to her and see her future as shown in *Parzival* as a life of atonement (Christoph 1981). Her desire for the leash has also been interpreted as a quest for her own identity, and Schionatulander's readiness to respond to her challenge as his attempt to prove himself, not only in her eyes, but also in a more abstract way. The name of the dog is, after all, Gardeviaz, which Wolfram translates as 'guard the path!' The message sent by Clauditte to her beloved – and Wolfram describes the hound itself as 'this wild letter' (153, 2) – is some kind of exhortation to all men and women, who, if they stay on the right path, will enjoy the favour of this world and earn true happiness in the next (144). Sigune and Schionatulander embark upon their path with hope and optimism, yet, as we know, something goes terribly wrong, at least in ordinary, human terms. *Titurel* provides no answer to the question of whether this was the right path or not, but the poem does appear to cast doubt on the validity of traditional love-service. What kind of love is it that sends the beloved to his death? And what kind of hero perishes in the pursuit of his goal? The puzzling closing strophe of the fragment is ambivalent about the prospects of Schionatulander in his pursuit of fame (*prîs*). Wolfram has already challenged established values in *Parzival*, which, with the emphasis on the Grail as the supreme spiritual goal, transcends the norm in several important respects, and it may be that he intends *Titurel* as a further critique of the Arthurian romance.

Everything about *Titurel* suggests that Wolfram may be attempting a daring experiment destined to remain incomplete. Its unique form, the complex four-line strophe, distinguishes it from all the courtly narratives which precede it and has more in common with the *Nibelungenlied* and some of the early lyric. The manner of his narrative, with its fusion of the epic and the lyrical, is remarkable, both for its intrinsic impact and for its striking uniqueness. Nineteenth-century critics praised the work for its poetic qualities, Jacob Grimm placing it above *Parzival* and *Willehalm* (Bumke 1997, 255). One of the first major studies of the poem concentrates on its elegiac mood and its lyric qualities, but also broaches the problem of its structure, venturing the suggestion that the two fragments constitute the greater part of a work which needed only the beginning of the first fragment and one further section to complete it (Wolff 1950, 118). Looking at the problem rather differently, Mohr (1977) argues that the fragments are a sketch ('ein Entwurf', 123) never intended for public consumption but pre-served, possibly out of deference for Wolfram's stature. A central article on the nature and structure of the poem goes further, suggesting that what we have is 'a lyrical recreation of epic material' and that Wolfram did not intend a full-scale epic but a series of episodes describing the phases of love (Richey 1961, 180). This view verges on the proposition, presented already in earlier criticism and not without its supporters even today, that he broke off because there was no more to be said or that precisely the fragmentary nature of the work accords with Wolfram's intention to present an open-ended, enigmatic situation (Mertens 1993, 203).

A deliberate fragment would make *Titurel* a unique work in its time, and most recent scholars dismiss the idea as too 'modern'. Increasingly, scholarship has concerned itself with the nature of *Titurel* and its place within Wolfram's œuvre: with the question of whether it can be seen to continue or even to retract stand-points adopted in *Parzival* and also in *Willehalm*. The article by Haug (1980a) is immensely thought-provoking, examining *Titurel* from the perspective of the Arthurian romance and concluding that Wolfram could not complete it because it represented a reversal of all the accepted norms of that genre: Schionatulander dies, his quest is not the process of transformation and growth of the Arthurian hero, and the backcloth is not the court but the world outside and beyond it. In the subtitle to his article, Haug refers to 'gebrochene Handlung und zerfallende Welt' ('broken action and a world falling to pieces') in *Titurel*. This is how the work looks if one reads it, as he suggests one should, as it was written, backwards from the perspective of death, backwards from *Parzival*. This view of *Titurel* comes close to the daring, almost iconoclastic, assessment of it as Wolfram's self-criticism (Wyss 1974). Schionatulander's adventure puts a question mark over the traditional Arthurian adventure, and Wolfram left the work incomplete because, leading, as we know it would, to the death of the hero, it was of no interest in its time and he knew that. In Haug's view (1980b), Wolfram's fragments represent the sketch for an anti-Arthurian romance, in which Sigune's dispatch of her lover in search of the leash represents 'ein irritierender Vorwurf' ('a disturbing reproach', 223). Both Haug and Wyss, in their respective probings of the meaning of the poem and its relationship to its literary context, are a long way from the gentler acclamation of early scholars, who saw it as an exquisite achievement, perfect in its evocation of young love and the bitter-sweetness of human existence, in which chivalry might play a central and legitimate role.

Wolfram's contemporaries are unlikely to have been satisfied with the two fragments, no matter how beautiful, and as in the case of other works – Gottfried's *Tristan* and Wolfram's own *Willehalm* – a bold man was on hand to take on the responsibility of fulfilling their need for completeness. Some would say that he took his responsibility overzealously, but the abundance of manuscripts of the work known as the *Jüngerer Titurel* speaks for its success during the later Middle Ages. It was composed about 1270–5, as much as fifty years after the death of Wolfram von Eschenbach, by one who, explicitly assuming the identity of Wolfram, maintains this pose – though there are occasional, possibly interpolated, hints at his subterfuge – until he reveals his name, Albrecht, in strophe 5883. That he is the Albrecht von Scharfenberg to whom Ulrich Füetrer, in his late fifteenth-century compilation *Das Buch der Abenteuer*, attributes two highly praised works no longer extant, is now largely disputed, and the two Albrechts are accorded separate identities. About the author of the *Jüngerer Titurel* we know nothing for certain, although important details can be gleaned from the work itself. His erudition is evident in a work which has been described as a compendium of medieval knowledge (Ebenbauer 1993, 363), and his command of both French and Latin is apparent, as is his familiarity with his literary predecessors in German. The early belief that he came from Bavaria was brought into question by the manuscript findings of Röll (1964) who argued for a provenance further north, possibly at Wittenberg, a view disputed by Nyholm, who in 1992 completed the vast task of editing the work, which had been left unfinished on Wolf's death in 1967. The complexity of textual matters, the abundance of manuscripts, and the absence until very recently of a complete edition to replace the unsatisfactory version of Hahn printed in 1842, have all hampered the work of scholars who have turned their attention to this enormous and in many ways puzzling work which has provoked diverse and sometimes vituperative assessments.

The early history of the reception of the *Jüngerer Titurel* is already intriguing. There are eleven manuscripts and forty-five fragments, some dating from around 1300 or just before, the preponderance belonging to the fourteenth century and some to the fifteenth, which also saw a printed version. This distribution speaks for the popularity of a work which was acclaimed in 1462 by the literary enthusiast Jakob Püterich von Reichertshausen as 'das haubt ob deutschen püechen' ('the crown of German books'), praise which is echoed in other contemporary records (Wolf 1955, I, x). Just as telling evidence for the esteem in which the work was held is the fact that Wolfram's own fragments are extant in only two manuscripts, both from the thirteenth century and one of them badly damaged. It seems fair to conclude that his work was subsumed into the vast 'continuation' and further independent transmission of his original deemed to be unnecessary. Large portions of Wolfram's *Titurel* are inserted, intact or in modified form, into Albrecht's work. When this was rediscovered in the early nineteenth century, it was accepted at its face value, as a work by the author of *Parzival* and *Willehalm*; indeed it was acclaimed as Wolfram's finest achievement. The turning point came when, in 1829, the great medievalist Karl

Lachmann wrote in response to an article by Karl Rosenkranz which had juxtaposed *Titurel* and Dante's *Divine Comedy*. In no uncertain terms he exposed the misconception and condemned Albrecht's achievement as 'ein langweiliges, todtes und geziertes Werk' ('a boring, dead and elaborate work'), the product of a foolish and insensitive author with inflated ideas of his ability, trying to imitate Wolfram.

It was a long time before Albrecht's work recovered from the damning assessment of Lachmann, whose admiration for Wolfram doubtless led to this onslaught on a work he saw as an affront to the master. Not until 1897 was the work the subject of a large-scale study, and then it was considered primarily in its relation to Wolfram (Borchling); in recent years, Parshall's thorough and measured analysis of narrative style is likewise based on a comparison (1981). Albrecht's work can even today evoke opinions as far apart as Schröder's scathing dismissal of it as 'a monstrous opus' (1982, 19) and Haug's description of it as 'the most significant Arthurian romance of the post-classical period' (1980b, 222). The subtitle to Schröder's book implies a question: was it devotion or arrogance that prompted Albrecht? Perhaps it was a bit of both, or perhaps it was neither, and possibly a true evaluation of the *Jüngerer Titurel* can be achieved only when it is divorced from the fragments which prompted its composition. Increasingly, this independent assessment of the work has been conducted by scholars such as Haug and Ebenbauer, and this must surely be the trend for the future, with the completed edition of Wolf and Nyholm now available and, despite any misgivings expressed about the procedure, providing a comprehensive presentation of the complex manuscript tradition. The *Jüngerer Titurel* needs to be considered, not as the clumsy ramblings of a third-rate imitator, but within a context such as that of the present volume, as a significant contribution to the Arthurian literature in Germany at the end of the thirteenth century. That said, it must be conceded that the obviously Arthurian content of the work is only a portion of its diverse material. Albrecht's attitude to the Arthurian world is one of ambivalence, or even indifference (Ebenbauer 1979, 396): the gradation between the court of Arthur and the Grail is levelled out by his insistence that Anfortas should be a member of the Round Table. Moreover, he changes the nature of his Arthurian material by placing Arthur in a quasi-historical context, borrowing from Geoffrey of Monmouth to relate him to the Roman Emperor Lucius. Even material familiar from his literary predecessors is treated in a manner which suggests a higher degree of reality: Gawain is still a child; the story of Erec is in the past; that of Iwein lies largely in the future, given that Ascalon and Laudine marry at the festival of Arthur. Structurally the work lacks the elements which had become established for the courtly romance: there are no parallel paths for the hero, no sense of rehabilitation after failure and thence the acquisition of a higher status. Apart from some supernatural features essential to the plot – magic gold, the 'bridge test', for example – the prevalent mood of fairy tale is absent. Even the leash itself is less remarkable for its extraordinary beauty than for the somewhat ponderous instructions it bears.

The work comprises many distinct areas of action, though all framing and emanating from the story of Tschionatulander which must be seen as the heart of the poem and which does, in fact, occupy about two-thirds of its enormous length. Much of the material is gleaned not only from Wolfram's *Titurel* but from his *Parzival* too, but what Albrecht has done is give to often familiar events a significance which depends on his own completely different conception of that material, and, if we judge him aright, his totally different purpose. His comment fairly early on (65), 'daz ist niht wan ein lêre' ('this is nothing but a piece of didactic writing'), has led some critics to place overriding emphasis on the poem as a work of pedantry but, although this is indisputably what he says, he can hardly have meant his audience to mistake his intention of offering them a narrative in which traditional ingredients – two great tournaments, three campaigns, the story of the love of Sigune and Tschionatulander, the activities of other named individuals – all play a part. If large portions of the work – and some would argue the best parts of it – are devoted to learned excursuses, commentaries of a moral and essentially didactic nature, these do not replace traditional narrative material but, existing side by side with it, determine the unique quality of the whole. Schröder is probably right when he suggests (1982, 75) that what Albrecht had in mind was 'ein Weltgedicht', a world-encompassing work which, like *Parzival*, was to embrace East and West, but constitute also 'ein Lehrbuch der Tugend' ('a moral textbook').

A lengthy Prologue contains distinct echoes of both Wolfram's *Willehalm* and his *Parzival*, with its address to God and praise of all Creation, the exhortation to banish *zwîvel* (doubt) and the rebuttal of negative critics. Sometimes there is blatant paraphrase, as in the borrowing of the image of the glass backed by tin, and the dreams of a blind man (51), the vanishing of dew in the hot sun and fire in a spring (58). Such reminders could well convince the listeners that they were hearing Wolfram himself. Then, in strophe 64, comes the reference to three princes, whose names he declines to divulge but who may well have been Margrave Heinrich von Wettin and his two sons (de Boor 1973). Late in the work he laments that his original patrons have abandoned him (5844–5). The separate piece known as the *Verfasserfragment,* in which Albrecht identifies himself, contains also a dedication to 'duc loys et palatinus', almost certainly Ludwig II of Bavaria ('Ludwig the Stern'), whom, it seems evident, Albrecht was attempting to gain as his new patron. Strophe 5961 of the *Jüngerer Titurel* suggests that this appeal was unsuccessful, possibly in part owing to Ludwig's failure to succeed to the imperial crown.

The essential action of the poem, the story of Tschionatulander, is preceded by the history of the Grail family, an account which ranges far in time and place, tracing the family of Titurel back to the Roman emperors. When Titurel receives the Grail from God, he constructs to house it the magnificent Grail Temple, which Albrecht describes at considerable length (112 strophes) and in elaborate detail. His emphasis on the lavish decoration and his insistence on architectural features invite an allegorical interpretation, though the precise meaning of this complex edifice is elusive, submerged in often overwhelming concrete details. Its extravagant splendour and the isolation of the description within the narrative accentuate the significance of the Grail itself as the embodiment of Christian virtue and spiritual ambition.

With the abdication of Titurel in favour of his son Frimutel, Albrecht has reached the point where his work takes account both of Wolfram's fragment and much which is told or implied in *Parzival*: the birth of Sigune; her love for the young page Tschionatulander who then departs with Gahmuret in the service of the Baruch; the death of Gahmuret, who entrusts to Tschionatulander his lands, his wife Herzeloyde and his unborn child. When Tschionatulander returns to Kanvoleiz, Parzival is born, amidst great sorrow, and Herzeloyde withdraws into the wilderness. The love between Tschionatulander and Sigune blossoms and – Albrecht's addition – the young man is invested as a knight (1128ff.). At this point Albrecht is still dependent upon Wolfram's second fragment, but, following Tschionatulander's undertaking to restore the hound's leash to Sigune, he launches into material largely his own, though with occasional hints at events known from *Parzival,* and, indeed, from the works of Hartmann von Aue and from other Arthurian romances.

In his pursuit of the leash, Tschionatulander is victorious in a series of combats which earn him membership of the Round Table. The action is complex, but what is clear is that Tschionatulander is the central character, the hero, who will nevertheless die. This is no Arthurian knight in the traditional mould, who comes through a succession of trials and emerges ultimately intact and triumphant, but one who adheres to a system of values and dies in upholding them. Moreover, the leash as his goal and inspiration loses its validity when the inscription is read out for all to hear, Sigune included. Nor is that inscription, as we might have believed it was, from *Titurel*, a story of tragic love, but a solemn proclamation of a code of honour and a catalogue of virtues.

Albrecht has placed at the heart of the Arthurian action an adventure recognizable as a traditional test of knightly honour, the 'bridge test', which proves the undoing of such redoubtable knights as Erec and Iwein, Segremors, Kalogreant and Lehelin (2348ff.), but the true ambience for the adventures which bring glory to Tschionatulander lies beyond the limits of the Arthurian domain. When Tschionatulander journeys once more to the East, where he engages in a

series of tournaments and combats, he is undertaking a further challenge: to take
revenge for the death of Gahmuret. This he does, but his glorious actions involve
him in new conflicts, both physical and ethical. Again and again he proves
himself worthy of the love of Sigune, who now in any case knows the content of
the inscription, but still his desire for fame presses him forward, until he dies,
rather as Wolfram's Gahmuret had done, by an act of fate. This comes when he
fails to receive the ring and the brooch made of magic gold which are on their way
to him from the Baruch to replace his earlier gift of the magic suit of armour
which he has likewise lost, thus forfeiting the supreme happiness which it was
meant to bestow upon him. What may be construed as ill fortune, when the
objects come into the possession of Orilus and Jeschute, may also be attributed to
negligence on the part of Tschionatulander, who has chosen to accompany King
Arthur on a campaign instead of remaining at home to defend the lands
bequeathed to him by the dying Gahmuret. By a misunderstanding, the messenger hands the objects over to Orilus, believing him to be the lord of those
lands, and so gives to him the means to defeat Tschionatulander. Only in this way
can the greatest of knights forfeit his supremacy.

With the central hero slain (5092), the remainder of the poem centres on
Parzival, using Wolfram's four episodes as the basis of this account of the grief
and death of Sigune, the adventures of Parzival which include his first visit to the
Grail and his later release of Anfortas, the death of Orilus at the hand of Ekunat
which brings with it the destruction of the leash which had come to adorn the
helmet of Orilus. Other motifs which resurface in Albrecht's work include the
Grail sword which Parzival passes to Ekunat and which presumably kills Orilus,
and the two objects which Parzival recovers from Jeschute. The question of
Sigune's guilt arises in her own self-accusations, yet her responsibility for
Tschionatulander's death has become blurred, as increasing importance is
attached to factors other than his pursuit of the leash.

As the extraordinary work nears its conclusion, its compass widens again. The
lands of Parzival pass into the hands of King Arthur, but the Grail, his true
domain, travels to India, where, in the now transposed Grail Temple, it is tended
first by Priester Johann and then, for ten years, by Parzival himself. Albrecht has
achieved his grandiose purpose, one might say, and in doing so he has left
behind him many of the conventions which gave him his inspiration. In creating
a work of such scope and proportions, Albrecht has attempted to fulfil his sense
of vocation, an almost sacred duty to art which he expresses somewhat
flamboyantly in the *Verfasserfragment*. The *Jüngerer Titurel* is not a failed
Arthurian romance, or a clumsy and ill-conceived attempt to outdo Wolfram,
though Albrecht's debt to Wolfram cannot be disputed in this work which
borrows so freely from *Parzival* and *Willehalm*, whose inspiration is clearly the
Titurel fragments, and whose strophic form is a more complex version of

Wolfram's own. With all its imperfections, it is a considerable achievement in its own right, and a testimony to the state of narrative literature in Germany towards the close of the thirteenth century.

Bibliography

I. *Titurel*

Primary Sources and Translations

Wolfram von Eschenbach, *Titurel*, in *Wolfram von Eschenbach*. Ed. by K. Lachmann, 1926. 6th edn. Berlin and Leipzig.

Wolfram von Eschenbach, '*Titurel' and the Songs.* Ed. and transl. by M. Gibbs and S. Johnson, 1988. New York and London.

Wolfram von Eschenbach, *Titurel. Lieder.* MHG text and translation by W. Mohr, 1978 (GAG, 250). Göppingen.

Titurel. Wolfram of Eschenbach. Translation and Studies by C. Passage, 1984. New York.

Other Literature

Bumke, J. 1968. *Die Wolfram von Eschenbach Forschung seit 1945. Bericht und Bibliographie,* Munich.

Bumke, J. 1971. 'Zur Überlieferung von Wolframs *Titurel*. Wolframs Dichtung und der *Jüngere Titurel*', *ZfdA*, 100, 390–431.

Bumke, J. 1973. '*Titurel*überlieferung und *Titurel*forschung', *ZfdA*, 92, 147–88.

Bumke, J. 1997. *Wolfram von Eschenbach*, Sammlung Metzler, 7th edn., Stuttgart.

Christoph, S. 1981. 'Wolfram's Sigune and the question of guilt', *GR*, 56, 62–9.

Harvey, R. 1980. 'Zu Sigunes Liebesklage (*Titurel* 117–119)', *WSt*, 6, 54–62.

Haug, W. 1980a. 'Erzählen vom Tod her. Sprachkrise, gebrochene Handlung und zerfallene Welt in Wolframs *Titurel*', *WSt*, 6, 8–24.

Haug, W. 1980b. See *Jüngerer Titurel*. Other Literature.

Heinzle, J. 1972. *Stellenkommentar zu Wolframs 'Titurel'*, Tübingen.

Heinzle, J. 1989. 'Nachlese zum *Titurel*-Kommentar', in Gärtner and Heinzle 1989 (see Gen. Bibl.), 485–500.

Johnson, S. 1989. 'Das Brackenseil des Gardeviaz zwischen Wirklichkeit und Phantasie', in Gärtner and Heinzle 1989 (see Gen. Bibl.), 513–19.

Mertens, V. 1993. 'Wolfram von Eschenbach: *Titurel*', in Brunner 1993 (see Gen. Bibl.), 196–211.

Mohr, W. 1977. 'Zur Textgeschichte von Wolframs *Titurel*', *WSt*, 4, 123–51 (repr. in Mohr 1979 (see Gen. Bibl.), 237–65).

Mohr, W. 1978. 'Zu Wolframs *Titurel*', see Primary Sources, *Titurel*, MHG text and translation by Mohr, 101–61.

Ortmann, C. 1980. '*Titurel* im *Parzival*-Kontext. Zur Frage nach einer möglichen Strukturdeutung der Fragmente', *WSt*, 6, 25–47.

Richey, M. 1961. 'The *Titurel* of Wolfram von Eschenbach: structure and character', *MLR*, 56, 180–93.

Ruh, K. 1989. 'Bemerkungen zur Liebessprache in Wolframs *Titurel*', in Gärtner and Heinzle 1989 (see Gen. Bibl.), 501–12.

Wehrli, M. 1974. *Wolframs 'Titurel'*, Opladen.

Wolff, L. 1950. 'Wolframs Schionatulander and Sigune', in Kienast, R., ed., *Studien zur deutschen*

Philologie des Mittelalters. Friedrich Panzer zum 80. Geburtstag, Heidelberg, 116–30 (repr. in Rupp, H., ed., *Wolfram von Eschenbach*, WdF, 57, Darmstadt 1966, 549–69).

Wyss, U. 1974. 'Selbstkritik des Erzählers. Ein Versuch über Wolframs *Titurel*-Fragment', *ZfdA*, 103, 249–89.

II. *Jüngerer Titurel*

Primary Sources

Albrecht von Scharfenberg, *Jüngerer Titurel*. 1–2, 2. Ed. by W. Wolf, 1955–68. Berlin.Vols. 3, 1–3, 2. Ed. by K. Nyholm, 1985–92. Berlin.

Albrecht von Scharfenberg. *Der Jüngere Titurel*. Ed. by W. Wolf, 1952. Berlin (Selections).

Other Literature

Borchling, C. 1897. *Der Jüngere Titurel und sein Verhältnis zu Wolfram von Eschenbach*, Göttingen.

de Boor, H. 1973. 'Drei Fürsten im mittleren Deutschland', in Schmidtke, D. and Schüppert, H., eds., *Festschrift für Ingeborg Schröbler zum 65. Geburtstag*, *PBB*, 95, Sonderheft, Tübingen, 238–57.

Buschinger, D. 1989. 'Zu Albrechts *Jüngerem Titurel*: Versuch einer Interpretation', in Gärtner and Heinzle 1989 (see Gen. Bibl.), 521–8.

Ebenbauer, A. 1979. 'Tschionatulander und Artus. Zur Gattungsstruktur und zur Interpretation des Tschionatulanderlebens im *Jüngeren Titurel*', *ZfdA*, 108, 374–407.

Ebenbauer, A. 1993. 'Albrecht: *Jüngerer Titurel*', in Brunner 1993 (see Gen. Bibl.), 353–72.

Fromm, H. 1984. '*Der Jüngere Titurel*. Das Werk und sein Dichter', WSt, 8, 11–33.

Haug, W. 1980b. 'Paradigmatische Poesie. Der spätere Artusroman auf dem Weg zu einer "nachklassischen" Ästhetik', *DVj*, 54, 204–31.

Hirschberg, D. 1984. 'Zum Aventiure-Gespräch von der Bedeutung *warer minne* im *Jüngeren Titurel*', WSt, 8, 107–19.

Huschenbett, D. 1977. 'Albrecht, Dichter des *Jüngeren Titurel*', in *VL*, I, cols. 200–6.

Huschenbett, D. 1979. *Albrechts 'Jüngerer Titurel'. Zu Stil und Komposition*, Munich.

Huschenbett, D. 1984. 'Der *Jüngere Titurel* als literaturgeschichtliches Problem', WSt, 8, 153–68.

Kern, P. 1984. 'Albrechts Gönner und die Wolfram-Rolle im *Jüngeren Titurel*', WSt, 8, 138–52.

Lachmann, K. 1829. '*Titurel* und Dante', in the *Hallesche Allgemeine Zeitung*, 238, December 1829. Also in Lachmann, *Kleinere Schriften I*, edited by K. Müllenhoff, Berlin, 1876 (repr. Berlin 1969, 351–7).

Nyholm, K. 1984. 'Pragmatische Isotypien im *Jüngeren Titurel*. Überlegungen zur Autor-Hörer/ Leser Situation', WSt, 8, 120–37.

Parshall, L. 1981. *The Art of Narration in Wolfram's 'Parzifal' and Albrecht's 'Jüngerer Titurel'*, Cambridge, London etc.

Passage, C. 1984. See Primary Sources, *Titurel*.

Ragotzky, H. 1971. *Studien zur Wolfram-Rezeption. Die Entstehung und Verwandlung der Wolfram-Rolle in der deutschen Literatur des 13. Jahrhunderts*, Stuttgart, Berlin etc.

Röll, W. 1964. *Studien zu Text und Überlieferung des sogenannten Jüngeren Titurel*, Heidelberg.

Röll, W. 1984. 'Quellen des Wortschatzes im *Jüngeren Titurel*', WSt, 8, 49–66.

Schröder, W. 1982. *Wolfram-Nachfolge im 'Jüngeren Titurel'. Devotion oder Arroganz*, Frankfurt.

Schröder, W. 1984. 'Textkritisches zum *Jüngeren Titurel*', WSt, 8, 34–48.

Schröder, W. 1985. 'Der Schluß des *Jüngeren Titurel*', *ZfdA*, 111, 103–34.

Thomas, N. 1992. See Gen. Bibl.

Wolf, W. 1955. See Primary Sources, *Jüngerer Titurel*, I.

Zatloukal, K. 1984. 'Eigennamen und Erzählwelten im *Jüngeren Titurel*', WSt, 8, 94–106.

5

THREE POST-CLASSICAL AUTHORS: HEINRICH VON DEM TÜRLIN, DER STRICKER, DER PLEIER

Rosemary E. Wallbank

The first wave of Arthurian writers in Germany was characterized by a youthful and beguiling confidence in the eternal values of chivalric society which, if embraced with integrity and pursued with boldness, might provide a solution to the problems of this world and even, as in Wolfram's *Parzival*, a stepping-stone to the next. Succeeding generations of writers continued to satisfy the hunger for Arthurian stories in which readers recognized familiar figures, motifs and settings, but they now began to explore new possibilities. The post-classical writers – Heinrich von dem Türlin, Der Stricker and Der Pleier – do not form a homogeneous group, though all were active in the Austrian region between about 1215 and 1270.

Heinrich von dem Türlin, *Diu Crône*

The title of Heinrich's long romance, *Diu Crône* (30,041 lines), stems from his own description of it as a crown set with precious jewels. Rudolf von Ems in his catalogue of authors, *c.* 1240, calls it *Allr Âventiure Krône* (*Alexander* v. 3219). Heinrich also gives his name in his poem, but of his social standing, patrons and provenance he says nothing. The theory that he was court poet to Duke Bernhard of Carinthia was demolished by Kratz (1977, 123–67), but Jillings (1981, 87–102) produces fresh clues that support a Carinthian connection. He was certainly addressing an audience of considerable literary sophistication and was himself widely read in German and above all French literature. He possessed a fund of knowledge on all manner of subjects both practical and abstruse, and at the end of his poem complains that he has not enjoyed the recognition his achievement deserves (*Crône* vv. 29990–30000). *Diu Crône* is preserved in only one complete manuscript (P= Heidelberg cpg 374, 1479), another comprising almost half the work and five fragments.

A fragment of another Arthurian poem known as *Der Mantel* ('The Cloak'), preserved in the 'Ambraser Heldenbuch', has traditionally been attributed to Heinrich, though reservations have been voiced, mainly on stylistic grounds

(Kratz 1977; Schröder 1992, 138). Yet the claim remains strong, since *Der Mantel* deals with the popular theme of the Virtue Test in a characteristically ironical and salacious manner not paralleled among writers of his day. Moreover, in *Diu Crône* he inserts another variation on the theme, a Glove Test, citing 'Cristiân von Trois' as his source (vv. 22990–24692)! His authorship of *Diu Crône* is undisputed. But almost every other aspect of this extraordinary work is the subject of controversy. The last thirty years have seen an encouraging growth of interest following generations of neglect: today's scholars are more willing to wrestle with Scholl's inadequate text, while awaiting the promised edition by Klaus Zatloukal. Meanwhile, a readable English prose translation by J. W. Thomas (1989) has made *Diu Crône* accessible to a wider range of Arthurian students, and much has been done to dispel the notion that it is little more than a superficial and long-winded conglomeration of traditional motifs.

Diu Crône falls clearly into two parts, both with Gawein as hero, but these do not constitute separate romances, being linked together by a complex system of cross-reference. Nor is this a variant of the double structure of 'classical' romance: there is no suggestion of moral crisis, alienation and reintegration into Arthurian society as in *Erec* and *Iwein*. The pattern is quite different: in both parts the hero's adventures are intertwined with a second (not secondary) plot, or plots, in the manner of the French prose romances. This technique of *entrelacement*, in which the narrative strands interrupt one another and are entwined together (Lot 1918, 17–28; Frappier 1959, 298f.), was new to Germany and is managed with dexterity by Heinrich. With the recognition of these underlying structures, much that appeared confused and arbitrary falls into place. Since it was first noted (Wallbank 1965, 303), Heinrich's use of this device has been often recognized (Kratz 1973, 141–53; Jillings 1980, 222–4) and it still appears the simplest way of confronting the intricacies of his narrative (see the table on pp. 84–5). It is a scheme based purely on content, without interpretative significance. Individual readings of the text may suggest a quite different structure. Cormeau (1977, 157–64), for example, prefers the simple scheme of four adventure series, each ending with a Court Feast, put forward by Heller in 1942. But for him Gawein's static 'preformed' character precludes any ethical or psychological progression and inhibits Heinrich from achieving a unified structure. Menzel-Reuters (1989, 36–8, 314–17), too, can only contemplate a narrative edifice supported by an infrastructure of ideas, and argues that *Diu Crône* provides no textual evidence of such organization. The scheme proposed here credits Heinrich with higher organizational ability. It also provides an economical oversight of the individual plots which interlock to create one of the most complicated of Arthurian romances. Heinrich was perhaps more familiar than any German writer of his age with French literature. Consequently, he was well placed to import innovative formal techniques into German romance, just as he gave a new direction to its content and attitudes.

French and German writers of Arthurian romance had long since evolved a system of signals, by means of which audience expectation could be both stimulated and reassured. Heinrich deftly introduces these type-constituents into the exposition of his story, placing it securely in the Arthurian setting so familiar to his public. He does it with a light touch (in contrast to the somewhat plodding didacticism of Stricker). But it becomes clear from the start that his design is not simply to satisfy reader expectation with a graceful and well-tempered series of variations on familiar themes: *minne* and *âventiure* to be sure, but there will be surprises and even shocks in his handling of traditional material. Choosing Gawein as hero gives rise to a discrepancy between that and his traditional role as a 'preformed' character, one of the essential ingredients of Arthurian fiction, through which the genre is defined (Cormeau 1977, 10f., 167; Schmolke-Hasselmann 1980, 35–41). Such characters may become increasingly differentiated, as Keie does in *Diu Crône*, but they remain open-ended, ill-adapted to the finite career of the classic Arthurian hero, who emerges through trials and errors to moral standing and acclaim. The choice of Gawein signals a conscious departure on Heinrich's part from the 'classical' mode of Arthurian romance.

The narrative begins with a Christmas Feast at Tintagel, with some of the liveliest depictions of court life in medieval romance. The celebrations are interrupted by the arrival of a grotesque dwarf, half man, half fish, bringing a present of a goblet from which the king and his court are to drink. Heinrich's readers will have been quick to recognize the Virtue Test, a theme that evidently fascinated him, for he used it (if we include *Der Mantel*) three times. His treatment shows his indebtedness both to Ulrich von Zatzikhoven's *Lanzelet* and to the twelfth-century French versions, as well as to the *Livre de Caradoc* in the First Continuation of Chrétien's *Perceval*. It also demonstrates the independent manner in which he customarily combines and manipulates his sources. The relatively harmless commentary that Ulrich put into the mouth of his messenger is allotted to Keie and expanded into a succession of virulent and sexually explicit attacks on Guinevere, Enite and the rest, refining at great length on the crude humour and anti-feminist tone of the *Lai du Cor* and *Le Mantel mautaillié* (or the *Lai du Cort Mantel*). But the episode is chiefly significant in signalling that from the outset of his romance Heinrich is taking a new direction, one that sets him apart from more deferential inheritors of the classical tradition, like Der Stricker and Der Pleier. Scholars have become increasingly aware of the satirical intention that underlies Heinrich's treatment of familiar Arthurian themes (e.g. Wallbank 1965, Kratz 1973, Schröder 1992 and, above all, Jillings 1980). Jillings (1980, 12) rightly draws attention to his secularism, to the disdain he often shows for chivalric ideals and 'the manner in which comic and satirical elements obtrude at the cost of any high moral significance'. The Goblet Test is more than an episode, amusing or offensive according to taste. In

The Structure of *Diu Crône*

Part One

Assiles (Giant) Adventure	Amurfina (Sisters' Strife) Adventure	Guinevere–Gasoein (Abduction) Adventure
		Arthur's Christmas Court; Goblet Test 466–3207.
Gawein leaves Court 3208–75.		
		Gasoein claims Guinevere; indecisive combat with Arthur; second combat agreed six weeks hence at Karidol 3276–5459.
Gawein's first contest with Assiles 5460–7659.		
	Gawein summoned by Amurfina as champion against Sgoidamur; his enchantment, oblivion and recovery 7660–9128.	
Gawein defeats monsters and Assiles 9129–10112.		Arthur's February Court; judicial combat with Gasoein; Guinevere rejects Gasoein 10113–11036. Guinevere abducted by her brother, then by Gasoein; rescued by Gawein; return to court; Gasoein retracts his claim to Guinevere 11037–12600.
	Sgoidamur at Arthur's Whitsun Court; demands Gawein as her champion 12601–890. Bridle Quest: in a series of contests Gawein wins the bridle and releases Amurfina's castle from enchantment 12891–13654. Double wedding at Arthur's Court: Gawein–Amurfina, Gasoein–Sgoidamur 13655–924.	

Part Two

Grail and Garland Adventure	Skeins of Marvels ('Wunderketten')	Fortune's Jewel Adventure
Gawein learns of Parzival's failure to ask the Grail question 13925–14021.		
	First 'Wunderkette' 14022–567.	
Gawein's first Grail visit ends in failure 14568–926.		
		Gawein is protected from Giramphiel's vengeance by the magic jewel he had won from Fimbeus's girdle (flashback) 14927-15649. Fortune receives Gawein; gives him a ring which will guarantee the survival of Arthur's court 15650–972.
	Second 'Wunderkette' 15973–16499.	
		Gawein's death reported; the head of his double shown at Arthur's court causes violent laments 16500–17311.
Gawein visits a Land of Women; settles a Rival Sisters dispute 17312–18679. Chessboard Adventure: Gawein takes over the Grail Quest 18680–19345. Schastel Marveil and Garland Adventure; return to Arthur's court; Guiremelanz's wedding 19346–22563.		
		Gawein gives Arthur Fortune's Ring. Glove Test; girdle, ring and glove stolen and regained 22564–28261.
Gawein instructed how to succeed in Grail Quest 28262–628.		
	Third 'Wunderkette' 28629–732.	
After several Enchanted Castle adventures, Gawein comes to the Grail Castle; sees the procession and lifts the spell, releasing the inmates; return to Arthur's court 28733–29909.		

the derision to which it holds up both knights and ladies of Arthur's court it is a declaration of Heinrich's intent to divert a new generation of readers by undermining the idealistic assumptions and outdated pretensions of Arthurian romance, and painting a more realistic picture of the world as he saw it – a world where success was less likely to come from noble aspirations than from a combination of good sense and good fortune.

The dynamic interplay of love and combat, which provides the ideal structure for Hartmann's romances, is transformed in the Guinevere–Gasoein adventure into irreverent comedy, in which Heinrich's anti-feminism and distaste for martial chivalry soon become apparent. In a hilarious parody of courtly love, Guinevere observes her husband raking the coals and stretching his hands to the fire after a day's hunting in the snow, and sarcastically wonders how he would ever keep warm in women's light clothes. 'The hottest woman is supposed to be / Colder than the coldest man' (*Crône* vv. 3379f.), so the learned doctors say; but the whole heath would have to go up in flames to warm her husband up – a sexual jibe she proceeds to illustrate by comparison with a knight she knows, who rides abroad in all weathers, wearing nothing but a white shirt and singing songs of love to his *amîe* (*Crône* vv. 3334–3427). This is Gasoein (the preferred reading, rather than Gasozein; Menzel-Reuters 1989), who unmistakably betrays his fairy origins (Wallbank 1981, 258f.), but who in *Diu Crône* is a mortal king, betrothed to Guinevere long before her marriage to Arthur – a singular motif, derived from an older tradition of the abduction myth, of which traces are preserved in Ulrich's *Lanzelet*. In a series of burlesque encounters, Gasoein easily disposes of Arthur's knights, demonstrating Heinrich's lack of regard for chivalric combat, which he consistently denigrates by rational rejection or parodistic exaggeration.

The Gasoein adventure is Heinrich's funniest and most tightly constructed plot and is clearly satirical in intent (for a contrary view, see Cormeau 1977, 228f.).The two targets of his parody, love and chivalric combat, are the themes of the Assiles and Amurfina adventures respectively, which the author ingeniously and with meticulous attention to chronology interweaves both with each other and with the Gasoein strand. The Assiles complex consists of a series of combats culminating in the destruction of the giant and his evil empire and presented in two stages, intersected by Gawein's enchantment in Amurfina's castle. Whether this sequence reveals a development in Gawein's character (Jillings 1980, 59) is questionable, for the status of the exemplary knight attaches to him from the start (Cormeau 1977, 142–4). What the author does demonstrate, through a variety of devices (excessive length of the fights, pointless reduplications, gruesome nature of injuries, gratuitous unpleasantness of opponents etc.) is the futility and irrationality of knightly combat.

Inserted between the two stages of the Assiles adventure and interlaced, too, with the Gasoein action is the tale of Gawein and the Rival Sisters. Heinrich evidently finds in the shorter French texts of the late twelfth and early thirteenth centuries not only novelty of subject matter, but an irreverent, humorous and often sceptical attitude to high chivalry and courtly love, which coincides with his own persuasions. Such tales provide the basis for both stages of the Amurfina story but, whereas the second part, the Bridle Quest, has been shown to derive from an earlier, lost version of *La Mule sans Frein* (Boll 1929; Jillings 1980, 62), the first stage is Heinrich's own compilation, an original combination of romance motifs, including an unusual version of the Beheading Game, exemplifying the destructive power of *minne* and the mischievous nature of woman. The courtly appearance of the heroine barely conceals the imperious and capricious temperament of the Irish fay. The two parts of the Amurfina adventure, basically a Fairy Mistress story and an Unspelling Quest, unite in displaying that alienation from courtly values inherent in the Assiles and Gasoein sections. We see the hero subdued and diminished by *minne*, not inspired by it, dwindling into a husband.

In the second part of *Diu Crône* there are two interlocking narrative strands: the Grail adventure and the Giramphiel or Fortune's Girdle adventure, which in turn are intersected not by a third adventure complex, as in Part One, but by a triple series of Marvels ('Wunderketten'). The Grail adventure corresponds to the Gawein and Grail sections of Chrétien's *Conte del Graal* and Wolfram's *Parzival*, and it is this part of Heinrich's poem on which in the past a disproportionate measure of scholarly attention has been focused. Indeed, before the 1960s most comment on Heinrich targeted his handling of the Grail theme and, as this was judged to be banal and superficial by comparison with Wolfram's, the epic as a whole was dismissed as an example of the formal and intellectual disintegration of post-classical romance (see Wallbank 1965, 300 and Jillings 1980, 1f. for references). In fact *Parzival* is only one among several sources on which Heinrich draws in this section. For the adventures which correspond to Wolfram's Books VII–VIII and X–XIV, including the Castle of Marvels, the Perilous Bed and the Garland adventure, he leans heavily on Chrétien (Buschinger 1981, 1–12), and in the Grail episodes he also uses the First and Second Continuators, the Didot *Perceval* and probably *Perlesvaus* and other prose versions (Jillings 1980, 109f., 123f.; Buschinger 1981, 12–29). He refers repeatedly to Parzival's cowardice and promotes Gawein as his more prudent and resolute successor. Even Gawein, however, can only achieve success with the assistance of all-powerful Fortune. His first visit, before he receives and recognizes her special protection, ends in failure. Apparently untroubled by guilt, he accomplishes, or more frequently merely observes (Zatloukal 1981; Andersen 1987, 38f.) a long succession of 'fine adventures' before coming a second time to the Grail. It is difficult to discern any moral or personal development in Gawain: what now ensures his success is the detailed instruction he has received from the Grail Princess (Heinrich calls her a 'goddess', his term for any female with magical or fairy connections). The wonders of the Grail are assembled from the wide variety of Heinrich's sources, with the evident intention of outshining all predecessors, but for him it is not a profound mystery, much less the spiritual climax of his hero's life. Gawein's aspirations remain centred on the Arthurian court, which he has no notion of relinquishing for a kingdom that is not of this world. As an episode it is not so dominant as to justify labelling the whole work an 'anti-Grail romance' (Ebenbauer 1977, 40), but it is a clear affirmation of Heinrich's secularism and implies a deliberate step back from the spiritualizing tendency both of the *Parzival* and of the French cyclical romances (Buschinger 1981, 27–9).

Heinrich's resolute refusal to open up secular romance to spiritual and moral problems finds its most striking expression in the figure of the goddess Fortuna. It is not until halfway through his story that he presents her to his audience in all her regal splendour. But this celebration of *Vrou Saelde* comes as no surprise, for every turn of the narrative exhibits her dominion over the affairs of this world. Gawein is as prudent as he is valiant, but the one quality that sets him apart from all others is that he is Fortune's favourite and that he recognizes her power. The Giramphiel adventure (Wallbank 1993), though it interweaves with the Grail story to form the content of the second part of *Diu Crône*, casts its shadow backwards over Gawein's whole career. For it is the jewel torn from a magic girdle that secures him a charmed life, a jewel presented to the fay Giramphiel by her sister, Lady Fortune. What Jillings (1980, 87–104) describes as 'the struggle for Fortune's trophies' now resolves itself into a struggle for the survival of Arthur's court, in which Gawein's ultimate triumph is due less to 'genuine self-reliant Arthurian chivalry' (Jillings 1980, 88f.) than to the repeated interventions of Fortuna. The court itself is never far from ridicule, whether in the parodistically exaggerated laments for Gawein's supposed death, or in its ludicrous ineptness in confronting the wiles of Giramphiel. In a remarkable scene, in which Gawein is received in audience by *Vrou Saelde*, Heinrich presents us with the most original evocation of the classical goddess in Middle High German courtly literature. In a sharp break with tradition he shows Lady Fortune divided against herself, richly adorned on the right, old, blind and pallid on the left, recalling the *ambiguus vultus* of Boethius or the double-sided Fortuna of iconographic tradition. Moreover, she is not turning her wheel, but is enthroned above it, holding her child, *daz heil*, 'good luck', on her lap, while her subjects sing her praises. This is a unique configuration among representations of Fortune, whether literary or pictorial (Pickering 1966, 141) and a daring one, for it cannot but conjure up the familiar image of the Madonna and Child in the mind of the reader. As in the celestial sphere the *regina caelis* lays her finger on the scales of justice and saves her faithful worshippers from retribution, so on earth does the queen of this world, in defiance of her appointed role, stop her wheel in token of the special grace accorded to her favourite, Gawein. It is a startling *contrafactura*, the transformation of a divine into a secular image and, whatever the provenance of individual motifs, in its entirety and in its impact, undoubtedly the poet's own, highly original creation (on Fortuna in *Diu Crône* see de Boor 1975, Ebenbauer 1977, Wallbank 1987).

Interspersed between various stages of the Grail and Girdle adventures are three curious excursuses, 'skeins of marvels' (*Wunderketten*), which have only the most tenuous link with either narrative, and which include such bizarre and gruesome tableaux as a naked maiden scaring away birds, who are tearing at the flesh of a chained giant; a hag riding a green tri-horned beast and whipping a naked Moor, whom she leads by a rope; and a crystal palace filled with singing maidens which is smashed to pieces by an ogre and consumed by fire, while the churl shovels the ladies into it. Gawein remains unmoved by these scenes of fire, flagellation and torment, obedient to Fortune's command never to deviate from his appointed goal. Whether these distractions are to be seen as 'pathological phantasizing' on the author's part or as Bosch-like images of Purgatory (Wyss 1981, 267–91) or simply as the literary equivalent of the *bizarreries* that decorate so many medieval manuscripts and churches, is one of many aspects of *Diu Crône* that invite further investigation.

Altogether, a consensus in the interpretation of Heinrich's work is still some way off. The tendency to view *Diu Crône* almost exclusively as an anti-Grail or anti-*Parzival* tract has given place to a more balanced perspective. This is not to overlook Heinrich's weaknesses as a writer, nor his rancorous jibes against *Parzival*. Reverence for Wolfram can still occasionally produce an unrelentingly severe judgement on Heinrich, with accusations of slander, plagiarism and wanton obscenity (Schröder 1992). But if his purpose was to create one of the most amusing of all adventure stories (Thomas 1989, xii), that he has achieved in some measure in this complex of interlocking tales that combine excitement and mystery with extravagant fantasy and wickedly irreverent humour.

Der Stricker, *Daniel von dem blühenden Tal*

Der Stricker, the 'Spinner of Yarns', was a professional poet, probably of Franconian extraction, but for much of his life – to judge from allusions in his works – at home in Austria. Over a period of twenty years or more, *c.* 1215–35, he produced a wide variety of works, that reflect the tastes of his clients, but his fame rests largely and legitimately on his *maeren*, popular and amusing tales of everyday life, with a moral, or sometimes amoral, *cauda*. His longer works include a version of the *Song of Roland* and his one Arthurian romance *Daniel von dem blühenden Tal*, preserved in five manuscripts from the fifteenth century.

The claim to a French source for the *Daniel* is entirely fictional, copied from Lamprecht's *Alexander*, with the evident intention of preparing the reader for the exotic content of the work and of forestalling doubts as to its authenticity. Not without cause, for the story is a compendium of fabulous and outlandish adventures, culled from a variety of sources, not necessarily Arthurian, with a dash of pure invention. These exploits are inserted into a larger framework of territorial conflict, a struggle between Arthur and the tyrant Matur of Cluse, whose giant envoy demands Arthur's submission, just as Daniel has won a place at the Round Table. Through his encounters with monsters, dwarfs and villains, Daniel acquires both men and magical aids and these, added to his native wit, are effective in securing Arthur's victory in the four battles of Cluse. The peace is sealed by his marriage to Matur's widow. But the happy end is delayed when Arthur and Parzival are abducted by a giant to an impregnable rock, to be rescued by Daniel with the help of his magic net. A Whitsun feast provides a traditional conclusion.

Daniel's triumph is in no sense a victory over self. He suffers no crisis and needs no regeneration. Alongside Arthur, who plays an active part in the struggle, he never falters in the fight against arrogance and oppression. His name too, with its Old Testament connotations, strikes a new note, alerting the reader to his most striking quality, that of cunning, *list*, perhaps better translated as 'astuteness' or 'cleverness', since, though deception and trickery are by no means excluded, his sharpness, like that of his biblical counterpart, is viewed in a positive light (Pingel 1994, 318). This regard for intellectual superiority sets Stricker's hero apart from his forebears in classical romance (Classen 1991). Like Gawein in *Diu Crône* he is often pitted against foes whose supernatural powers make them immune to strength and prowess, who can be vanquished only by magic or, as so often in the *Daniel*, by tactics. Thus the 'bûchlôse', monsters with huge heads and no stomachs, are disposed of without a blow struck, by the classic device of a mirror to counter the deadly glance of their Medusa-like severed head (*Daniel* vv. 2075–165). The necromancer whose medicinal bath requires the blood of 600 knights a week, is likewise dispatched by guile (*Daniel* vv. 4329–795). Courage and skill at arms are taken for granted, but example on example shows how much higher Der Stricker rates an agile brain. It is a new departure for an Arthurian hero and is underlined through authorial commentary: 'Anyone who is clever and resourceful deserves to be highly regarded by men and women alike. A man can achieve by clever tricks what a thousand could not, however strong they might be' (*Daniel* vv. 7487–92).

The triumph of native wit over stupidity is a constant theme of the popular verse tale and it is not surprising that Der Stricker has transposed it so effectively into his romances. Single combat as a way of settling differences appears much diminished, and a second innovation renders it almost irrelevant: this is the prominence given to mass warfare in the *Daniel*. Here Arthur emerges from his traditional static role to lead his army in a series of bloody encounters reminiscent of heroic epic and the *chansons de geste:* 'They rode in blood up to their horses' knees. All those who were hewn down drowned in it' (*Daniel* vv. 5628–31). The sense of chivalry as a noble sport, pursued for the joy and the honour of it, has given place to the dualistic opposition of good and evil (Pingel 1994, 319). The adversaries, however fantastic, have shed their other-world aura to become devils incarnate, to be crushed by all means and at all costs.

The elevation of the intellect at the expense of chivalric notions of fair play has long been recognized in the *Daniel* (de Boor 1957, 193; Schmidt 1979, 192). Its significance in terms of social function and the history of ideas is not in equal degree a matter of consent. It may be seen as an index of Der Stricker's 'bourgeois' mentality, more specifically of his appeal to urban audiences in southern Germany (Buschinger 1989a, 23) or as a means of personal enrichment on the part of the landless gentry and rising middle class (Moelleken/Henderson 1973, 199). On the other hand, it may, in the changed conditions of the 1220s and 1230s, simply be a modern method of upholding traditional Arthurian values (Pingel 1994, 318f.). In any event, *list* is presented as an acceptable means of ensuring the victory of good over evil, the rightful king over upstart princes, in a struggle in which fundamental legal and moral values are at stake.

The assumption of a wider, less exclusively aristocratic audience might go some way to explain Der Stricker's handling of the fictive Arthurian world into which his new-style knight is inserted. There is an oddly pedagogical tone in his description of the Round Table, for instance. The code of chivalry is reduced in the *Daniel* to a set of rigidly formulated rules, whose infringement is visited with prescribed penalties. Genre-defining motifs, such as Arthur's custom of fasting and the institution of the Round Table, are furnished with a pedantically ration-alizing gloss: Arthur fasted each day until he heard a fresh adventure, in order to spur his knights to action and prevent their lapsing into sloth. The Round Table was likewise a means of keeping them up to scratch: every man setting out on an adventure was given a shield and might not return until it was convincingly battered; and knights were not allowed to boast of their own successes, but were obliged to confess publicly any shame that had befallen them. It is a precept pursued *ad absurdum* when Gawain, introducing Daniel to the court, men-daciously declares that he has just been unhorsed by the stranger. Perhaps the humour is intended (Buschinger 1989a; Mertens 1990, 92f.). But this view is hard to reconcile with Der Stricker's earnest rationalizing, of which there are endless examples: the King of Clûse takes his palace with him – by loading it onto elephants; the golden monster who guards his land is a miracle of technology and so on. The fragile magic of Arthurian romance is constantly at risk from pedantic explanation by a narrator, who seems to come from outside the charmed circle of Arthurian chivalry and to be expounding its values to a public in need of enlightenment as much as entertainment.

Der Pleier, *Garel, Tandareis und Flordibel, Meleranz*

Der Pleier is the author of three long verse romances, *Garel von dem blühenden Tal*, *Tandareis und Flordibel* and *Meleranz*. From his language he appears to be Austrian, but proposed connections with specific patrons or local families are now largely discredited (see, however, Herles 1981, vii–lx). The name by which he calls himself, the 'Glass Blower', is more likely to be one of the many fanciful pen-names used by professional poets to indicate their calling. Attempts to associate his works with historical events, notably the political upheavals of the *interregnum* in Germany (1256–73), remain speculative, and they are cautiously placed between 1240 and 1280. *Garel* is preserved in one fourteenth-century manuscript and a small fragment; *Meleranz* in one fifteenth-century manuscript. *Tandareis* exists in four fifteenth-century manuscripts and an earlier fragment, as well as in an abbreviated rendering in Czech.

In *Garel* the hero sets out to reconnoitre the land of King Ekunaver, who has declared war on Arthur to avenge his father. As in Stricker's *Daniel*, the large-scale conflict between Arthur and the tyrant provides a framework within which Garel encounters a succession of adventures, e.g. he vanquishes the aggressive suitor of Sabie of Merchanie; he liberates 400 knights confined in a garden by Eskilabon of Belamunt; he chops off the heads of the giant couple Purdan and Fidegart, and releases their captives, including a host of dwarfs, from whose king, Albewin, he receives a magic ring and sword; he destroys the scaly monster Vulganus, whose shield bears a death-dealing Medusa head, and marries Laudamie, queen of Anferre. With the aid of the troops amassed through his conquests, Garel finally defeats Ekunaver and succeeds in reconciling him with Arthur. Guinevere, carried off earlier by Meljakanz, a victim of the Rash Boon trick, is restored in time to organize the celebrations, after which Garel and Ekunaver establish a cloister on the battlefield.

Tandareis und Flordibel is a love story, with *minne* as the spur to chivalric endeavour, as well as its reward. The Indian princess Flordibel commits herself to Arthur's protection, with the condition that no man shall seek her love. But she and Tandareis fall in love and take refuge with Tandareis's parents, furiously pursued by Arthur. In the ensuing conflict Tandareis demonstrates his superiority in battle and his magnanimity as victor. He is legally vindicated, but exiled from court. A sequence of noble adventures earns him forgiveness, but he continues to champion hard-pressed ladies, like Queen Albiun of the Wild Mountains, until he is captured by guile by the lustful Kandalion, imprisoned and left to starve. Freed by Kandalion's sister, he acquits himself honourably at a three-day tournament before Arthur and is at last restored to favour and to Flordibel.

In *Meleranz*, too, love is the prize, and adventure the way to win it. On his way to Arthur's court Meleranz, son of the king of France, comes upon Tydomie of Kamarie lying in a magnificent bath in a forest glade, a glamorous setting for love at first sight. Meleranz goes on to become a knight, but leaves Arthur's court to rejoin Tydomie. On his way he encounters three interconnected adventures. He kills the tyrant Godomas, who has conscripted a family of giants to abduct and enslave knights and ladies. He liberates Tydomie's cousin Dulceflor from the heathen oppressor Verangoz. Learning that Tydomie is to be forced by her uncle Malloas to marry Libers of Lorgan, he vanquishes Libers, reveals his own identity and is accepted as a suitable match for Tydomie.

Of this chapter's trio of Arthurian writers, Der Pleier is the most conventional. To readers with tastes formed by Hartmann and Wolfram he offers elegant and undemanding variations on familiar themes, ingeniously reworking well-used material to create diverting if leisurely narratives. The resulting bland fare has attracted scant attention from critics (see Herles 1981, xi), but like other neglected texts they are beginning to reward closer scrutiny (e.g. Kern 1981, Müller 1981). Like other post-classical writers, Der Pleier has to reckon with the literary expectations of his audience; like them he cannot point to a well-known French model for his offerings, and achieves credibility by demonstrating his solidarity with the genre. He is massively indebted to Hartmann and Wolfram and is familiar, too, with Ulrich von Zatzikhoven, Gottfried von Straßburg and Wirnt von Grafenberg, though not apparently with Heinrich von dem Türlin. His design is neither to modernize like Der Stricker, nor to undermine like Heinrich, but to vindicate and perpetuate the inherited fictional world in which he and his readers are at home. The result is not invariably drab imitation or dreary compilation. Frequent quotation from 'classical' romances is part of an extensive system of intertextual reference. Accusations of plagiarism cannot wholly be set aside (Schröder 1985), but for the most part such reminiscences are designed to sustain the integrity of a genre which the author feels to be under threat (Mertens 1990, 96f.). The same principle seems to guide his choice of theme and his handling of plot and character. Naturally, he presents us with new protagonists and new combinations of adventures to test their courage and loyalty. *Tandareis* is a story of star-crossed lovers, whose predicament is based on a curious variation of the Rash Boon motif, with Arthur cast in the role of stern guardian. *Meleranz* is a characteristically Arthurian mix of romantic love and high adventure. But whatever is new here is carefully tailored to slot into received patterns, to supplement, as it were, an existing scenario (Kern 1981, 84, 89). Der Pleier is, of all Arthurian writers, the least inclined to tamper with the overarching fictions which guarantee the genre. Preformed characters, places and motifs provide a firm framework into which his own narratives slot comfortably (Kern 1981, 312f.). Chronology is as important to him as it is to Heinrich von dem Türlin, but not primarily to ensure self-consistency within his own works; rather he sees these as part of a historical *continuum* embracing the totality of Arthurian romance, and slots them into a time frame deduced from *Erec* and *Iwein*, *Lanzelet* and *Parzival* (Müller 1981, 115; Kern 1981, 132–5). Garel, Tandareis and Meleranz are secured in a web of family relationships largely derived from *Parzival* and painstakingly expanded to accommodate the new heroes and heroines (Kern 1981 especially 114–30).

Beyond such conservatism, there is discernible a corrective tendency, an effort to shore up the Arthurian dream and to fend off the decline of courtly behaviour in all Der Pleier's romances. But most explicitly in *Garel von dem blühenden Tal*, which, as the name implies, was conceived as a counter-attack, to limit the damage done by the (in Pleier's view) uncourtly and un-Arthurian antics of Der Stricker's *Daniel*. In *Garel* guile is replaced by old-fashioned chivalry, and mass slaughter by individual prowess (de Boor 1957, 78f.; Kern 1981, 44–76). This particular interest of *Garel* has tended to overshadow the other two romances, which however similarly demonstrate Der Pleier's talent in the field of courtly *Unterhaltungsliteratur*. Romance for him offers an escape, not into 'faery lands', for there is little residue of Celtic magic, but into a vanished world of beauty and order, with much lingering over courtly dress and etiquette and the rituals of aristocratic society (Zimmermann 1988, 354). There is an elegiac as well as a didactic tone in the leisurely verse, a feeling of decline, of 'each year being worse than the last' (*Meleranz* v. 24), from which Arthurian story offers a desired refuge. His influence is discernible in *Wigamur* and in Konrad von Stoffel's *Gauriel von Muntabel*; themes from his romances recur centuries later in *Flordimar* and in Ulrich Füetrer's *Buch der Abenteuer*, and his *Tandareis und Flordibel* was adapted into Czech in the late fourteenth century.

Bibliography

I. Heinrich von dem Türlin

Primary Source and Translation

Heinrich von dem Türlin, *Diu Crône*. Ed. by G. H. F. Scholl, 1852 (BLV, 27). Stuttgart (repr. Amsterdam 1966).

Heinrich von dem Türlin, *The Crown: A Tale of Sir Gawein and King Arthur's Court*. Transl. with an Introduction by J. W. Thomas, 1989. Lincoln and London.

Other Literature

Andersen, E. 1987. 'Heinrich von dem Türlin's *Diu Crône* and the Prose *Lancelot*: an intertextual study', *AL*, 7, 23–49.

Boll, L. L. 1929. *The Relation of 'Diu Krone' of Heinrich von dem Türlin to 'La Mule sanz Frain': A Study of its Sources*, Catholic University of America Studies in German, 2 (repr. New York 1960).

de Boor, H. 1975. 'Fortuna in mittelhochdeutscher Dichtung, insbesondere in der *Crone* des Heinrich von dem Türlin', in H. Fromm et al., eds., *Verbum et Signum. Festschrift für F. Ohly*, Munich, II, 311–28.

Buschinger, D. 1981. 'Burg Salîe und Gral. Zwei Erlösungstaten Gaweins in der *Crône* Heinrichs von dem Türlin' in Krämer 1981, 1–32.

Cormeau, Ch. 1977. *'Wigalois' und 'Diu Crône'. Zwei Kapitel zur Gattungsgeschichte des nachklassischen Aventiureromans*, Münchener Texte und Untersuchungen, 57, Munich.

Ebenbauer, A. 1977. 'Fortuna und Artushof. Bemerkungen zum "Sinn" der *Krone* Heinrichs von dem Türlin', in Ebenbauer, A. et al., eds., *Österreichische Literatur zur Zeit der Babenberger*, Wiener Arbeiten zur germanischen Altertumskumde und Philologie, 10, Vienna, 25–49.

Frappier, J. 1959. 'The Vulgate Cycle', in Loomis 1959 (see Gen. Bibl.), 295–319.

Heller, E. K. 1942. 'A vindication of Heinrich von dem Türlin, based on a survey of his sources', *MLQ*, 3, 67–82.

Jillings, L. 1980. *'Diu Crone' of Heinrich von dem Türlein: The Attempted Emancipation of Secular Narrative*, GAG, 258, Göppingen.

Jillings, L. 1981. 'Heinrich von dem Türlein. Zum Problem der biographischen Forschung', in Krämer 1981, 87–102.

Knapp, F. P. 1981. 'Literarische Beziehungen und mögliche Auftraggeber', in Krämer 1981, 145–87.

Krämer, P., ed. 1981. *Die mittelalterliche Literatur in Kärnten*, Wiener Arbeiten zur germanischen Altertumskunde und Philologie, 16, Vienna.

Kratz, B. 1973. 'Zur Kompositionstechnik Heinrichs von dem Türlin', *ABäG*, 5, 141–53.

Kratz, B. 1977. 'Zur Biographie Heinrichs von dem Türlin', *ABäG*, 11, 123–67.

Lot, F. 1918. *Etude sur le Lancelot en prose*, Paris (repr. 1954).

Menzel-Reuters, A. 1989. *Vröude, Artusbild, Fortuna- und Gralkonzeption in der 'Crône' des Heinrich von dem Türlin als Verteidigung des höfischen Ideals*, Europäische Hochschulschriften, Reihe 1, Deutsche Sprache und Literatur, 1134, Frankfurt.

Pickering, F. P. 1966. *Literatur und darstellende Kunst im Mittelalter*, Grundlagen der Germanistik, 4, Berlin.

Schmolke-Hasselmann, B. 1980. *Der arthurische Versroman von Chrestien bis Froissart*, Beihefte zur *ZfrPh*, 177, Tübingen.

Schröder, W. 1992. 'Zur Literaturverarbeitung durch Heinrich von dem Türlin in seinem Gawein-Roman *Diu Crône*', *ZfdA*, 121, 131–74.

Thomas 1989. See Primary Sources, Heinrich von dem Türlin, *The Crown*.

Wallbank, R. E. 1965. 'The composition of *Diu Krône*. Heinrich von dem Türlin's narrative technique', in Whitehead, F. et al., eds., *Medieval Miscellany presented to E. Vinaver*, Manchester 300–20.

Wallbank, R. E. 1981. 'Heinrichs von dem Türlin *Crône* und die irische Sage von Etain und Midar', in Krämer, 1981, 251–68.

Wallbank, R. E. 1987. 'König Artus und Frau Saelde in der *Crône* Heinrichs von dem Türlin', in McLintock, D. et al., eds., *Geistliche und weltliche Epik des Mittelalters in Österreich*, GAG, 446, Göppingen, 129–36.

Wallbank-Turner R. E. 1993. 'An Irish fairy in Austria: Vrou Giramphiel and Lady Fortuna in

Diu Crône', in Skrine, P. et al., eds., *Connections: Essays in Honour of Eda Sagarra,* Stuttgarter Arbeiten zur Germanistik, 281, Stuttgart, 285–96.

Wyss, U. 1981. 'Die Wunderketten in der *Crône*', in Krämer 1981, 269–91.

Zach, C. 1990. *Die Erzählmotive der 'Crône' Heinrichs von dem Türlin und ihre altfranzösischen Quellen,* Passauer Schriften zu Sprache und Literatur, 5. Passau.

Zatloukal, K. 1981. 'Gedanken über den Gedanken. Der reflektierende Held in Heinrichs von dem Türlin *Crône*', in Krämer, 293–316.

(Earlier literature is listed in Jillings 1980 and Menzel-Reuters 1989.)

II. Der Stricker

Primary Source and Translations

Der Stricker, *Daniel von dem Blühenden Tal.* Ed. by M. Resler, 1983 (ATB, 92). Tübingen.

Der Stricker, *Daniel of the Blossoming Valley (Daniel von dem Blühenden Tal).* Transl. by M. Resler, 1990 (Garland Library of Medieval Literature, 58). New York.

Der Stricker, *Daniel von dem Blühenden Tal.* Transl. by H. Birkhan with introduction and notes, 1992 (Erzählungen des Mittelalters, 5). Kettwig.

Other Literature

Birkhan, H. 1994. 'Motiv- und Handlungsgeschichten in Strickers *Daniel*', in Honeman, V. et al., eds., *German Narrative Literature of the Twelfth and Thirteenth Centuries: Studies for R. Wisbey,* Tübingen, 363–89.

de Boor, H. 1957. 'Der *Daniel* des Stricker und der *Garel* des Pleier', *PBB* (Tübingen), 79, 67–84.

Brall, H. 1984. 'Höfische Ideologie und feudale Herrschaftsgewalt. Überlegungen zum Strukturwandel höfischer Epik im Werk des Stricker', in Ebenbauer, A., ed., *Philologische Untersuchungen gewidmet Elfriede Stutz,* Philologica Germanica, 7, Vienna, 102–30.

Buschinger, D. 1989a. 'Parodie und Satire im *Daniel von dem Blühenden Tal* des Stricker', *Wissenschaftliche Beiträge der Ernst-Moritz-Arndt Universität Greifswald. Deutsche Literatur des Mittelalters,* 5, 15–23.

Classen, A. 1991. 'Transformation des arthurischen Romans zum frühneuzeitlichen Unterhaltungs- und Belehrungswerk. Der Fall *Daniel von dem Blühenden Tal*', *ABäG*, 33, 167–92.

Mertens, V. 1990. ' "gewisse lêre". Zum Verhältnis von Fiktion und Didaxe im späten Artusroman', in Wolfzettel 1990 (see Gen. Bibl.), 85–106.

Moelleken, W. and Henderson I. 1973. 'Die Bedeutung der "liste" im *Daniel* des Strickers', *ABäG*, 4, 187–201.

Müller, D. 1981. *'Daniel von dem Blühenden Tal' und 'Garel von dem Blühenden Tal'. Die Artusromane des Stricker und des Pleier unter gattungsgeschichtlichen Aspekten,* GAG, 334, Göppingen.

Pingel, R. 1994. *Ritterliche Werte zwischen Tradition und Transformation. Zur veränderten Konzeption von Artusheld und Artushof in Strickers 'Daniel von dem Blühenden Tal',* Mikrokosmos, Beiträge zur Literaturwissenschaft und Bedeutungsforschung, 40, Frankfurt.

Schmidt, W. 1979. *Untersuchungen zu Aufbauformen und Erzählstil im 'Daniel von dem Blühenden Tal' des Stricker,* GAG, 266, Göppingen.

Schröder, W. 1986. ' "und zuckte in uf als einen schoup". Parodierte Artus-Herrlichkeit in Strickers *Daniel*', in Hauck, K., ed., *Sprache und Recht. Beiträge zur Kulturgeschichte des Mittelalters. Festschrift für Ruth Schmidt-Wiegand,* Berlin, II, 814–30.

Wailes, S. 1977. 'Stricker and the virtue "Prudentia": a critical review', *Seminar* 13, 136–53.

III. Der Pleier

Primary Sources and Translations

Der Pleier, *Garel von dem bluenden Tal.* Ed. by W. Herles, 1981 (Wiener Arbeiten zur germanischen Altertumskunde und Philologie, 17). Vienna.

Der Pleier, *Tandareis und Flordibel. Ein höfischer Roman.* Ed. by F. Khull, 1885. Graz.

Der Pleier, *Meleranz.* Ed. by K. Bartsch, 1861 (BLV). Stuttgart (repr. Hildesheim 1974).

The Pleier's Arthurian Romances: Garel of the Blooming Valley, Tandareis and Flordibel, Meleranz. Transl. and introduced by J. W. Thomas, 1992 (Garland Library of Medieval Literature, B 91). New York.

Other Literature

de Boor, H. 1957. 'Der *Daniel* des Stricker und der *Garel* des Pleier', *PBB* (Tübingen), 79, 68–84.

Buschinger, D. 1988. 'Ein Dichter des Übergangs. Einige Bemerkungen zum Pleier', in Honsze, N. et al., eds., *Festschrift für M. Syrocki*, Amsterdam, 137–49.

Buschinger, D. 1989b. 'Die Wiederspiegelung mittelalterlicher Herrschaftsstrukturen im *Garel* des Pleier', *Wissenschaftliche Beiträge der Ernst-Moritz-Arndt-Universität Greifswald. Deutsche Literatur des Mittelalters*, 4, 21–31.

Cormeau, Ch. 1991. '*Tandareis und Flordibel* von dem Pleier. Eine poetologische Reflexion über Liebe im Artusroman', in Haug and Wachinger 1991 (see Gen. Bibl.), 39–53.

Herles 1981. See Primary Sources, Der Pleier.

Kern, P. 1981. *Die Artusromane des Pleier. Untersuchung über den Zusammenhang von Dichtung und literarischer Situation*, Philologische Studien und Quellen, 100, Berlin.

Mertens, V. 1990. '"gewisse lere". Zum Verhältnis von Fiktion und Didaxe im späten Artusroman', in Wolfzettel 1990 (see Gen. Bibl.), 85–106.

Müller, D. 1981. '*Daniel vom blühenden Tal*' und '*Garel vom blühenden Tal*'. *Die Artusromane des Stricker und des Pleier unter gattungsgeschichtlichen Aspekten*, GAG, 334, Göppingen.

Pütz, H. P. 1982. 'Pleiers *Garel von dem blühenden Tal.* Protest oder Anpassung?', in Kühebacher, E., ed., *Literatur und bildende Kunst im Tiroler Mittelalter*, Innsbruck, 29–44.

Riordan, J. L. 1948. 'A vindication of the Pleier', *JEGP*, 47, 29–43.

Schröder, W. 1985. 'Das *Willehalm*-Plagiat im *Garel* des Pleier oder die vergeblich geleugnete Epigonalität', *ZfdA*, 114, 119–41.

Thomas, N. 1992. *The Defence of Camelot: Ideology and Intertextuality in the 'Post-Classical' German Romances of the Matter of Britain Cycle*, Deutsche Literatur von den Anfängen bis 1700, 14, Berne, 44–69.

Zimmermann, M. 1988. 'Ritter Garel von dem blühenden Tal. Arthurische Idealität aus der Steiermark', in Ebenbauer, A. et al., eds., *Die mittelalterliche Literatur in der Steiermark*, Jahrbuch für Internationale Germanistik, Reihe A. Kongressberichte, 23, 337–56.

6

INTERTEXTUALITY IN THE LATER THIRTEENTH CENTURY: *WIGAMUR, GAURIEL, LOHENGRIN* AND THE FRAGMENTS OF ARTHURIAN ROMANCES

Matthias Meyer

The texts treated in this chapter have enjoyed little literary success. While cursory critical interest has been accorded to *Lohengrin* as an offspring of the immensely popular *Parzival*, the other texts have been largely neglected in past research, and *Wigamur* and *Gauriel* have both been regarded as the worst German Arthurian romances. However, there has been a considerable increase in understanding of the 'minor' Arthurian romances in recent years, and *Wigamur* is by now the only such work not to have undergone a fundamental reappraisal. The fragments have received little more than codicological attention.

Wigamur

The romance is preserved anonymously in a single manuscript (W: Wolfenbüttel, fifteenth century, paper, illustrated; see Henderson 1989) and two fragments (M: Munich, fourteenth century, parchment; S: Vienna, fourteenth century, parchment). Several pages are missing from W, including at least four pages missing before the last page. Since there is no prologue, the usual source of information about author, patron and context is lacking. *Wigamur* is mentioned in Tannhäuser's parodistic fourth lay and in the *Jüngerer Titurel*, in *Friedrich von Schwaben* and in Füetrer's strophic *Lannzilet*. The mention by Tannhäuser, the literary style and the mixture of genres suggest a dating in the middle of the thirteenth century. The dialect points to eastern Swabia or Franconia as the possible home of the author. There is no known French source for the text, and a brief synopsis illustrates that well-established literary motifs have been reworked by the author.

The text opens with the birth of the hero, Wigamur, son of King Paltriot of Lendrie. When Paltriot attends a Whit feast at Arthur's court Wigamur is kidnapped by Lespia, a wild woman, who searches for a future spouse for one of her daughters. Lespia also holds captive a *merwunder*, a marvellous creature. Later, she is herself taken hostage by Wigamur's father. The *merwunder* frees himself, kills the two daughters and frees Wigamur. On returning with King Paltriot and finding her daughters dead and Wigamur missing, Lespia commits suicide. Wigamur is raised and educated in courtly behaviour by the *merwunder*. Wigamur obviously knows his own name (see v. 3884), but not his lineage, and he departs in search of his father. In keeping with the tradition of the Fair Unknown, the youth of unknown parentage, he has no knowledge of knighthood. He is fascinated to see the destruction of a castle by a band of knights, captures a riderless horse and takes the armour from a dead knight. He is victorious in his first combat but shows himself ignorant of the convention of submission. In the ruins of the castle he finds the sole survivor of the massacre, a maiden named Pioles, whom he tries to comfort. Wigamur leaves Pioles alone three times. After the third occasion (narrated in a missing passage which is recounted later) he entrusts Pioles to the care of dwarfs whose oppressor he has defeated in combat. In the next extant episode Wigamur receives a knightly education from Yttra, which is modelled on Parzival's education by Gurnemanz. He then encounters an eagle struggling with a vulture, he kills the vulture, and the eagle becomes his constant companion. The next episode leads him to Arthur's court where a woman, Eudis, seeks a champion in a judicial combat over an inheritance. The object of the quarrel between the two female relatives is a wondrous fountain. Wigamur wins the combat and is offered Eudis's hand in marriage and lordship over her land, but he declines the offer because knowledge of his kin eludes him. The next two episodes, a tournament with the prize of a kingdom and a battle in aid of a besieged queen, repeat this pattern. Even though the court sees his deeds as proof of his worth, Wigamur wishes to spare any kingdom the possible embarrassment of being ruled by someone of low birth. Furthermore, Wigamur refuses to stay at Arthur's court and leaves for the wilderness to discover his lineage. The search does not take long, for he reaches a land that is the subject of a feud between two neighbouring kings as the old ruler has died without an heir. Wigamur joins the party of King Atroclas, unaware that the contender is King Paltriot, his father. After a fierce battle it is agreed that the conflict should be decided by a duel. While Paltriot himself will fight the duel, Atroclas yields this right to Wigamur. Before the combat begins, Wigamur is asked to reveal his lineage as proof of his right to fight against a king. To his shame, Wigamur is unable to provide the necessary information. However, he tells the story of his life as far as he knows it and is recognized by his father, who reveals his royal lineage to him. A peace is negotiated and sealed with the marriage of Wigamur and the daughter of Atroclas, Dulceflor. Atroclas, Dulceflor and Wigamur then attend a tournament where Dulceflor is kidnapped. During the pursuit of the kidnapper, Wigamur meets a knight who

turns out to be the lover of Pioles. The lovers are reunited, as are Wigamur and
Dulceflor. A court feast celebrating the reunion may have been described in the
four missing pages of the manuscript; in the epilogue the birth of a son,
Dulciweygar, is reported.

Wigamur is a reworking of several Arthurian themes, including the search for
the father and the connection of marriage and kingship; and parallels to earlier
texts can be established for almost every scene in the romance, with the Eudis
episode, for instance, echoing Hartmann's *Iwein*. Material is drawn in *Wigamur*
chiefly from Arthurian romance, but also from other genres: the heroic motif of
battle between father and son is alluded to yet deftly avoided. The changes
introduced by the author when combining Arthurian material with motifs from
other genres are consistent, if drastic when compared to the Arthurian norm,
and while the style of the romance is simple, the story itself is well constructed
and coherent, and leaves no open ends, as the unfolding of the Pioles episodes
demonstrates. Indeed, the work shows more literary merit than some earlier
judgements have suggested. Although some motifs seem to be handled
ironically, the general style makes the parodistic interpretation suggested by
Classen (1993) unlikely.

The treatment of some familiar features of Arthurian romance in *Wigamur*
warrants further comment. First, the motif of the Fair Unknown (Thomas, N.
1992) is used in reduced form: Wigamur knows his name but not his lineage.
Consequently the quest is not one of self-realization, but a search for lineage
(Ebenbauer 1984). Wigamur resists invitations of Arthur's court to pursue the
'normal' career of an Arthurian knight. He is obsessed by his own enigmatic
kinship, and author and protagonist reject the idea that lordship and nobility
can be won by individual merit alone. Second, the concept of *âventiure* is also
refashioned. The knight errant is no longer doing battle against a more or less
well-defined 'Other' and either conquering it or integrating the opponents into
society, but his tasks are always clearly related to the clash of opposing groups in
power: judicial combat, tournament over a fiefdom, war about sovereignty
(Martin 1987). The conventional Arthurian correlation between adventure and
love no longer holds for the protagonist, who not only avoids marriages that are
offered to him but also obtains his bride in an episode where the central combat
fails to take place. His marriage is purely political, the result of peace
negotiations. The motif of love goes unmentioned – until the very end.

Women also have minimal significance in the plot. Wigamur's mother is
mentioned only in passing. While the abduction is performed by a female figure,
this episode is one of the strangest reworkings by the author. The world of
Lespia is clearly female-dominated: the mother procures the bridegroom for her
daughters. This female world is destroyed by the *merwunder*. The text uses
masculine or neuter pronouns to describe this figure, but the illustrations of the

Wolfenbüttel manuscript are unequivocal: the wild woman is a naked, blond female figure; the *merwunder* is a scaled, thus armoured, manly creature. The motif of a young man in a female-dominated world consequently seems to be avoided, although Wigamur still exhibits the shortcomings associated with this motif.

The role of Arthur's court is similarly marginalized. Although the plot starts with the journey of Wigamur's father to Arthur's feast, the court remains somewhat obscure. It is still an institution of juridical importance, but the arrival at Arthur's court has little significance for the protagonist. In fact, he has to distance himself from the court to reach the end of his quest for kinship. Arthur then vanishes from the romance, unless one assumes that the final marriage celebrations take place at Arthur's court (Mertens 1998, 248f.). If the marriage is assumed to take place at one of the other kingdoms there is little reason to describe the text as an Arthurian romance proper; it would more aptly be termed a heroic romance with Arthurian episodes.

Finally, the role of society is strongly emphasized compared with that of the individual. Society is governed less by courtly ideals than by kinship structures, and it is shown to be ravaged by war and destruction. It is the task of the protagonist to take sides in this warfare, but it is increasingly difficult to choose among the available options with any moral certainty, as the beginning of the dénouement makes clear. The social focus is also evident in the dominance of battle scenes and mass tournaments compared to the individual combats of the knight errant.

All these points confirm the conservative ethos of *Wigamur*. In *Wigamur* images are taken from the core of Arthurian romance to underpin an ethos that has close affinities with heroic epic, and the text is highly anti-individualistic. Ulrich von Zatzikhoven's Lanzelet discovers his name, his identity and his individual love. Wigamur's name is known all the time; he discovers his kin and becomes the object of negotiations to enhance the standing of his clan. It is indeed plausible to describe *Wigamur* as a reaction against an individualistic tendency in Arthurian romance, a reaction which may have been prompted in part by concern about the cohesion of aristocratic society, for the world of this text seems threatened by forces of disintegration.

Konrad von Stoffeln, *Gauriel von Muntabel*

The text is transmitted in two complete though highly divergent manuscripts and two fragments. D, Donaueschingen, Hofbibliothek, Cod. 86, last quarter of fifteenth century, paper, contains the long version of *Gauriel* (5634 vv.) and the *Historie des kuniges Appollonij* in the redaction of Heinrich Steinhöwel;

I, Innsbruck, Tiroler Landesmuseum Ferdinandeum, Cod. FB 32001, around 1457, paper, contains a collection of short tales, the short version of *Gauriel* (3807 vv.) and some verses of Rudolf von Ems's *Willehalm*. Fragment M, Bayerische Staatsbibliothek, Cgm 5249/9a, fourteenth century, parchment, contains vv. 1093–1214; fragment m, Bayerische Staatsbibliothek, Cgm 5249/9b, late fourteenth century, paper, contains 585 vv., 3369–873, largely following the longer version in D (Achnitz/Schiewer 1989).

The name of the author is given only in the longer Donaueschingen version as 'von stoffel maister Cuonrat' (v. 5667) and was regarded as identical with a Konrad von Hohenstoffeln (from Hegau) named in charters from Strasbourg. In his new edition, Achnitz makes a case for the Swabian Konrad von Stöffeln/Gönningen (*c.* 1250–after 1300). The text of this romance poses a major problem since the two extant versions differ greatly in length. Khull's old edition (4172 vv.) created a new text that was unknown in the Middle Ages, using hardly justifiable criteria. The new edition by Achnitz (used here) offers a synoptical presentation of the manuscript tradition and a new critical text (5670 vv., mostly following D, with additions).

In the prologue Konrad opens a fictional window in the Arthurian world by announcing his plan to tell the story of a valiant Arthurian knight who has been strangely forgotten by the canonical writers. Gauriel, the knight with the goat (an offshoot of Iwein's lion), encounters a group of beautiful ladies to whom he praises the beauty of his own lady. However, she is a fairy creature, and Gauriel has broken a taboo by talking about her, for which he is punished by the absence of his beloved, and by becoming hideously ugly so that no other lady will love him. After a year he receives a message from his lady that they can be reunited if he accomplishes a task set by the 'order of gods', to which she belongs: he has to capture the best three Arthurian knights and bring them to her country, Fluratrone. He sets up camp near Arthur's court and captures one of Ginover's damsels. All knights who fight against Gauriel are either severely wounded or killed (v. 912); in the fight between Iwein and Gauriel the lion and the goat kill each other. Only when Arthur himself wishes to fight against Gauriel does Gauriel surrender. When Gauriel tells his story, he is readily pardoned and the three best knights (Walban, Gawan and Iwein) agree to follow him. However, Gauriel promises to return and serve the queen for one year as atonement for the havoc he has wreaked. Interspersed is an adventure of Erec who is not present during Gauriel's *âventiure*, but later joins the knights on their way to Fluratrone. After a number of fights which overcome the defence of his lady's realm, the lovers are reunited and Gauriel leaves for Arthur's court. The returning knights experience three major encounters – one concerning the country Pronaias, which is beleaguered by heathens, the second concerning the count Asterian in a dark wood from which no one has ever escaped (a classic realm of death), the last a *merfeie* in Geldipant. Gauriel's fairy-love appears with much pomp at Arthur's court, and the two are married before returning to her realm.

The romance was probably written in the decades around 1250; Achnitz (1997) argues for a later date: between 1280 and the early fourteenth century. It has been widely ignored in research, following Panzer's judgement (1902, LXXXVII) that *Gauriel* was the worst of many bad Arthurian romances, and in view of Khull's problematical edition. The sources of the romance have been surveyed in detail (Demtröder 1964). *Gauriel* is not a translation but a typical late Arthurian romance composed according to the 'Poetik der Verfügbarkeit' ('the poetics of availability', Meyer 1994). Although the work contains a high incidence of literary allusions, it is often difficult to name specific sources (Neugart 1992). Schöning (1991, 210) speaks of a confusion of structures, and the text certainly combines divergent narrative types: Arthurian romance, *chanson de geste*, the relationship of fairy woman and knight. *Gauriel* is in part a variation on *Iwein*, but it is matter of debate whether Konrad's work is a criticism of *Iwein* (Thomas, N. 1988) or simply takes Hartmann's romance as a starting point (Zimmermann 1992). A tendency to unbridled violence on the part of the protagonist and other knights sets *Gauriel* apart from many Arthurian romances. Whether this constitutes a serious fault in the construction of the romance that hinders successful communication between author and audience (Meyer 1993) or whether it is part of a meaningful de-idealization is still an open question.

Gauriel can be read as a correction of *Iwein*, especially with regard to Laudine's role. Gauriel's lady acts capriciously but offers the possibility of reconciliation. Like Laudine she accepts a one-year period of absence, but instead of waiting for her lover's return she surprises him at Arthur's court (Egerding 1991). The marriage that takes place at Arthur's court can be seen as the incorporation of personal love into knightly society. Achnitz reads the text as closely following the structure of Chrétien/Hartmann romances; its theme is the integration of the individual (presented in the outcast Gauriel) into society. However, the reader is never sure how to interpret the romance, for the text offers numerous inconsistencies and ironies, and generally seems to resist the notion of an underlying significance. Its main function was probably to provide good, if at times heavy-handed, entertainment by exploiting stock material. This could hold true for *Wigamur* as well, though the more consistent thematic emphasis on 'law and order' in *Wigamur* suggests a stronger social ideology.

Lohengrin

The text is transmitted in three complete manuscripts and two fragments from a fourth manuscript. A, Heidelberg, cpg 364, early fourteenth century, parchment, contains Wolfram's *Parzival* (G^x) and *Lohengrin*. B, Heidelberg, cpg 345, around 1475, paper, contains *Lohengrin* and *Friedrich von Schwaben*. M, Munich, cgm 4871, contains *Lohengrin* and a few short texts. The dating of the fragments Cf is hotly debated since the date of the text is affected, and varies between late thirteenth century (recently Bertelsmeier-Kirst/Heinzle 1996) and early fourteenth century (recently Thomas, H. 1995).

The text (7670 vv. in a ten-line stanza form drawn from the *Wartburgkrieg*) begins with a long exchange in riddle form between 'Wolfram von Eschenbach' and 'Klingsor', after which 'Wolfram' tells the story of *Lohengrin*. Thus *Lohengrin* is one of several thirteenth-century texts, e.g. *Wolfdietrich D* and the *Jüngerer Titurel*, which are more or less successfully passed off as works of the revered Wolfram. The author of *Lohengrin* is believed to be one Nouhusius or Nouhuwius (Neuhaus), a name derived from an acrostic in stanzas 763–65. These stanzas form an epilogue in which the author talks about his work and its style. It has not proved possible to match the name of this author – possibly of Bavarian origin – with a historical person.

The story falls into two main parts: the tale of Lohengrin and Elsam of Brabant is the story of a marriage between an otherworldly and a human partner, whilst a historical part depicts two battles of the emperor's armies against invading heathens. There is no clear distinction between fictional and historical narrative, since the 'historical' parts are heavily fictionalized as well.

Elsam seeks a champion to defend her in a judicial combat. She nurses a wounded falcon which carries a bell, and as she sighs and prays for a champion the bell announces her plight to the realm of the Grail, where Arthur and his knights are in attendance. An inscription on the Grail nominates Lohengrin as a champion for Elsam. A swan-boat carries him to Antwerp, and he is victorious in the combat, which takes place at a diet of Emperor Henry I at Mainz. Lohengrin then agrees to marry Elsam after she has promised to obey a command which is not specified at this point in the narrative. This opening (about 250 stanzas) leads to the 'historical' centre of the text. Heinrich, still not a true emperor as he has not yet been consecrated by the pope, leads an army to victory against Hungarian invaders. After the victorious return another session of the emperor's court is described in detail, and the first 'historical' part of *Lohengrin* ends here. The second 'historical' part is a fictional account of a battle against a heathen invasion in Italy, which threatens the pope. The style of the battle scenes is influenced by Wolfram's *Willehalm*. Lohengrin and other German nobles, the German emperor and the kings of France and Arles take part, and again the Christians are victorious, aided by divine intervention in the shape of two strange knights who are later revealed as the apostles St Peter and St Paul. After the victory, Henry I is finally consecrated as emperor by the pope, and the festive return of the heroes to Germany is reported in great detail.

Finally, the fictional story of Elsam and Lohengrin is taken up again when the countess of Cleve calls Lohengrin's nobility into question (stanza 692). Elsam, affected by this slander, breaks the promise she has made, and asks Lohengrin to tell her his name and kin. Lohengrin announces his parentage in the presence of the emperor in Antwerp, linking the taboo he placed on a question in his marriage (which appears already in Wolfram's *Parzival*) with Parzival's failure to ask a question on his first visit to the Grail. In a scene of great drama and emotion, Lohengrin takes leave of wife and emperor and is taken back by the swan to the Grail realm. The text closes with a brief account of German emperors from Henry I to Henry II.

No direct German or French source has been found for *Lohengrin*, save for some historical passages where the author uses especially the *Sächsische Weltchronik*, a thirteenth-century narrative chronicle. The text is only indirectly related to other versions of the Swan Knight motif. Even the connection to the close of Wolfram's *Parzival* is tentative. There is hardly any medieval reception of the work, though the fifteenth-century *Lorengel* draws on *Lohengrin* for its beginning.

Research has focused on the historical elements of the text, particularly on dating and on the political tendencies (Cramer 1971, Thomas, H. 1973 – with different contextualization), which at times override concerns for historical accuracy (Kerdelhué 1991). In its historical and political dimension, *Lohengrin* is a crusading epic in which knighthood is described as 'more austere' than all religious orders (stanza 538), and it is above all an 'emperor's epic'. The emperor is idealized as the central figure. He has harmonious relations with the pope, and his political actions are described in extensive detail and without any trace of criticism, as he leads the Christians into battle, holds court and successfully manages the affairs of his realm.

Questions of style and genre have received less attention in recent research, though there are useful discussions in Kerdelhué (1986) and Unger (1990). The author of *Lohengrin* clearly imitates Wolfram's style. The text also brings the hybrid tendencies of late Arthurian romances into sharp relief. Indeed, it is hardly appropriate to describe *Lohengrin* as an Arthurian romance. It is in part a reduced Grail romance that follows the *Jüngerer Titurel* to show the political actions instigated by the Grail. However, it is clear that the Grail story merely provides the frame in *Lohengrin* for a literary experiment in creating historical fiction. *Lohengrin* may well have been successful as a political work in its own time, and this could explain its meagre reception in the later Middle Ages: *Lohengrin* is less the tale of a fairy marriage than a political romance which has lost its context.

The central role of Emperor Henry I explains the marginal role of King Arthur and the Grail in the work. The story of Lohengrin, Elsam, the Grail and the taboo is less an autonomous narrative than a functional framework. Arthur is mentioned in the early account of the Grail realm, and personages of his court (especially the Queen, Key, Gawein, Parzival, Lanzelet) are alluded to in their usual roles, but this Arthurian world fades from the narrative once Lohengrin sets out with the swan (stanza 64). The geographical location of the Grail realm is unclear at the beginning of the text, though it is possibly in France, and at the end it is in *Indîâ* (v. 7142). A double location of the Grail realm could spring from the author's reading of the *Jüngerer Titurel* (Cramer 1971, 34–6). The status of Arthur's court in relation to the Grail is unclear, and in his farewell speech in Antwerp Lohengrin refers to his father, Parzival, as 'lord with the Grail' ('herre zuo dem grâl', v. 7102).

It is revealing of the direction of the work that the Grail realm is no longer described when Lohengrin returns to it; rather the narrative ends in the history of German emperors.The marginalization of the Arthurian world in the Grail romances is a well-known feature of thirteenth-century literature. The author of *Lohengrin* goes one step further by marginalizing the Grail as well, thus gaining political immediacy and losing narrative impact in his romance. Finally, the combination of fiction and history in *Lohengrin* is typical of a tendency in German romances from the late thirteenth century onward. *Reinfried von Braunschweig*, *Willhelm von Österreich* and *Friedrich von Schwaben* (transmitted in the *Lohengrin* manuscript B) are further examples of this mixture.

The Fragments of Arthurian Romances

If the testimony of Rudolf von Ems in his catalogues of names and works is reliable, two Arthurian romances may have been quite lost to us. In the authors' catalogue in *Willehalm von Orlens*, Rudolf names a Gottfried von Hohenlohe ('En Gotfrit von Hohenloch', v. 2239) who has supposedly described all the notable knights at Arthur's court. This text may have been a mere list of names like the fifteenth-century *Spruch von den Tafelrundern* (Schiewer 1988, 225), but it could have been an Arthurian romance. Even more obscure is Heinrich von Leinau and his work *Der Wallære* ('her Heinrich von Lînouwe', Rudolf von Ems, *Alexander* vv. 3254–6). According to Rudolf's *Willehalm* (vv. 7100–8) the hero of *Der Wallaere* was called Ekken or similar (the name appears in the genitive case as Ekkenes) and the text contained a tournament episode reminiscent of the beginning of *Erec*.

In addition to these lost works there are a number of extant fragments of German Arthurian romances. In most cases the fragments are reduced to no more than a couple of hundred lines and little can be inferred about the story as a whole. They will be discussed briefly with regard to questions of content and genre.

Abor und das Meerweib. One fragment (beginning of fourteenth century, Copenhagen, Kongelige Bibliotek, Ny kgl. Saml. cod. 4843,4°, 136 vv.)

The strange text was believed to be an invention of the nineteenth century until the fragment was rediscovered in 1974. The wounded knight Abor is found by a *merwip* (a fairy-creature) at a fountain of youth. She takes him to her castle, nurses him and procures a wondrous root which enables Abor to understand all animals. After a period of six weeks and two days he has to leave her since her husband is due to come home. He receives a magical bathrobe that makes him invulnerable, and a bow and arrow, probably to shoot a wild bird – and here the fragment ends. Most likely this is part of a story resembling the adventurous epics of the Dietrich von Bern cycle. The healing of the severely wounded protagonist by a *merwip* is a central episode in the *Eckenlied*. But it is equally possible that this is part of a later Arthurian romance which incorporates motifs (and landscapes) of the heroic epics.

Blanschandin. Three fragments of a manuscript (Vienna, ÖNB, cod. s.n. 102) from the late thirteenth century, 384 partly truncated vv.

This piece is a translation of the French romance *Blancandin et l'Orgueilleuse d'Amor*, which combines motifs of Arthurian romances, Byzantine romances and *chansons de geste*. The mixture is typical of the late German Arthurian romance as well. The fragments are all from the beginning of the romance (vv. 72–154, 292–353 and 379–440 of the French text) and start with a dialogue on knighthood between the young Blanschandin and a master, which leads to the furtive departure of the protagonist from his parents' court. Fragments of his first fight and its aftermath follow.

Cligès (Konrad Fleck? Ulrich von Türheim?). Three fragments (Kalocsa, Kathedralbibl., MS 312/a, 242 vv.; St. Paul, Stiftsbibl. Sign. 27/8; Zurich, Zentralbibl., MS Z XIV 12: around 1300/20)

The text is attributed to Ulrich von Türheim in the Kalocsa fragment. However, since all fragments stem from the last third of a translation of Chrétien's *Cligès*, the disputed question of whether there were two German *Cligès* versions or whether there was a *Cligès* by Konrad Fleck which was continued by Ulrich von Türheim remains unanswered. The Zurich fragment contains part of Kliges's request for permission to leave for Arthur's court (Chrétien vv. 4230ff.); the St Paul fragment describes the combat between Kliges and Kawein (Chrétien vv. 4940–90). Fenice's faked death is found in the Kalocsa fragments with an intermission where Ulrich discloses his name. The first part of this fragment can be reconstructed and contains a dialogue between Kliges and Jehan (Chrétien vv. 5490–5652). The text is too truncated to gain an impression of any alterations brought in by the German translation.

Edolanz. Two fragments (Seitenstetten, Stiftsbibliothek, around 1300, 124 vv.; this fragment still exists (Schiewer 1988) and is not missing as reported in *VL*; Vienna, ÖNB, cod. s.n. 4001, first half fourteenth century, 255 vv.)

The first fragment reports Edolanz's victory over a giant whereby he frees Gawan and a noblewoman. Edolanz and Gawan then depart and separate. Edolanz meets a dwarf on a deer, but the ensuing adventure is missing. A headline announces that Edolanz has slain two dragons and four lions. The second fragment reports Edolanz helping a beleaguered town against Pontschur, whom he later defeats at Arthur's court in a sparrowhawk contest. The status of the town and the identity of 'Pontschur' remain unclear.

The texts belong to an Arthurian romance in the manner of Heinrich von dem Türlin's *Crône*. Some motifs (dwarf on a deer, battle against a succession of dragons and lions) stem either from the *Crône* or from the same tradition. This gives a tentative *terminus post quem*; the references to Edolanz in Konrad von Stoffeln's *Gauriel* and in Albrecht's *Jüngerer Titurel,* where his beloved, Karfite, is also mentioned, point to a date between 1230 and 1250. The style is accessible and action-oriented. In short, the fragments belong to a typical Arthurian romance of the thirteenth century.

Loccumer Artusromanfragment. A single fragment, end of thirteenth century (Loccum, Klosterbibliothek, MS 20), about 150 vv.

Two pages found in a prayer book from around 1500 contain a text in early Middle Low German. A more precise identification of the dialect is impossible since most of the rhymes are missing. The contents of the story are hardly recognizable. A fight between Oriental and Arthurian knights is reported. There are some French lines in the dialogue, some Arthurian names, like Gamuret, Anyowe, Isenhart, which suggest an influence of Wolfram's *Parzival*, and five lines are a quotation from Hartmann von Aue's *Der arme Heinrich*. The text could be a late offshoot of the postulated (though not extant) early German Arthurian romances of the Middle Rhenish area.

Der Mantel, 994 vv.

The text is recorded as an introduction to Hartmann's *Erec* in the 'Ambraser Heldenbuch' (1515). It is an incomplete adaptation of the French fabliau *Du mantel mautaillié* and treats with humour the motif of a test of virtue at Arthur's court by means of a cloak that will fit only one who is perfectly virtuous. The motif figures in German also in Ulrich von Zatzikhoven's *Lanzelet*, and in later *Meisterlied* and *Fastnachtspiel* versions, and tests of virtue involving a goblet and a glove appear in Heinrich von dem Türlin's *Crône*. Since Erec and Enite play a major role in the testing episode in the *Mantel* and show deficiencies in Hartmann's romance, the choice of the *Mantel* as an introduction to *Erec* is plausible, if eccentric.

Despite earlier attribution to Heinrich von Türlin, the author of *Der Mantel* remains unknown (Kratz 1977, Kasper 1995). The German adaptation may have been intended to stand on its own, or to be placed in a larger framework. The third possibility is that the text is, after all, a translation by Heinrich von dem Türlin who later incorporated features from it into his romance. If this is really the case, it would provide a rare glimpse of a thirteenth-century author at work constructing an intertextual *mélange*.

Manuel und Amande. Three fragments from one manuscript, early fourteenth century (Schwaz, Klosterbibliothek, Archiv, Lade O), 292 vv.
The fragments contain two incomplete dialogues – the first involving a figure named Jonas and reporting allegations of unknightly behaviour, the second showing a lady accepting the service of a knight (here the king of Navarre is mentioned) – and a passage probably from the close of the romance, where Manuel of Greece marries Amande, daughter of a Spanish nobleman, at Arthur's court. Arthur and his queen are cited as examples of faithful love, thus negating the tradition of Guinevere as adulteress. Tullius (=Cicero) and Seneca are cited as authorities. The passage about Arthur contains a reflection on his death, an incomplete account of the fight between Arthur and a huge cat, and a comparison of the wealth of stories related about Arthur with a *wunder bovme* ('wondrous tree', v. 129).The text has affinities with *Cligès* and the Byzantine romances in its use of pseudo-historical figures and its emphasis on love. No French source has been found.

Parcheval. Fragments of a Middle Franconian version of the Middle Dutch adaptation of Chrétien's *Perceval* (Prague, Strahov cloister, 392/zl, 71 vv., and Düsseldorf, UB, F 23, 192 vv., fifteenth century)
The Middle Dutch *Perchevael* exists only in fragments and as an adaptation in the *Lancelot* compilation. Thus the German fragments are a further indication of the popularity of early Dutch versions of French Arthurian romances. The fragments do not play a significant role in German studies since it is evident that they have not been used by Wolfram as a source. They nevertheless provide evidence of cultural contact and exchange in the area of the Lower Rhine, where French, Dutch and German works form a close intertextual relationship that was made possible by an audience fluent in several languages.

Der Rheinische Merlin. One fragment (Berlin, Staatsbibliothek, mgq 1409, 232 vv., first half fourteenth century)
This text is the odd one out in the list of German Arthurian fragments. It is not an Arthurian romance but the only German example of the *Prophecies of Merlin*. No direct French, Latin or English source has been found. The

prophecies reported are well known, such as the one about the man who is to die in three different ways – and does so by falling from his horse, being hanged on a tree while falling from a cliff and, finally, drowning in a river. They are followed by a prophecy *post factum* about the death of Richard the Lionheart and a rather veiled reference to an Emperor Heinrich (which one is unclear). The beginning of the text is missing. Directly following, and clearly to be read together with the *Merlin* as one text, is a legend of St Lüthild, a Rhenish local saint. This has led to the *Merlin*'s being interpreted as a kind of secular legend, which can be supported by significant alterations in the portrayal of Merlin: there is no hint of Merlin's demonic parentage, and he chooses the life of a hermit. However, the beginning of the text, where the devil might have already played his role in the conception of Merlin, is missing, and since the epilogue is also missing it is left unclear how we are intended to interpret the strange combination of Merlin and Lüthild. Although it adds to the spectrum of German Arthurian literature, *Der Rheinische Merlin* poses more questions than it answers.

Segremors. Three fragments of two manuscripts; one manuscript (first half fourteenth century: Gotha, Forschungsbibliothek, Memb. I 133: 288 vv.; Weimar, Staatsarchiv, Reg. 1, 144 vv.) was produced in the same workshop as the *Jenaer Liederhandschrift* and was originally a larger compendium of narrative texts, a companion piece to the song collection. The *Parzival* fragments from Gotha (Memb. I 130) were in all likelihood part of the same codex. The other fragment (around 1300, Krakow, Biblioteka Jagiellonska, MS germ. 4° 662) contains another 139 vv.

The text is remarkable because it is a free translation of the French *Meraugis de Portlesguez* of Raoul des Houdenc, attributing the adventures to the Arthurian knight Segremors, who plays a minor role in Hartmann's *Erec* and Wolfram's *Parzival*. The stories connected with Segremors in the *Third Continuation* and in the *Prose Lancelot* are not reflected in the fragments. The departure of the young Segremors to the aid of Gawan is opposed by Malgrim. Segremors's beloved Nyobe thinks about giving him a token of her love to help him on his way but then decides that her presence would be a greater help. The second fragment tells of a promise of revenge given to a severely wounded knight and the arrival of Segremors at a feast. Here the victor in a fight gains permission to appoint the partners in marriage amongst those present and willing to marry. The second half of this fragment tells of a fairy island where a knight is the lover of an unnamed fairy until he is killed in combat; the victor then becomes his successor. Segremors has to undertake this adventure, much to the chagrin of Nyobe. The last fragment shows a battle in which Gawan and a group of fellow knights are taken captive by Segremors. The knights are in some way supposed to be able to help Segremors. *Segremors* (like *Edolanz*) is a romance in which Gawan plays an important role along with the hero; thus these texts follow in the wake of Wolfram's *Parzival* and especially Heinrich's *Crône*.

Tirol und Fridebrant. Fragments of a manuscript in folio, greatly damaged by cutting (Berlin, SB Preuß. Kulturbesitz, Grimm-Nachlaß 127, 1): 18 complete, 39 fragmentary stanzas

The fragments of the romance are linked to a riddle and a didactic poem (transmitted only in the Codex Manesse) by the use of the same seven-line Tirol-stanzas. It is possible that the didactic poem was originally part of a larger narrative work, a romance of indefinable genre, with the riddles as its introduction (cf. *Lohengrin*). While King Tirol is not an Arthurian name, Fridebrant is reminiscent of Wolfram's *Parzival* (*Parz.* 16, 16 etc.). The action involves heathen and Christian knights, the names Tervigant and [G]amuret also refer to Wolfram. The fragments contain a court feast held by a queen, a battle against two monsters and a *merwunder*, and a chaplain fleeing from an apparition of the devil. Style and content make this author one of the many imitators of Wolfram in the thirteenth century. The text dates from around 1250 and may have taken an intermediate stance between *Wolfdietrich D* and later Arthurian romances.

Although little can be said about any one piece, taken as a whole the fragments illustrate the remarkable breadth of German Arthurian literature. The fact that they have often been of only local importance should not lead to their being excluded from literary study. Rather, they offer precious glimpses into the rich literary landscape of the thirteenth century where, parallel to the reception of the 'classical' Arthurian works, many romances were written in the intertextual mode that was characteristic of the time. Seen in the context of *Segremors* and *Edolanz*, *Diu Crône* loses much of its singularity; and the existence of so many of these works confirms that patrons wished to have their own Arthurian romance. The romances have become 'available', not only in a poetic, but also in a practical sense. For the figure of Arthur this development testifies to the fact that he has, by this time, largely lost his significant role as the once and future king and is reduced to a symbol of adventure. In this role he remains an influential figure until he is marginalized once again through the increasing historical contextualization in fictional literature in the late thirteenth century.

Bibliography

Primary Sources

Abor und das Meerweib, in Meyer-Benfey, 180–3.

Blancandin et l'Orgueilleuse d'Amour. Ed. by F. P. Sweetser, 1964. Geneva and Paris.

Blanschandin, in Meyer-Benfey, 155–65.

Edolanz, in Meyer-Benfey, 145–50.

Konrad von Stoffeln, *Gauriel von Muntabel*. Fragm. m. See Other Literature II, Achnitz and Schiewer 1989.

Konrad von Stoffeln, *Gauriel von Muntabel. Eine höfische Erzählung*. Ed. by F. Khull, 1885. Graz (repr. with 'Nachwort' and bibliography by Hildebrand, A., Osnabrück 1969).

Konrad von Stoffeln, *Gauriel von Muntabel*. See Other Literature II, Achnitz 1997.

Loccumer Artusromanfragment, in Beckers, H. 1974. 'Ein vergessenes mittelniederdeutsches Artuseposfragment (Loccum, Klosterbibl., Ms. 20)', *NdW*, 14, 23–52.

Lohengrin. Ed. by H. Rückert, 1858. Quedlinburg/Leipzig (reprint Darmstadt 1970).

Lohengrin. See Other Literature III, Cramer 1971.

Lorengel. Ed. by D. Buschinger. Melody ed. by H. Brunner, 1979 (GAG, 253). Göppingen.

Der Mantel, in Warnatsch, O. 1883. *Der Mantel. Bruchstück eines Lanzeletromans des Heinrich von dem Türlin, nebst einer Abhandlung über die Sage von Trinkhorn und Mantel und die Quelle der Krone* (Germanistische Abhandlungen, 2). Breslau.

Manuel und Amande, in Meyer-Benfey, 151–4.

Meyer-Benfey, H., ed., 1920. *Mittelhochdeutsche Übungsstücke*. 2nd edn. Halle a.d. Saale.

Parcheval. Düsseldorf fragments, in *Carminum Epicorum Germanicorum nederlandicorum Saeculi XIII et XIIII fragmenta*. Ed. by F. Deycks, 1859. Regensberg.

Parcheval. Prague fragments, in Zatocil, L. 1968. 'Prager Bruchstück einer bisher unbekannten mfrk. Übertragung der mndl. Versbearbeitung von Chrétien des Troyes Percevalroman (Li contes del Graal)', *Germanistische Studien und Texte*, 1. Brno, 247–80.

Der Rheinische Merlin. Text, Übersetzung, Untersuchungen der 'Merlin' und 'Lüthild'-Fragmente. Nach der Handschrift Ms.germ.qu. 1409 der Staatsbibliothek Preußischer Kulturbesitz. Ed. by H. Beckers. Translation and Studies by G. Bauer et al., 1991 (Schöninghs Mediävistische Editionen, 1). Paderborn.

Segremors, in Meyer-Benfey, 166–80; in Beyer, P. G. 1909. *Die mitteldeutschen Segremorsfragmente*, Diss. Marburg.

Tirol und Fridebrant, in Meyer-Benfey, 140–4; in Maync, H. 1910. *Die altdeutschen Fragmente von König Tirol und Fridebrant* (Sprache und Dichtung, 1). Tübingen.

Ulrich von Türheim, *Cliges. Ausgabe der bisher bekannten Fragmente vermehrt um den Neufund aus St. Paul im Lavanttal*. Ed. by H. Gröchening and P. H. Pascher, 1984 (armarium, 2). Klagenfurt.

Ulrich von Türheim, *Cliges*. Kalocsa fragments, in Vizkelety, A. 1969. 'Neue Fragmente des mittelhochdeutschen Cligès-Epos aus Kalocsa', *ZfdPh*, 88, 409–32.

Wigamur. (Fragments M and S), in *Mittelhochdeutsches Übungsbuch*. Ed. by C. v. Kraus, 1926, 2nd edn. Heidelberg, 109–61, 287–8.

Wigamur. Ed. by J. G. Büsching, 1808, in *Deutsche Gedichte des Mittelalters*. Ed. by F. v. d. Hagen and J. G. Büsching, vol. I. Berlin, III–VIII, 1–80.

Wigamur. Ed. with introduction and index by D. Buschinger, 1987 (GAG, 320). Göppingen.

Other Literature

I. *Wigamur*

Blamires, D. 1973. 'The sources and literary structure of *Wigamur*', in Rothwell, W. et al., *Studies in Medieval Literature and Languages in Memory of Frederick Whitehead*, Manchester, 27–46.

Classen, A. 1993. 'Der komische Held Wigamur – Ironie oder Parodie? Strukturelle und thematische Untersuchungen zu einem spätmittelalterlichen Artus-Roman', *Euph*, 87, 200–24.

Ebenbauer, A. 1984. 'Wigamur und die Familie', in Wolfzettel 1984 (see Gen. Bibl.), 28–46.

Henderson, I. 1989. 'Illustrationsprogramm und Text der Wolfenbütteler *Wigamur*-Handschrift', in McConnell, W., ed., *in hôhem prîse. Festschrift Ernst S. Dick*, GAG, 480, Göppingen, 163–81.

Martin, A. G. 1987. 'The concept of *reht* in *Wigamur*', *ColG*, 20, 1–14.

Mertens, V. 1998. *Der deutsche Artusroman*, RUB 17609, Stuttgart.

Thomas, N. 1992. See Gen. Bibl. (pp. 12–43 on Wigamur).

II. Konrad von Stoffeln, *Gauriel von Muntabel*

Achnitz, W. 1997. *Der Ritter mit dem Bock. Konrads von Stoffeln 'Gauriel von Muntabel'*. New edition, introduction and commentary, Texte und Textgeschichte 46, Tübingen.

Achnitz, W. and Schiewer, H.-J. 1989. 'Ein bisher unbekanntes "Gauriel"-Fragment in München', *ZfdA*, 118, 57–76.

Demtröder, H.-A. 1964. *Untersuchungen zu Stoff und Stil des 'Gauriel von Muntabel' des Konrad von Stoffeln*, Diss. Bonn.

Egerding, M. 1991. 'Konflikt und Krise im *Gauriel von Muntabel* des Konrad von Stoffeln', *ABäG*, 34, 111–25.

Karnein, A. 1984. 'Minne, Aventiure und Artusidealität in den Romanen des späten 13. Jahrhunderts', in Wolfzettel 1984 (see Gen Bibl.), 114–25.

Lichtblau, K. 1998. 'Das "Minnegericht" in Fluratrône: die domestizierte Fee', in Tuczay, C., Hirtager, U. und Lichtblau, K., eds., *Ir sult sprechen willekommen. Fs. Helmut Birkhan*, Berne, 263–83.

Meyer, M. 1993. '*Sô dunke ich mich ein werltgot.* Überlegungen zum Verhältnis Autor-Erzähler-Fiktion', in Mertens and Wolfzettel 1993 (see Gen. Bibl.), 185–202.

Meyer, M. 1994. *Die Verfügbarkeit der Fiktion. Interpretationen und poetologische Untersuchungen zum Artusroman und zur aventiurehaften Dietrichepik des 13. Jahrhunderts*, Beihefte zur *GRM*, 12, 2–19, 271–90.

Neugart, I. 1992. 'Beobachtungen zum "Gauriel von Muntabel"', in Janota, J., ed., *Festschrift Walter Haug / Burghart Wachinger*, Tübingen, II, 603–16.

Panzer, F., ed. 1902. *Merlin und Seifrid de Ardemont. Von Albrecht von Scharfenberg. In der Bearbeitung Ulrich Füetrers*, BLV Stuttgart, 227, Tübingen, LXXXVI–LXXXIX.

Schöning, B. 1991. *'Friedrich von Schwaben'. Aspekte des Erzählens im spätmittelalterlichen Versroman*, Erlanger Studien, 90, Erlangen, 210–17.

Thomas, N. 1988. 'Konrad von Stoffeln's *Gauriel von Muntabel*: a comment on Hartmann's *Iwein*', *OGS*, 17, 1–9.

Zimmermann, G. 1992. 'Some aspects of Konrad von Stoffeln's *Gauriel von Muntabel*: a reply to Neil Thomas', *OGS*, 20/1, 1–6.

III. *Lohengrin*

Bertelsmeier-Kierst, Ch. and Heinzle, J. 1996. 'Paläographische Tücken! Noch einmal zur Datierung des *Lohengrin*', *ZfdPh*, 115, 42–54.

Cramer, Th. 1971. *Lohengrin. Edition und Untersuchungen*, Munich.

Goulet, D. 1984. 'Le Rôle d'Arthur et du Graal dans *Lohengrin*', *MA*, 90, 39–63.

Kerdelhué, A. 1986. *Lohengrin, Analyse interne et étude critique des sources du poème moyen-haut-allemand de la fin du 13ième siècle*, GAG, 444, Göppingen.

Kerdelhué, A. 1991. '*Lohengrin* et la *Sächsische Weltchronik*', in Buschinger, D., ed., *Histoire et littérature au Moyen Age. Actes du colloque du Centre d'Etudes Médiévales de l'Université de Picardie (Amiens 20–24 mars 1985)*, GAG, 546, Göppingen, 195–203.

Salvini-Plawen, L. von 1990. 'Zur Historizität des "Schwanritters" ', *AfK*, 72, 297–322.

Thomas, H. 1973. 'Der *Lohengrin*, eine politische Dichtung der Zeit Ludwigs des Bayern', *RhVjbl*, 37, 152–90.

Thomas, H. 1995. 'Paläographische Tücken: zur Datierung des *Lohengrin*', *ZfdPh*, 114, 110–16.

Unger, R. 1990. *Wolfram-Rezeption und Utopie. Studien zum spätmittelalterlichen bayerischen 'Lohengrin' Epos*, GAG, 544, Göppingen.

Wyss, U. 1979. 'Parzivals Sohn. Zur strukturalen Lektüre des Lohengrin-Mythos', WSt, 96–115.

IV. The Fragments of Arthurian Romances

Beckers, H. 1977. 'Mittelniederdeutsche Literatur. Versuch einer Bestandsaufnahme', *NdW*, 17, 1–58.

Besamusca, B. 1985. *Repertorium van de Middelnederlandse Arturepiek*, Utrecht.

Draak, M. 1969. 'Een onbekend Praags Perchevaelfragment', *NTg*, 62, 175–6.

Kasper, Ch. 1995. *Von miesen Rittern und sündhaften Frauen und solchen, die besser waren. Tugend–und Keuschheitsproben in der mittelalterlichen Literatur vornehmlich des deutschen Sprachraums*, GAG, 547, Göppingen.

Kratz, B. 1977. 'Die Ambraser *Mantel*-Erzählung und ihr Autor', *Euph* 71, 1–17.

Rocher, D. 1993. '*Cligès* in Deutschland', in Jones and Wisbey 1993 (see Gen. Bibl.), 111–19.

Schiewer, H.-J. 1988. ' "Ein ris ich dar vmbe abe brach / von sinem wunder bovme". Beobachtungen zur Überlieferung des nachklassischen Artusromans im 13. und 14. Jahrhundert', in Honemann and Palmer 1988 (see Gen. Bibl.), 222–78.

Schröder, E. 1925a. 'Abor und das Meerweib', *Nachrichten der Gesellschaft der Wissenschaften zu Göttingen*, 161–5.

Schröder, E. 1925b. 'Manuel und Amande', *Nachrichten der Gesellschaft der Wissenschaften zu Göttingen*, 166–8.

Steinhoff, H. H. 1984. 'Ein neues Fragment von *Manuel und Amande*', *ZfdA*, 113, 242–5.

Thiele, G. 1940. 'Ein ostmitteldeutscher Artusroman des 13. Jahrhunderts', *ZfdA*, 77, 61–3 (on *Segremors*).

Winkelmann, J. H. 1998. 'Chrétien de Troyes, Perceval und die Niederlande. Adaption als didaktisches Verfahren', in Kasten, I., Paravicini, W. and Pérennec, R., eds., *Kultureller Austausch und Literaturgeschichte im Mittelalter. Transferts culturels et histoire littéraire au moyen âge*, Sigmaringen, 245–8.

Part Two

Continuity and Change in the Later Middle Ages

7

TRISTAN NARRATIVES FROM THE HIGH TO THE LATE MIDDLE AGES

Mark Chinca

Stories of Tristan and his love for Isolde, the wife of his uncle King Mark, enter German literature from France in the later twelfth century, at the same time as Arthurian themes and as part of the same cultural development: the emergence of a vernacular literary scene at the courts of the secular aristocracy. The production of different versions of the story (including manuscript redactions of the same work) into the fifteenth century attests to its enduring fascination for a German literary public; it also reflects the intractable quality of the story's constitutive problem. Tristan and Isolde become lovers when they accidentally drink a love-potion intended for Isolde and Mark; their love is thus simultaneously unavoidable (because compelled by the potion) and impossible (because illicit). This problem, which can never be resolved definitively, provokes repeated attempts at negotiation through narrative.

Eilhart von Oberg, *Tristrant*

This romance, probably composed in the late twelfth century, is the earliest known narrative treatment of the Tristan theme in German. Eilhart does not describe his source, but it is presumed to be a French romance that has not survived. It is impossible to determine whether this romance represented the original written version of the story, if such a thing ever existed, nor is it clear whether the meanings implicit in the thematic and narrative organization of Eilhart's romance reflect the story's pristine symbolism (Schindele 1971).

Eilhart's romance was never totally eclipsed by the more grandiose treatment of the Tristan story by Gottfried von Strassburg. In common with other twelfth-century texts it underwent redaction in the thirteenth century in order to bring its style and diction into line with contemporary standards (Bumke 1997, 98–100); it appears to have been known to Gottfried's continuators Ulrich von Türheim and Heinrich von Freiberg and is one of the sources of the fourteenth-century Czech Tristan romance; it continued to be current in the fifteenth century, when it was also recast as a prose version.

The complete text of *Tristrant* is preserved in two fifteenth-century manuscripts; in addition there are four fragments from the late twelfth and the thirteenth century, as well as a fifteenth-century manuscript which includes the final part of the narrative in continuation of Gottfried's unfinished romance (*Tristrant*, ed. Bußmann, xxx–xxxix, xliii–il; Brandstetter 1988). The fifteenth-century manuscripts transmit significantly variant texts; modern textual philology does not view variants such as these as more or less corrupt representations of the author's original composition, but as parallel versions of equal interest.

The author's name is contained only in the fifteenth-century versions; in the manuscripts it is given variously as *von Hobergin her Eylhart*, *von Oberengen Enthartte*, *von Baubemberg Segehart*; the prose adaptation has *Filhart von Oberet*, presumably a corruption of *Eilhart von Oberg*. This last form has established itself in preference to the others because a ministerial *Eilhardus de Oberch* (= Oberg, between Hildesheim and Brunswick) is attested in Welf charters between 1189 and 1209/27. It is conceivable that Eilhart von Oberg may be the name of the romance's thirteenth-century redactor, though there are arguments for continuing to regard it as the name of the author (Bumke 1979, 108f.).

The exact place and time of composition in the twelfth century are controversial; recent opinions are divided between the Lower Rhineland in the early 1170s (Wolff and Schröder 1980), and the Brunswick court of the Welf princes either *c.* 1170 (Buschinger 1991) or *c.* 1190 (Mertens 1987) or even *c.* 1208 (Hucker 1995, 382f., 395). Both places were significant centres of literary patronage in the second half of the twelfth century (Tervooren and Beckers 1989, Schneidmüller 1995), and both were active in the mediation of French literature: the geographical position of the Lower Rhine–Maas region made it one of the earliest and most important zones of cultural contact with France, and the Brunswick court had close links to Anglo-Norman culture through the marriage of Henry the Lion to Matilda, daughter of Henry II of England. A German adaptation of a French Tristan romance is therefore plausible in either place, though the language of the early manuscript fragments, which points to Eastphalia, tips the scales in Brunswick's favour (Klein 1988, 133). These same fragments do not necessarily require the romance to have been composed by the 1170s; the Regensburg fragment, often dated to the 1180s, could be as late as the first decade of the thirteenth century (Mertens 1987, 264).

The romance provides its own plot summary in its prologue: it tells the story of Tristrant's life from birth to death, his wondrous and cunning exploits, his love for Isalde and how each died for the sake of the other (ed. Buschinger vv. 36–45). The accent is on the extraordinariness and incomparability of the contents, vividly and dramatically realized before a listening public in the immediate present of narration. The prologue evokes recital to an audience of listeners: the narrator is to tell a story to the people he sees before him (vv. 1f.), he warns troublemakers to desist (vv. 6–29) and pleads for silence (v. 31) before prefacing the narrative proper with an inventory of its themes (joy, sorrow, worldly wisdom, manly prowess, love) to which the audience are exhorted to listen (vv. 47–53). This narratorial stance, maintained throughout the narrative by means of ejaculations and further injunctions of the type 'vornemet' ('listen'), connects Eilhart's romance with the immediacy of orality. That is only part of the picture, however, because the author had literate training and a knowledge of formal rhetoric. Both the source of the story and the romance based upon it are designated as books (vv. 35, 1806, 4576, 4731, 9447), and the emphasis placed on the story's extraordinary (and hence memorable) quality may reflect learned Latin rhetoric, which recommends stressing the enormity of the subject matter, the *magnitudo rerum*, as a way of gaining the listeners' attention. The authorial presence in Eilhart's text therefore combines literate compositional activity with a narratorial role conditioned by oral recital.

Tristrant performs his memorable deeds of prowess in two contexts: in the feudal kingdoms of Cornwall, Ireland and Karahes and, for a brief interlude, as a member of Arthur's court. Although Arthur's kingdom of 'Britania' is geographically contiguous with the other kingdoms, the distinctive form in which knightly prowess manifests itself there suggests that this world is of a different order. In the feudal kingdoms Tristrant demonstrates his prowess in the role of helper, assisting kings against various challenges to their power and their realm: external enemies, rebel nobles, famine, dragons. In Arthur's realm prowess is realized through 'adventure' (v. 5048), combat sought out by the knights in order to establish their relative ranking. In one of these adventurous encounters, Tristrant unhorses Delekors, an exemplary knight who has never before been defeated; he does not, however, claim the deed as his own until Walwan asks him to tell the truth for the love of Isalde – a demand that Tristrant cannot refuse. The incident illustrates how honour won by fighting is articulated at Arthur's court through an etiquette of modesty; it also points to the different status of love in the feudal and the Arthurian context. In the feudal context, Tristrant's love always threatens to undermine the position of the king: Mark is disgraced by his wife's adultery; Havelin, Tristrant's father-in-law, is dishonoured by his daughter's unconsummated marriage. In the Arthurian realm, by contrast, the same love is compatible with the accumulation of honour at court; its invocation by Walwan produces confirmation of what Arthur suspects and wants to know for certain: that the knight who was good enough to beat Delekors can only be Tristrant. Moreover, Arthur and his court are complicit in facilitating Tristrant's love. Walwan arranges a hunt that strays into Mark's territory, and Arthur negotiates permission for Tristrant to stay overnight at Tintagel with him and his party. When Tristrant cuts himself on the blades of the trap that has been set for him by Isalde's bed, all the Arthurian knights cut themselves; thus they neutralize the signs that would otherwise incriminate Tristrant, and enable him to make love to the queen in the king's hall.

Recent interpretations of *Tristrant* have suggested that it is primarily concerned with the possibility of accommodation between the feudal order and a love which, because it furthers no political or dynastic purpose, is in opposition to that order as its absolute, unintegrable other. The romance has been said to propose various kinds of accommodation: an acknowledgement that love can inspire the hero to great deeds coupled with a reminder that the lovers will be outlived by the feudal order (Mertens 1987); separation of love from the exercise of feudal lordship, a policy successfully maintained by Tristrant during most of his exile and marriage (Strohschneider 1993), though arguably at the price of the disintegration of his feudal-aristocratic identity (Müller 1990). The Arthurian interlude suggests a further possible accommodation: love can be integrated in a society organized around chivalrous adventure, at least temporarily (Mikasch-Köthner 1991, 101–3).

Gottfried von Strassburg, *Tristan*

Although incomplete, Gottfried's early thirteenth-century romance is the most ambitious and sophisticated treatment of the story in German. Its source is the Anglo-Norman *Roman de Tristran* by Thomas (*c.* 1150/70). In the prologue Gottfried states that he is following the version of 'Thomas von Britanje', which he singles out from other accounts as the only one that is correct and true (vv. 131–62). Among these other versions Gottfried may be including Eilhart; later on in the work (vv. 8601–15) he polemicizes against an alternative account of events which recalls Eilhart's narrative (Chinca 1993, 94–6). Comparison between Gottfried and his source is difficult because of the fragmentary survival of Thomas's romance, but it is clear that Gottfried was an independent adaptor (Jantzen and Kröner 1997). Gottfried's *Tristan* is not the only German adaptation of Thomas: there are fragments from the second half of the thirteenth century of a Low Frankish version (Steinhoff 1987).

Gottfried's romance reveals its author's name only obliquely, in an acrostic which entwines the names GOTE(FRIT), TRIS(TAN), ISOL(DEN) and DIETERICH (Schirok 1984). The letters in brackets show how the acrostic would probably have continued if the work had been finished. The last character is generally assumed to be the patron, though he cannot be reliably identified with any known historical person. Gottfried is identified as the author of *Tristan* by his continuators Ulrich von Türheim and Heinrich von Freiberg and also by other narrative authors of the later thirteenth century. The only biographical detail we possess about Gottfried is the continuators' statement that he died before completing *Tristan* (Ulrich von Türheim, *Tristan*, vv. 1–18; Heinrich von Freiberg, *Tristan*, vv. 30–44). The title *meister*, which the later authors apply to Gottfried, expresses their admiration for his artistic mastery; in addition it may also designate social rank (a burgher rather than a nobleman) and educational status (a *magister artium*, a graduate who had completed the traditional school curriculum of the seven liberal arts). There can be no doubt that he was highly educated: *Tristan* is full of learned allusions, and the style and mode of presentation bear the imprint of academic rhetoric, poetics and dialectics (Christ 1977, Glendinning 1987, Stevens 1990). An author like this fits into the cultural milieu of an episcopal city like Strasbourg, with its ecclesiastical foundations and schools; Strasbourg became an important literary centre in the thirteenth century (Bumke 1979, 283–5).

Gottfried is thought to have written *Tristan c.* 1210. There is no external evidence for this date; it is a conjecture based on what are believed to be allusions to contemporary literature and politics: disparaging remarks on the style of Wolfram's *Parzival* (*c.* 1200–10) (vv. 4638–90), and an ironic commentary on the practice of trial by ordeal (vv. 15733–44) which may have resonance against the background of heresy trials at Strasbourg in 1212 and the debates preceding the abolition of ordeals by the Lateran Council of 1215.

There are fourteen complete manuscripts of *Tristan* (this figure includes three now lost) and twenty-one fragments from seventeen manuscripts. They date from the thirteenth to the fifteenth century, with two peaks of production, one around the end of the thirteenth and the beginning of the fourteenth century and the other in the fifteenth century. The geographical provenance of the manuscripts, concentrated in the Upper Rhineland and Central Germany, suggests that Gottfried's *Tristan* may have had a more restricted reception than other major literary works of the period, although it is transmitted in a comparable number of manuscripts (Wetzel 1992, 39–56, 396, 401). In the thirteenth century Gottfried became a canonical vernacular author, alongside Hartmann and Wolfram, and attracted both continuators and imitators (Wachinger 1975).

The narrative begins with the story of the hero's parents Riwalin and Blanscheflur, which is told as a prelude to Tristan's own love affair; the main part of the romance recounts Tristan's life and exploits from his birth up to his separation from Isolde and exile; the remainder of the plot – Tristan's marriage, his returns to Isolde, the lovers' death – can be reconstructed in outline from Thomas. Unlike many other German Tristan narratives, there is no Arthurian connection; in fact Gottfried asserts that during their sojourn in the cave of lovers, an idyllic and allegorical landscape, Tristan and Isolde form a society equal to and even surpassing Arthur's court (vv. 16859–65, 16896–901). The allegory of the cave is an instance of the work's salient structural characteristic: the insertion into the narrative of extensive authorial commentaries, including a literary excursus, the earliest example of literary criticism in the vernacular.

No consensus exists about even basic lines of interpretation. The difficulty of interpreting *Tristan* arises from a combination of factors.

1. The incompleteness of the work means that no interpretation can ever be more than provisional. The narrative breaks off as Tristan is contemplating an attachment to Isolde Whitehand. This course of action entails being untrue not only to Isolde, but also to himself. Tristan speculates that by devoting himself to more than one love he can become 'ein triureloser Tristan' ('a sorrowless Tristan') (v. 19464). This would amount to a negation of his identity. Tristan's name, it is explained at his baptism, is derived from 'triste' meaning 'triure' ('sorrow') (vv. 1998–2001); the name encapsulates the essence of its bearer (vv. 2021f.). The baptism scene throws a further term into the equation. The proof of the name's aptness is provided by the story, which is said to demonstrate how the hero's life is defined by sorrow at every stage (vv. 2001–17). At the point where the fragment breaks off, however, the plot is potentially on course to demonstrate the opposite; thus the integrity of the very story is in jeopardy. One can argue that if Gottfried had continued, then Tristan's plan to be rid of his sorrow would fail and the concordance of name, identity and story would be restored. That argument, though probable, necessarily remains hypothetical.

2. The interpretative commentary which accompanies the story is inconsistent. It sometimes appears to have an ad hoc quality, as though it were made up solely for the particular incident under consideration. An example is Gottfried's presentation of the lovers' circumspect behaviour after Isolde's ordeal and their reconciliation with Mark. Gottfried relates that whenever Tristan and Isolde lack the opportunity to be together, they make do with the will instead (vv. 16411–14). His commentary generalizes their practice of taking the will for the deed into advice for other lovers in similar circumstances (vv. 16420–39). This advice posits that lovers are rational beings, aware of and able to estimate risk. Yet it is at variance with other commentary which characterizes lovers as blind and reckless, for example when Tristan persists in trying to join Isolde in her bed even though he has been warned about the flour strewn on the floor (vv. 15165–8). Inconsistencies like this can be explained as the effect of Gottfried's 'rhetorical particularism' (Christ 1977, 117): his practice of embellishing and amplifying individual episodes apparently without regard to the consistency of the whole work. Although this explanation gives insight into Gottfried's *modus tractandi*, it does not abolish the fundamental problem of interpretation: how to extract a general authorial 'line' out of commentaries based on irreconcilable

postulates. An alternative explanation invokes irony: the remarks about love's blindness are not to be taken at face value but as ironic ridicule of Tristan's attitude (Wessel 1984, 399). The problem of apparently contradictory statements is certainly solved if at least one of them can be discounted as not intended; yet this solution comes at the price of introducing another kind of discrepancy which adds a new layer to the work's complexity. Instead of an inconsistent authorial voice, split between irreconcilable positions, we have an ironic voice divided between statement and intention.

3. Some of Gottfried's commentaries are consistent with each other; these are the prologue, the 'short discourse on good love' which accompanies the lovers' first night together after drinking the potion, the allegory of the cave, and the excursus on surveillance (*huote*) which precedes the narrative of Mark's discovery of Tristan and Isolde in the orchard. The common factor in all these commentaries is the proposition that love based on loyalty and mutuality is good. Yet it is uncertain how this commentary relates to the narrative with which it is interwoven, for the commentary posits love as good, as the only path to virtue and honour (vv. 187–90), whereas in the narrative the lovers appear as neither virtuous nor honourable, but as deceiving adulterers. Attempts at treating the discrepancy fall typically into one of two patterns: either they try to resolve it, or they allow it to stand.

Attempts at resolution take various forms. It has been argued that it is not the lovers who are at fault, but the society in which they live; if Tristan and Isolde are considered purely as lovers, without regard to their social interactions, they exemplify the virtues promoted by the commentaries (Jackson 1971). But this resolution is based on a move of doubtful legitimacy: the lovers cannot be isolated from their society, because they share its values and desire the esteem of others (Haug 1986, 42f.). Another form of resolution is to argue that the lovers are indeed at fault and fall short of the ideal of love commended in the commentary (Tomasek 1985); the difficulty here is that the narrative loses its connection with the commentary and threatens to become redundant (Haug 1986, 43). A third kind of resolution consists in saying that the divergence between commentary and narrative is a perspectival illusion; the two levels of discourse illustrate the same principle – that conduct should be guided and judged by one's inner intentions – from different points of view. The narrative demonstrates this for the lovers' relationship to each other, whereas the commentary extends the principle to provide the basis for a utopian society. The realization of this utopia is impeded by the inadequacies of human perception: our limited perspective prevents us from recognizing others' intentions. This is where love comes in, for it renders the hearts and minds of others transparent in a 'mystery of understanding' (Schnell 1992, 13–56, 226–8). The debatable point in this interpretation is the assumption that the limitations of perspective can and must be overcome in order to get at the truth; yet where Gottfried does thematize the limitations of human understanding, in the various stories that Tristan invents about himself, the opposite seems to be the case: there is no experience of truth that is not a function of perspective (Chinca 1993, 110–17).

If this last point is admitted, it lends encouragement to the kind of interpretation that allows the discrepancy between commentary and narrative to stand. Haug (1986) interprets the discrepancy as a symptom of the paradoxical structure of all of Gottfried's thought: perfection and corruption, innocence and guilt, retribution and grace, salvation and damnation are simultaneously co-present in the same person or act. Mertens (1995) reads Gottfried's work as a collage of contradictory positions; on the one hand love is an irrational force, symbolized by the potion; on the other it is compatible with a rational ethical system, allegorized in the cave. In relation to the 'modern' Arthurian romance and love-lyric of the late twelfth century, which optimistically accommodate love within an ethical system, this collage is distinctly 'postmodern'.

4. The last-mentioned interpretations suggest that Gottfried's writing may be inherently dialogic. The term was used by Bakhtin (1981) in order to define the characteristic quality of the novel. The novelist has no discourse of his own; rather the novel is composed of representations of other discourses which the novelist 'dialogizes': each discourse that he deploys is set in relation to another point of view with which it may be said to be in dialogue. This dialogue can take many different forms, for example agreement, complicity, antagonism, parody, irony, critique. The result is a text comprising multiple voices and points of view, each of which can never lay claim to more than relative validity. Bakhtin sketches the history of this mode of discourse from its roots in antiquity, noting that medieval literature is richly dialogic; this hint has been followed up in several recent treatments of the Arthurian romance in Germany (Groos 1993, Stevens 1993, Kasten 1995).

Gottfried's *Tristan* is certainly full of the representations of many different discourses, for instance religious allegory (Ranke 1925), saint's life (de Boor 1940), mysticism (Schwietering 1943), Ovidian love-discourse (Ganz 1971), classical historiography (Jaffe 1978), medieval Platonism (Jaeger 1977, Wisbey 1980, Huber 1988), Christian salvation history (Tomasek 1985), Arthurian romance (Haug 1990). The list is nothing like exhaustive. These discourses have often been treated as though one of them holds the key to understanding the entire romance. Thus the presence in the work of allegorical modes of signification or hagiographical narrative structures has authorized the conclusion that Gottfried's purpose consists in propagating a religion of love (Ranke 1925) or sacralizing love so that it appears as a transcendental value (de Boor 1940). The most recent discussions of Christian thought-structures in *Tristan* also seek to uncover the work's underlying rationale, though they differ from their predecessors in arguing that religious forms of thought and experience are being secularized. The major commentaries are held to articulate a process of loss and restitution conceived along the same lines as Christian salvation history; the difference is that the process concerns a secular value, love, and its telos is not salvation in the kingdom of heaven but 'living paradise' (v. 18067), a utopian vision of harmony and reconciliation between self, other and society (Tomasek 1985, Huber 1988).

What these interpretations neglect is that the commentaries articulating this 'innerworldly salvation history' (Tomasek 1985, 206) are dialogized; they are placed in relation to another point of view. The relation is established through Gottfried's choice of imagery. The living paradise is described as a place where nothing grows that does not please the eye (vv. 18079–82), as 'vröudebære' ('joyful') (v. 18089) and 'gemeiet' ('May-like') (v. 18090). This imagery belongs to the rhetorical topos of the nature idyll or *locus amoenus*, and it recurs in all the major commentaries on love; it is also prominent in the literary excursus, where Gottfried characterizes his ideal of eloquence as verdant, florid and pleasurable (vv. 4673–82, 4913–22). Thus the message becomes associated with the medium; the association is not, however, one of mutual reinforcement. The message of living paradise offers the prospect of a condition from which all suffering is removed; the medium of that message, however, promises to preserve the antinomy of joy and sorrow. In the prologue Gottfried describes the effect of his story on his chosen public of 'edele herzen', the 'noble hearts' for whom love is a compound of joy and sorrow: their condition is stimulated by reading about the joy and the sorrow of the lovers Tristan and Isolde (vv. 45–122). Gottfried's artistic medium is therefore productive not of harmony or resolution, but of a disposition that is itself a dialogue of irreducible opposites (Chinca 1997, 50–3).

Ulrich von Türheim, *Tristan*; *Tristan als Mönch*; Heinrich von Freiberg, *Tristan*

All except one of the complete manuscripts of Gottfried's *Tristan* also transmit one or more other Tristan narratives in whole or in part: the verse romances of Eilhart, Ulrich von Türheim and Heinrich von Freiberg, and the anonymous episodic poem *Tristan als Mönch*. These narratives continue or supplement Gottfried's unfinished romance, suggesting that medieval readers recognized a category superordinate to the work of a single author, namely the whole story of the hero (Bumke 1997, 110f.).

The romances of Ulrich and Heinrich were conceived expressly as continuations of Gottfried and present themselves in these terms (Ulrich vv. 23f.; Heinrich vv. 45–7); *Tristan als Mönch* was originally a self-contained narrative unconnected with Gottfried. Nevertheless, all three narratives have important features in common. None has any manuscript transmission independent of Gottfried's *Tristan*. All their narratives unfold during the phase of Tristan's career that begins where Gottfried breaks off. All three narratives combine the same elements of the hero's disguise and death (the latter is real in the case of the continuators and feigned in *Tristan als Mönch*). That justifies considering them as a group and in relation to Gottfried.

These narratives not only continue Gottfried's romance, they also introduce discontinuity. This is most obvious in their introduction, without explanation, of characters from the Eilhart tradition who do not appear in Gottfried, for example Tristan's enemy Antret, and his friend Tinas. There are also thematic refocusings and discontinuities of attitude. These changes are often interpreted negatively, as symptoms of a 'falling away' from Gottfried's achievement (Wachinger 1975, 64). If, however, continuation is not just a question of giving readers more of the same, but also an opportunity for introducing distance from what is being continued, then the way is open to reading these works as a creative commentary on Gottfried (Strohschneider 1991).

Ulrich von Türheim, *Tristan*

The author names himself 'ich von Türeheim Uolrich' (v. 3598); he is probably identical with the Swabian ministerial of the same name who is attested in two Augsburg charters of 1236 and 1244. Other works of his are *Rennewart*, a sequel to Wolfram von Eschenbach's uncompleted epic *Willehalm*, and a version of Chrétien de Troyes's *Cligès*. All of Ulrich's activity as an author can be connected with the court of the Hohenstaufen kings Henry VII and Conrad IV, which was a centre for literature in the thirteenth century (Bumke 1979, 250–2). In the *Tristan* prologue Ulrich names his patron as Conrad of Winterstetten (v. 26), a high-ranking ministerial at the court with literary interests. Conrad's death in 1243 gives a likely date for *Tristan* of *c.* 1240.

Ulrich's continuation follows Gottfried's *Tristan* in seven manuscripts (*Tristan*, ed. Kerth, viii–xiii); in three of them it is abridged, most drastically in the Berlin manuscript, which gives only the first fourteen lines of the prologue; Ulrich is thus reduced to providing an obituary notice for Gottfried, before the narrative continues with Eilhart.

The story narrates Tristan's marriage to Isolde Whitehand; his expedition with Kaedin to Cornwall and their exploits there; his fatal involvement in Kaedin's illicit love affair; the death of the lovers and their burial by Mark.

These episodes are also found in Eilhart, but Ulrich has amalgamated the hero's four separate returns to Cornwall into a single visit. This structural change, together with the lack of precise correspondences to Eilhart's text, lends support to the hypothesis that Ulrich's source was not (or not only) Eilhart but some other related version (Deighton 1997, 141–52).

For almost all of the plot Tristan is accompanied by his brother-in-law Kaedin. Ulrich's continuation is largely the story of the fortunes of their relationship, which is directly affected by their exploits with women. Companionship between the two men is threatened when Isolde Whitehand reveals to her brother the secret of her unconsummated marriage, repaired by Tristan's demonstration of his true love's superiority, disturbed again when Kaedin is piqued at his failure with Isolde's lady-in-waiting Kamele, and restored once more when Tristan helps Kaedin to see his lover Kassie. This pattern brings out the similarity and also the difference between the two companions: each loves another man's wife, but Kaedin cannot realize his desire without Tristan's help. He is a copy of Tristan, but a less competent one. Moreover, the fatal outcome of Kaedin's love affair demonstrates the rule to which Tristan is the exception: that the prevailing social order will punish those who violate it. Kaedin is killed by Kassie's avenging husband, whereas Tristan dies because he believes Isolde has not come to cure him; his death alone demonstrates the special quality of his love. Kaedin's story is therefore a warning against the consequences of imitating Tristan, and thus also a statement about how not to read Gottfried (Strohschneider 1991, 78–83).

The difference between the rule, illustrated by Kaedin, and the exception, represented by Tristan, also informs Ulrich's ambivalent attitude to love. On the one hand love brings only 'wandelungen' ('vicissitudes') (v. 246) which all right-thinking people do well to avoid (vv. 248f.); its influence leads Tristan into 'unsin' ('folly') (v. 3582). This conception of love as a fickle, destructive force is commonplace in thirteenth-century literature (Grubmüller 1985). On the other hand, love is praised by Ulrich as a source of 'saelde und gelückes vil' ('much happiness and good fortune') (v. 1723), as 'bezzer danne guot' ('better than good') (v. 1731); Tristan and Isolde provide true lovers with an unsurpassed example of its power (vv. 3628–34). But this love is exceptional, a 'wonder' by which the hero Tristan is distinguished (Müller 1992, 534–40).

Tristan als Mönch

This is an example of an episodic Tristan narrative in which the exiled hero disguises himself to see Isolde; other representatives of the type in Old French are *Tristan menestrel* and the two versions of the *Folie Tristan* (Wolf 1989, 19–54). Literary allusions and influences (*Prose Lancelot*, Der Stricker) indicate a date *c.* 1250. Although originally an independent poem, *Tristan als Mönch* is transmitted only in two fifteenth-century manuscripts of Gottfried's *Tristan*. In both of them it is preceded by Gottfried and followed by the conclusion of Ulrich von Türheim's continuation; thus it fills the space between the lovers' separation and their death with an episode that is typologically similar to the equivalent phase of the romance narratives.

The action is given an Arthurian frame. Guinevere persuades Arthur to hold a court to which each knight will come accompanied by the lady he loves most; she does this in the hope of attracting her own lover. The invitation places Tristan in a quandary: if he does not attend, he offends Guinevere; if he attends without Isolde, he offends her; if he attends with her, he offends his wife. He decides to attend with his wife, but arrives at Karidol riding a magnificent horse which was a gift from his lover. The attempt at doing right by all three ladies does not work: Tristan dreams that Isolde is angry with him and sets out in search of adventure. In the forest he finds the body of a dead knight, disfigures it beyond recognition, dresses it in his own armour and has it presented to the court as his own; disguised as a monk he accompanies the corpse to Tintagel for burial and uses the opportunity to see Isolde. After this, he returns to his homeland Parmenie and never becomes a monk again.

The plot is open-ended (McDonald 1990): both the Arthurian frame and Tristan's predicament are unresolved. The scene does not return to Arthur's court and nothing more is said about Guinevere's lover; Tristan withdraws to Parmenie, away from all three women whose demands he cannot reconcile. This ending has been interpreted as a pragmatic solution to the problem of how to be married and have a lover (Jungreithmayr 1980, 423f.); more plausibly it marks a withdrawal from the problem (and the resulting disintegration of the hero's identity) into the stable world of feudal lordship (Strohschneider 1991, 83–7). Not only is the plot weakly executed; it is also weakly foregrounded. A disproportionate amount of space is devoted to scenes that do not move the story along: the description of Tristan's horse and equipment (modelled on Hartmann's *Erec*), the splendour of Arthur's court, the plaints for the supposedly dead Tristan. These passages create a series of thematic backdrops (chivalry, courtliness, love) to the central figure. The poem's original purpose in evoking these typically romance themes may have been to ironize them (Jungreithmayr 1980, Buschinger 1987a); in the manuscript context these scenes read as amplifications of what the hero Tristan incorporates and hence what will be lost when he dies in reality.

Heinrich von Freiberg, *Tristan*

This continuation follows Gottfried in three manuscripts from the fourteenth and fifteenth centuries; there is also a fourteenth-century fragment (*Tristan*, ed.

Buschinger, xiii–xviii). The author is not attested independently of his works which include, in addition to *Tristan*, a legend of the holy cross and a panegyric of the Bohemian ministerial John of Michelsberg. All of Heinrich's works are connected with the Prague court of Wenceslas II of Bohemia (d. 1305), which was at the time an unrivalled centre of German literary culture (Bumke 1979, 202). The patron of *Tristan* is Raymond of Lichtenburg (*Tristan* vv. 75–7), a nobleman with close ties to the Prague court and possessions in Leitmeritz and Deutschbrod; Heinrich's reference to his patron's youth (Raimund is attested between 1261 and 1329) allows us to date *Tristan* between 1285 and 1290. Heinrich appears to have known Eilhart's romance, but he describes his source as 'Thomas of Britain . . . in the Lombard tongue' (vv. 6842–4); the most recent theory is that Heinrich used a version of the romance related to Thomas, whose *Tristan* circulated in northern Italy in the thirteenth century (Deighton 1997, 152–64).

Heinrich's continuation begins with Tristan's marriage; the revelation of its non-consummation is, however, delayed until after the hero returns from a sojourn at Arthur's court. The extensive development of the Arthurian episodes may reflect the interest of the Bohemian nobility in chivalrous ideals (Grothues 1991, 69–139): hearing that Arthur is founding the Round Table for perfect knights, Tristan is driven by his manly courage and his love of Isolde to seek out chivalry; he performs valorous adventures, visits Isolde at Tintagel with Gawan's help, and rescues her from the death sentence imposed by Mark. After Tristan's return to his wife, there follow his expedition to Cornwall with Kaedin, his fateful involvement in the latter's affair with Kassie, the lovers' death and their burial by Mark.

The first episode establishes Heinrich's programmatic distance from Gottfried. Heinrich is confronted with the problem of explaining Tristan's decision to give up his lover and marry Isolde Whitehand, although this is 'sêre wider sîn art des trankes' ('completely against the potion's nature') (vv. 217f.). Heinrich speculates that, just as there are eclipses of the sun and the moon, so perhaps there is a star governing the potion which has been eclipsed long enough for Tristan to stop loving Isolde (vv. 225–58). Heinrich does not present his astronomical analogy as anything more than a hypothesis, the best explanation he can offer for something he knows ought not to be possible (vv. 259–68). This stance, careful to distinguish between fact and speculation, reveals the author's distance from Gottfried, whose telling of the story amounts to a problem which Heinrich now must try to solve.

Heinrich's hypothetical answer goes beyond the immediate problem to suggest a resolution of all the tangled relationships between the principal characters. Heinrich speculates that the eclipse might also affect Isolde, causing her love for Tristan to be extinguished and allowing her to live happily with her husband (vv. 286–302). Into the story that celebrates adultery Heinrich has therefore injected a speculative counternarrative in which all the major actors live in lawful matrimony. The whole of the continuation is haunted by the tension between the story that Heinrich has to narrate and the legitimate dénouement he desires (Strohschneider 1991, 87–93); this tension is finally negotiated in the closing image of the rose and the vine. The two plants, fed by the potion, grow out of the buried lovers' hearts and entwine above their graves (vv. 6822–41). They are therefore symptoms of the force about the end of whose effects Heinrich has speculated; these effects are transient earthly love which brought Tristan and Isolde to their unhappy end and against which Heinrich warns his public in the following epilogue (vv. 6847–55). But in this same epilogue the entwining of the plants is further said to symbolize the coming together of Christ (the rose) and his believers (the vine) in true, incorruptible love (vv. 6856–90); this kind of love, which is commended by Heinrich, is analogous to the marriage sacrament, in which the union of husband and wife in the flesh symbolizes the spiritual union of Christ with his church. Thus the lovers are simultaneously a cautionary example and a reminder of the means of attaining divine grace; the two poles, adultery and marriage, sin and salvation, coexist in Heinrich's concluding image.

Tristrant und Isalde

This romance is a fifteenth-century prose adaptation of Eilhart. The earliest edition known today was printed at Augsburg by Anton Sorg in 1484; there are thirteen further editions before 1664. Prose reworkings of older verse romances are common in the fifteenth century (von Ertzdorff 1989, 75f.); the anonymous (and unidentified) author of *Tristrant und Isalde* declares that he has put the rhymed 'hystorj' into this form for those who do not care for or cannot understand verse (pp. 197f.). The designation 'history' is typical for late medieval and early modern narrative prose (Müller 1985, 61–71).

The preface of the 1484 edition announces that the story will be told 'auff das kürtzt' ('as briefly as possible') (p. 1), and this principle of brevity is frequently invoked and defended in the course of the narrative. For example: the author does not need to expand on what everybody knows and can imagine for himself (p. 22); his self-acknowledged stylistic limitations constrain him to be brief (p. 139); his emotional vulnerability precludes a long description of love which would only rekindle painful memories for him (pp. 158f.). These examples also illustrate one of the author's principal strategies for making the story comprehensible: Tristrant and Isalde are drawn into the lived experience of the author and his imagined public, whose commonsense notions of normality and verisimilitude provide the criteria for understanding the lovers and their actions (Plate 1977, 81–3). Their passion may be initially caused by the potion, but the force that drives it permanently is 'der natürlich flammen der liebe' ('the natural flame of love'), which the author thinks must inevitably take hold whenever two people have been intimate for so long (p. 43). The effect is to highlight the ordinariness of extraordinary passion.

Precisely this approximation to the familiar world inhabited by the author and his public enables the history to perform a didactic function. The narrative concludes by stating the moral: the lovers' fate is a warning to the target readership of young men and women not to let worldly love dominate them to the point where they neglect God and meet a premature death (p. 197). Yet this moralization provides at most a partial perspective on the whole story (Müller 1985, 76f.), which also presents the lovers as paragons of devotion who are unfairly persecuted by their enemies (Plate 1977, 85–9) and who deserve understanding and sympathy (von Ertzdorff 1989, 84–7); this positive appraisal of the lovers is made possible by the same principle of ordinariness that enables them to function as a moral example.

Bibliography

Primary Sources and Translations

Eilhart von Oberg, *Tristrant*. Ed. by D. Buschinger, 1976 (GAG, 202). Göppingen.
Eilhart von Oberg, *Tristrant. Synoptischer Druck der ergänzten Fragmente mit der gesamten Parallelüberlieferung*. Ed. by H. Bußmann, 1969 (ATB, 70). Tübingen.
Eilhart von Oberg, *Tristrant*. Transl. by J. W. Thomas, 1978. Lincoln, Nebr.
Gottfried von Strassburg, *Tristan und Isold*. Ed. by F. Ranke, 1978, 15th edn. Dublin and Zurich.
Gottfried von Strassburg, *Tristan*. Ed. by R. Krohn, 1995 (Reclams Universal-Bibliothek, 4471–3), 4th edn. Stuttgart.
Gottfried von Strassburg, *Tristan*. Transl. by A. T. Hatto, 1960 (Penguin Classics). Harmondsworth.
Heinrich von Freiberg, *Tristan*. Ed. by D. Buschinger, 1982 (GAG, 270). Göppingen.
Tristan als Mönch. Ed. by B. Bushey, 1974 (GAG, 119). Göppingen.
Tristant (= Low Frankish Tristan fragments). Ed. by M. Gysseling, 1980 (*Corpus van middelnederlandse teksten*, II,1, 337–42). 'S-Gravenhage.
Tristrant und Isalde. Prosaroman. Ed. by A. Brandstetter, 1966 (ATB Ergänzungsreihe, 3). Tübingen.
Ulrich von Türheim, *Tristan*. Ed. by T. Kerth, 1979 (ATB, 89). Tübingen.

Other literature

Bakhtin, M. M. 1981. 'From the prehistory of novelistic discourse', in Bakhtin, *The Dialogic Imagination: Four Essays*, ed. by M. Holquist, University of Texas Press Slavic Series, 1, Austin, 41–83.

de Boor, H. 1940. 'Die Grundauffassung von Gottfrieds *Tristan*', *DVj*, 18, 262–306.

Brandstetter, A. 1988. 'Über den Stellenwert des neugefundenen St Pauler Fragments in der Überlieferung von Eilharts *Tristrant*', in Stein, P. K., Weiss, A. and Hayer, G., eds., *Festschrift für Ingo Reiffenstein zum 60. Geburtstag*, GAG, 478, Göppingen, 339–52.

Bumke, J. 1979. *Mäzene im Mittelalter. Die Gönner und Auftraggeber der höfischen Literatur in Deutschland 1150–1300*, Munich.

Bumke, J. 1997. 'Autor und Werk. Beobachtungen und Überlegungen zur höfischen Epik', in Tervooren, H. and Wenzel, H., eds., *Philologie als Textwissenschaft. Alte und neue Horizonte*, *ZfdPh*, 116, Sonderheft, Berlin, 87–114.

Buschinger, D. 1987a. 'Tristan le Moine', in Buschinger 1987b, 75–86.

Buschinger, D., ed., 1987b. *Tristan et Iseut, mythe européen et mondial. Actes du Colloque des 10, 11 et 12 janvier 1986*, GAG, 474, Göppingen.

Buschinger, D. 1991. 'Conjectures sur Eilhart von Oberg', in Buschinger, ed., *Figures de l'écrivain au moyen âge. Actes du Colloque du Centre d'Etudes Médiévales de l'Université de Picardie, Amiens 18–20 mars 1988*, GAG, 510, Göppingen, 63–72.

Buschinger, D. and Spiewok, W., eds, 1993. *Tristan-Studien*, Wodan, 19, Ser. 3, 7, Greifswald.

Chinca, M. 1993. *History, Fiction, Verisimilitude: Studies in the Poetics of Gottfried's 'Tristan'*, MHRA Texts and Dissertations, 35/Bithell Series of Dissertations, 18, London.

Chinca, M. 1997. *Gottfried von Strassburg: Tristan*, Landmarks of World Literature, Cambridge.

Christ, W. 1977. *Rhetorik und Roman. Untersuchungen zu Gottfrieds von Straßburg 'Tristan'*, Deutsche Studien, 31, Meisenheim.

Deighton, A. 1997. 'Die Quellen der Tristan-Fortsetzungen Ulrichs von Türheim und Heinrichs von Freiberg', *ZfdA*, 126, 140–65.

von Ertzdorff, X. 1989. *Romane und Novellen des 15. und 16. Jahrhunderts in Deutschland*, Darmstadt.

Ganz, P. F. 1971. 'Tristan, Isolde und Ovid. Zu Gottfrieds *Tristan* Z. 17182ff.', in Hennig, U. and Kolb, H., eds., *Mediaevalia litteraria. Festschrift für H. de Boor zum 80. Geburtstag*, Munich, 397–412.

Glendinning, R. 1987. 'Gottfried von Strassburg and the school tradition', *DVj*, 61, 617–38.

Groos, A. 1993. 'Dialogic transpositions: the Grail hero wins a wife', in Jones and Wisbey 1993 (see Gen. Bibl.), 257–76.

Grothues, S. 1991. *Der arthurische Tristanroman. Werkabschluß zu Gottfrieds 'Tristan' und Gattungswechsel in Heinrichs von Freiberg Tristan-Fortsetzung*, Europäische Hochschulschriften, Reihe 1: Deutsche Sprache und Literatur, 1202, Frankfurt, Berne and New York.

Grubmüller, K. 1985. 'Probleme einer Fortsetzung. Anmerkungen zu Ulrichs von Türheim *Tristan*-Schluß', *ZfdA*, 114, 338–48.

Haug, W. 1986. 'Gottfrieds von Straßburg *Tristan*. Sexueller Sündenfall oder erotische Utopie', in Schöne, A., ed., *Kontroversen, alte und neue. Akten des VII. Internationalen Germanisten Kongresses Göttingen 1985*, vol. 1: *Ansprachen – Plenarvorträge – Berichte*. Tübingen, 41–52.

Haug, W. 1990. 'Der *Tristan* – eine interarthurische Lektüre', in Wolfzettel 1990 (see Gen. Bibl.), 57–72.

Huber, C. 1988. *Die Aufnahme und Verarbeitung des Alanus ab Insulis in mittelhochdeutschen Dichtungen. Untersuchungen zu Thomasin von Zerklære, Gottfried von Straßburg, Frauenlob, Heinrich von Neustadt, Heinrich von St Gallen, Heinrich von Mügeln und Johannes von Tepl*, Münchener Texte und Untersuchungen zur deutschen Literatur des Mittelalters, 89, Munich.

Hucker, B. U. 1995. 'Literatur im Umkreis Kaiser Ottos IV.', in Schneidmüller 1995, 377–406.

Jackson, W. T. H. 1971. *The Anatomy of Love: The 'Tristan' of Gottfried von Strassburg*, New York and London.

Jaeger, C. S. 1977. *Medieval Humanism in Gottfried von Strassburg's 'Tristan und Isolde'*, Germanische Bibliothek, Reihe 3: Untersuchungen und Einzeldarstellungen, Heidelberg.

Jaffe, S. 1978. 'Gottfried von Strassburg and the rhetoric of history', in Murphy, J. J., ed., *Medieval Eloquence: Studies in the Theory and Practice of Medieval Rhetoric*, Berkeley, Los Angeles and London, 288–318.

Jantzen, U. and Kröner, N. 1997. 'Zum neugefundenen *Tristan*-Fragment des Thomas d'Angleterre. Editionskritik und Vergleich mit Gottfrieds Bearbeitung', *Euph*, 91, 291–309.

Jungreithmayr, A. 1980. '*Tristan als Mönch*. Ansätze zu einem Textverständnis', in Stein, P. K., ed., *Sprache – Text – Geschichte. Beiträge zur Mediävistik und germanistischer Sprachwissenschaft aus dem Kreis der Mitarbeiter 1964–1979 des Instituts für Germanistik an der Universität Salzburg*, GAG, 304, Göppingen, 409–40.

Kasten, I. 1995. 'Bachtin und der höfische Roman', in Lindemann, D., Volkmann, B. and Wegera, K.-P., eds., *'bickelwort' und 'wildiu mære'. Festschrift für Eberhard Nellmann zum 65. Geburtstag*, GAG, 618, Göppingen, 51–70.

Klein, T. 1988. 'Ermittlung, Darstellung und Deutung von Verbreitungstypen in der Handschriftenüberlieferung mittelhochdeutscher Epik', in Honemann and Palmer 1988 (see Gen. Bibl.), 110–67.

McDonald, W. C. 1990. 'A reconsideration of *Tristan als Mönch*', in McDonald, W. C. and McConnell, W., eds., *Fide et amore: A Festschrift for Hugo Bekker on his Sixty-Fifth Birthday*, GAG, 526, Göppingen, 235–60.

Mertens, V. 1987. 'Eilhart, der Herzog und der Truchseß. Der *Tristrant* am Welfenhof', in Buschinger 1987b, 262–81.

Mertens, V. 1995. 'Bildersaal – Minnegrotte – Liebestrank: Zu Symbol, Allegorie und Mythos im Tristanroman', *PBB*, 117, 40–64.

Mertens, V. 1998. 'Exkurs. Artus in den Tristanromanen', in Mertens 1998 (see Gen. Bibl.), 250–61.

Mikasch-Köthner, D. 1991. *Zur Konzeption der Tristanminne bei Eilhart von Oberg und Gottfried von Straßburg*, Helfant Studien, S7, Stuttgart.

Müller, J.-D. 1985. 'Volksbuch/Prosaroman im 15./16. Jahrhundert. Perspektiven der Forschung', in Frühwald, W., Jäger, G. and Martino, A., eds., *Forschungsreferate*, IASL Sonderhefte, 1, Tübingen, 1–128.

Müller, J.-D. 1990. 'Die Destruktion des Heros oder wie erzählt Eilhart von passionierter Liebe?' in Schulze-Belli, P. and Dallapiazza, M., eds., *Il romanzo di Tristano nella letteratura del Medioevo – Der 'Tristan' in der Literatur des Mittelalters. Atti del convegno – Beiträge der Triester Tagung 1989*, Trieste, 19–37.

Müller, J.-D. 1992. 'Tristans Rückkehr. Zu den Fortsetzern Gottfrieds von Straßburg', in Janota, J., ed., *Festschrift Walter Haug und Burghart Wachinger*, Tübingen, 2, 529–48.

Okken, L. 1996. *Kommentar zum Tristan-Roman Gottfrieds von Strassburg*, Amsterdamer Publikationen zur Sprache und Literatur, 57–8, Amsterdam.

Plate, B. 1977. 'Verstehensprinzipien im Prosa-Tristrant von 1484', in Kaiser, G., ed., *Literatur – Publikum – historischer Kontext*, Beiträge zur Älteren Deutschen Literaturgeschichte, 1, Berne, Frankfurt and Las Vegas, 79–89.

Ranke, F. 1925. 'Die Allegorie der Minnegrotte in Gottfrieds *Tristan*', Schriften der Königsberger gelehrten Gesellschaft, Geisteswissenschaftliche Klasse, 2. Jg., H. 2, 21–39, Berlin.

Schindele, G. 1971. *Tristan. Metamorphose und Tradition*, Studien zur Poetik und Geschichte der Literatur, 12, Stuttgart.

Schirok, B. 1984. 'Zu den Akrosticha in Gottfrieds *Tristan*', *ZfdA*, 113, 188–213.

Schneidmüller, B., ed. 1995. *Die Welfen und ihr Braunschweiger Hof im hohen Mittelalter*, Wolfenbütteler Mittelalter-Studien, 7, Wiesbaden.

Schnell, R. 1992. *Suche nach Wahrheit. Gottfrieds 'Tristan' als erkenntniskritischer Roman*, Hermaea, n.s. 67, Tübingen.

Schwietering, J. 1943. *Der Tristan Gottfrieds von Straßburg und die Bernhardische Mystik*, Berlin.

Sedlmeyer, M. 1976. *Heinrichs von Freiberg Tristanfortsetzung im Vergleich zu anderen Tristandichtungen*, Europäische Hochschulschriften, Reihe 1: Deutsche Sprache und Literatur, 159, Berne and Frankfurt.

Steinhoff, H.-H. 1976. *Bibliographie zu Gottfried von Straßburg*, Bibliographien zur deutschen Literatur des Mittelalters, 5, Berlin.

Steinhoff, H.-H. 1986. *Bibliographie zu Gottfried von Straßburg. Berichtszeitraum 1970–1983*, Bibliographien zur deutschen Literatur des Mittelalters, 9, Berlin.

Steinhoff, H.-H. 1987. 'Niederfränkischer Tristan', in *VL*, 6, 994–5.

Stevens, A. 1990. 'The renewal of the classic: aspects of rhetorical and dialectical composition in Gottfried's *Tristan*', in Stevens and Wisbey 1990 (see Gen. Bibl.), 67–89.

Stevens, A. 1993. 'Heteroglossia and clerical narrative in Wolfram's adaptation of Chrétien', in Jones and Wisbey 1993 (see Gen. Bibl.), 241–55.

Strohschneider, P. 1991. 'Gotfrit-Fortsetzungen. Tristans Ende im 13. Jahrhundert und die Möglichkeiten nachklassischer Epik', *DVj*, 65, 70–98.

Strohschneider, P. 1993. 'Herrschaft und Liebe: Strukturprobleme des Tristanromans bei Eilhart von Oberg', *ZfdA*, 122, 36–61.

Tervooren, H. and Beckers, H., eds. 1989. *Literatur und Sprache im rheinisch-maasländischen Raum zwischen 1150 und 1450*, *ZfdPh*, 108, Sonderheft, Berlin.

Tomasek, T. 1985. *Die Utopie im 'Tristan' Gottfrieds von Straßburg*, Hermaea, n.s. 49, Tübingen.

Wachinger, B. 1975. 'Zur Rezeption Gottfrieds von Straßburg im 13. Jahrhundert', in Harms, W. and Johnson, L. P., eds., *Deutsche Literatur des späten Mittelalters. Hamburger Colloquium 1973*, Berlin, 56–82.

Wessel, F. 1984. *Probleme der Metaphorik und die Minnemetaphorik in Gottfrieds von Straßburg 'Tristan und Isolde'*, Münstersche Mittelalter-Schriften, 54, Munich.

Wetzel, R. 1992. *Die handschriftliche Überlieferung des 'Tristan' Gottfrieds von Straßburg untersucht an ihren Fragmenten*, Germanistica Friburgensia, 13, Freiburg.

Wisbey, R. A. 1980. 'The *renovatio amoris* in Gottfried's *Tristan*', *London German Studies*, 1, 1–66.

Wolf, A. 1989. *Gottfried von Straßburg und die Mythe von Tristan und Isolde*, Darmstadt.

Wolff, L. and Schröder, W. 1980. 'Eilhart von Oberg' in *VL*, 2, 410–18.

Wolfzettel 1990. See Gen. Bibl.

APPENDIX TO CHAPTER 7: ARTHUR IN THE TRISTAN TRADITION

Volker Mertens

Although it is not clear at what stage in their development the stories of Tristan and of Arthur first came together, the two complexes were already associated in twelfth-century works, and the appearance of Arthurian motifs and figures in Tristan romances forms an illuminating strand in the history of Arthurian literature. It is generally held that a lost *Estoire de Tristan*, written in French *c.* 1150, was the basis from which later, existing versions derived. Béroul's *Tristan* (incomplete), the oldest French Prose *Tristan*, and Eilhart von Oberg's *Tristrant*, which is considered the most faithful representative of the lost work, are versions which emphasize adventure and dramatic action, whilst the 'courtly' or clerical version by the Anglo-Norman poet Thomas, from which Gottfried von Strassburg's *Tristan* derives, has a more psychological and rational bent.

In Thomas's *Tristan* King Arthur appears only in a retrospective passage, based on Wace's *Brut*, which tells of him killing a giant who had claimed his beard. In the versions of Béroul and Eilhart, by contrast, the worlds of Arthur and Tristan come together, Arthurian episodes play a direct part, and Arthur and his knights aid the lovers. In Béroul, they come to Yseut's aid when she acquits herself of the charge of adultery in the trial by ordeal, an episode which Eilhart omits, probably for religious reasons.

In Eilhart's version Arthur plays an important part in the chain of adventures that lead Tristrant back to Cornwall in order to meet Isalde – a part of the poem not included in the incomplete Béroul manuscript. Following the pattern of Arthurian romances, Eilhart's *Tristrant* gains the friendship of Gawain (Walwan) and acquires a chivalric reputation comparable to his. Impressed by the courtly attitude shown by Tristrant when (after his victory over Delekors) he asserts that he will undertake anything he is asked to do for the sake of his mistress (vv. 5339–44), Walwan arranges a meeting between the lovers which shows Arthurian kingship in an interesting light. When Arthur's company arrives at Mark's court with Tristrant, Mark asks Arthur to ensure that none of his men should do anything detrimental to his (Mark's) honour (vv. 5474–77), and Arthur promises that anyone who brings disgrace to Mark shall be punished (vv. 5488–91). This amounts to a legal contract between the kings, but Tristrant disregards it when he goes to the queen's bed. When Tristrant is at risk of discovery by the blood that flows from the wound he received on visiting Isalde's bed, Arthur's knights help him hide the offence by arranging a fight in which they voluntarily wound themselves on the iron trap set by Mark to guard Isalde's bed, and Arthur covers up for his knights' deception by telling Mark that it is their habit to behave like that. The Arthurian knights return to Brittany and, despite offers of fief and land, Tristrant leaves the court.

Eilhart thus presents Arthur as an accomplice in Tristrant's adultery, and the breach of trust is intensified by the fact that Arthur had expressly promised to avenge any offence against Mark's honour. The solidarity of the knights of the Round Table overrides legal propriety, and Tristrant has a claim to this solidarity because of his knightly feats and because of his perfect courtly conduct in love as shown in the Delekors episode. Love is here not a goal in itself but an incentive to knightly deeds and knightly perfection; love has become functionalized as courtly service within the system of Arthurian values. By becoming a member of the Round Table Tristrant is transformed into a courtly knight, and this accords with his general characterization, for Eilhart shows him primarily as a hero without equal and only in a secondary way as the great lover. In the prologue 'the marvellous feats' performed by Tristrant rank before the love story, which itself is reduced to the winning of the beloved and the death that results from love (vv. 38–47). The image of the valiant hero concurs with that of the Arthurian Tristrant who has transformed his love into an incentive for knightly achievement and himself into a model of courtliness.

However, this transformation is possible only in the later stages of the work. In Eilhart's romance the most powerful, life-threatening effects of the love-potion fade after four years, to give place to a more 'natural' love. Even if this love now has a courtly dimension, it is still strong enough to force Tristrant into violations of social and moral laws in order to be with Isalde, and time and again Eilhart excuses these offences by reference to the potion that induced love 'against their will' (v. 9697). King Arthur's complicity in Tristrant's adultery points forward to the end of the romance when King Mark's regret at having banned Tristrant from his court and caused the death of his wife and his nephew signals Tristrant's and Isalde's love as an innocent fate. Indeed, two worlds come together in the concept of the Arthurian Tristrant: on the one hand, the magic love of the potion acquires courtly qualities and, on the other, the Arthurian court becomes 'Tristanized' in its support of an adulterous love. Eilhart has probably shifted the compromise between love and courtliness from an earlier position in the story to its present place. In the *Estoire* the episode of the iron trap took place at Mark's court soon after the marriage to Isolde. This is its position in the oldest prose *Tristan*, where it also has no Arthurian connection. Eilhart seems deliberately to have changed the episode in order to have King

Arthur himself sanction the adulterous love. The episode of the trap takes the place of the ordeal in which God helps the lovers, and which Eilhart has omitted probably because of religious scruples. Arthur was less problematic as an accomplice than God himself and, as Eilhart needed an authority to sanction the love between Tristrant and Isalde, he chose the king so as to legitimize his telling a story in which adultery plays such a prominent part. This interpretation matches what we know about the Welf court, for which Eilhart probably produced the romance, for the Welfs' cultural self-understanding was character-ized by religiosity, aristocratic pride and the dignity of lordship.

In Gottfried von Strassburg's *Tristan* Arthur plays no part in the narrative, he is referred to only in the episode of the lovers' cave, when the narrator comments that the lovers' joy is greater than that of Arthur's court and his Round Table (vv. 16859–65, 16896–901). Gottfried's lovers accept the destiny of their love with their full being. They do not need an external recognition of their love by an exemplary King Arthur. However, in other works Tristan is often associated with Arthur's court. Tristan is present among the knights of the Round Table already in the work that established the genre of Arthurian romance – the *Erec* of Chrétien de Troyes and its adaptation by Hartmann von Aue – and in Ulrich von Zatzikhoven's *Lanzelet*, which also represents an early stage of the genre.

In his continuation of Gottfried's *Tristan* Heinrich von Freiberg goes so far as to narrate Arthur's inauguration of the Round Table and to present Tristan as one of its founding members (vv. 1307–20, 1981–2000). The table can seat 500 knights; its roundness places all members in a position of equal dignity; and in order to gain a seat the knight must demonstrate military prowess, nobility of birth and true loyalty ('triwe', v. 1372) as well as the courtly qualities of generosity and good bearing. Arthur invites all knights who wish to win membership of the Round Table to seek adventure in his realm as proof of their worth. Spurred on by his manly courage and his love for Isolde the Blonde, Tristan travels to Karidol, where the knights of the Round Table are engaged in competitive combats in a kind of park of adventure, where any knight who rides in armour is bound to give combat (vv. 1606–15). This is an expansion of the motif of knightly adventure that was introduced as a typical practice of Arthur's knights already in Eilhart's work. Tristan engages in a brilliant combat against Gawan, with neither recognizing the other until Tristan reveals himself by his war cry, whereupon Gawan breaks off the combat, and Tristan is received into the company of the Round Table, where he quickly gains the highest renown among the knights.

Tristan is able to pass the Arthurian test because he has the proper qualifica-tions: a thirst for action inspired by love, prowess as shown in the indecisive combat with Gawan (which is modelled on the combat between Gawan and Parzival in Wolfram's *Parzival*) and noble descent. Indeed Tristan is drawn into a family relationship with Arthur's court because he is not only the special friend but also a relative ('mac', v. 1936) of Arthur's nephew Gawan, and Arthur himself speaks of Tristan in terms of kinship ('neve', v. 2287). In addition, Tristan's career thus far is sufficient proof of his worthiness for acceptance into the company of the Round Table. Tristan is a model Arthurian knight, and his love for Isolde the Blonde fits that concept, because it motivates him to knightly deeds, like the loves of the other knights. As well as friendship with Gawan, the classic career of the Arthurian hero includes a combat with Keie, and this, too, Tristan undertakes. Only after this combat does Tristan meet the knight Delekors. Heinrich largely follows Eilhart in the Delekors episode. In comparison with Eilhart, Heinrich leaves out the agreement between Mark and Arthur that the latter will protect the honour of his host. However, Heinrich does have Tristan himself reflect inwardly on the consequences that will follow if he goes to Isolde: he will endanger her reputation and bring anger to Mark and sadness to Arthur; but these scruples are vanquished by love (vv. 2726–50). What was an external, juridical conflict in Eilhart has become an inner conflict in Heinrich's work, and this shift from the outer to the inner dimension echoes the treatment of Tristan in Gottfried's work.

The love potion does not, in Heinrich's work, lose its power. The lovers meet as often as possible, and when they seek refuge in the forest after escaping Mark's sentence of death the narrator comments that, even though they were unable to find the lovers' cave of Gottfried's romance, they nevertheless delighted in each other's company (vv. 3321–33). Indeed, it is clear that Heinrich von Freiberg sought to include the entire Tristan tradition in his continuation and thus to write a *summa* of Tristan material. This tendency is typical of authors of the thirteenth century, and it indicates not only a desire to possess the whole tradition, but also that fiction is now at the disposal of the author and not to be derived faithfully from a source. In terms of narrative composition this disposability means that individual motifs can be rearranged in new connections and new relations. In terms of broader thematic structures it means that the Arthurian tradition is available to the author as well as that of Tristan. Heinrich equips Tristan with characteristic attributes of the classical Arthurian hero and in doing so he brings together two different literary projects which represent different conceptions of the world: Tristan stands for the supremacy of love above the law, Arthur for the courtly ideal and the upholding of peace and justice.

Heinrich goes further than Eilhart in integrating Tristan's love into the courtly realm. It is not first at Arthur's court that Tristan becomes a knight servitor of his lady-love, but he is driven there already by a similar motivation in his love for Isolde. The functionalization of love thus begins not in the courtly milieu of Arthur's court but earlier, in Tristan himself. Just as the autonomy of

Tristan's love is reduced, so is Arthur's position impaired. Although he does not break a formal promise (as in Eilhart's work) when he helps Tristan, he is apparently content to go even further by arranging a reconciliation between Tristan and Marke (vv. 2980–3000) and thus covering up not merely for the folly of one night but for a long-term adulterous relationship. When Arthur is 'saddened' ('betruebet', v. 2837) that Tristan has been wounded in Mark's trap, it is not because of the offence against Mark's hospitality but out of concern for his knights, including Tristan. King Arthur is no longer a regal embodiment of universal justice but reduced to solidarity with the knights of the Round Table and with their internal code of honour. The founding charter of the Round Table (vv. 1329–48) speaks of valour and noble-mindedness, but not of functions of the ruler such as the defence of peace and justice. Chivalric combats aim only at the accretion of honour; they have no overarching purpose, and consequently Arthur's knights do not ride through the world in order to help those in need, but stay in their realm and compete with each other for eminence. It is in keeping with this perspective that the episode of the iron trap has comical aspects (Arthur and his knights fighting with cushions, bedclothes and garments).

The bringing together of the two realms, that of Tristan and Isolde and that of Arthur, thus has a mutually corrosive effect. However, in the further course of the action Tristan and Isolde's love regains some of its absoluteness: for instance Heinrich refrains from taking over the quarrel of the lovers from Eilhart. He plays a double game, on the one hand reducing the absoluteness and self-sufficiency of love, on the other hand building it up again, and thus preventing the establishment of a firm doctrine in the course of the narrative (the 'gewisse lêre' promised in the prologue to Hartmann's *Iwein*), as neither the Arthurian court nor the love of Tristan and Isolde provides an absolute norm. It lies in the logic of this stance that the end of the work is orientated towards transcendental values, as the narrator reminds the audience of the transience of earthly love and interprets the rose and the vine that entwine on the graves of Tristan and Isolde allegorically as an appeal to Christians to entwine themseves with Christ (vv. 6847–90). The religious turn at the end of Heinrich's work has been criticized as unfitting, but it is the logical consequence of the relativity of values in the romance: only Christ (and here Heinrich differs from Gottfried) is not 'at the author's disposal'; his grace remains a necessity for mankind.

Heinrich wrote his romance for the Bohemian noble Raimund von Lichtenburg, and the account of the foundation of the Round Table and the self-directed activities of the knights have been seen as reflections of the knightly societies of the time, to one of which Raimund may have belonged (Grothues 1991, 131–5). The initial Arthurian ideal has become a confirmatory ritual for an exclusive body of noblemen – that matches the spirit of the knightly societies.

The political aims of the societies were avowedly particularist and could not well be represented by the traditional Arthurian concept of a Round Table that fought for peace and justice for all.

The only German episodic Tristan poem is *Tristan als Mönch* (2705 vv.). The opening of the narrative uses the Arthurian court to show a courtly conflict between honour and love. This conflict, however, does not determine the action for long, and for the most part the work is characterized by a sequence of ostentatious episodes rather than by any consistent thematic programme. The work begins like an Arthurian romance, with the name of the king as an indicator of genre (v. 3) and a typical court meeting. The meeting, however, is summoned not by the king, but by the queen in order to meet her lover again (Lancelot, who remains unnamed in this work). Tristan experiences the conflict between honour and love when he receives an invitation to attend the court: shall he attend with his wife, Isolde with the White Hands, as honour demands, or with Isolde the Blonde, as love demands? Kornewal counsels Tristan that Queen Isolde would not be angry if he were to follow the dictate of honour (vv. 275–7), and Tristan takes his wife to the court, where he receives a seat at the Round Table. (For an outline of the remainder of the action see Chinca, chapter 7 above.)

In *Tristan als Mönch*, even if adultery exists at Arthur's court in the form of the love between Guinevere and Lancelot, the adultery has to remain concealed: it is possible only in secrecy. In the case of Tristan, this means that it would have brought a loss of honour had he made his adulterous relationship public by choosing Queen Isolde as his companion for the feast. Arthur does not become an accomplice in adultery (as he did in the versions of Eilhart and Heinrich von Freiberg); rather, the episodic poem preserves Arthur's role as the guarantor of honour and custom, as is indicated in the prologue, where it is stated that his country enjoyed high esteem (v. 4). The courtly ideal represented by the king has marginalized the conflict between love and honour, or relegated it into the secret realm of the love between Guinevere and Lancelot. It is this conflict that underlies Guinevere's words when she mourns the supposed death of Tristan: 'What I must conceal hurts me more than anything else. Alas, how will she react, alas, how will she mourn you? Alas, what am I saying! What did I almost accuse you of? From now it is better that I remain silent' (vv. 1172–8). Guinevere is here referring to adulterous love, which has to be kept secret in order to maintain the honour of the court.

The text of *Tristan als Mönch* is transmitted in one manuscript which dates from the middle of the fifteenth century; a second, slightly later one has been lost. The free play with literary motifs and the dominance of the public and representative dimension which characteristically follows from the introduction of Arthur into the Tristan tradition could suggest a date of origin for the work around the middle of the thirteenth century.

Bibliographical Note

Line numbers in this contribution refer to Eilhart von Oberg, *Tristrant und Isalde*. Middle High German/New High German. Ed. and transl. by D. Buschinger and W. Spiewok, 1993 (Wodan, 27, Ser. 1, 7). Greifswald.

For other Primary Sources and for Other Literature see Chinca, the bibliography to chapter 7 above.

8

THE WIGALOIS NARRATIVES

Volker Honemann

Wirnt von Grafenberg, *Wigalois*

Wigalois occupies a unique place in German Arthurian literature, perplexing modern scholars with its failure to conform to their expectations of such works: although written within a few years of Hartmann's *Iwein*, it fails to depict its hero on the sort of twofold journey which, on the basis of the works of Chrétien de Troyes and Hartmann himself, is held to give meaning to the narrative structures of Arthurian romance. As such, it may be said to have been written too soon. Instead of a protagonist who undergoes a crisis and proves his worth as a knight by winning wife, land and ultimate happiness, Wirnt presents a hero who suffers no crisis and who inhabits a world of wondrous beings and events, with King Arthur and his realm playing only a relatively minor role. In the opinion of many critics, the poem lacks depth, yet it was extraordinarily popular with listeners and readers from the thirteenth to the seventeenth century, a popularity attested not only by the many surviving manuscripts but also by the existence of a prose redaction (*Wigoleis vom Rade*), a strophic retelling (*Floreis und Wigoleis*) and, virtually without parallel, a Yiddish adaptation (*Widuwilt*).

The poet gives his name as 'Wirnt von Grâvenberc' at the end of the Prologue (v. 141; see also v. 10576). There is no other documentary evidence of such an individual, but 'Grâvenberc' is presumably the town of Gräfenberg to the northeast of Nuremberg. It is unclear whether Wirnt was a knight, although Konrad von Würzburg treats him as one in *Der Welt Lohn* (c. 1260), and Wirnt himself, in a *laudatio temporis acti*, insists with some vehemence on knighthood as an inherited status and criticizes the granting of knighthood to those not qualified by birth (vv. 2319–48). The dating of *Wigalois* is beset by problems. The two earliest manuscripts, which are not directly related, are no later than 1225–30. Heinrich von dem Türlin mentions Wirnt in *Diu Crône* as 'my lord Wirnt' ('mîn herre Wirnde', v. 2942; see also v. 2949). Since *Diu Crône* can be dated to the period between 1215 and 1230, Wirnt's reference to 'a most noble prince . . . of Meran', whose funeral he himself attended (vv. 8063f.), must be to Duke

Berthold IV of Andechs-Meranien, who died in 1204, rather than to Berthold's son, Otto, who died in 1234. Since Wirnt goes on to express the hope that the duke's soul may find eternal salvation, he or his family may have been Wirnt's patron. Wirnt also includes a literary excursus (vv. 6284–605) that reveals him to have been well read. He mentions Hartmann's Arthurian romances as well as the Jeschute episode from Wolfram's *Parzival* (vv. 129, 18ff.), so that he must have been familiar with at least the first six books of *Parzival*. In short, *Wigalois* probably arose no later than the second decade of the thirteenth century, although it remains unclear whether it was written at Andechs in Bavaria or at the nearby Augustinian monastery of Dießen. (It is from this area that the oldest surviving manuscript comes, a circumstance that might similarly suggest the patronage of the Andechs-Meranien family.)

Wirnt is keen to convey an image of himself as an inexperienced poet. He has 'not mastered rhetoric' (v. 38) and can speak only 'as a child' (v. 47), hence his appeal to God to help him with his 'first work' (v. 140) (see, in general, vv. 33–144 and 5753f.: 'my feeble mind'). Bound up with these expressions of modesty is Wirnt's extravagant praise of Wolfram von Eschenbach ('layman's mouth never spoke better', v. 6346). That his protestations of inexperience are examples of a topos becomes clear from his modern, sophisticated approach to the phenomenon of literacy. It is the book itself that speaks the opening lines: 'What good man has opened me?' (v. 1; this speech by the book in vv. 1–19 is found only in the oldest manuscript, A, and in the Leiden manuscript, B); and the work is specifically described as a 'buoch' in the very last line (v. 11708). Throughout the poem as a whole, literacy and books repeatedly play a role (see Ziegeler 1998b, 1253–4).

Among the challenges faced by scholars continues to be that of Wirnt's sources. He himself indicates his intention to tell a 'tale' ('mære') that was 'told' ('geseit') to him (vv. 131f.), and later he claims that a squire ('knappe') told him the story so that he could put it into literary form ('tihten', v. 11688). In spite of extensive inquiries, scholars have discovered only a handful of parallels with the opening section of *Le Bel Inconnu*, an Old French verse romance by Renaut de Beaujeu dating from around 1190. These parallels include the figure of Gawein's son, who is told about his father; the motif of the female messenger who, together with her dwarf, begs for assistance; the journey with her; and the three succeeding episodes (the fight with the giant, the fight over the hunting dog and the beauty contest) in which Wigalois proves his worth as a knight and impresses the messenger, who had in fact wanted Gawein to help her (Cormeau 1977, 95f.). These parallels cover vv. 1500–3150 of *Wigalois*. It is worth noting that one of the prizes in the beauty contest is a parrot ('sitich', v. 2517). None the less, it seems more likely that the French prose romance, *Le chevalier du papegau*, which shares other motifs with *Wigalois* and which is first attested in the fifteenth century, is dependent upon *Wigalois*, rather than the other way round (see Cormeau 1977, 94f.). Certainly, the exceptional popularity of the German poem makes this possible, even though it represents a reversal of the usual line of influence. That Wirnt himself conceived at least part of his narrative independently is clear from the lengthy episode in which Wigalois demonstrates his valour by engaging in combat with the Red Knight, Hojir von Mannesvelt (vv. 2349–3285). Hojir is modelled on Count Hoyer II of Mansfeld who fell at the Battle of Welfesholz in 1115. In this way, Wirnt introduces a historical character into his narrative, a figure, moreover, around whom a whole series of legends must already have accrued by his day (Honemann 1994).

In terms of its manuscript tradition, *Wigalois* is something of a special case, as Schiewer has noted (1988, 235–7 and 241). Not only have a remarkably large number of manuscripts survived (in total, there are forty-one, of which twenty-eight are incomplete, a figure that surpasses the thirty-two of Hartmann's *Iwein* and is exceeded in the corpus of Arthurian, Grail and Tristan romances only by *Parzival* and the *Jüngerer Titurel*), but the tradition also begins at a very early date, with two manuscripts dating back to between 1220 and 1230 or even earlier. The manuscripts in question are A = Cologne W 6* and E = Vienna 14612 (Ziegeler 1998b, 1256f.). According to Schneider, A was probably written 'soon after *Wigalois* was first set down'; as a likely location she suggests 'the territories of the counts of Andechs', that is, 'the area on the border between Bavaria and Swabia' (1987, 85 and 47). If we include the codices written around 1300, more than half the manuscripts (twenty-one) date from the thirteenth century (for full details, see Schiewer 1988 and Hilgers 1971). These statistics, taken together with the large number of times that *Wigalois* is mentioned in thirteenth-century texts by Heinrich von dem Türlin, Rudolf von Ems, Der Tannhäuser, Konrad von Würzburg and others (Ziegeler 1998b, 1265f.), indicate that Wirnt's poem was one of the most popular romances of the High Middle Ages in Germany. It retained its appeal well into the fourteenth century, with twelve surviving manuscripts, each of them apparently individually transmitted and often in reduced format (Schiewer 1988, 241), in other words, as the medieval equivalent of a portable paperback. Of particular interest in this context is a manuscript commissioned by Duke Albrecht II of Braunschweig-Grubenhagen and prepared in 1372 at the Cistercian monastery at Amelungsborn (B = Leiden, Ltk 537). It includes forty-seven half-page and (exceptionally) full-page miniatures of a very high quality, albeit of an unusual style. Not until the fifteenth century does the number of new manuscript copies – eight – show signs of declining, but even in this period the appearance of a prose recension, first printed in 1493, gave the work a new lease of life more in keeping with the times. Alongside the textual transmission, reception of the subject in other branches of art, including a series of frescos dating from around

1400 at Burg Runkelstein in the south Tyrol (drawings of the Wigalois frescos reproduced in Waldstein 1982; commentary by Huschenbett 1982, 170–7), indicate that interest in Wirnt's work was still very much alive in the late Middle Ages. (On pictorializations of the Wigalois story see below, chapter 16.)

The plot of Wirnt's *Wigalois* is so complicated that space allows only a brief summary here (for a detailed paraphrase, see Ziegeler 1998b, 1257–61 and Kapteyn 1926, 77*–91*). An introductory Prologue (vv. 1–144) is followed by the story of Wigalois's parents, Gawein and Florie, beginning with the challenge issued to Arthur's court by Florie's uncle, King Joram (vv. 145–1219). Wigalois himself is then introduced ('I am called Gwi of Galois', v. 1574; thereafter the name appears as Gwigalois, or in forms without initial G in many manuscripts). He arrives at Arthur's court, becomes a member of the Round Table and rides out in search of adventure, a dangerous undertaking which, if successful, promises to reward him with a wife and country (vv. 1220–709). In a series of contests comparable to those of the initial cycle of adventures in Hartmann's romances, he proves his eligibility to undertake such adventures (vv. 1710–3884). He meets Larie, who is living in exile in an impregnable castle at Roimunt, bordering on Korntin, the country over which she is queen and which Wigalois now sets out to restore to her. Inflamed with love for her, he is extravagantly armed for the dangerous adventures that lie ahead (vv. 3885–4479). After overcoming great dangers, including fights with dragons and giantesses, he defeats the heathen usurper of Korntin, Roaz of Glois, who is in league with the devil (vv. 4480–7903). In terms of the structural model of Hartmann's romances, this section of Wirnt's narrative could be interpreted as the second cycle of adventures. Wigalois now marries Larie and becomes king of Korntin, a development that seems to presage a happy ending (vv. 7904–9798), but the hero must first defeat Lion of Namur, who has attacked his wife's kinsmen, and capture Namur (vv. 9799–11284). With his wife and father and other Arthurian knights, he then travels to Arthur's court (vv. 11285–517), before returning to Korntin and ruling his country in exemplary fashion (vv. 11518–708).

Although Wirnt's work should not be judged by the standards of Hartmann's Arthurian romances, comparison with these romances can throw light on *Wigalois*, and the following interpretative comments focus on the most important differences and peculiarities vis-à-vis *Erec* and *Iwein*.

Wirnt creates a new type of hero with his protagonist (see above). Wigalois is predestined for the task that presents itself to him: he can sit on the Stone of Virtue on which only Arthur himself, but not the latter's knights, can sit (vv. 1489–524). From his mother Florie he receives a magic belt that grants 'joy and wisdom' and dispels 'every kind of sorrow' (vv. 331–3 and 1367–77). As a sign of his lasting good fortune, his coat of arms bears a wheel of fortune (see below).

Before leaving for Korntin and Glois to fight with Roaz, he is equipped with a series of magic gifts: a 'letter' that wards off spells ('brief', v. 4428), a 'loaf of bread' that drives away hunger and grants him 'good spirits' and 'strength' ('muot' and 'maht', v. 4475), a flower from the tree of paradise that protects him from the dragon's fiery breath and a lance brought to him by an angel with which he can kill the monster (vv. 4736–59). It is clear from this that, as the romance progresses, Wigalois turns increasingly into a hero who not only needs God's help but who can count on receiving it. In response to his prayer to God (which Wirnt quotes in full), the fetters that the giantess Ruel had used to bind him fall away (vv. 6494–508). The sword-wheel that blocks the road stops turning when Wigalois humbly accepts God's will and commends himself to God's care (vv. 6835–40). Before entering the castle at Glois he protects himself with a crucifix and a brief prayer (vv. 7267–70). Together with the 'letter', they help him to overcome Roaz, who is assisted in their fight by a devil (vv. 7334–41). The adventure at Korntin is thus clearly presented as a journey into the hereafter, with Wigalois himself as a saviour and redeemer (Grubmüller 1985; Thomas 1987, 65–75). In his actions, he is additionally motivated by his love of Larie, although Wirnt treats love and religion as two distinct entities, rather than as a combined force: love inspires Wigalois to acquire a wife and land, while religion leads him to free the country and its inhabitants from the oppressive yoke of the heathen magician, Roaz. As the narrative unfolds, the Arthurian court progressively loses its normative function, a function replaced by the hero's growing commitment to his role as a Christian saviour. During his first series of adventures, Wigalois proves himself not in the eyes of the Arthurian court, but in the estimation of Nereja, the messenger from the kingdom of Korntin: it is she whom he must convince of his worthiness to ride out in search of adventure. Although he sends a number of his defeated opponents back to Arthur's court, no consequences flow from this action, which seems, rather, to be taken over unthinkingly from Hartmann. Similarly, it is not until Wigalois's coronation that Erec, Iwein and Lanzelet appear. Gawein is invited to the festivity by letter, at the same time that he is informed that his son has recaptured Korntin (vv. 9561–71 and 9615–40). The way in which this reunion between father and son is structured (Gawein asks after the fate of Wigalois's mother, Florie, whom he had earlier abandoned) shows that Wirnt is more concerned here with family history than with any links with the Arthurian court. Not even the fact that at the end of the romance Wigalois and Larie and a large number of their followers spend a week at Nantes, visiting Arthur (vv. 11395–480), alters this emphasis in any appreciable way.

Wigalois is thus a hero who undergoes no crisis: Wirnt's romance is concerned not with a symbolic structure of success, crisis, self-affirmation and ultimate happiness, but with a hero who pursues his course with one-dimensional single-mindedness. Initially he does so unthinkingly (this is clear from his at times unintentional killing of his knightly adversaries in his first series of adventures), but as the challenges increase (the Korntin adventure is said to be 'like unto death itself', v. 1764), so he grows more and more self-aware and acts with increasing resolve, while relying on God's help (symbolized by his numerous supernatural aids) and inspired by Larie's love (which strengthens his resolve). By the end, he stands before the reader as a mature ruler over several kingdoms, with Wirnt repeatedly stressing what a good king he is (Wigalois orders his vassals to obey Carolingian law (vv. 9520–60) and to spare the lives of the inhabitants of Namur (vv. 11157–60), while his own benevolent reign is symbolized by post-war reconstruction in Korntin (vv. 11605–25)). As a result, the scene in which Wigalois recovers his senses by a lake, where he has been left by the dying dragon, and thinks that his former life was a dream, that he himself is 'loathsome' (v. 5831) and that his father was a peasant, whereupon his discovery of his bag containing his magic loaf plunges him further into despair (vv. 5802–57), should not be seen as analogous to the scene of Iwein's 'awakening', even though Wirnt evidently modelled his own account on Hartmann. It appears, rather, that Wirnt was keen to include this Arthurian motif in his narrative but was unable to invest it with a proper function. Hartmann's structure of the twofold path is replaced, therefore, with what is essentially a linear structure (Mertens 1981), but it is a framework which, far more than with Hartmann, is filled by the protagonist and his actions: Enite and Laudine have no counterpart with Wirnt; and Larie, who inspires Wigalois's deeds of valour and later marries him, plays a far less important role than Hartmann's womenfolk, remaining relatively colourless as a character, even though it is to serve her that Wigalois fights Roaz (vv. 7588–95) and even though he later sends her a letter (v. 8696) in which he reaffirms his love and announces that he has liberated her country (vv. 8759–79). Love is relativized in importance not least by the fact that, in fighting Wigalois, the heathen sorcerer Roaz is explicitly said to be serving his own wife, Japhite (vv. 7581–7), who feels the profoundest grief on his death and dies of a broken heart soon afterwards (vv. 7673–744); see also the narrator's comments in vv. 7745–52 and the posthumous paean to Japhite as a great lover who unfortunately died unbaptized (vv. 8017–37); see, finally, the description of her burial and the inscription on her grave (vv. 8227–89).

In general, *Wigalois* may be said to show an 'appropriation of the Arthurian narrative model' (Fuchs 1997, 213). Above all, however, Wirnt juxtaposes narrative elements and motivations of very different provenance, even when they do not belong together structurally or conceptually. The result is a 'multiplicity of motivation' and 'glaring contradictions':

Each time there is the suggestion that the various adventures in which the hero proves his worth as a knight may serve as the basis of an ethical discussion, the author immediately moves on, trumping what he has just said, because his hero has to play not only the role of the young Arthurian débutant but also that of the chosen, predeterminedly perfect redeemer who leads an unproblematical existence and, therefore, has no scruples . . . The hero is at once a knight who acts in the name of love, a fairy-tale Arthurian hero and an elect protagonist invested with religious traits. (Fuchs, 216)

In consequence, it is possible to speak of an 'overloading' ('Überdetermination') of the hero, resulting in a romance 'defined by the life of a single hero' (Fuchs 1997, 217f., 222).

If this conclusion reflects the unease that more recent scholars have felt with regard to *Wigalois* (earlier generations dismissed the romance as epigonic), it is clear from the poem's immense popularity in the High Middle Ages that contemporary audiences evidently did not share this unease. The following considerations can throw light on why *Wigalois* was evidently such an attractive read.

In comparison with Hartmann's romances, Wirnt's poem has a far more complicated plot and far more characters, scenes, narrative motifs and symbols, all of which create a highly colourful impression, even for today's reader. Attention has already been drawn to some of these features. Also worth mentioning here are the narrative episodes that are recounted with great attention to detail such as the one involving a fisherman and his wife who steal Wigalois's clothes as he lies unconscious following his fight with the dragon; the woman's first inclination is to kill him, but his physical beauty melts her heart. He is finally 'bought' by Beleare, the wife of Count Moral, whose lady-in-waiting had seen the fisherfolk drag Wigalois into their hut (vv. 5287–781). In general, these elements make the plot far more complex than that of any Hartmannesque romance: it contains far more episodes and motifs and is far less single-minded in its structure. In addition, Wirnt's list of characters includes not only the usual Arthurian entourage, but also a whole series of strange and fearsome figures, some of whom inhabit an exotic otherworld: here one thinks of King Lar, who, turned into a stag, helps Wigalois by acting as his guide and interpreter (vv. 4480–835), or of the monster Marrien, who is half beast and half man (vv. 6927–7027). The creation of an alternative world inhabited by monsters and devils (a world that will later be even more colourfully depicted by Der Stricker in *Daniel von dem blühenden Tal*) and the related profusion of narrative sequences and characters must have contributed substantially to the work's appeal. The result is a concentration on the individual scene and on what Fuchs terms an effectively staged 'dramatization' (1997, 214) that repeatedly loses sight of the hero's long-term objective of gaining a wife and country, but which none the less ensures a high degree of tension. Listeners, in particular, must have been drawn to a narrative method that is geared to the individual scene.

It is also worth stressing that Wirnt provides his characters with a vast panoply of magnificent armour, clothes and various other attributes, many of which are described in often elaborate detail. Especially notable in this context are the 'very tall round castle erected on an elephant' (vv. 10346–8) in which Larie takes part in the military expedition to Namur and the description of her clothes in this episode (vv. 10531–80).

Wirnt is especially fond of describing coats of arms, above all in the form of the turning wheel of fortune on King Joram's castle that signifies the king's success (vv. 1036–52). Later, as he sets out on his great adventure, Wigalois is armed with a shield that shows a gold wheel on a black field (vv. 1826–9). Gawein buckles on him a helmet on which 'a gold wheel' turns, and from now on he wears this symbol constantly to remind him of the wheel of fortune on Joram's castle (vv. 1860–9). In this way, it comes to symbolize his own good fortune, too. When Wigalois defeats the Red Knight and dispatches him and his lady to Arthur's court, Hojir is instructed to report that he has been defeated by 'the knight with the wheel' (v. 3103). Other coats of arms (and armour) that play a role in *Wigalois* include those belonging to Roimunt (vv. 3891–915, 10631f.), those of the knights killed by Roaz (vv. 4558–62), the arms of Glois that betoken heathendom by depicting Mohammed on a gold column on a lapis lazuli field (vv. 6567–76) and Roaz's own coat of arms (vv. 7363–6).

Wirnt's romance also features an extremely active narrator who intersperses the action with comments that relate critically to contemporary issues or to more general matters. When Wigalois defeats a giant and extracts from him a promise to accompany a maiden back to Arthur's court and not molest her on the way, the narrator interjects with a remark to the effect that at that time, unlike today, people who broke their word were cast out from society (vv. 2146–58). When Wigalois kills a knight and ties his horse to a bush, the narrator comments that horse and armour would nowadays be stolen, that men are made knights who are unworthy of the honour, and that 'the old laws' ('reht') have been lost (vv. 2319–48). The narrator also comments on the relationship between idleness and honour ('gemach' and 'êre'), for instance in the critique of sloth (*sich verligen*) in lines 2875–96, and on loyalty and falsehood, which, he notes, can be detected by looking the other person in the eyes (vv. 4244–69). The narrator additionally condemns bad women and praises good ones (vv. 5393–412; see also vv. 9697–715); he also discusses in a dialogue between himself and his own mind whether a man who has no possessions can be pleasing in the sight of his fellow human beings (vv. 5753–81); towards the end of the poem, he laments the world's disloyalty, brute force, treachery and greed, suggesting that the world's end is nigh, as in the days when God's mysteries were revealed to St John (vv. 10245–305); and finally in the Epilogue he laments the 'greed that causes ill feeling and malice' (vv. 10683–4). Even if these comments may be seen against the background of comparable remarks in Hartmann's works, their impact on the audience should not be underestimated, not least because they can be related to the poet's clear, if understated, emphasis on Wigalois's good and just rule. Although *Wigalois* may well, in its combination of diverse elements, be a 'syncretistic' work (Schröder 1986) with a 'hybrid' hero (Fuchs 1997), for listeners and readers of the thirteenth and fourteenth centuries its colour and narrative variety clearly made it an attractive work of considerable entertainment value.

Wigoleis vom Rade

That interest in *Wigalois* was still very much alive in the second half of the fifteenth century is clear from the fact that in 1493 the Augsburg printer Johann Schönsperger the Elder published a prose version of the text. This first printed edition was followed by a dozen others in a sequence reaching into the seventeenth century. In this way, *Wigoleis* was part of the wave of prose recensions of court epics wrongly described until recently as 'Volksbücher' (see Brandstetter 1971). Consciously concealing his own identity ('jch vngenant', Brandstetter 1971, 234, v. 38 and Melzer 1973, A ii^r, vv. 4–5), the adaptor explains that he has been asked by his aristocratic (and equally anonymous) patrons to tell 'the story (*histori*) of the much-praised knight, Sir Wigoleys of the Wheel, of whom the worthy man from Grafenberg [the German 'erwirdig' may also contain a pun on the name Wirnt] wrote and most prettily put into verse' (Brandstetter 1971, 234, vv. 35–8), turning it 'from rhyme into unrhymed prose' (Melzer 1973, A ii^r, v. 9), a task which, in view of his 'slight intelligence', he claims to have needed twelve years to complete (A ii^v, vv.3 and 14). If this is so, the adaptor must have started work on *Wigoleis* in 1481. Everyone, he goes on, who feels that he could improve on his work 'has the power and authority to change the words and put them in whatever form he likes', but he should 'leave the sense of the story untouched, as this already seems to me right' (Brandstetter 1971, 235, vv. 3–5).

The adaptor puts Wirnt's verse into readable and, its sometimes complex hypotactic structures notwithstanding, clear prose, bringing it into line with 'the changed formal and functional norms of a later and newer audience' (Cormeau 1978, 29) and making abundant use of direct speech. He reduces the text to a little more than a third of the original, without losing any essential aspects of the plot, but dispensing with 'the names of characters who appear in only a single episode, together with individual strands in the action (armour, coats of arms and legal acts) and parts of the rhetorical framework' as well as the whole idea of predestination on which Wirnt expatiates at such length (Ziegeler 1998a, 1069). Drawing on the tradition of biography that was becoming increasingly popular in the fifteenth century as well as on the tradition of historical writing, the adaptor clearly reworks the romance as a biography of its hero, Wigoleis, a reworking underlined by the emphasis placed on his personal attribute, the wheel of fortune.

As in other 'Volksbücher' of the fifteenth and sixteenth centuries, the text is divided into chapters, virtually all of which begin with a chapter heading printed in a larger type. In turn, these headings refer the reader to a woodcut that follows immediately afterwards and occupies around one-third of the page. For example, the scene in which the giantess Ruel binds Wigoleis and plans to kill him is introduced with the words: 'Here Sir Wigoleyß lies bound hand and foot and the evil woman Ruel makes to strike off his head.' The woodcut beneath it shows Wigoleis bound, with his armour (including the wheel of fortune) lying beside him. To the left of the picture is his horse, apparently on the point of whinnying and thereby saving his life by frightening away Ruel. To his right is the naked figure of Ruel, baring her boar's teeth and wielding a club with which to kill him (see facsimile in Melzer 1973, F i^v). Given the large number of headings and woodcuts (thirty-three headings and thirty-five woodcuts, including the title-page; five of the woodcuts are repeated), the text acquires the character of an illustrated sequence of scenes. These two features – the lucid structure and the illustrations – must have contributed in no small way to the continuing popularity of the subject and to its continuing reception in the repertoire of literary entertainment down to collections of romances such as Sigmund Feyerabend's *Buch der Liebe* of 1587 and Reichard's *Bibliothek der Romane* of 1778 (Cormeau 1978, 29).

In view of the popularity of *Wigoleis vom Rade*, it comes as no surprise to discover that a second adaptation of Wirnt's poem, the strophic *Floreis und Wigoleis* prepared by the Munich poet Ulrich Füetrer only a few years after Schönsperger's edition of 1493 and incorporated into his monumental *Buch der Abenteuer*, failed to find a publisher and circulated in only a handful of manuscript copies, some of them sumptuously produced. Here 'the text was made topical for members of the court and higher aristocracy as part of a historicist cultural programme' designed to 'reclaim the subject matter retrospectively' (Cormeau 1978, 30; on the *Buch der Abenteuer* see also Bastert, chapter 10 below).

Widuwilt

The continuing appeal of *Wigalois* is highlighted by a Yiddish version, *(Ritter) Widuwilt* or *(Kinig) Artus hof*, a version that may be as old as the fifteenth century and that is the only known Yiddish translation of an Arthurian romance. It survives in three sixteenth-century manuscripts and a number of printed versions from the seventeenth and eighteenth centuries. The sixteenth-century manuscripts 'point to northern Italy, then a centre for Yiddish literary production, as their place of origin' (Warnock 1996, 512); the later printed versions appeared in places further north (including Amsterdam, Königsberg, Hanau and Prague). The various versions may be divided into further subgroups by reference to their form and content. (One of them turns the usual rhyming pairs of *Knittelverse* into stanzas, while the rhymed-couplet versions form the basis of later prose versions; for full details, see Dreessen 1998, 1006 and especially Cormeau 1978, 30–1.) The hero's name, which has been changed from Wigalois to Widuwilt, is explained as follows: on leaving home, Giwein (= Gawein) tells his wife that their unborn child shall be called 'wi du wilt' ('as you like'; see Wolf 1974, 27, stanza 49, v. 12). The text appears to derive from Wirnt's romance, rather than – as one might have expected – from its prose recension. The unknown Jewish adaptor follows the plot of *Wigalois* in all its essential features, omitting only the Namur episode, cutting back his source to something over 4,000 lines and recounting the contents in a linguistically simple style, suggesting that he was a professional entertainer and that the work was performed within the context of some celebration such as a wedding. It ends with a wedding complicated by a 'double bridegroom' (Warnock 1981, 104 and 108). In the process, the author reveals certain idiosyncrasies, including a predilection for triadic elements (Dreessen 1998, 1007) and a tendency to demythologize and reduce tensions. In contrast to Wigalois, Widuwilt kills only giants and dragons, not humans. With its removal of explicitly Christian elements and its emphasis on the role of King Arthur, the work acquires a certain innocent, fairy-tale quality, imbued with comic elements, that continued to entertain listeners and readers until well into the eighteenth century, once again confirming the exceptional status of *Wigalois* within the German Arthurian tradition.

Bibliography

Primary Sources

Wirnt von Grafenberg, *Wigalois*

Wirnt von Grafenberg, *Wigalois der Ritter mit dem Rade.* Ed. by J. M. N. Kapteyn, 1926 (Rheinische Beiträge und Hülfsbücher zur germanischen Philologie und Volkskunde, 9). Bonn.

Wirnt von Grafenberg, *Wigalois, the Knight of Fortune's Wheel*. Transl. by J. W. Thomas, 1977. Lincoln, Nebr.

Wigoleis vom Rade

Text of the 1493 edition, Augsburg: Schönsperger, in Brandstetter 1971 (see Other Literature), 190–235.

Facsimile of the 1519 edition, Strasbourg: Johannes Knoblouch, in *Wigalois. Mit einem Vorwort von H. Melzer*, 1973 (Deutsche Volksbücher in Faksimiledrucken, A, 10). Hildesheim and New York.

Widuwilt

Widuwilt, in Landau, L., ed. 1912. *Hebrew-German Romances and Tales and their Relation to the Romantic Literature of the Middle Ages. Part I. Arthurian Legends or the Hebrew-German Rhymed Version of the Legend of King Arthur* (Teutonia 21), Leipzig.

Ritter Widuwilt. Die westjiddische Fassung des 'Wigalois' des Wirnt von Gravenberc. Nach dem jiddischen Druck von 1699. Ed. by S. A. Wolf, 1974. Bochum.

Other Literature

Brandstetter, A. 1971. *Prosaauflösung. Studien zur Rezeption der höfischen Epik im frühneuhochdeutschen Prosaroman*, Frankfurt.

Cormeau, Ch. 1977. *'Wigalois' und 'Diu Crone'. Zwei Kapitel zur Gattungsgeschichte des nachklassischen Artusromans*, Münchener Texte und Untersuchungen zur deutschen Literatur des Mittelalter, 57, Munich.

Cormeau, Ch. 1978. 'Die jiddische Tradition von Wirnts *Wigalois*', *LiLi*, 8, H. 32, 28–44.

Dreessen, W.-O. 1998. '*Widuwilt*', in *VL*, 10, 1006–8.

Fuchs, S. 1997. *Hybride Helden. Gwigalois und Willehalm*, Frankfurter Beiträge zur Germanistik, 31, Frankfurt.

Grubmüller, K. 1985. 'Artusroman und Heilsbringerethos. Zum *Wigalois* des Wirnt von Gravenberg', *PBB* (Tübingen), 107, 218–39.

Hilgers, H. 1971. 'Materialien zur Überlieferung von Wirnts *Wigalois*', *PBB* (Tübingen), 93, 228–88.

Honemann, V. 1994. '*Wigalois'* Kampf mit dem roten Ritter. Zum Verständnis der Hojir-Aventiure in Wirnts *Wigalois*', in Honemann et al. 1994 (see Gen. Bibl.), 347–62.

Huschenbett, D. 1982. 'Beschreibung der Bilder des *Wigalois*-Zyklus', in Haug et al. 1982 (see Gen. Bibl.), 170–7.

Kapteyn 1926. See Primary Sources, Wirnt von Grafenberg.

Melzer 1973. See Primary Sources, *Wigalois*, 1519 edn.

Mertens, V. 1981. 'Iwein und Gwigalois. Der Weg zur Landesherrschaft', *GRM* 31, 14–31.

Schiewer 1988. See Gen. Bibl.

Schneider, K. 1987. *Gotische Schriften in deutscher Sprache. I. Vom späten 12. Jahrhundert bis um 1300*, Wiesbaden.

Schröder, W. 1986. 'Der synkretistische Roman des Wirnt von Gravenberg. Unerledigte Fragen an den *Wigalois*', *Euph* 80, 235–77.

Thomas, N. 1987. *A German View of Camelot: Wirnt von Gravenberg's 'Wigalois' and Arthurian Tradition*, European University Studies, Ser. 1, 963, Berne.

Waldstein, E. K. 1982. 'Zeichnungen zum *Wigalois*-Zyklus', in Haug et al. 1982 (see Gen. Bibl.), 178–93.

Warnock, R. G. 1981. 'Wirkungsabsicht und Bearbeitungstechnik im altjiddsichen Artushof', *ZfdPh*, 100, Sonderheft, 98–109.

Warnock, R. G. 1996. '*Widuwilt*', in Lacy, N. J., ed., *The New Arthurian Encyclopedia*, revised
    edn, New York and London, 512f.
Wolf, 1974. See Primary Sources, *Ritter Widuwilt*.
Ziegeler, H.-J. 1998a. '*Wigoleis vom Rade*', in *VL* 10, 1067–70.
Ziegeler, H.-J. 1998b. 'Wirnt von Grafenberg', in *VL* 10, 1252–67.

9

THE RECEPTION OF PROSE:
THE *PROSA-LANCELOT*

Elizabeth A. Andersen

The thirteenth century saw a further development in the popular Arthurian romance in Old French literature. Romancers fused the two existing genres of Arthurian literature, the pseudo-historical tradition and the verse romance. They welded together figures, episodes and motifs from discrete works and of new invention into a coherent narrative and encased this in a chronicle framework. The voluminous and panoramic prose romance was, however, not merely a *summa*, for it interpreted the Arthurian material from a new and radically different perspective. The greatest example of these Arthurian cycles is the one thought to have been composed between 1215 and 1235 and known variously as the Vulgate Cycle, the Lancelot-Grail or the Pseudo-Map Cycle (the text purports to be the work of Walter Map, Archdeacon of Oxford, d. 1209, whose patron was ostensibly Henry II of England, d. 1189). In its fullest version, preserved in only six manuscripts, the Vulgate Cycle consists of five romances. The *Lancelot del Lac*, the *Queste del Saint Graal* and the *Mort le Roi Artu* form the oldest part of the cycle and are often known collectively as the *Lancelot en prose*, though some scholars use this term for the first of these three sections only. The later additions of the *Estoire del Saint Graal* and the *Estoire de Merlin* have a prefatory function for the *Lancelot en prose* within the context of the cycle. The former gives an account of the early history of the Grail and links it with that of Lancelot's ancestors. The latter recounts the life of the magician Merlin and the history of Arthur's reign down to Lancelot's birth. The survival of over 100 manuscripts, dating from the thirteenth through to the fifteenth century (Micha 1960, 1963), testifies to the popularity of the Old French *Lancelot en prose*. Furthermore, it appeared in print in seven editions between 1488 and 1533 before interest in the work flagged.

Only the trilogy of the *Lancelot en prose* was translated into German. The *Prosa-Lancelot* did not enjoy the popularity of its Old French source and has survived in only ten manuscripts which date from the thirteenth to the sixteenth centuries (Kluge 1948 I, XIV–LIII). Nor was it taken up by the newly invented printing presses of the fifteenth century. Kluge based his three-volume edition of the *Prosa-Lancelot* on P (Heidelberg, Codex Palatinus Germanicus 147), the first entire manuscript in German, which, although not completed until the fifteenth century, shows evidence of being based, at least in part, on a translation dating from the thirteenth century. The only other complete version in German, the Bavarian manuscript a (Bibliothèque de l'Arsenal, Paris), is a translation from the sixteenth century which does not follow the same source as P (Steinhoff 1995, 770–3). Kluge's volumes correspond to the three 'books' of P as they appear in the codex; *Lancelot* I and II comprise the so-called *Lancelot* proper and *Lancelot* III the *Gral-Queste* and the *Tod des König Artus*.

Research has revealed a complex picture of the relationship of P to the Old French text. Linguistic analyses and the lacuna (about one-tenth of the trilogy) between *Lancelot* I and *Lancelot* II have led to the conclusion that the translation into German was not executed at one time, and neither was there one source manuscript (Keinästö 1986a, 90–101). The existence of the thirteenth-century manuscripts M and A vouch for the antiquity of *Lancelot* I, thought to have been translated around 1250. It is now generally accepted that Lancelot I had as its source text a Middle Dutch version of the *Lancelot en prose* (Tilvis 1951; Steinhoff 1968; chapter 12 below). Three extant Middle Dutch adaptations of the *Lancelot en prose* are evidence of the widespread interest in this material in the Netherlands, although none of these manuscripts can be regarded as the source for the Middle High German *Lancelot* I (Lie 1987, 404–18). There is not the same compelling evidence of a Dutch source for the *Lancelot* II and *Lancelot* III (Steinhoff 1995, 766). Evidence of a later phase of translation is provided by the fourteenth-century fragments m and w which contain material from the *Lancelot* II section. The lack of earlier manuscripts for the *Lancelot* II suggests that this part of the trilogy was perhaps translated for the first time in the fifteenth century (Keinästö 1986b, 287–95). It has proved impossible to establish a clear stemma for the extant Old French manuscripts (Kennedy 1980, II, 11; Micha, 1962, 99–106) and, consequently, for the relationship of P to the Old French source. Extant long and short versions of the False Guinevere episode, the death of Galahot and the Cart episode have led to controversy about the possible existence of a non-cyclic version which was later expanded into the full-blown *Lancelot en prose* (Kennedy 1986). In the Middle High German *Lancelot* proper the narrative from the *Falsche Ginover* to the *Karrenritter* episode (L I, 482–633) follows the Old French long version, but the section entitled *Galahots Tod* and the *Karrenritter* episode follow the short version. Although knowledge of the precise channels of transmission of the Old French text remains obscure, there is a growing consensus that P was executed between 1455 and 1475. A Rhenish Franconian manuscript of 1476, k, provides circumstantial evidence that P might have been translated for Friedrich I, known as 'the Victorious', who presided over the Heidelberg court from 1449 to 1476, or perhaps for his sister the Archduchess Mechthild of Rottenburg (Beckers 1986).

The identity of the German translators is as unknown to us as that of the Old French author(s). However, the clear influence of Cistercian thought in the trilogy and the use of prose might point to Cistercian circles, perhaps to the monasteries of Gottesthal in the Duchy of Limburg, Heisterbach in the Siebengebirge and Himmerod in the southern Eifel (Steinhoff 1995, 768).

Although Germanists have undertaken much research on the basis of Kluge's edition, there has been some disquiet amongst scholars (Heinzle 1986, 8) about the extent to which the *Prosa-Lancelot*, a translation rather than an adaptation, may be considered a work of German literature, and thus whether it can be regarded as a proper subject for literary analysis. The *Lancelot en prose* purports to be the transcription and translation by Walter Map of the adventures of Arthur's knights, as Arthur had them recorded by his clerks. This claim to historicity, the absence of the original author's identity, the concept of Walter Map as the second transmitter of the histories of Arthur's knights, together with the familiarity of the source material, probably encouraged readers to regard the work as a common heritage. That the *Lancelot en prose* was a text particularly susceptible to scribal intervention has been established by the thorough examination of the manuscripts undertaken by Kennedy (1980, II, 10). Just as the scribes were not passive transmitters, so the German translator(s) appear to have had a relatively independent attitude (Buschinger 1986). The protean quality, vitality and continuity of the Arthurian tradition are reflected in the history of the text of the *Lancelot* trilogy. The scribes and, in the case of the German version, the scribe-translators were faithful to the bedrock of the original romance, but they did not hesitate to exploit the potential for original variation allowed them by the conventions of the time. The Middle High German text may be regarded as a variant (and in part an early one) of the original within the scribal tradition of Old French manuscripts. Germanists in the early years of research on the *Prosa-Lancelot* regarded the quality of the translation of the *Lancelot* I as grounds for treating it as a literary work in its own right (e.g. Ruh 1970, 242–44). Since the publication of *Lancelot* II and III closer analysis of the text has revealed that the quality of translation is variable in the trilogy (Steinhoff 1995, 773f.). In recent research there has been a growing insistence that the Middle High German text must be read in conjunction with the Old French (e.g. Unzeitig-Herzog 1990, 15; Reil 1996, 8–11).

Prose and anonymity became the hallmarks of those Old French Arthurian romances which incorporated the chronicle tradition of Arthurian history, the tales of individual knights and the history of the Grail. The use of prose was undoubtedly partly a response to a movement in contemporary historiography to distance itself from the fiction of verse (Haug 1978, 77–82). The *Prosa-Lancelot* encompasses the history of Artus's reign, the development and decline of the company of the Round Table, the salvation-history of the Grail and how the quest for it was achieved. Within this broad canvas the focus of the narrative is determined largely by the career of Lancelot.[1]

The trilogy relates how Lancelot's father, King Ban, is driven from his kingdom by Claudas, king of the 'Wúst Lant' (Waste Land), how Lancelot is brought up by the Lady of the Lake and how, when he is knighted at Artus's court, he falls irrevocably in love with Queen Ginover. Once Lancelot has been knighted, the narrative follows his exploits and relates how he discovers his name in achieving the adventure of the 'Dolorose Garde' ('Dolorous Guard'). Galahot, the lord of the 'Fremden Einlande' ('Foreign Isles') invades Artus's kingdom. His aggression towards Artus is halted by the admiration he feels for Lancelot, with whom he develops a remarkable friendship. He is instrumental in bringing about the consummation of Lancelot and Ginover's love. At the request of the queen, Lancelot becomes a member of the Round Table and he is successful in a great number of adventures. As the best knight of the Round Table, he is a constant and invaluable support to Artus in his battles against invading foes. Artus helps Lancelot to win back his patrimony from Claudas. The quest for the Grail is initiated, but Lancelot, although originally destined to be the Grail winner, is unsuccessful because of his sinful relationship with the queen. However, his son Galaad achieves what Lancelot could not. Once the quest for the Grail has been completed, attention is focused on Artus's court. The discovery of Lancelot's adultery with the queen triggers off the sequence of events which disrupts the fellowship of the Round Table and causes Artus's downfall.

It is Lancelot's love for Ginover which is the mainspring of his life. This love is characterized by its inherent ambivalence. On the one hand, it inspires Lancelot to great deeds which benefit King Artus and the Round Table. On the other, it is a constant threat to the very heart of the Arthurian world, a threat which is eventually realized. The delineation of this love illustrates the prose romancer's characteristic and creative use of existing literary paradigms. Lancelot's love for Ginover is a subtle and yet distinctive blend of the three literary models of love in Old French literature of the twelfth century, 'fin' amors', 'amour courtois' and the love characterized by Tristan and Isolde's relationship (Remakel 1995, 57–62).

The three constituent parts of the *Prosa-Lancelot* are all markedly different in content, tone and spirit. The *Lancelot* proper is the largest (it is three times the combined length of the *Gral-Queste* and the *Tod des König Artus*) and the most diversified. On a first reading, the *Lancelot* proper bewilders with its multiplicity of knights and their adventures. However, the majority of knights whose presence is constant in the entire work and who advance the action belong to one of two kin groups, either to the House of King Ban or that of King Artus. Contact between the Houses is established through two channels, a feudal relationship and non-hierarchical membership of the Round Table. Throughout the trilogy, Lancelot, the son of King Ban, and Gawan, the nephew of King Artus, are the leading protagonists around whom the knights of their respective kin are grouped. Gawan has three brothers, Agravain, Gaheries and Guerrehes, who are balanced by a similar constellation round Lancelot, for Lancelot has close and loyal companions in his two cousins, Lionel and Bohort, and his half-brother Hector. Kinship is one of the major organizing principles of the *Prosa-Lancelot*. This structural principle is, furthermore, a thematic one, for the *Prosa-Lancelot*, in its broadest terms, is about the impact of Ban's lineage with its Grail connections on the world of Arthurian chivalry.

The narrative space of the *Lancelot* proper is such that there is room to explore in considerable detail the ties of kinship, friendship and love, the implications of the secular code of chivalry, the fellowship of the Round Table, the legal obligations of the feudal relationship between vassal and overlord and the nature of territorial aggression. The focus of the narrative is largely concentrated on the career of Lancelot – his disinheritance by Claudas, his overwhelming love for Ginover, his friendship with Galahot, his services to Artus, his conduct as a knight, his membership of the Round Table, his relations with his kin and his fathering of Galaad, the Grail winner. The events of Lancelot's life are related as a series of adventures, which are interwoven with those of his kin and the knights of the Round Table within a narrative pattern of quests, tournaments and battles.

The broad canvas of the *Lancelot* proper is supplanted in the *Gral-Queste* by the concentration of the narrative on one quest only – that for the Grail. The values of secular chivalry in the *Lancelot* proper, subsumed from the verse romances and given further definition by the Lady of the Lake (L I, 120–4), are superseded by those of an ascetic and mystic religious chivalry. The romance is concerned solely with the adventures of the Round Table knights as they attempt to achieve the quest for the Grail. The degree of their success is seen to be in proportion to the extent of their spiritual virtue and awareness. In the exegeses of the omnipresent hermits, chastity, humility, patience, justice and love of one's neighbour emerge as the criteria against which the activity of the knights is assessed. Lancelot's success in the quest can only be partial, but his bastard son, Galaad, eventually completes the quest with Perceval and Bohort, Lancelot's cousin, in attendance.

In the *Lancelot* proper we learn that the Round Table was founded for the express purpose of achieving the quest for the Grail. With the completion of this quest its function is at an end and in the *Tod des König Artus* there are no further adventures or quests in the Kingdom of Logres. The absence of these results in the more constant presence of the Round Table knights at Artus's court. Consequently, tensions that exist within the community of the Round Table, most notably the adulterous love of Lancelot and the queen, become more apparent and eventually trigger a series of events which wreck the harmonious but fragile fellowship of knights. A blood feud between Lancelot and Gawan, territorial aggression by the Romans and treason on the part of Artus' bastard and incestuous son, Mordret, culminate in the downfall of Artus and the destruction of the Round Table fellowship.

The intertwining of the life of Lancelot, the history of the Grail and the history of Artus's reign, provides the broad parameters within which the diverse episodes of the narrative are realized, but the interlinking of the three romances is not merely achieved by a common framework and common *dramatis personae*. The skill with which the prose romancer has harmonized so many diverse elements of the rich Arthurian material and created a coherence and cohesion of themes has fascinated researchers. Lot (1954) recognized the two fundamental narrative devices in the *Lancelot en prose* as being the 'principe d'entrelacement' and the 'procédé du chronologique'. Together these determine the form and explicate the meaning of the trilogy. The attention to chronological detail ensures the temporal progression of the narrative, and in doing so underpins the greater sense of history as conveyed by the framework of Lancelot's biography, the chronicle of Arthur's reign and the typological perspective of the Grail legend. In addition to the prominence given to the recording of the passage of time in the *Prosa-Lancelot*, the whole work is bound together by a complex system of recalling and foreshadowing, of dream vision and predestination, of prophecy and fulfilment (Ruberg 1965, 184f.). Genealogy is also used as an effective poetic resource, linking the early history of the Grail with the Arthurian world. The acentric principle of interlacing allows an apparently simultaneous exposition of events; the adventures of various knights, the interaction of a number of contexts and levels of narrative reality are interwoven in such a way as to produce an intricate polyphony of action and meaning (Lewis 1966, 133). This narrative technique facilitates thematic development by analogy. An understanding of how this aspect of interlacing functions has become one of the interpretative keys to the *Lancelot* trilogy (Vinaver 1971, 105). Analysis of the structure of the *Prosa-Lancelot* reveals that the myriad of sub-plots reflect and explore further the central themes of the trilogy. Thus, issues raised by the complexities of Lancelot's relations with the king and queen and his fathering of the Grail winner are made fundamental to the portrayal of other main protagonists in the narrative (Andersen 1986 and 1990).

Narrative shape is given to the multifarious events of the *Prosa-Lancelot* by structuring them within a rhythm of quests, tournaments and battles. In the *Lancelot* proper the individual adventures of various knights are grouped together within shared quests (Ruberg 1963). The quests, essentially an individualistic exercise, are interrupted by and interspersed with the collective gatherings of tournaments and battles. Once the Grail has been achieved there are no further adventures and no quests in the Kingdom of Logres. Consequently, in the *Tod des König Artus* individual chivalric activity virtually ceases and the action unfolds in court, tournament and battle scenes.

Although the *Prosa-Lancelot* purports to be the work of Walter Map, authorial activity is apparently limited to the role of a scribe. The trilogy is ostensibly an accurate account of events, and needs no reference beyond itself and, in the case of the *Gral-Queste*, the Latin chronicle of which it is supposed to be a translation, to substantiate its truthfulness. The timeless world of the verse romances has been superseded by a world subject to the laws of history, and the identity of the author has disappeared behind the persona of the objective chronicler (Ruberg 1965, 135). Research into the identity of the narrator's voice in the *Lancelot* trilogy has revealed a complex fiction built around the 'author' of the narrative (Leupin 1939).

The question of the authorship of the *Lancelot* trilogy has been fundamental to the direction research has taken. Lot (1954, 107) and Micha (1961, 357 and 365) concluded that a single author was responsible for the entire work, whereas Pauphilet (1950, 212–17) saw a fundamental split in the Vulgate Cycle. He grouped together the *Queste del Saint Graal* and the *Estoire del Saint Graal* on the one hand and the *Lancelot* proper and the *Mort le Roi Artu* on the other. Frappier's (1961, 122–46) compromise solution of an 'architect' who probably wrote the *Lancelot* proper (or at least the greater part of it), while two collaborators wrote the *Queste del Saint Graal* and the *Mort le Roi Artu* respectively has been most widely accepted by Romanists and Germanists alike (Ruberg 1985, 533).

Interpretations of the *Prosa-Lancelot* as a coherent and consistent work of art have been complicated by the striking antinomy between the courtly chivalric ethic of the *Lancelot* proper, as evolved in the Arthurian verse romances, and the ascetic, religious and chivalric ethic, as expounded in the *Gral-Queste*. Where Lot was content to accept this 'double esprit' as 'inhérente au moyen âge' (1954, 106), two conflicting models of interpretation have emerged amongst Germanists. The dualist approach (Voß 1970) sees in the trilogy an unavoidable clash of mutually exclusive value-systems. The gradualist approach (Steinhoff 1977) interprets the chivalric code of the *Gral-Queste* as the typological successor to the secular chivalry of the Arthurian world, expressed through the portrayal of the adulterous Lancelot as the father of the chaste Grail winner Galaad. Both these schools of thought place the *Gral-Queste* at the centre of their inquiries. In more recent research there has been a move away from regarding the *Gral-Queste* as the pivotal section of the trilogy (e.g. Ehlert 1986; Huber 1991, 37). Instead, there has been more interest in attempting an inclusive interpretation of the whole work which demonstrates a conceptual unity for the trilogy (Remakel 1995; Reil 1996). The summative nature of the *Prosa-Lancelot* has fostered an interest in the poetological dynamics of the trilogy. From this angle the finality of the downfall of the Arthurian world in the *Tod des König Artus* may be interpreted as an intended conclusion to a literary tradition. The reworking of the conventions of the verse romance according to the different emphases of the prose romance, particularly evident in the shaping of Chrétien's *Chevalier de la Charrette*, culminates in the 'Auserzählen', the 'telling to an end', of the material (Unzeitig-Herzog 1990, 173–5; Haug 1995).

The Arthurian prose romance continued to flourish in Old French literature despite this poetological conclusion. However, the *Prosa-Lancelot*, as it was translated in the thirteenth century, remained the sole prose romance in German literature until the late fifteenth century. It has generally been regarded as an anomaly (e.g. Wehrli 1980, 499; Heinzle 1984a, 223f.), standing 'at the head of a discontinuous tradition of prose romance' (Blamires 1986, 68). However, within the German context the contemporary use of prose in religious writing and the writing of world histories may provide a broader literary context against which the phenomenon of the *Prosa-Lancelot* may be more properly assessed (Heinzle 1984b, 110).

The Lancelot legend does not appear to have taken root in German soil in the way it did in France, the Netherlands and England. The lack of resonance of the Lancelot material in the German-speaking world has been attributed to a number of factors that were peculiar to the German development of Arthurian romance (Blank 1993, 134–6). The fact that the *Prosa-Lancelot* did not achieve the popularity of its Old French source, and that it did not exercise a corresponding influence on the development of Arthurian literature in Germany, must be in part attributable to the pre-eminence of the Grail tradition as developed by Wolfram von Eschenbach (Thomas 1994, 29–33) and to the masterly exploration of adulterous love by Gottfried von Strassburg in his version of the Tristan story. Differing socio-political circumstances amongst the German ruling class may also account to some extent for the apparent lack of interest in the *Prosa-Lancelot* (Remakel 1995, 226–7). And, at the end of the day, this most central of European Arthurian texts is in German a translation rather than an adaptation of French sources, as the works of Hartmann von Aue, Gottfried von Strassburg and Wolfram von Eschenbach are.

In *c.* 1467 Ulrich Füetrer produced an abridged prose version of the *Prosa-Lancelot*, and some twenty years later he recast the material in strophic form, modifying it to agree with the sequence of events as related in his Arthurian compendium, the *Buch der Abenteuer*. These works of Füetrer are the only extant literary successors to the magnificent *Lancelot* trilogy in German.

Note

1 Bruce 1923, 2, 308–79 provides a detailed plot summary.

Bibliography

Primary Sources and Translations

The Non-cyclic *Lancelot en prose*
Lancelot do Lac: The Non-cyclic Old French Prose Romance, 2 vols. (I: Text; II: Introduction, Bibliography, Notes and Variants, Glossary and Index of Proper Names). Ed. by E. Kennedy, 1980. Oxford.

The Cyclic *Lancelot en prose*
The Vulgate Version of the Arthurian Romances, 8 vols. Ed. by H. O. Sommer, 1909–16. Washington.
Lancelot. Roman en prose du XIIIe siècle, 9 vols. Ed. by A. Micha, 1978–83 (Textes littéraires français, 247, 249, 262, 278, 283, 286, 288, 307, 315). Geneva and Paris.
La Queste del Saint Graal. Ed. by A. Pauphilet, 1984 (CFMA, 33), 2nd edn. Paris.
La Mort le roi Artu. Ed. by J. Frappier, 1964 (TLF 58), 3rd edn. Geneva and Paris.
Lancelot of the Lake. Transl. by C. Corley, 1989 (The World's Classics). Oxford and New York.
The Quest of the Holy Grail. Transl. by P. Matarasso, 1969 (Penguin Classics). Harmondsworth.
The Death of King Arthur. Transl. by J. Cable, 1971 (Penguin Classics). Harmondsworth.

Prosa-Lancelot
L= *Lancelot. Nach der Heidelberger Pergamenthandschrift Pal. Germ. 147*, 3 vols. Ed. by R. Kluge, 1948, 1963, 1974 (Deutsche Texte des Mittelalters, 42, 47, 63). Berlin.
Lancelot und Ginover [*Prosalancelot*], 2 vols. Ed. and transl. by H.-H. Steinhoff, 1995 (Bibliothek des Mittelalters, 14, 15). Frankfurt. (This edition includes only the *Lancelot* proper.)

Middle Dutch Prose *Lancelot*
Lie, O. S. H. 1987. *The Middle Dutch Prose Lancelot: A Study of the Rotterdam Fragments and their Place in the French, German and Dutch Lancelot en prose Tradition. With an edition of the text* (Middelnederlandse Lancelotromans, 3). Amsterdam, Oxford and New York.

Other Literature

Andersen, E. A. 1986. 'Väter und Söhne im Prosa-Lancelot', WSt, 9, 213–27.
Andersen, E. A. 1990. 'Brothers and cousins in the German Prose *Lancelot*', *FMLS*, 26, 144–59.
Beckers, H. 1986. ' "Der püecher haubet, die von der Tafelrunde wunder sagen". Wirich von Stein und die Verbreitung des *Prosa-Lancelot* im 15. Jahrhundert', WSt, 9, 17–45.
Blamires, D. 1986. 'The German Arthurian prose romances in their literary context', in Adams A., ed., *The Changing Face of Arthurian Romance. Essays on Arthurian Prose Romances in Memory of Cedric E. Pickford*, Woodbridge, 66–77.
Blank, W. 1993. 'Zu den Schwierigkeiten der Lancelot-Rezeption in Deutschland', in Jones and Wisbey 1993 (see Gen. Bibl.), 121–36.
Bruce, J. D. 1923. *The Evolution of Arthurian Romance from the Beginnings down to the Year 1300*, 2 vols., Göttingen.

Buschinger, D. 1986. 'Zum Verhältnis des deutschen Prosa-Lancelot zur altfranzösischen Vorlage', WSt, 9, 46–89.

Ehlert, T. 1986. 'Normenkonstituierung und Normenwandel im Prosa-Lancelot', WSt, 9, 102–18.

Frappier, J. 1961. *Etude sur la Mort le Roi Artu, roman du XIIIe siècle, dernière partie du Lancelot en prose*, 2nd edn, Geneva and Paris.

Haug, W. 1978. '*Das Land von welchem niemand wiederkehrt'. Mythos, Fiktion und Wahrheit in Chrétien's 'Chevalier de la Charrete', im 'Lanzelet' Ulrichs von Zatzikhoven und im 'Lancelot'-Prosaroman*, Untersuchungen zur deutschen Literaturgeschichte, 21, Tübingen.

Haug, W. 1995. 'Das Endspiel der arthurischen Tradition im Prosalancelot', in Haug, *Brechungen auf dem Weg zur Individualität. Kleine Schriften zur Literatur des Mittelalters*, Tübingen, 288–300.

Heinzle, J. 1984a. *Vom hohen zum späten Mittelalter. Teil 2: Wandlungen und Neuansätze im 13. Jahrhundert (1220/30–1280/90)*, Geschichte der deutschen Literatur von den Anfängen bis zum Beginn der Neuzeit, II, 2, Königstein.

Heinzle, J. 1984b. 'Zur Stellung des Prosa-Lancelot in der deutschen Literatur des 13. Jahrhunderts', in Wolfzettel 1984 (see Gen. Bibl.), 104–13.

Heinzle, J. 1986. 'Einleitung' (= introduction to volume of papers from the Schweinfurt *Lancelot* Colloquium, 1984), WSt, 9, 7–9.

Huber, C. 1991. 'Von der "Gral-Queste" zum "Tod des König Artus". Zum Einheitsproblem des "Prosa-Lancelot"', in Haug and Wachinger 1991 (see Gen. Bibl.), 21–38.

Keinästo, K. 1986a. 'Zu Infinitivkonstruktionen und Übersetzungsschichten im mittelhochdeutschen Prosa-Lancelot', WSt, 9, 90–101.

Keinästo, K. 1986b. *Studien zu Infinitivkonstruktionen im mittelhochdeutschen Prosa-Lancelot*, Frankfurt.

Kennedy, E. 1980. See Primary Sources, *Lancelot do Lac*, ed. E. Kennedy.

Kennedy, E. 1986. *Lancelot and the Grail: A Study of the Prose Lancelot*, Oxford.

Kluge, R. 1948. See Primary Sources, *Lancelot*, ed. R. Kluge.

Leupin, A. 1939. 'Narrateurs et scripteurs dans la Vulgate "Arthurienne"', *Digraphe*, 20, 83–109.

Lewis, C. S. 1966. *Studies in Medieval and Renaissance Literature*, Cambridge.

Lie, O. S. H. 1987. See Primary Sources, *The Middle Dutch Prose Lancelot*, ed. O. S. H. Lie.

Lot, F. 1954. *Etude sur le Lancelot en prose*, 2nd edn, Paris.

Micha, A. 1960; 1963. 'Les manuscrits du *Lancelot en prose*', *Rom*, 81, 145–87; 84, 28–60, 478–99.

Micha, A. 1961. 'Etudes sur le *Lancelot en prose*. II. L'Esprit du *Lancelot-Graal*', *Rom*, 82, 357–78.

Micha, A. 1962. 'Tradition manuscrite et versions du *Lancelot en prose*', *BBIAS*, 14, 99–106.

Pauphilet, A. 1921. *Etudes sur la Queste del Saint Graal, attribuée à Gautier Map*, Paris (repr. Paris 1968).

Pauphilet, A. 1950. *Le Legs du Moyen Age*, Melun.

Reil. C. 1996. *Liebe und Herrschaft. Studien zum altfranzösischen und mittelhochdeutschen Prosa-Lancelot*, Tübingen.

Remakel, M. 1995. *Rittertum zwischen Minne und Gral. Untersuchungen zum mittelhochdeutschen Prosa-Lancelot*, Mikrokosmos, 42, Frankfurt, Berlin, Berne.

Ruberg, U. 1963. 'Die Suche im Prosa-Lancelot', *ZfdA*, 92, 122–57.

Ruberg, U. 1965. *Raum und Zeit im Prosa-Lancelot*, Medium Aevum, 9, Munich.

Ruberg, U. 1985. 'Lancelot' ('Lancelot-Gral-Prosaroman'), in *VL*, V, 530–46.

Ruh, K. 1970. 'Lancelot', in Wais, K., ed., *Der arthurische Roman*, WdF, 157, Darmstadt, 237–55.

Steinhoff, H.-H. 1968. 'Zur Entstehungsgeschichte des deutschen Prosa-Lancelot', in Ganz, P. F. and Schröder, W., eds., *Probleme mittelalterlicher Überlieferung und Textkritik. Oxforder Colloquium 1966*, Berlin, 81–95.

Steinhoff, H.-H. 1977. 'Artusritter und Gralsheld. Zur Bewertung des höfischen Rittertums im *Prosa-Lancelot*', in Scholler, H., ed., *The Epic in Medieval Society: Aesthetic and Moral Values*, Tübingen, 271–89.

Steinhoff, H.-H. 1995. See Primary Sources, *Prosa-Lancelot. Lancelot und Ginover.*

Thomas, N. 1994. 'The reception of the Prose *Lancelot* in France and Germany: a contest between visible and invisible worlds', in Maber, R., ed., *Nouveaux Mondes from the Twelfth to the Twentieth Century*, Durham French Colloquies, 4, Durham, 19–36.

Tilvis, P. 1951. 'Mittelniederländisches im Prosa-Lancelot I', *NM*, 52, 195–205.

Unzeitig-Herzog, M. 1990. *Jungfrauen und Einsiedler. Studien zur Organisation der Aventiurewelt im Prosalancelot*, Heidelberg.

Vinaver, E. 1971. *The Rise of Romance*, Oxford.

Voß, R. 1970. *Der Prosa-Lancelot. Eine strukturanalytische und strukturvergleichende Studie auf der Grundlage des deutschen Textes* [I+II], Deutsche Studien, 12, Meisenheim am Glan.

Wehrli, M. 1980. *Geschichte der deutschen Literatur vom frühen Mittelalter bis zum Ende des 16. Jahrhunderts*, Stuttgart.

10

LATE MEDIEVAL SUMMATIONS: *RAPPOLTSTEINER PARZIFAL* AND ULRICH FÜETRER'S *BUCH DER ABENTEUER*

Bernd Bastert

At first glance it may appear as if interest in Arthurian literature had all but died out in the final two centuries of the Middle Ages in Germany. Although the work of Hartmann, Wolfram or Wirnt von Grafenberg that had been written in the twelfth and thirteenth centuries continued to be copied and read, there seems to have been a lack of outstanding writers to take up and recast the Arthurian material. The only two Arthurian romances of the fourteenth and fifteenth centuries that emerged in German-speaking countries are a case in point. The first is an almost word-for-word translation from French sources which was incorporated into an already existing German work (the *Rappoltsteiner Parzifal*, from the first half of the fourteenth century); the second consists of an abridged adaptation and compilation of several older German Arthurian romances from the classical and so-called post-classical periods (the *Buch der Abenteuer*, from the latter part of the fifteenth century). The authors concerned are not considered to be particularly original writers; and it was this lack of originality that has until recently prevented literary critics, schooled in a modern aesthetic of individual creativity, from taking a greater interest in work considered as merely derivative.

Furthermore, German historians have long viewed the later Middle Ages as a time of crisis and decline for the nobility, trapped as they were between the rising wealthy towns on the one side and the concentration of power in the hands of sovereign princes on the other. This loss of political and economic influence was further accelerated by the invention of gunpowder and the subsequent decline in the military importance of knighthood. The alleged political, economic and military crisis found its counterpart in the apparently crisis-prone Arthurian romance, the aristocratic literary form *par excellence*, and its creative deficiencies. The romances that did emerge in the fourteenth and fifteenth centuries were thus of interest only as indicators of the so-called 'chivalric revival' which was described impressively by Johan Huizinga in his influential study, *The Waning of the Middle Ages,* as a nostalgic and highly idealistic longing on the part of the nobility for a golden age that had disappeared.

This view has been revised. It is now thought that the nobility did not in general lose their political influence, their economic power or their military function. Although this may, indeed, have happened in some cases, in others individual nobles or entire families profited from the situation and increased their social prestige and wealth. Similarly, literary scholarship has revalued the late medieval romances on the basis of advances in narratological theory and a deeper insight into the production and reception of medieval literature. They are no longer dismissed as mere imitations, but are seen as independent treatments of the original romance genre as found in the works of Chrétien, Hartmann or Wolfram and, therefore, as worthy of scholarly attention. The romances of the thirteenth century, such as *Wigalois, Daniel, Diu Crône* and others, have already been the subject of intensive scholarly analysis employing new and more adequate categorizations. Although the *Rappoltsteiner Parzifal* and the *Buch der Abenteuer* have not yet received the same degree of attention, the increasing number of studies and new editions of the works that have appeared in recent years signal a similar change in attitude.

Rappoltsteiner Parzifal

The *Rappoltsteiner Parzifal* (*RP*) – also called, somewhat misleadingly, *Niuwer Parzifal*[1] – has been preserved in two manuscripts from the fourteenth century. One manuscript, formerly in Donaueschingen (Hs. 97) and now in the Baden State Library in Karlsruhe, is considered to be an 'original manuscript' on the basis of its careful editing and its use of dialect features; as such, it would represent the only original example of a courtly epic from the thirteenth and fourteenth centuries. Another manuscript generally regarded as a copy of the Karlsruhe text is held in the Bibliotheca Casatanense in Rome (MS 1409); it comprises only the second half of the work, the *Perceval* supplements as translated from the French, whereas the first part, which consists largely of Books I to XIV from Wolfram's *Parzival* and which is part of the Karlsruhe manuscript, is missing (Wittman-Klemm 1977, 1–9).

Critical attention has mainly focused on the Epilogue of the *Rappoltsteiner Parzifal*, on account of its uniquely detailed information on the origin of the text. According to the Epilogue, the romance was written between 1331 and 1336 and was commissioned by a certain Ulrich von Rappoltstein (hence *Rappoltsteiner Parzifal*), who appears to have been a member of a wealthy and influential aristocratic family whose ancestral castle was situated close to present-day Ribeauvillé, about fifty kilometres south of Strasbourg. It is, however, impossible to establish with certainty the identity of this 'von Rapoltzstein Uolriche' (*RP* 858, 4). There are, in fact, three members of the family who might

have been the person in question. Ulrich von Rappoltstein V (documented
1310–45) had studied in Bologna and was a canon in Strasbourg. A relative of
his, Ulrich von Rappoltstein VI (documented 1313–33), was commander of the
Knights of St John of Jerusalem in Dorlisheim (about twenty kilometres east of
Strasbourg). Ulrich von Rappoltstein VII, first mentioned in 1337, was a canon
in Basle, and after 1348 was referred to as Herr zu Rappoltstein ('Lord of
Rappoltstein'); around 1350 he married a Duchess of Fürstenberg, whose name,
Herzelaude, was the same as that of Parzival's mother. A daughter of this
marriage was also called Herzelaude (Schorbach 1888, XXII–XXIV), and most
scholars, doubtless motivated by this correspondence of real and fictional
names, have opted for Ulrich von Rappoltstein VII as the patron in question.
The choice of Ulrich V (Wittman-Klemm 1977, 2–4) is partly based on the
identification of the copyist referred to at the end of the *Rappoltsteiner Parzifal*
as 'Henselin' (a diminutive of 'Hans' or 'Johann'), with a copyist by the name of
Johann who worked for Ulrich V. Scholz (1987, 108–10) disputes this choice.

Apart from 'Henselin' there is mention not only of a second copyist named 'von
Onheim' (Schorbach 1888, XVI; Wittman-Klemm 1977, 3), but also of an
adaptation or translation team consisting of the following members: 'von
Straszburg Philippez Colin' ('Philipp Colin from Strasbourg', *RP* 846, 21), who
calls himself 'ein cluoger goltsmit' ('a clever goldsmith', *RP* 846, 20), 'Clawez
Wisze' ('Klaus Wisse', *RP* 854, 7); and finally 'ein jude ist Sampson Pine genant'
('a Jew by the name of Samson Pine', *RP* 854, 27). Prompted by the comment 'er
tet unz die stüre' ('he supported us', *RP* 854, 30), early scholars thought that Wisse
and Colin were responsible for producing the text and that they consulted Pine in
matters of translation. However, Bumke (1996) has drawn attention to the fact
that in medieval times the production of a work was understood as a *compilatio*, as
a new organization of already existing materials, rather than as the free invention
of individual artists.[2] Such a concept of authorship is undoubtedly reflected in the
team of compilers mentioned in the epilogue to the *Rappoltsteiner Parzifal*.

The starting point of their work was Wolfram's *Parzival* (Wittman-Klemm
1977, 9–28). After the first two Books, the story of Parzival's father, Gahmuret,
a *prologus* to the actual Parzival plot is inserted. It is a faithful translation of the
so-called *Elucidation*, which in French manuscripts served as an introduction to
Chrétien's *Perceval*. The narrative of Wolfram's romance is then resumed and
followed to the end of Book XIV, with only a few lines (twenty-nine in total)
from Chrétien's *Perceval* intercalated (after *Parzival* 175, 4 and 319, 18). The
ending of Book XIV of *Parzival*, with the completion of the Gawein narrative,
forms something of a break, which the compilers of the *Rappoltsteiner Parzifal*
also highlight through graphic means: a prose section written in red ink marks a
new beginning:

. . . alles daz hie nach geschriben stat, das ist ouch Parzefal und ist von welsche zuo tüzsche braht und volletihtet und zuo ende braht. (Schorbach, XIII)

(*Everything that follows is also called 'Parzifal'. It has been translated from the French into German in its entirety and narrated to the very end.*)

Before the new narrative line begins, however, seven strophes of courtly love lyric (*Minnesang*) are inserted, which can be ascribed to such well-known authors as Walther von der Vogelweide and Reinmar. These strophes play an important role in the overall structure of the work (Holtorf 1967, Holznagel 1995).

The narrative that follows is a predominantly literal translation of the French *Perceval* Continuations, which supplement some French manuscripts of Chrétien's incomplete *Perceval*. The so-called First Continuation (also known as the *Gauvain Continuation*) tells of the deeds and the fate of Gawein, who twice ends up at the Grail castle without being able to fulfil the task of putting back together a sword that was broken (*RP* 1, 1–313, 40). Various love stories, some successful, some not, are inserted into the narrative. The Second Continuation (sometimes referred to as the *Perceval Continuation*) follows without a break linked by a short bridging section (*RP* 313, 41–314, 25). Here, too, the compilers follow the plot and wording of the French source: Parzifal, after a long search filled with fantastical adventures, finally succeeds in reaching the Grail castle and putting together the broken sword (*RP* 314, 26–610, 26). The long narrative of his adventures is interrupted only by a single passage telling of Gawein's search for Parzifal (*RP* 525, 9–582, 12). A variety of love stories also play a significant role. The German version of the Third Continuation (also called the *Manessier Continuation* after its alleged author) again follows the French original in switching back and forth between the Parzifal and Gawein narrative strands (*RP* 610, 27–846, 9). This part depicts Parzifal's successful fight with the devil and his deliverance of the Grail King besides treating the theme of love, which here is usually unrequited love, or even connected with violence. After Parzifal's return to King Arthur's court the narrative goes back to Wolfram's romance. Books XV and XVI of that text are interspersed with a few passages from the *Manessier Continuation* (Schorbach 1888, LI–LVI). From them we learn how Arthur has the adventures of Parzifal and the other knights of the Round Table carefully recorded in a book, how Parzifal and the entire Round Table set off for the Grail castle, where he is crowned Grail King and how he entertains Arthur and all the knights with the help of the Grail, before they ride back to court while Parzifal remains with the Grail. The Epilogue and an anonymous *Minnesang* strophe round off the compilation.

This sweeping panoramic history of the Grail and of some of the Arthurian knights (mainly Parzifal and Gawein) comprises about 63,000 lines on 320 folio

pages. The vast narrative is held together by the recurring personnel, the search
for the Grail, and the theme of love. Yet there are contradictions and inconsistencies, some of which were already present in the French sources and which are
aggravated through the use of material from Wolfram's *Parzival*. The compilers
managed to achieve unity in certain respects, such as in the use of proper names
– for example, the name of Parzival's wife is changed from the French
Blanchefleur to Wolfram's Kundewiramurs. Some contradictions remain; there
are differences in the German and French concept of the Grail and in its physical
appearance. However, Wittman-Klemm (1977, 96–110) has shown that the main
aim of the project was not to overcome such discontinuities, but rather to put
together a complete collection of available material, which was then systematically restructured, and the organization made visible through the employment
of carefully ordered headings and titles. As such, the *Rappoltsteiner Parzifal* is a
not untypical representative of late medieval literature, which as a whole
developed new attitudes towards both the written word and the older vernacular
literature. This can be seen in changes in the arrangement of newly produced
manuscripts, and in the organization of often voluminous codices, with the
intention of bringing already existing texts into a comprehensive state of
completion.

No conclusive answer has been found to the question of why the lengthy and
costly task of compiling the *Rappoltsteiner Parzifal* was undertaken. One
hypothesis is that the project represents a secularization of the French and
German Parzival tradition, a form of entertainment for a private circle of
literary enthusiasts (Thomas 1992, 110–13; Buschinger 1994, 76f.). This view is
based on two features: the compilers did not include the final passage of the
Manessier Continuation, where Perceval is ordained as sub-deacon, deacon and
finally priest, and where as saint he enters paradise after his death; furthermore,
in contrast to Wolfram's romance, King Arthur's entire Round Table manages,
at least for a period of time, to acquire the Grail and to be taken care of by it.
With respect to these two features, it seems fitting that in the Epilogue Ulrich
von Rappoltstein is referred to as the rightful heir to King Arthur – not,
however, in a genealogical but rather in a literary sense:

> Wir beide daz vernommen hant,
> daz dir ein welsch buoch ist gesant,
> das der künig Artus
> hiez schriben von orte unze ende uz
> von ir aller munde
> der von der tofelrunde.
> daz buoch er alle zit gerne laz,
> wan ez wor und bewert waz . . .

> künig Artus mueste din mog sin,
> wan er ouch sine stunde
> domitte kürzen begunde,
> daz er lesendez sich gewag,
> so er hofierendez nüt enpflag,
> so waz ez sine kurzewile groz.
> daran bist du sin genoz,
> du hest von imme geerbet daz.   (*RP*, 850, 11–31)

(*The two of us* [Frau Minne *and* Frau Milte] *have heard that you have been sent a French book in which King Arthur – according to what the Knights of the Round Table reported – had the entire adventures recorded from beginning to end. He enjoyed reading this book because it was true and verified . . . King Arthur might be called a kinsman of yours, for he too spent his time reading when his official duties allowed him time to do so. Then he enjoyed this book immensely. You are very similar to him in this respect; this you have inherited from him.*)

Frau Minne ('Lady Love') and *Frau Milte* ('Lady Generosity') commissioned Ulrich von Rappoltstein to translate into German a French book that can be traced directly back to Arthur – this book is obviously the *Perceval* and its Continuations (*RP* 850, 32–35). He agrees to do so and engages a 'tihtere' (an 'author' or 'writer', *RP* 853, 31), namely Philipp Colin, who is one of the compilers and who also writes the Epilogue. This fictional genealogy of the text is of course primarily a strategy of authentication; in addition, however, it also allows us a glimpse into the notions of literature current at the time. The reference to the allegorical Lady Love and Lady Generosity as the inspirational forces behind the German translation is at the same time a reference to the primary conditions for the production of literature. Lady Generosity clearly refers to the enormous cost of such an undertaking. It is, however, more difficult to determine what Lady Love is supposed to signify here. For a long time it was suspected that the production of the *Rappoltsteiner Parzifal* came about on account of the patron's love for a lady; but this is rather problematic given the religious offices of Ulrich V, Ulrich VI and Ulrich VII (Scholz 1987, 110). It is now assumed that such references deal merely with a 'stylization of the patron, a role-play' (Wittman-Klemm 1977, 119), which must be connected with the repeated appearance of the romance theme in both the narrative and the *Minnesang* strophes. Moreover, the romance is described in the Epilogue as a 'minnebuoch' (a 'book of courtly love', *RP* 849, 44), or even more strongly as a 'bildere' ('model'), as a 'schuole' ('school'), or as 'letze' ('lesson, instruction') in courtly love, or *minne* (*RP* 856, 21–35). The relevance of *minne* for the work's reception is thereby emphasized (Wittman-Klemm 1977, 119–29; Holznagel 1995, 72f.).

This still does not explain the central role that the Epilogue attributes to Lady Love in the production of the *Rappoltsteiner Parzifal*, next to that of Lady Generosity (that is, next to the material requirements). All of the participants in the planning and creation of the work are associated with *minne* in some manner. Apart from the patron, there is also Klaus Wisse, for whom continued success as 'ein cluoger minnere' ('an experienced courtly lover', *RP* 854, 10–12) is hoped for. The copyist 'Henselin' is humorously referred to as 'den vinen vröwelin zart' ('beloved by the young noble ladies'), while it is claimed of the other copyist 'von Onheim' that 'er trüeget die vrowen mit sinem growen hore' ('his grey hair helps him to deceive the ladies'; Schorbach 1888, XVI). Last but not least, Colin, the author of the Epilogue, also asserts

> so lert die Minne tihten mich,
> daz diz werg wurt vollebroht.   (*RP* 854, 24f.)

(Love instructed me in the art of creation, so that this work could be completed.)

Minne, love, is thus the decisive element in all the literary processes. Moreover, *minne* is also decisive for the reception of the work on the basis of the emphasis placed on love in the various plots and sub-plots of the romance, in the employment of several *Minnesang* strophes at decisive points in the manuscript, and finally in the description of the work as an instruction book for *minne*. *Minne* becomes both the premise and the result of the involvement with literature. As such, *minne* must be seen as a literary phenomenon. Those who are acquainted with the relevant literature belong to a circle of courtly lovers – Ulrich von Rappoltstein, Colin, Wisse, as well as the readers of such works. Together with the literary characters, they all form an exclusive group of connoisseurs, of 'edele herzen' ('noble hearts', *RP* 850, 38; 852, 30; 853, 4; 858, 8). But this means that even in the fourteenth century *minne* plays a very similar role to the one it had had in the preceding two centuries, and which is most clearly seen in the *Minnesang* strophes. Participation in the discourse of love converged with membership of a social elite; conversely, the social elite was characterized by its knowledge of and proper involvement with literature concerned with love.

Ulrich Füetrer, *Buch der Abenteuer*

With its 11,655 so-called *Titurel* strophes (81,585 lines), the *Buch der Abenteuer* (*BdA*) combines several Grail and Arthurian romances and is even more comprehensive than the *Rappoltsteiner Parzifal*. Two complete manuscripts have been preserved (Munich, Cgm 1 and Vienna, Cod. Vind. 3037/38) with 348 and 516 folio pages respectively. Three further manuscripts contain scattered parts of the voluminous work (Munich, Cgm 247: Book I; Vienna, Cod. Vind. 2888: *Mörlin*; Karlsruhe, previously Donaueschingen, Cod. 140: *Poytislier* and *Flordimar*), and there is also a fragment (Berlin, MS germ. fol. 757) with some lines from the third Book (*Lannzilet*) (Nyholm 1964, XXXV–LXXXV; Lenk 1989, IX–XXVII; Voß 1996, 2–9).

The Munich painter and author Ulrich Füetrer (d. *c.* 1495/6?) composed his *Buch der Abenteuer* in the last quarter of the fifteenth century. Before or during the work on the *Buch* he wrote a prose version of *Lantzilet* and a *Bayerische Chronik* (a 'Chronicle of Bavaria'). It is tempting to compare Füetrer's activity as historiographer with that as adaptor of Arthurian literature (Wenzel 1986). Füetrer was born in Landshut and was a master painter in Munich by the middle of the fifteenth century; it was probably in this capacity that Füetrer first came into contact with the duke's court there (Bastert 1993, 139–51). How and where Füetrer acquired the knowledge of literature that enabled him to take on such an ambitious project as the *Buch der Abenteuer* remains an open question. It is fairly certain that he received the commission for the work from Albrecht IV (1449–1508), the Duke of Upper Bavaria, who is enthusiastically praised by Füetrer in several prominent passages in the *Buch der Abenteuer*.

The title of the work, *Buch der Abenteuer* ('Book of Adventures'), was first given to it in the nineteenth century and is misleading inasmuch as it suggests a simple collection of adventure stories featuring various knights. To view it this way would not do justice to Füetrer's work. One can get a glimpse of his aims and the structure of the gigantic undertaking in one of the opening stanzas of the work, when the narrator announces that he wishes first to describe the origins of the Grail lineage:

> . . . wie sich die auss erkoren
> ritterschaft erhueb zum ersten male,
> ich main in Salva terra,
> die dort wonten pey dem edeln grale.   (*BdA* 5, 4–7)

(. . . *how the select group of knights, who lived there by the noble grail – I mean, in Salva terra – appeared for the first time.*)

To this end Füetrer used Albrecht's *Jüngerer Titurel* and Wolfram's *Parzival* as sources (*BdA* 10–120). In contrast to the compilers of the *Rappoltsteiner Parzifal*, Füetrer did not simply take over such sources more or less unchanged into the new work, but instead adapted them to the metrical schema of the so-called *Titurel* strophe. Moreover, he trimmed the plots of the sources down to their core without, however, altering their intended meaning in any essential way. The Prologue also speaks of the portrayal of the 'anfang der pritoneysen' ('origins of the British', *BdA* 6, 3), that is, of the commonplace medieval notion that Arthur's lineage can be traced back to the Trojans. Füetrer accordingly inserted a depiction of the Trojan War, for the most part following Konrad von Würzburg (*BdA* 121–706) before describing Arthur's birth and first exploits, the most important of which is the founding of the Round Table (*BdA* 707–969). Thereafter the narrative shifts its focus back to the history of the Grail. Once again Wolfram's *Parzival* and the *Jüngerer Titurel* serve as primary sources, with additional sections taken from Heinrich von dem Türlin's *Crône* and the *Lohengrin*. At the centre of the narrative are the changing fortunes of the Grail family and, in particular, of its most important representative, Parzival, though the text does not neglect the heroic deeds of Gawein (*BdA* 970–2955). Füetrer shows considerable skill in solving the problems presented in bringing together and harmonizing the various sources, which at times diverge considerably in this part of the narrative (Bastert 1993, 164–70). The first book ends with the arrival of the knights of the Round Table at the Grail and the removal of the Grail to India (*BdA* 2955ff.). The connection of the book that immediately follows ('annder puech', *BdA* 3004ff.) with the rest of the work has long been a matter of dispute; it uses seven autonomous narratives, the sources of which are only partly known: *Wigoleis* (*BdA* 3004–320), based on Wirnt von Grafenberg's *Wigalois* and/or the *Volksbuch* ('chap book') (Borgnet 1994); *Seyfrid von Ardemont* (*BdA* 3321–839), based on a lost Arthurian romance by Albrecht von Scharfenberg, *Melerans* (*BdA* 3840–4111), based on Pleier's *Meleranz*; *Iban* (*BdA* 4112–408), based on Hartmann von Aue's *Iwein* (Voß 1994b); *Persibein* (*BdA* 4409–938); *Poytislier* (*BdA* 4939–5293) and *Flordimar* (*BdA* 5294–646; Kern, 1988). The second Book of the *Buch der Abenteuer* describes the tremendous success of young knights who had been accepted as members of the Round Table, something the Prologue had already announced:

> wer geselleschaft dartzue begerte,
> der muest mit ritters ellen
> vil preis bejagen mit sper unnd auch mit schwerte   (*BdA* 6, 5–7)

(To belong to the Round Table, one had to display chivalry and courage and win praise with lance and sword.)

Each of the seven narratives portrays the aims of knighthood as the winning of women and land. These narratives are connected to Book I through the use of identical characters and genealogies; Füetrer differs from his sources in part by declaring the protagonists of the second Book to be related to those in Book I

(Bastert 1993, 178–90). By means of this strategy, Book II depicts the fortunes of the next generation of Arthurian knights. Together with the ancestors of both the Arthurian and the Grail family as described in the introductory sections, a genealogical tree covering several generations of these two important families is fleshed out in the sequel. The final third Book (*Lannz.* I, 1–1122 and *Lannz.* II, 1123–6009) is often treated as an autonomous work under the name of *Lannzilet*, but can be considered as an integral part of the larger undertaking for formal as well as internal narratological reasons. Using the *Prosa-Lancelot* as its model, it follows the further and ever darker destinies of familiar Arthurian and Grail heroes and heroines, up to the death of the most important protagonists and thus to the approaching decline of the Arthurian world (Voß 1988 and 1990, Ziegeler 1996).

With his *Buch der Abenteuer* Füetrer strives to present a comprehensive over-all view of the literary cosmos that had been handed down by the various authors preceding him. The romance cycle tends towards an all-encompassing presentation without losing sight of the chronological succession that extends from the origins of the Arthurian and the Grail knighthood, through its glorious peak to its final decline. Although certain discontinuities, especially between Books I and III, must be acknowledged (Voß 1994a), Füetrer's literary history of King Arthur's knights and the Grail manages to achieve a better and more coherent structure than the *Rappoltsteiner Parzifal*. It does so through the use of both forward and backward referencing, adaptations of differing passages to its overall narratological concept, and other unifying strategies. By means of this kind of coherent structure Füetrer's *Buch der Abenteuer* joins similar Arthurian and Grail cycles that appeared throughout Europe in the fourteenth and fifteenth centuries. Prominent examples are the Dutch *Lancelot* compilation, which integrates another seven originally independent romances (Besamusca 1994), and several French compilations, which similarly unite various older Arthurian and Grail romances in a comprehensive whole (Walters 1994a, 1994b). Like the *Buch der Abenteuer*, for example, Codex BN MS 450, held in the Bibliothèque Nationale in Paris, uses the history of Troy as the prehistory for the *Roman de Brut* (Walters 1985). The best-known of these large cycles is without doubt that of Thomas Malory, written about 1470 and later published by Caxton under the title of *Morte D'Arthur*. This immense work is structurally very similar to the *Buch der Abenteuer* and follows the histories of Arthur and the Grail from the legendary birth of the King through to the decline and fall of his empire. The relationship between these narrative cycles and the *Buch der Abenteuer* has not been adequately addressed, nor has it been clarified whether and how Füetrer or his patron had or might have had knowledge of them.

Instead, discussion has focused on the question of what possible function Füetrer's romance cycle might have had at the Munich court at the end of the

fifteenth century. The long-held position was that the *Buch der Abenteuer* represents the anachronistic and escapist literary strivings of a nobility shaken by the
crisis of the late Middle Ages (Rupprich 1970, 55). But, because many historians
consider Füetrer's patron to have been one of the first humanistically educated
German princes, one already displaying tendencies characteristic of the early
absolutist period (Kraus 1969), the *Buch der Abenteuer* has also been interpreted
as a work that itself shows traces of this humanist influence (Nyholm 1965; Harms
1966), or as a deliberate attempt on the part of a modern prince to celebrate
himself and his government in the image of literary heroes (Rischer 1973). A third
line of interpretation even sees in Albrecht's demonstrative preservation of
aristocratic literature of centuries past a possible attempt to convince a Bavarian
aristocracy, fearful of losing its old rights and freedoms, of its duke's mindful
adherence to tradition as well as of his concern to preserve a 'classic' feudal
ideology (Müller 1980; Behr 1986). However, it is by no means certain that
Albrecht IV can be seen as a sovereign influenced by humanism and with
absolutist aspirations. His methods of governing did not differ significantly from
those of previous sovereigns or of his contemporaries, who continued to come into
conflict with the nobility over territorial claims (Stauber 1997). The allegedly
absolutist Albrecht was forced in the end to acknowledge these claims.

Such political conflicts have not, however, left any noticeable trace on
Füetrer's work. Passages allegedly evincing tendencies towards the concentration of sovereign power are flatly contradicted by other passages. In general,
contemporary events and issues play only a marginal role; the multilayered and
richly textured romance does not lend itself to sweeping socio-historical
interpretations. A rather more promising approach is perhaps to be found in the
aesthetics of reception. The single major 'variation' that Füetrer permits himself
to make is the reduction of his sources to their narrative core. The abridgements
are at times so radical that listeners or readers must have been thoroughly
acquainted with the original texts in order to be able to follow the plots in their
condensed fifteenth-century versions (Bastert 1993, 226–72). Similarly, Füetrer
probably counted on the recipients' prior knowledge when he repeatedly
undermines the narrator, who is called Ulrich and is acting in a role reminiscent
of Wolfram the narrator, in Ulrich's many disputes with Lady Adventure. To
the extent that Ulrich's opinions and predictions were seen against the
background of the romances of the High Middle Ages, the literary incompetence
of a narrator seemingly unaware of the details of such texts, is exposed. If,
however, in contrast to the foolish Ulrich, one understands the narrative
contexts, then one can not only predict subsequent plot developments with
precision; one can also impressively demonstrate one's literary expertise. Thus
when the narrator complains to Lady Love that Uterpandragon's love for
Ygrena, who is married to the Duke of Tyntayol, demonstrates once again the

perils and unhappiness caused by the allegorical lady (*BdA* 880), Lady Love answers him:

> An not dein haupt du prichest,
> mercken wol all die weysen.   (*BdA* 882, 1–2)

(*You concern yourself needlessly, as knowledgeable people will notice.*)

One may surmise that these 'weysen' made up a segment of the *BdA*'s intended public. It would have been obvious even to those with only a passing acquaintance with the tradition that Lady Love is correct in admonishing the simple-minded Ulrich, since the love affair will have a happy end and lead to the birth of Arthur. This suggests that the gaps left in the text by Füetrer were intended to be filled by literary connoisseurs – in other words, by a public characterized at the beginning of his work as follows:

> Graf, ritter unnd auch chnechte,
> die kunste sich verstandt.   (*BdA* 19, 1–2)

(*Counts, knights and squires too, who know something of art.*)

Füetrer's *Buch der Abenteuer* from the late fifteenth century and the *Rappolt-steiner Parzifal* from the first half of the fourteenth century are thus comparable from two points of view: both demonstrate structural similarities in their task of compiling existing textual material in the most complete fashion possible, and both may be interpreted in terms of their reception by an elite group of literary specialists. If, however, the authors or compilers of both works thus presuppose the knowledge of such existing material on the part of their audiences, then this testifies to a continuity in the German reception of Arthurian and Grail literature, a literature that in no way appears to have lost its topicality in the late Middle Ages. Despite, or perhaps even precisely because of, observable changes in the production of literature and the arrangement of texts, the function of the Arthurian and Grail romances that emerged in the fourteenth and fifteenth centuries hardly changed at all. They continued to affirm and constitute the identity of a social elite, which defined itself by cultural knowledge. Thus the *Rappoltsteiner Parzifal* and the *Buch der Abenteuer* point to a milieu that recently and with some justification has been described as an 'educated knight-hood', since a kind of 'scholarly expertise' manifested itself in this milieu, deliberately linking the cultural traditions of the court with a specific 'imaginary world of literature, iconography and history' (Paravicini 1994, 18).

Notes

[1] Bumke 1996, 92f. points out that the division in the manuscript between an 'old' and a 'new' *Parzifal* is nothing more than a way of counting pages.

[2] Bumke 1996, 88 n. 2 points out that Colin's portrayal of himself as a goldsmith should not be understood as a description of his actual trade but rather as a metaphorical description of his literary activity. Both Wisse and Colin belonged to important Strasbourg patrician families. It is by no means certain, as Schorbach (1888, XXVIIIf.) assumes, that the Philipp Colin named in the text is identical with the person whose name occurs in Strasbourg documents of 1307 and 1309 and who apparently found himself in financial straits. It is also unclear to what extent Samson Pine contributed to the project. One may not limit his participation to that of a mere translator simply on the basis of the phrase 'er tet unz die stüre' (RP 854, 30), since this can also mean: 'he directed us, set out the guidelines.' This notion of a Jewish translator seems implicitly to assume that Samson Pine, as a member of a marginalized religious and social group, lacked the necessary knowledge of an elite literary form like the Arthurian romance. However, the recognition that Jews could indeed take part in the cultural activities of the social elite – as the example of the *Widuwilt*, a Yiddish version of the Arthurian romance *Wigalois*, shows – probably calls for a revision of this assessment.

Bibliography

Rappoltsteiner Parzifal

Primary Source

Parzifal von Claus Wisse und Philipp Colin (1331–1336). Eine Ergänzung der Dichtung Wolframs von Eschenbach. Ed. by Karl Schorbach, 1888 (Elsässische Literaturdenkmäler aus dem XIV.–XVI. Jahrhundert, 5). Strasbourg [*RP*].

Other Literature

Besamusca et al. 1994. See Gen. Bibl.
Besch, W. 1962. 'Vom "Alten" zum "Nüwen" Parzival', *Der Deutschunterricht*, 14, 91–104.
Bumke, J. 1996. 'Autor und Werk. Beobachtungen und Überlegungen zur höfischen Epik (ausgehend von der Donaueschinger Parzivalhandschrift G$^\delta$)', *ZfdPh*, 116, *Sonderheft*, 87–114.
Buschinger, D. 1994. 'Zum Rappoltsteiner Parzival', in Buschinger and Spiewok 1994b, 71–8.
Buschinger and Spiewok 1994b. See Gen. Bibl.
Cramer, Th. 1983. 'Aspekte des höfischen Romans im 14. Jahrhundert', in Haug, W., Jackson, T. R. and Janota, J., eds., *Zur deutschen Literatur und Sprache des 14. Jahrhunderts. Dubliner Colloquium 1981*. Heidelberg, 208–20.
Holtorf, A. 1967. 'Eine Strophe Reinmars von Brennenberg im Rappoltsteiner Parzival', *ZfdA*, 96, 321–8.
Holznagel, F.-J., 1995. 'Minnesang-Florilegien. Zur Lyriküberlieferung im Rappoltsteiner Parzifal, im Berner Hausbuch und in der Berliner Tristan-Handschrift N', in Krohn, R., ed., *'Dâ hœret ouch geloube zuo'. Überlieferungs- und Echtheitsfragen zum Minnesang. Beiträge zum Festcolloquium für Günther Schweikle anläßlich seines 65. Geburtstags*. Stuttgart and Leipzig, 65–88.
Scholz, M. G. 1987. *Zum Verhältnis von Mäzen, Autor und Publikum im 14. und 15. Jahrhundert. 'Wilhelm von Österreich' – 'Rappoltsteiner Parzifal' – Michel Beheim*. Darmstadt.

Schorbach, K. 1888. 'Einleitung', in *Parzifal* (see Primary Source), VII–LXX.
Thomas, N. 1992. 'Patronage and literary context in a fourteenth-century German Arthurian romance: the *Rappoltstein Parzifal'*, *Parergon*, 10, 103–13.
Wittmann-Klemm, D. 1977. *Studien zum 'Rappoltsteiner Parzifal'*, GAG, 224, Göppingen.

Buch der Abenteuer

Primary Sources

Ulrich Füetrer, *Das Buch der Abenteuer*. 2 vols. Ed. by H. Thoelen, 1997 (GAG, 638). Göppingen [*BdA*].
Ulrich Füetrer, *Lannzilet. (Aus dem 'Buch der Abenteuer')* Str. *1–1122*. Ed. by K.-E. Lenk, 1989 (ATB, 102). Tübingen [*Lannz*. I].
Ulrich Füetrer, *Lannzilet aus dem 'Buch der Abenteuer'* Str. *1123–6009*. Ed. by R. Voß, 1996 (Schönings Mediävistische Editionen, 3). Paderborn [*Lannz*. II].
Die Gralepen in Ulrich Füetrers Bearbeitung (Buch der Abenteuer). Ed. by K. Nyholm, 1964 (Deutsche Texte des Mittelalters, 57). Berlin.
Ulrich Füetrer, *Prosaroman von Lanzelot*. Ed. By A. Peter, 1885 (BLV, 175). Tübingen.

Other Literature

Bastert, B. 1993. *Der Münchner Hof und Fuetrers 'Buch der Abenteuer'. Literarische Kontinuität im Spätmittelalter*, Mikrokosmos, 33, Frankfurt.
Bastert, B. 1996. '"es ist ain krieg vil starck in disen maeren". Ein Versuch über die Merlin-Adaptation Ulrich Füetrers', *GRM*, 46, 336–44.
Behr, H.-J. 1986. 'Von der *aventiure* zum *abenteur*. Überlegungen zum Wandel des Artusromans in Ulrich Füetrers *Buch der Abenteuer'*, *IASL*, 11, 1–20.
Besamusca, B. 1994. 'Cyclification in Middle Dutch literature: the case of the *Lancelot* compilation', in Besamusca et al. 1994 (see Gen. Bibl.), 82–91.
Borgnet, G. 1994. 'Le *Wigoleis* d'Ulrich Füetrer. Étude comparative des trois versions du chevalier à la roue: Wirnt von Grafenberg, Volksbuch, Ulrich Füetrer', in Buschinger and Spiewok 1994a (see Gen. Bibl.), 51–64.
Buschinger, D. 1995. 'Quelques aspects du *Lantzilet* en prose et du *Lantzilet* strophique d'Ulrich Füetrer', in Buschinger and Zink 1995 (see Gen. Bibl.), 87–99.
Buschinger and Spiewok 1994b. See Gen. Bibl.
Harms, W. 1966. 'Anagnorisis-Szenen des mittelalterlichen Romans und Ulrich Füetrers *Buch der Abenteuer'*, *ZfdA*, 95, 301–18.
Harms, W. 1974. 'Zu Ulrich Füetrers Auffassung vom Erzählen und von der Historie', *ZfdPh*, 93, Sonderheft, 185–97.
Kern, P. 1988. 'Ulrich Füetrers *Flordimar*: Bearbeitung eines Artusromans des 13. Jahrhunderts?', *ZfdPh*, 107, 410–31.
Kraus, A. 1969. 'Sammlung der Kräfte und Aufschwung', in Spindler, M., ed., *Handbuch der bayerischen Geschichte*, Munich 2, 269–97.
Lenk, K.-E. 1989. 'Einleitung', in Ulrich Füetrer, *Lannzilet* (see Primary Sources), IX–XXXII.
Müller, J.-D. 1980. 'Funktionswandel ritterlicher Epik am Ausgang des Mittelalters', in Kaiser, G., ed., *Gesellschaftliche Sinnangebote mittelalterlicher Literatur. Mediaevistisches Symposium an der Universität Düsseldorf*, Forschungen zur Geschichte der Älteren Deutschen Literatur, 1, Munich, 11–75.
Nyholm, K. 1964. 'Einleitung', in *Die Gralepen* (see Primary Sources), VII–CXII.
Nyholm, K. 1965. 'Das höfische Epos im Zeitalter des Humanismus', *NM* 66, 297–313.

Paravicini, W. 1994. *Die ritterlich-höfische Kultur des Mittelalters*, Enzyklopädie deutscher Geschichte, 32, Munich.

Rischer, C. 1973. *Literarische Rezeption und kulturelles Selbstverständnis in der deutschen Literatur der 'Ritterrenaissance' des 15. Jahrhunderts. Untersuchungen zu Ulrich Füetrers 'Buch der Abenteuer' und dem 'Ehrenbrief' des Jakob Püterich zu Reichertshausen*, Studien zur Poetik und Geschichte der Literatur, 29, Stuttgart.

Rupprich, H. 1970. *Die deutsche Literatur vom späten Mittelalter bis zum Barock. Erster Teil. Das ausgehende Mittelalter, Humanismus und Renaissance 1370–1520*, Geschichte der deutschen Literatur von den Anfängen bis zur Gegenwart, 4.1, Munich.

Stauber, R. 1997. 'Staat und Dynastie. Herzog Albrecht IV. und die Einheit des "Hauses Bayern" um 1500', *Zeitschrift für bayerische Landesgeschichte*, 60, 539–65.

Strohschneider, P. 1986. *Ritterromantische Versepik im ausgehenden Mittelalter. Studien zu einer funktionsgeschichtlichen Textinterpretation der 'Mörin' Hermanns von Sachsenheim sowie zu Ulrich Fuetrers 'Persibein' und Maximilians I. 'Teuerdank'*, Mikrokosmos, 14, Frankfurt.

Strohschneider, P. 1988. '"Lebt Artus noch zu Karydol, So stünd es in der welte baß." Von der Aktualität des Vergangenen in der höfischen Versepik des ausgehenden Mittelalters', *LiLi*, 70, 70–94.

Voß, R. 1988. 'Problematische Konstellationen. Zu Ulrich Füetrers Rezeption des Prosa-Lancelot', *LiLi*, 70, 26–53.

Voß, R. 1990. 'Literarische Referenzen in Ulrich Füetrers strophischem Lannzilet', in Wolfzettel 1990, 195–214.

Voß, R. 1994a. 'Werkkontinuum und Diskontinuität des Einzelwerks. Zum Ensemble von Ulrich Füetrers *Buch der Abenteuer*', in Besamusca et al. 1994 (see Gen. Bibl.), 221–7.

Voß, R. 1994b. 'Die *Iwein*-Rezeption Ulrich Füetrers. Der *Iban* im Kontext des *Buchs der Abenteuer*', in Ertzdorff, X. v., ed., *Die Romane von dem Ritter mit dem Löwen*, Chloe, Beihefte zum *Daphnis*, 20, Amsterdam, 331–52.

Voß, R. 1996. 'Einleitung', in Ulrich Füetrer, *Lannzilet* (see Primary Sources), 1–14.

Walters, L. 1985. 'Le rôle du scribe dans l'organisation des manuscrits des romans de Chrétien de Troyes', *Rom*, 106, 303–25.

Walters, L. 1994a. 'The formation of a Gauvain cycle in Chantilly manuscript 472', *Neophil*, 78, 29–43.

Walters, L. 1994b. 'Chantilly MS. 472 as a cyclic work', in Besamusca et al. 1994 (see Gen. Bibl.), 135–9.

Wenzel, H. 1986. '"Alls in ein summ zu pringen". Füetrers *Bayerische Chronik* und sein *Buch der Abenteuer* am Hof Albrechts IV.', in Wapnewski, P., ed., *Mittelalter-Rezeption. Ein Symposion*, Germanistische Symposien, 6, Stuttgart, 10–31.

Wolfzettel, F., ed. 1990. *Artusroman und Intertextualität*. Giessen.

Ziegeler, H.-J. 1996. '*fraw Fortun, fraw Wer, fraw Awentewr* und *fraw Mynne*. Darstellung und Interpretation von Konflikten und ihren Ursachen in Ulrich Fuetrers *Lannzilet*-Versionen', in Gärtner, K., Kasten, I. and Shaw, F., eds., *Spannungen und Konflikte menschlichen Zusammenlebens in der deutschen Literatur des Mittelalters. Bristoler Colloquium 1993*, Tübingen, 321–39.

11

LORENGEL AND THE
SPRUCH VON DEN TAFELRUNDERN

W. H. Jackson

Lorengel is an anonymous fifteenth-century narrative variant of the Swan Knight story treated earlier in *Lohengrin*. The work is transmitted almost complete in 207 ten-line stanzas (with four leaves missing) in the Austrian National Library Vienna, Cod. Vindob. 15478 (W = 'Linhart Scheubels Heldenbuch', 1480–90); forty-one stanzas of the opening section appear in Bavarian State Library Munich, cgm 4997 (K = 'Kolmarer Liederhandschrift', *c.* 1460). W and K probably derive independently of each other from a common source (Buschinger 1979, VII).

The precise relationship of *Lorengel* to *Lohengrin* is not clear (Elster 1896; Cramer 1971, 34–45). There are close verbal correspondences between the two in the opening, which includes an account of Arthur's court, whence Lorengel sets out to champion the cause of Else, or Isilie, Duchess of Brabant. *Lorengel* also follows the basic pattern of the earlier work in presenting the hero's victory over the duchess's disloyal protector Friderich in a duel approved by the emperor. However, this pattern is filled out independently in *Lorengel* with a retrospective account of King Etzel's attacking the Rhinelands, France and Spain, and fighting a fierce battle before Cologne, the account of which draws on the legend of 11,000 virgins martyred in Cologne. Of particular Arthurian interest is the report that it was ultimately Partzefal who, carrying the Grail in his hand, prevented Etzel from subjugating the whole of Christendom (st. 78, 8–10). The foremost Grail knight is thus pitted, as a defender of Christendom, against one of the major figures from German legend. *Lorengel* also differs from *Lohengrin* in the conclusion, for *Lorengel* has no account of the hero's returning to the Grail realm; instead the work ends with his marriage and lordship in Brabant. The subjugation of Arthurian and Grail matters to German story and history, which was evident already in *Lohengrin* (see Meyer, chapter 6 above), is no less pronounced in *Lorengel* a century or more later.

Lorengel has received little detailed interpretative attention. For Cramer, the main interest of the poem lies in the urban setting and the important role ascribed to burghers in the action (Cramer 1985). Against this view, Thomas points out that the main action takes place in courtly contexts and is carried by aristocratic figures, and he hypothesizes that the work, as it is transmitted in W, reflects the marriage of Maximilian of Habsburg to Maria of Burgundy in 1477 (Thomas 1987). Like the other works transmitted in Linhart Scheubel's 'Helden-buch', *Lorengel* is much concerned with the noble hero's self-assertion in combat and with the etiquette and material luxury of aristocratic life (Ertzdorff 1972); on the other hand Linhart Scheubel himself, who is named in the manuscript as owner, was in all likelihood a burgher of Nuremberg (Hoffmann 1979). The internal evidence of *Lorengel*, with its sympathetic portrayal of the wealthy burgher Callebrand beside the work's knightly ethos, thus matches the external evidence of its transmission to point to a social milieu in which urban and aristocratic interests merged.

The *Spruch von den Tafelrundern* is a descriptive verse list, 256 lines long, of some 160 figures from courtly literature, composed by an unknown author at the end of the fifteenth century (Henkel 1995). The work opens with a genealogy of the Grail dynasty (vv. 1–23), proceeds to a genealogy of the Arthurian dynasty and a list of figures from Arthurian literature who embody the values of chivalry (vv. 24–158) and closes with hero-figures from other branches of courtly narrative (vv. 159–256). The work has affinities with a name list in the fourteenth-century romance *Friedrich von Schwaben*, a name list published by Singer (1894), and with the close of Ulrich Füetrer's *Lannzilet* (Menhardt 1955, 147). It was probably produced in connection with the Wittelsbach court of Duke Albrecht IV at Munich (for which Füetrer also wrote) in the last years of the fifteenth century.

The *Spruch* has little poetic merit, but it is an illuminating attempt to provide an inventory of the mass of Arthurian (and other courtly) literature. Arthur is praised more extensively than any other figure (vv. 32–42). Chivalry is idealized as the service of ladies (v. 42) but remains a matter of military force: Gawein's prowess is marked by the men he wounded or killed (vv. 43–6). The leading position of Parzival, who won ('erstrait', v. 88) the Grail, is indicated by the epithet 'a crown of knighthood' (v. 86). Most figures are referred to with one leading characteristic: Erec is linked with 'Eneyt sein amey' (v. 120), 'Herr Iban' is characterized by his defeat of Aschalun (vv. 136f.) and Lantzelet appears not as the adulterous lover of Guinevere, but in the tradition of Ulrich von Zatzikhoven as the partner of Iblis (vv. 122f.).

The *Spruch* is transmitted in three manuscripts: Austrian National Library Vienna, Cod. Vindob. 7692 (a), and Bavarian State Library Munich clm 1231 (b) and clm 28699 (c). Manuscript a is a 244-folio collection of various texts, particularly of a genealogical nature, that was assembled in 1508–10 by Ladislaus Sunthaym. The *Spruch* is on three folios. Manuscript b is a fair copy of a, prepared by Sunthaym for Emperor Maximilian I (Eheim 1959, 86); c is an eighteenth-century copy of b. Sunthaym was one of the foremost scholars who worked on the historical and genealogical projects mounted by Maximilian with the aim of linking the Habsburg dynasty to as many other leading dynasties as possible. Although the figures in the *Spruch* are largely drawn from literary works, they are introduced in a historical way as 'the best who ever lived' ('den tewristn so gelebt haben'). King Arthur was the most celebrated ancestor of Maximilian's English relatives in the emperor's genealogical project, and it may have been largely a genealogical interest that prompted Sunthaym to include the *Spruch* in his collection, so as to shed greater glory on Maximilian's dynasty by association with the Arthurian family (Müller 1982, 196).

Lorengel and the *Spruch von den Tafelrundern* are very different works, but they show major features of the Arthurian material in the German world at a time when this material was soon to fade into the past: the prominence of the Grail theme; the integration of Arthurian motifs and themes into larger frameworks, both in individual works and in anthologizing manuscripts; the continuing relevance of Arthurian figures in the aristocratic world (particularly around Emperor Maximilian I) and also the reception of Arthurian literature in burgher circles.

Bibliography

Primary Sources

Lorengel. Ed. by E. Steinmeyer, 1872. *ZfdA*, 15, 181–245.
Lorengel. Edité avec introduction et index par D. Buschinger, 1979 (GAG 253). Göppingen.
Spruch von den Tafelrundern. Ed. by H. Menhardt, 1955. *PBB* (Tübingen), 77, 136–164, 316–32.

Other Literature

Buschinger, D. 1979. See Primary Sources, *Lorengel*.
Cramer, T. 1971. *Lohengrin. Edition und Untersuchungen*, Munich.
Cramer, T. 1985. '*Lorengel*', *VL*, V, 907–9.
Eheim, F. 1959. 'Ladislaus Sunthaym. Ein Historiker aus dem Gelehrtenkreis um Maximilian I.', *Mitteilungen des Instituts für Österreichische Geschichte*, 67, 53–91.
Elster, E. 1896. 'Das Verhältnis des *Lorengel* zum *Lohengrin*', in *Philologische Studien. Festgabe für Eduard Sievers*, Halle, 252–76.
Ertzdorff, X. von 1972. 'Linhart Scheubels Heldenbuch', in O. Bandle et al., eds., *Festschrift Siegfried Gutenbrunner*, Heidelberg, 33–46.
Henkel, N. 1995. '*Spruch von den Tafelrundern*', *VL*, IX, 188–90.
Hoffmann, W. 1979. 'Die spätmittelalterliche Bearbeitung des Nibelungenliedes in Lienhart Scheubels Heldenbuch', *GRM*, NF 29, 129–45.
Menhardt, H. 1955. See Primary Sources, *Spruch von den Tafelrundern*.
Müller, J.-D. 1982. *Gedechtnus. Literatur und Hofgesellschaft um Maximilian I.*, Forschungen zur Geschichte der älteren deutschen Literatur, 2, Munich.
Singer, S. 1894. 'Zu Ulrich Füetrer', *ZfdA*, 38, 205–6.
Thomas, H. 1987. 'Maximilian als Schwanritter. Zur Deutung und zur Datierung des *Lorengel*', *ZfdA*, 98, 303–16.

Part Three

The Medieval Dutch Arthurian Material

12

THE MEDIEVAL DUTCH ARTHURIAN MATERIAL

Bart Besamusca

Introduction

Flemish proper names like Iwanus of Waldripont (1114) and Vualauuaynus of Melne (1118) – i.e. Walewein of Melle – appearing in charters from the beginning of the twelfth century indicate that Arthurian stories must have been popular in the Low Countries very early (Verbeke et al. 1987, 113–18). At least some of these orally circulating stories were in Dutch (Gerritsen 1984). In some form such stories were still in existence around the middle of the thirteenth century. After all, Penninc states in the prologue to his *Walewein* (*c*. 1250) that 'Many stories about King Arthur have not yet been put into writing' ('Vanden coninc Arture / Es bleven menighe avonture / Die nemmer mee ne wert bescreven', vv. 1–3). We would dearly like to know more about these tales, but Penninc remains silent with regard to their contents. The oral tradition of Dutch Arthurian stories is an elusive phenomenon.

Almost all Dutch Arthurian texts that have come down to us were written in the thirteenth century. Four traditions can be distinguished. First, the historiographical works are adaptations of Latin sources into Middle Dutch verse. Second, the Middle Dutch renditions of Old French prose romances include not only faithful translations but also very free reworkings of the Old French texts, virtually all of them rendered in verse form. Third, other Middle Dutch romances are based on Old French verse romances, and it appears that in most cases the authors of these texts have taken the liberty of changing their Old French source drastically. Fourth, from the middle of the thirteenth century onwards indigenous romances were being written; the poets of these verse romances were thoroughly familiar with the Old French and Middle Dutch Arthurian romances, to which they freely referred. The material in this chapter is presented according to these four traditions and a closing section will give a short account of the development of Dutch Arthurian literature after the Middle Ages.

It will become clear that most Middle Dutch authors were of Flemish origin. This need not surprise us. Indeed, interest in Arthurian literature was markedly greater in Flanders than in the other areas of the Low Countries (van den Berg

1987). This does not mean, however, that we know where and how these Flemish romances were received. With regard to Middle Dutch literature, literary patronage at the Flemish courts is problematical. The court of the Flemish count was clearly French-orientated, as appears for example from Chrétien's *Perceval*, Gautier d'Arras's *Eracle*, Manessier's *Perceval* Continuation and the work of Adenet le Roi. Did Middle Dutch literature, too, function at this court, or only at the smaller courts? Was the Flemish court bilingual? Further research will have to answer these questions. Then it may also become clear if there were any other centres of literary activity outside the court of the Flemish count. Perhaps we should search for patrons of Middle Dutch Arthurian literature in the milieu of the urbanized nobility and the bourgeois élite in towns like Bruges and Ghent (Janssens 1988, 169–73; Prevenier 1994; van den Berg 1998; Besamusca 1998).

The Middle Dutch Arthurian texts have come down to us in a few codices and a great many fragments. With the exception of *Perchevael, Wrake van Ragisel* and *Tristant* fragments, which date from the thirteenth century, the texts were copied in the fourteenth century (Besamusca 1985, Kienhorst 1988). If the manuscript transmission does not deceive us, enthusiasm for Arthurian literature in the Low Countries reached its peak in the first half of the fourteenth century (Klein, J. W. 1995, 19). The absence of fifteenth-century Middle Dutch manuscripts shows that the popularity of Dutch Arthurian romances was waning rapidly after the fourteenth century.

The Middle Dutch Arthurian texts were previously discussed by Hendricus Sparnaay in *Arthurian Literature in the Middle Ages* (Loomis 1959, 443–61). Unfortunately, his essay contains a number of factual inaccuracies and it is, moreover, very outdated. During the last thirty years the study of Arthurian literature in the Low Countries has developed enormously. J. D. Janssens's contributions on Middle Dutch Arthurian literature in *Arturus Rex* show more expert knowledge (Verbeke et al. 1987). In *The New Arthurian Encyclopedia* (Lacy 1991) Janssens and I have used the entries on Dutch Arthurian literature (medieval and modern) to provide ample factual information. In *Medieval Arthurian Literature: A Guide to Recent Research* I have discussed the state of Dutch scholarship on Arthurian romances (Lacy 1996, 211–37). As a follow-up to these publications, the present contribution tries to reflect the wealth of recent research.

The Historiographical Tradition

Jacob van Maerlant, *Spiegel historiael*

Around 1285 the Flemish poet Jacob van Maerlant, working between *c.* 1260 and 1290, adapted Vincent of Beauvais's *Speculum historiale*. In the prologue to his *magnum opus*, commissioned by Count Floris V of Holland (1266–96),

Maerlant writes that his *Spiegel historiael* ('Mirror of History') should be preferred to the nonsense of the Grail, the lies about Perceval, the trifles of Lanval, and many other false stories (Part I, Book I, Prologue, vv. 55–60). Apparently, the aristocratic circles around Floris, who resided in The Hague, were familiar with these tales. (Incidentally no Middle Dutch version of the *Lai de Lanval* has come down to us.) As a contrast to these objectionable but popular stories, the Flemish poet offered his extensive world history, which provided not only entertainment but valuable and truthful information as well.

In the third part of the *Spiegel historiael*, which begins with the fall of the Roman empire and ends with Charlemagne's coronation as emperor in Rome, Maerlant deals with early British history (Gerritsen 1981, 379–80). His account is spread over three books. In Book I the poet devotes eight chapters to Brutus and British history (chapters 9–16). Fifteen chapters of Book V deal with the Saxon invasions, Vortiger, Merlin, Aurelius Ambrosius, Uther Pendragon, Arthur's accession to the throne, his conquests, his court and his war against the Romans (chapters 7–9, 13, 14, 19, 31, 32, 34, 48, 50–4). In chapters 29 and 30 of Book VI the war between Arthur and Mordred and the final battle on Salisbury Plain are described.

When Maerlant has reached the point where Arthur, then a fifteen-year-old youth, is crowned king, the poet interrupts his account with a comment on truth and fiction. He states that, although there exist many fabricated stories about Arthur, written by minstrels and buffoons who like to invent nonsensical stories, the truth about the king should not be disdained (Part III, Book V, chapter XLVIII, vv. 67–74). A little later Maerlant once more turns against the untruthful Arthurian romances, when he remarks that he will not write about Lancelot, Perceval and Agravain, because they are not historical figures; about Walewein (as Gawain/Gauvain is called in Dutch), Mordred and Keye (= Kay/Keu), however, he has found reliable information in Latin sources (Book V, chapter XLIX, vv. 18–24).

As Maerlant saw it, historical truth was to be found only in the Latin historiographical tradition. Of course, this tradition was in the first place represented by Vincent of Beauvais's *Speculum historiale*. But in his account of Arthurian history, of all places, Vincent was rather sparing with his information: his treatment of early British history, based on an enlarged version of Sigebert of Gembloux's *Chronographia*, is very concise. Unlike Vincent, however, Maerlant had a copy of Geoffrey of Monmouth's *Historia regum Britanniae* at his disposal. He used this source to extend Vincent's short account to 1,500 lines. The chapters in Book V, for example, are based mainly on Geoffrey's text (Gerritsen 1981, 378–9).

Maerlant's description of Arthur's rule is exceedingly positive. The poet depicts him as an admirable monarch, who was wise, generous, brave and forceful. Maerlant took this characterization from Geoffrey, but his exalted view of King Arthur probably also originated in his desire to provide his patron, Floris V, with a historically reliable model of princely excellence (Gerritsen 1981, 381–2; van Oostrom 1996, 316–18).

The *Spiegel historiael* has come down to us in nine manuscripts and around 250 fragments (Biemans 1998). Only one codex, however, is an illustrated copy of Maerlant's text. This manuscript, which is kept at the Royal Library in The Hague (MS K.A. XX) contains sixty-four illuminations of high quality. In all probability the codex was made in Ghent in the first decades of the fourteenth century. It has been suggested that the main illuminator had decorated French and Latin manuscripts as well, which would explain his great iconographical knowledge. Maerlant's story about Arthur is illustrated with four miniatures (Meuwese 1995; Meuwese 1996, 155–8; Janssens and Meuwese 1997). The first one (fol. 153v) depicts festivities at King Arthur's court. The miniature on fol. 154r shows the commander-in-chief of the Roman army, Lucius, sitting in his tent, and Walewein killing a Roman soldier. The third miniature (fol. 154v) depicts the battle between Arthur's army and the Romans. With the miniature on fol. 163v, we have arrived at the battle on Salisbury Plain. Two scenes are depicted: the fight between Arthur and Mordred, and Arthur's departure from the battlefield, lying on a cart and accompanied by the surviving knights. The importance of these four illuminations is clear if one realizes that in total there are no more than seven Arthurian illustrations in Middle Dutch manuscripts (Meuwese 1996).

Lodewijk van Velthem, *Spiegel historiael*

Maerlant ceased work on his *Spiegel historiael*, probably because of his declining health, when he had reached the year 1113. But the *Spiegel historiael* did not remain unfinished. Around 1300 the Flemish author Philip Utenbroeke translated the second part, which Maerlant had skipped. Later, in 1315, the Brabantine poet Lodewijk van Velthem finished the fourth part by describing the last period of Vincent's chronicle, which covered the years from 1113 to 1256. Velthem had been commissioned by Maria van Berlaer, a noblewoman from Antwerp. A year later Velthem even added a fifth part to Maerlant's *Spiegel historiael*. In this lengthy work (*c.* 30,000 lines) he described events between 1256 and 1316 (Lodewijk van Velthem, *Voortzetting van den Spiegel historiael*). Velthem dedicated his text, which has come down to us more or less complete in a manuscript dating from around 1325 (Deschamps 1972, 98–100), to Gerard van Voorne, viscount of Zeeland.

In the fifth part of the *Spiegel historiael* Velthem describes, among other things, events which took place in England in the days of Edward I. Of particular Arthurian interest is Velthem's report in Book II of a Round Table on the occasion of Edward's first marriage. The Brabantine poet tells us that Edward took on the identity of King Arthur, while members of his retinue became knights of the Round Table. During the meal, following the tournament, strange characters appeared, assigning tasks to Lancelot, Perceval and Walewein. All these tasks concerned the consolidation of royal power in distant parts of the country (Cornwall, Wales, Ireland). Accompanied by their king, the knights set out and fulfilled their tasks successfully.

Scholars have pointed out that Velthem's account of the events in England is historically inaccurate. Moreover, it has been assumed that Velthem's report of the Round Table is based on confusion with the Arthurian festivities which Edward is known to have organized on the occasion of his second marriage (Loomis 1953). Recently, however, the question of Velthem's historical reliability has been abandoned in favour of a narrative perspective (Summerfield 1998). Velthem appears to have linked the report of Edward's Round Table with the conflict between Edward and the nobleman Simon de Montfort who between 1263 and 1265 acted as the leader of a group of barons who strove for reforms during the reign of Edward's father King Henry III (1216–72).

In Book I Montfort betrays the young and inexperienced heir to the throne, Edward, and stirs up trouble in England. In Book II the emphasis is on the importance of co-operation. Edward is no longer a naive youth, but a powerful king, who settles his score with Montfort's followers in the guise of Arthur. The king is generous and hospitable, and he offers those knights who respect his authority the opportunity to prove themselves and to gain honour in battle. Thus it becomes clear that Velthem aimed at more than a faithful representation of historical events. In a narrative manner he presented his ideas on the ideal relationship between a sovereign and his knights. It is very likely that Velthem's views on kingship and the balance of power were of particular relevance to his audience. Around 1315 the Brabantine aristocracy saw themselves confronted with serious political problems, caused by the youthful age of Duke Jan III, who had succeeded his father at the age of twelve in 1312.

Translations and Adaptations of the French Prose Romances

Jacob van Maerlant, *Historie van den Grale* and *Boek van Merline*

The *Spiegel historiael* is not the only work by Jacob van Maerlant that was continued by Lodewijk van Velthem. This is also the case with two romances that Maerlant wrote around 1261: the *Historie van den Grale* and the *Boek van Merline*. These two texts were made for Albrecht van Voorne, viscount of Zeeland. In 1326 Velthem followed in Maerlant's footsteps with his *Merlijn*

Continuation, which was probably made for Albrecht's son Gerard van Voorne.
Velthem's text was meant to complement Maerlant's romances.

The *Historie van den Grale* and the *Boek van Merline* are Middle Dutch verse
renderings of the Old French prose versions of Robert de Boron's *Joseph
d'Arimathie* and *Merlin*. In the Prologue to these two romances, which form a
unity (*c.* 10,100 lines), Maerlant remarks:

> Jck wille dat gij des zeker zijt
> Dat ick de historie vele valsch
> Ge vonden hebbe in dat walsch
> Dar ze van gode onsen heren sprak
> Dat ene dat volck van rome wrack.
>> (Jacob van Maerlant, *Historie van den Grale und
>> Boek van Merline* vv. 20–4)

(*I want to assure you that I found the story in the French to be false in many respects
where it says of God, our Lord, that the people of Rome avenged him.*)

In this way the poet makes it clear already in his Prologue that his attitude
towards his French source is a critical one. Indeed, in the first 600 lines of the
Historie van den Grale the Flemish poet argues at length with Robert de Boron
(te Winkel 1881; Gerritsen 1981, 369–74). Maerlant gives credence to 'Der
waeren ewangelien woert' ('the true text of the gospel', v. 254), the *Gesta Pilati*
and Flavius Josephus' *Bellum Judaïcum*. Whenever the French author departs
from the content of the Latin texts, Maerlant intervenes, and tries to bring his
romance into agreement with Sacred History.

Maerlant's criticism only refers to the first part of the prose *Joseph
d'Arimathie*, in which the story of the Grail is linked with Christ's passion and
with Joseph of Arimathea. Maerlant follows his source closely from the moment
that God advises Joseph to construct the Grail table, in imitation of the table
that was used at the Last Supper. The second part of the *Historie van den Grale*
(from v. 640 onwards) and the *Boek van Merline* are faithful translations of
the Old French sources. The only exception is an interpolation of about 900
lines (vv. 1694–2581), the so-called *Processus Satanae* ('Satan's Lawsuit') or
Maskeroen (Gerritsen 1981, 374–6). Maerlant's *Maskeroen* is based on a lost
Latin source that has come down to us in the form of a late medieval printed
text, the *Litigacio Mascaron contra genus humanum* (van Oostrom 1996, 41–6).

At the beginning of the *Boek van Merline* the devils wonder how they can
restore their hold on the souls of the dead after Christ's harrowing of hell. At
this point Maerlant's interpolation follows. The devils decide to take legal action
and plead their case before God. They send Maskeroen, who summons Man
before God. On the appointed day, Good Friday, Man does not appear and is

therefore in danger of losing the case. Mary, however, speaks up for the accused. After a long debate she finally points to the fact that Man shall always be saved if he is baptized, has faith and has confessed his sins. When God confirms this, Maskeroen has lost the case. Here Maerlant's interpolation ends. The narrative continues with the devils' decision to engender a man who shall do their will (Merlin).

Why did Maerlant interpolate the *Maskeroen*? It is not unlikely that he wanted to stress the abundance of forgiveness that God offers the repentant sinner through Mary. And this is not the only lesson contained in the *Historie van den Grale* and the *Boek van Merline*. Maerlant emphasizes the need for timely confession, stresses the good influence that priests and clerics have on others, and provides examples of how young noblemen and kings should behave, how they should make the best use of advice, and which counsellors they should trust (Besamusca and Brandsma 1998). In short, Maerlant's romances may have had a didactic purpose. This is understandable if we assume that he wrote the *Historie van den Grale* and the *Book van Merline* for the education of a group of young noblemen, Albrecht van Voorne and Floris V among them (van Oostrom 1996, 127–36).

It is doubtful whether Maerlant still appreciated the didactic merit of his narrative about the Grail and Merlin when he was writing his *Spiegel historiael*. When in this world history he has reached the point where Uther Pendragon begets Arthur, he tells how French sources claim that Arthur had been nursed by Keye's mother, that Keye was wicked because he had had a wicked wet-nurse and that Arthur had pulled the sword from the stone. Because these particulars are lacking in the Latin, the poet dismisses them to the world of fantasy (Jacob van Maerlant, *Spiegel historiael*, Part III, Book V, chapter XXXII, vv. 77–90). At the same time, however, he must have realized that he himself had told such nonsensical tales (Gerritsen 1981, 380) for, twenty years earlier, in the *Boek van Merline*, he had written the same about Keye and Arthur, without showing a trace of doubt (vv. 9421–10079).

Lodewijk van Velthem, *Merlijn* Continuation

After Arthur had pulled the sword from the stone and been chosen as king, Maerlant concluded his *Book van Merline* by saying that for a long period of time Arthur ruled his country in peace, a statement which accords with his Old French source, the *Estoire de Merlin* (*The Vulgate Version of the Arthurian Romances*, 2, 88). Some sixty years later Lodewijk van Velthem replaced 'vreden' with 'onvreden' ('strife', v. 10082) and added a lengthy narrative in which young King Arthur, assisted by Merlin, tries to subdue his rebellious noblemen. Velthem's *Merlijn* Continuation counts around 26,000 lines (Jacob van Maerlant, *Merlijn* vv. 10409–36218).

Velthem's romance is a faithful verse translation of the *Suite-Vulgate du Merlin*. This Old French text forms the link between the coronation of Arthur (in the *Estoire de Merlin*) and Lancelot's birth (in the prose *Lancelot*). This raises the question of whether Velthem's *Merlijn* Continuation was meant to fulfil the same function in Middle Dutch literature. If this is the case, Velthem may have wanted to link his work and Maerlant's (*Historie van den Grale* and *Boek van Merline*) to the *Lancelot* Compilation, which contains a Middle Dutch translation of the prose *Lancelot* (see below). The fact that Velthem owned the only manuscript in which the compilation has been transmitted to us is in favour of this suggestion. On the other hand, it is strange that Velthem's *Merlijn* Continuation does not end with a transition to the prose *Lancelot*, as is usual in the *Suite-Vulgate du Merlin* (*The Vulgate Version of the Arthurian Romances*, 2, 465–6). Because of Merlin's fateful love for Viviane, Velthem ends his translation lamenting that women are capable of deceiving any man, however wise he may be (vv. 36192–207). He then writes that he finished his translation in 1326 (vv. 36208–18), without announcing a sequel (the *Lancelot* Compilation). Whether there is a connection between the three romances by Maerlant and Velthem on the one hand and the *Lancelot* Compilation on the other, is still an unsolved matter (Draak 1976, 6–10).

In Middle Dutch, Maerlant's *Historie van den Grale* and *Boek van Merline* and Velthem's *Merlijn* Continuation have been transmitted in fragmentary form only (Besamusca 1985, 34–9, 65–9; Kienhorst 1988, 66–7, 140–3; Klein, J. W. 1995, 9–10). In addition, an almost complete version of this trilogy has been preserved in a Middle Low German rendering from the Middle Dutch, in a codex from *c.* 1425 (Deschamps 1972, 33–5). This manuscript (Burgsteinfurt, Fürst zu Bentheimsche Schlossbibliothek, B 37) has always remained in the possession of the counts of Bentheim-Steinfurt.

A note at the end of the codex informs us that 'joncher Euerwyn van guterswick Greue to benthem' (referring to Everwin I of Bentheim (1397–1454) or his grandson Everwin II (1461–98)) owned more books containing Arthurian texts (Jacob van Maerlant, *Historie van den Grale und Boek van Merline*, 425). Besides 'dit boeck merlijn' ('this book Merlin'), 'twe nye boke van lantslotte' ('two new books about Lancelot') and 'eyn olt boek van lantslotte' ('an old book about Lancelot') are mentioned. In addition, the count owned a book about 'perceuale' (Perceval). We do not know what texts are referred to in this book list. Are the new books about Lancelot perhaps prose romances, and does the old book contain a verse romance about Lancelot? And does the name Perceval perhaps refer to (a translation of) Chrétien's *Conte du Graal*? Neither do we know in which language these works were written. However that may be, the book list proves that the counts of Bentheim-Steinfurt were very interested in Arthurian literature.

Historie van Merlijn

The events narrated in Maerlant's *Boek van Merline* are also the subject of the only printed Arthurian romance from the Low Countries that has survived. This is the *Historie van Merlijn*, which was published between 1534 and 1544 by the Antwerp printer Symon Cock (Pesch 1985). Of this print only two quires have survived. In quire B Vortigher is crowned king. He marries King Angis of Denmark's daughter and decides to build a castle to protect himself against Uther and Pendragon. In quire D Merlin is born. When he is six months old, he convinces the judge that his mother should not be executed for adultery.

The *Historie van Merlijn* is not based on Maerlant's *Boek van Merline*. This can be shown by the many differences which Maerlant's romance and the Old French *Estoire de Merlin* together show when compared with the printed text (Pesch 1985). The *Historie van Merlijn* has far more similarities with an English text about Merlin, *Of Arthour and Merlin*. The Middle Dutch romance turns out to be a prose translation of one of the different versions of the English text, *A lytel treatyse of ye byrth and the prophecye of Marlyn*. This text had been published in London in 1510 by Wynkyn de Worde. The Middle Dutch translator usually followed his source rather faithfully. When he departed from the original, he intended to correct inconsistencies and describe the events more concisely.

In Old French literature the *Estoire de Merlin* and the *Suite-Vulgate du Merlin* are part of a cycle of prose romances known as the Vulgate Cycle (Frappier 1959). Together with the *Estoire del Saint Graal* they precede the texts which form the three-part core of the cycle: *Lancelot en prose*, *Queste del Saint Graal* and *Mort le roi Artu*. The first part of the trilogy is about Lancelot, who, inspired by his love for the queen, becomes the world's best knight. In the middle part the knights of the Round Table search for the Grail; the chosen Grail hero is Lancelot's son Galaad. In the final part the fall of Arthur's kingdom is described. This trilogy was very popular in the Low Countries. Between *c.* 1235 and *c.* 1350 the *Lancelot en prose* was rendered into Middle Dutch at least three times and it is by no means ruled out that the work existed in five different translations (Draak 1954). The extant translations were written independently (Lie 1987).

Lantsloot vander Haghedochte

Lantsloot vander Haghedochte ('Lancelot of the Cave') is presumed to be the oldest (*c.* 1260?) extant Middle Dutch translation of the *Lancelot en prose*. It is a very free adaptation in verse by a Flemish poet, which must have consisted of more than 100,000 lines in total. What has come down to us are fragments from one codex of *c.* 1350, with almost 6,100 lines (Kienhorst 1988, 94–101). The existence of this romance was discovered in the mid-1930s by the German scholar Friedrich Meuser, who named the translation after its main hero. It is of course remarkable that Lancelot, in contrast to the Old French, does not bear the surname 'du Lac' ('of the Lake'), but 'vander Haghedochte' ('of the Cave'). In the Middle Dutch version the fairy who kidnaps Lancelot did not give her magical world the illusion of a lake. Consequently, she is not called the 'Dame du Lac', but the 'Joncfrouwe vander Haghedochte'; her domain has become a cave which cannot be found unless she wishes it. This is the place where Lancelot is raised. The adaptor probably opted for a different magical world because he considered the optical illusion of a non-existing lake too hard to imagine (van Oostrom 1981, 89–91).

In other passages, too, the adaptor tries to tell a story in which the events have a plausible explanation. As a result of this tendency towards rationalization, the Middle Dutch poet eliminates badly motivated elements and gives new and acceptable motivations for the behaviour of his characters (van Oostrom 1981, 69–95). When Hector, for example, comes to a plank leading across the water, he descends from his horse (*Lancelot*, 2, 350). In *Lantsloot vander Haghedochte* we are told why he acts like this: he sees a beautiful castle on the other side and wants to know who lives there (vv. 5820–3). Another example concerns Galehot. Searching for Lancelot, he sees a company of people paying homage to his friend's shield, which has been hung in a tree. After he has been politely informed about this show of honour, he tries to seize the shield, which leads to a fight (*Lancelot*, 3, 229–33). In *Lantsloot vander Haghedochte* the course of events has been made more natural. As soon as Galehot sees the shield, he tries to take it. The talking is left until after the fighting (vv. 3443–563).

The second major tendency in the poet's adaptation technique may be labelled blurring (van Oostrom 1981, 97–125). In the *Lancelot en prose* the knights act within a well-defined geographical and chronological framework. The Middle Dutch adaptor, however, blurs the exact references to place and time. When Sagremor, for example, rides on a narrow path, the Old French remarks that both horse and rider suffer from the thorns. After a long while the path broadens and the knight beholds a beautiful pavilion (*Lancelot*, 2, 281). In *Lantsloot vander Hagedochte* we read that Sagremor strayed completely from the right course and came upon a pavilion that had been erected (vv. 5089–92). The poet's description of roads and places is vague, too, and frequently names of places are omitted. With regard to the treatment of time, the subtle and exact chronological structure of the Old French work is completely lacking in *Lantsloot vander Haghedochte*.

In the *Lancelot en prose* we are told that we owe our knowledge of the exploits of Arthur's knights to the four clerks who recorded the accounts of knightly adventures. The suggestion that the romance is directly based on the stories of eye-witnesses is strengthened by the precise chronology and geography, and by the absence of an omnipresent first-person narrator who might endanger the text's reliability. In the *Lancelot en prose* the narrator hides behind 'li contes' ('the story'). This is clearly demonstrated by the formal switches, the formulaic transitions which serve to interweave the different strands of adventures, with phrases such as 'Or dist li contes' ('Now the tale tells') and 'Or se taist li contes' ('Now the tale is silent'). In *Lantsloot vander Haghedochte*, however, 'li contes' is replaced by the first-person narrator. The story is told by an omniscient 'I', who speaks directly to his audience (Gerritsen and van Oostrom 1980, 107f.; van Oostrom 1981, 119–23; Besamusca and Brandsma 1994, 18–20).

The most prominent tendency in the poet's adaptation technique is idealization (van Oostrom 1981, 127–59). The Middle Dutch author strove to make the manners, speech, valour and self-control of his characters meet the standards of perfect courtly behaviour. A characteristic example can be found in a meeting between Lancelot and a damsel. In the Old French romance the damsel addresses Lancelot as soon as she recognizes him (*Lancelot*, 2, 310). The corresponding passage in *Lantsloot vander Haghedochte* reads as follows:

> Doe si hem quam bet ghehende,
> Lantslote, ende siene kende
> Groete hi se eer si hem dede;
> Het was altoos sine zede
> Dat hi joncfrouwen groete
> Teersten dat hi se ghemoete.
> Ende si seide . . .
>   (*Lantsloot vander Haghedochte* vv. 5433–39)

(*When she came closer and recognized him, Lancelot, he greeted her before she did; it was his wont to greet damsels as soon as he met them. And she said . . .*)

The Middle Dutch adaptor makes the lesson more explicit by emphasizing the greeting that precedes the conversation, and through the person of Lancelot he demonstrates how one can behave in a perfect courtly manner. This tendency towards idealization may reveal what the adaptor intended with his work: *Lantsloot vander Haghedochte* was perhaps meant as a mirror of courtly behaviour for a court that was not yet familiar with courtly ideals (van Oostrom 1981, 221–30).

Lanceloet

Like *Lantsloot vander Haghedochte*, the second rhymed translation of the *Lancelot en prose* was produced (probably around 1280) by a Flemish poet. Its author, however, accepted most of the innovations of his Old French original and gave a more faithful translation. *Lanceloet*, as the romance is called, is an extensive yet incompletely preserved text of almost 37,000 verse lines (*Roman van Lancelot*, Book II, vv. 1–36947; *Lanceloet*, parts 1–4). The Middle Dutch translation corresponds with the last section of the *Lancelot en prose*, the 'Préparation à la Queste'. Together with Flemish verse translations of the *Queste del Saint Graal* (*c.* 11,000 lines) and the *Mort le roi Artu* (*c.* 13,000 lines), *Lanceloet* forms the core of the *Lancelot* Compilation. These three translations originated from one and the same author.

Lanceloet is the work of a virtuoso Flemish poet, who rendered his source as literally as possible into Middle Dutch, while at the same time observing the demands of rhyme and metre (*Lanceloet*, part 2, 35–73). For example, he changes the word order of the original in order to place a suitable word in rhyming position. Other stylistic devices include translating an Old French word with a Middle Dutch tautology, replacing an Old French word with a paraphrase, expanding one or two French words into a whole verse, and adapting the usage of direct and indirect speech to meet the requirements of versification. These translating procedures were mainly used to produce rhyme-words. It is evidence of craftsmanship that almost a quarter of the rhyming couplets are formed by a literal translation of two French words. Moreover, more than half of the rhyme pairs in the work consist of one translated French word and one Middle Dutch rhyme complement.

As to the poet's narrative technique, it is clear that he generally intended to follow his source in its depersonalization of the narrative voice. In *Lanceloet*, 'li contes' becomes 'daventure' ('the adventure', i.e. 'the story'), a word that resembles the French terminology in its ability to refer both to the source of the story and to the narrative itself. But the first-person narrator in *Lanceloet* does not completely hide behind 'daventure' (*Lanceloet*, part 3, 55–7; Besamusca and Brandsma 1994). When he uses line-filling rhyming formulas the Middle Dutch translator has a tendency to use phrases in which the first-person narrator shows up: 'dat seggic u' ('I tell you this') and 'als ict las' ('as I read it'). The narrator appears, moreover, in the transitions from one narrative thread to another. In about half of the formal switches 'daventure' leads the audience across the transition; in the other half 'daventure' and the first-person narrator both pull the strings. For example, when Hestor and Walewein, who are searching for Lancelot, part company, the formal switch reads as follows:

> Nu sal ic van Waleweine bedieden
> Wat avonturen hem gescieden.
>   Nu gewaget davonture das:
> Alse Walewein gesceden was
> Van Hestore, hi maecte sine vart
> Recht ten foreeste wart.   (*Lanceloet* vv. 3537–42)

(*Now I shall tell [you] about Walewein, what adventures befell him. Now the story tells that Walewein rode to the forest when he had taken leave of Hestor.*)

In formal switches like this, the first-person narrator speaks to his audience, and then moves to the background in favour of 'daventure'.

Queeste vanden Grale

Whereas *Lanceloet* is a faithful translation of the *Lancelot en prose*, the *Queeste vanden Grale* differs in many places from the Old French source. Although the Middle Dutch romance (*Roman van Lancelot*, Book III, vv. 1–11160) contains many examples of very close translations, the Flemish poet generally tries to shorten the story, for example by eliminating repetitions. In particular, he leaves out large parts of the theological discussions between the ubiquitous hermits and the knights. Moreover, he omits expressions of devotion and religious sentiments on the part of the knights, and descriptions of daily life and scenery (Prins-s'Jacob 1980).

In an interesting passage which has been added to the Middle Dutch, the narrator informs his audience about his narrative technique (vv. 1181–206). What is the best way to tell the adventures of the individual knights? In the opinion of the first-person narrator it is not wise to unwind the separate threads in the story quickly, for 'Quade haeste es dicke onspoet' ('More haste, less speed', v. 1191). But on the other hand, 'daert glat es moet men gliden' ('where it is slippery, one has to slide', v. 1194). The narrator takes up a modest position and apologizes for his mistakes in advance.

Outside the *Lancelot* Compilation, the translation of the *Queste del Saint Graal* has only been preserved in a fourteenth-century fragment (Besamusca 1985, 57–8; Kienhorst 1988, 169–70).

Arturs doet

In the *Lancelot* Compilation, *Arturs doet* ('Arthur's death') is the romance which concludes the cycle (*Roman van Lancelot*, Book IV, vv. 1–13054). This Flemish translation of the *Mort le roi Artu* has not only been transmitted in the compilation. A fourteenth-century small fragment of the text was discovered a few years ago (Croenen and Janssens 1994, Biemans 1995).

The poet of *Arturs doet* used an Old French text which differed strongly from the common version of the *Mort Artu*. One of the French manuscripts containing a condensed version of the story was on his desk. Consequently, the Middle Dutch romance lacks, for example, one of the best-known scenes in Arthurian literature (Groninger neerlandici 1983, 201). The common version of the *Mort Artu* contains a passage in which a beautiful boat arrives at Arthur's court with the body of the damsel of Escalot. From the letter which she carries upon her person, it appears that she died because Lancelot did not return her love. This episode appears neither in the condensed version of the *Mort Artu* nor in *Arturs doet*.

The translation of the *Mort Artu* is preceded by a remarkable religious argument of almost 300 lines (vv. 1–296), based on the first chapter of *De modo orandi*, a Latin treatise by Hugh of Saint-Victor (Vekeman and Schröder 1997). The poet, in all probability the same person as the one who translated the *Mort le roi Artu*, deals with the question of how people should pray to God in order to be heard. The treatise forms a clue for the interpretation of *Arturs doet*. The idea that prayer is of crucial importance for the eternal salvation of man is confirmed by the following story. All worldly matters turn out to be fleeting, all courtly ideals fall short of expectations in the end, and only God's mercy is boundless and endless. At the end of the romance, Lancelot, the paragon of worldly knighthood, cuts himself off from the world. The four years which he spends praying and fasting save his soul. In the end, prayers are more valuable than chivalrous deeds (Besamusca and Lie 1994).

Lancelot Compilation

The three thirteenth-century Flemish romances *Lanceloet*, *Queeste vanden Grale* and *Arturs doet* were used as the framework for the *Lancelot* Compilation. This is a Brabantine narrative cycle of ten Arthurian romances, which was compiled around 1320 (Deschamps 1972, 47–50; Klein, J. W, 1995, 6–10). As far as we know, the creator of this cycle did not write the individual romances himself; he made use of already existing Middle Dutch works. Between *Lanceloet* and *Queeste* two texts have been inserted: *Perchevael* and *Moriaen*; between *Queeste* and *Arturs doet* five romances have been placed: *Wrake van Ragisel*, *Ridder metter mouwen*, *Walewein ende Keye*, *Lanceloet en het hert met de witte voet* and *Torec*. These seven romances will be discussed separately; here the *Lancelot* Compilation as a whole is dealt with.

The compiler has divided the cycle into four books. *Lanceloet*, *Perchevael* and *Moriaen* together make up the second book. The third book consists of *Queeste vanden Grale* and the following five inserted romances. The fourth book consists of only one work, *Arturs doet*. With about 87,300 lines the cycle is a lengthy work (*Roman van Lancelot*), yet it is incompletely preserved. The *Lancelot* Compilation was originally divided over two volumes. The first volume, containing two-thirds of *Lanceloet*, was lost.

The *Lancelot* Compilation is a fine example of a narrative cycle (Besamusca 1994 and Besamusca 1996). For one thing, the order of the texts has been determined with care. The romances in which Perceval plays an important part, viz. *Perchevael* and *Moriaen*, have been placed before *Queeste vanden Grale*, because he dies in the latter romance. Moreover, and this is more important, the ten romances have been linked by transitional passages. The transition that precedes *Moriaen* is a typical example. *Perchevael* ends with a feast. The narrator then says:

> Ende nu oec in dese feeste
> Suldi horen vele oreeste,
> Die een riddere maecte omtrent,
> Die Perchevale te hove nu sent,
> Ende van hem sal vort sijn die tale
> Ende oec mede van Perchevale:
> Van dat sine soeken varen
> Sal ic u hier al oppenbaren.
> (*Roman van Lancelot*, Book II, vv. 42539–46)

(And now you shall hear about the commotion which a knight, sent to the court by Perceval, caused during the feast. And about him and Perceval the story will continue. I shall tell you how they were going to search for him [=Perceval].)

After this linking passage, *Moriaen* starts with a court festival, at which a robber knight arrives, who has been defeated by Perceval. When the king laments Perceval's absence, Lancelot and Walewein decide to go and search for him, and this starts off the Moriaen story.

In addition a system of cross-references is used to present the individual romances in the *Lancelot* Compilation as one coherent unity. In *Queeste vanden Grale*, for example, Walewein meets a hermit who urges him to confess his sins. In both the Middle Dutch text and the Old French source (*La Queste del Saint Graal*, 55) Arthur's nephew refuses to follow this advice. Contrary to the Old French, the Middle Dutch hermit then predicts that Walewein will get into trouble because of his stubborn behaviour. A damsel will fall in love with him and imprison his brother (*Roman van Lancelot*, Book III, vv. 2578–95). Thereupon the narrator remarks that this adventure will be recounted later. The narrator's words announce the first episode of *Wrake van Ragisel*, in which the Lady of Galestroet keeps Gaheriet prisoner in order to lure his brother Walewein to her castle.

It is still unclear for what purpose the *Lancelot* Compilation was assembled. Why did the compiler insert the romances? One possibility is that he aimed at an alternation between the adventures of Lancelot and those of Walewein (Gerritsen 1963, 252). It is also conceivable that he inserted romances in which Walewein had the principal part in order to pay ample attention to Arthur's nephew as a positive hero. In this way he may have wanted to correct the negative image of Walewein in the core of the *Lancelot* Compilation (Zemel 1992, 95–7). As an explanation for the romances inserted between *Queeste vanden Grale* and *Arturs doet*, it has been suggested that the compiler thought that Wace's twelve-year period of peace – during which the adventures of the individual knights took place – lay between the two romances (Koekman 1991). This, however, is improbable, as *Queeste vanden Grale* stresses the Grail quest as the most important and final adventure (*Lanceloet*, part 3, 202; Besamusca 1994, 90). In order to explain why romances were inserted between the three main parts of the *Lancelot* compilation, further study is necessary.

Opinions also vary as to the identity of the compiler. Two persons qualify as candidates: the aforementioned poet Lodewijk van Velthem and the most important copyist of the codex (the writing was executed by five scribes), known as B (*Lanceloet*, part 1, 16–19). Velthem's candidacy is supported by his being a poet and by the fact that he owned the *Lancelot* Compilation at one time: on the last page of the codex, B has noted: 'Hier indet boec van Lancelote, dat heren Lodewijcs es van Velthem' ('Here ends the Book of Lancelot, which belongs to Sir Lodewijc of Velthem'). Scribe B produced the largest part of the codex and supervised the work of the other scribes. He also wrote the transitional passages, corrected a narrative error in *Wrake van Ragisel*, and rewrote (on an erasure) part of *Perchevael*. All this points to the possibility that he was the compiler. Recently it has been suggested that Velthem and scribe B were one and the same person (Klein, J. W. 1998).

Velthem's name is also connected with an aspect of the *Lancelot* Compilation that is unique in the medieval manuscript tradition. Substantial parts of the text have been revised by a person known as the corrector (Gerritsen 1976; *Lanceloet*, part 1, 19–22). It has been argued convincingly that he took an active part in the original production of the manuscript (Klein, J. W. 1990; *Lanceloet*, part 1, 105). This corrector may have been Velthem himself. Be that as it may, the corrector not only corrected scribal errors, he also smoothed away Flemish dialectical features and added marginal signs (dots, for instance) and short words. These words are vocatives like 'here' ('Sir') and 'vrouwe' ('Lady'), interjections like 'ay' ('ah'), and, above all, conjunctions like 'ende' ('and'), 'mer' ('but') and 'want' ('because'). In all probability these marginal signs and words were added by the corrector to facilitate the text's oral delivery.

The Middle Dutch Prose *Lancelot*

Unlike *Lantsloot vander Haghedochte* and *Lanceloet*, the third extant Middle Dutch translation of the *Lancelot en prose* is a prose text; when and where the author worked is not known. A very small part of the text has been preserved in the so-called Rotterdam Fragments (Besamusca 1985, 28–30; Kienhorst 1988, 90–1). The prose translator favoured a word-for-word translation, although occasionally he replaced a French phrase by a more condensed paraphrase (Lie 1987).

The Middle Dutch *Lancelot en prose* tradition included more than the three extant translations of the Old French text (Draak 1954). A lost translation probably underlies the German *Lancelot* romance in the so-called Blankenheim codex of the Stadtarchiv in Cologne (Lie 1991). From the colophon it appears that the text is based on a Flemish original:

> Diss buchelin zu einer stonden
> Hain ich inn flemische geschrieben fonden,
> Von eyme kostigen [konstigen?] meister verricht,
> Der es uss franczose darczu hait gedicht.
> Dwile das alle dutschen nit konden verstan,
> Habe ich unnutzeliche zcijt darczu versliessen und gethan,
> Biss das ich es herczu bracht hain.   (*Lancelot* II, 115)

(*This book is based on a book that I found a while ago, which was written in Flemish by a skilful (?) master, who translated it from the French. Because the German people cannot understand it, I have devoted much time and effort to bringing this book to this state of completion.*)

This is the only explicit reference to Middle Dutch intermediation in the German prose *Lancelot* tradition (see also Tilvis 1957).

Probably a second Middle Dutch translation was lost. This text was the source for the German *Lancelot* fragment housed in Munich. As this fragment dates from about 1250, the Middle Dutch translation must have been made in the first half of the thirteenth century. The remarkable implication of this is that the Old French *Lancelot en prose* was rendered into Middle Dutch almost immediately after its creation (Klein, Th. 1994, 228–9).

Translations and Adaptations of the French Verse Romances

Tristant

Judging by the manuscript tradition Lancelot enjoyed a much greater popularity in the Low Countries than Tristan. Of the latter only one text, and a fragmentary one at that, has been preserved. It consists of no more than 158 partly damaged lines from a manuscript that was written in the eastern part of the Low Countries around the middle of the thirteenth century (Besamusca 1985, 63–4; Kienhorst 1988, 192–3). The fragment contains a passage from the end of the Tristan story. The hero meets a namesake who is on his way to Arthur's court to find help against a knight who has abducted his wife. Tristan is severely wounded in his efforts to assist (Gysseling, *Corpus*, 337–42; Winkelman, 'Zu den Wiener *Tristant*-Fragmenten', 822–7).

The Middle Dutch episode shows close similarities with the version which Thomas d'Angleterre wrote around 1175. In Thomas's romance Tristan and Kaherdin meet Tristan the Dwarf, who is searching for Tristan to ask him for help because of the abduction of his wife. However, the Middle Dutch differs from the French text on salient points. In the Middle Dutch *Tristant* the man whose wife has been abducted is not a dwarf, and rumour has it that Tristan is dead. The most important difference between Thomas and the Middle Dutch version is that Tristan and Arthur are contemporaries in the Middle Dutch text, as in the versions of Béroul and Eilhart. Because of this it has been suggested that the Middle Dutch poet was acquainted with an oral version of the Tristan story (Gerritsen 1994, 159–61; see also Winkelman 1998).

Although only one Middle Dutch text about Tristan has come down to us, Middle Dutch literature often refers to the story of Tristan and Isolde. References are found not only in some Arthurian romances (*Perchevael*, *Ridder metter mouwen*, *Walewein*), but also outside the domain of Arthurian literature. A fine example can be found in a text by Dirc Potter (*c.* 1370–1428), who was employed as a civil servant and diplomat by the Count of Holland (van Buuren 1994). In his treatise on love, *Der minnen loep* ('The Course of Love'), written in 1411–12, Potter exemplifies his discussion of the characteristics of good love with, among other stories, that of Tristan's and Iseut's rendezvous under the tree in which King Mark is hiding to entrap them. Iseut sees the reflection of her husband's head in the well, and draws attention to this by pointing to the fish in the water. After this the only thing the lovers do is praise the king. In Potter's view, cunning is permitted to preserve a woman's honour (Winkelman 1986, 166–8, 187–8). This Tristan scene is depicted in the Leiden manuscript of *Der minnen loep* (Meuwese 1996, 158–60).

The tryst-beneath-the-tree scene is also depicted on leather slippers from the second half of the fourteenth century. One of these slippers, moreover, has an inscription which reads 'Triestram siedi niet dat viselkiin' ('Tristan, don't you see the little fish'). The motif of the fish matches Potter's version of the scene. It is thought that Potter did not invent this reference to the fish himself, but was influenced by an iconographical source (Winkelman 1995, 250, 256; Meuwese 1996, 159–60).

Perchevael

Tristan also plays a role in the Middle Dutch *Perchevael*, which is part of the *Lancelot* Compilation. This text consists of a translation of the Gauvain part of Chrétien's *Perceval*, followed by several Gauvain adventures from the First *Perceval* Continuation. In addition, the compiler has added episodes of his own invention. In one of these inserted episodes Tristan is challenged to a duel by Lancelot.

The Middle Dutch *Perchevael* numbers about 5,600 lines of the *Lancelot* Compilation (*Roman van Lancelot*, Book II, vv. 36951–42546). The romance begins with the arrival of the Loathly Lady at Arthur's court, announcing several adventures. At the same time, Walewein is challenged to a duel by Giganbrisiel at the court of the king of Escavalon. While Walewein is riding to Escavalon, the other knights, such as Keu and Agravain, try to accomplish the adventures. They succeed, owing especially to the brave deeds of Perceval. At Escavalon the duel between Walewein and Giganbrisiel is postponed for a year. Walewein must find the Bleeding Lance. At Montesclare, where a damsel is being besieged, he saves the lives of Mordret and Griflet. When the damsel has been freed with the assistance of other knights of King Arthur, Walewein continues his search. He reaches a castle which is inhabited by Arthur's mother and her daughter Clariane, and fights against Griromelant. When Arthur arranges a marriage between Griromelant and Clariane, Walewein leaves indignantly. A search for him is organized. During this quest an unknown knight, who will afterwards turn out to be Lancelot, challenges a number of knights, among them Tristan, to a duel. Walewein visits the Grail castle. Afterwards he fights with Dyandras; eventually they decide to postpone their duel. While those participating in the search for Walewein return to Arthur's court, Arthur's nephew reaches Escavalon, where, in the presence of Arthur, he takes on two opponents simultaneously: Giganbrisiel and Dyandras. After his victory Walewein returns to Carlioen with the king.

In the first half of the thirteenth century Chrétien's *Perceval* was translated by a Brabantine poet (van den Berg 1983, 208–9; van den Berg 1987, 5–6). His text has been preserved as a fragment (Besamusca 1985, 50–5; Kienhorst 1988, 164–8). The Middle Dutch poet seems to have made a rather faithful translation of Chrétien's text (Hogenhout-Mulder 1984, 167–290). It was this translation that was incorporated within the *Lancelot* Compilation, drastically abridged and with radical changes (*Lanceloet*, part 1, 15).

The compiler had to modify the *Perceval* translation radically in order to adjust it to the *Lancelot* Compilation. In accordance with Chrétien's *Perceval*, the Middle Dutch translation described how Perceval as a young man travelled to Arthur's court to become a knight. He killed the Red Knight and met

Blancheflor, who appeared at his bedside during the night. At the Grail castle he failed to ask questions about the Grail and the Bleeding Lance. All these events have been omitted from the compiler's version of *Perchevael*, because they were incompatible with the story of Perceval in the core of the *Lancelot* Compilation. It is for narrative reasons that the compiler's *Perchevael* begins with the arrival of the hideous damsel at Arthur's court.

When the Loathly Lady turns up at Arthur's court, we read in Chrétien's *Perceval* and in the Middle Dutch translation that she greets all those present with the exception of Perceval. She reproves him for having remained silent at the castle of the Fisher King. As a consequence, a great disaster will befall the world. Since Perceval's visit to the Grail Castle has been left out by the compiler, the damsel cannot but greet all those present in the compilaton version of *Perchevael*, with the exception of no one. Her reproaches to Perceval have also been omitted by the compiler.

When the Loathly Lady has left Arthur's court, Perceval vows in Chrétien's romance that he will solve the secret of the Grail and the Bleeding Lance. In the compiler's *Perchevael* he declares that he will search for knightly adventures (*Roman van Lancelot*, Book II, vv. 37017–24). At this point in the *Lancelot* Compilation Perceval has not yet embarked on his quest for the Grail.

One of the best-known passages in the Perceval story is the so-called Good Friday episode. After having travelled around for years it happens one Good Friday that the hero meets his uncle, who is a hermit. The latter enlightens him as to the mystery of the Grail and presents to him a form of knighthood that is based on the love of God. Perceval repents and does penance for his sins. Perceval's stay with his uncle does not fit within the context of the compilation and therefore this episode is omitted from the compiler's *Perchevael*.

Not only does the compiler change Perceval's role to a great extent, he also adds adventures of other knights. He uses the narrative technique of *entrelacement*, the interweaving of narrative threads, to insert new episodes into the Middle Dutch translation (Brandsma 1995, 37). When Walewein is on his way to Escavalon, knights such as Agravain and Keye have several adventures, which are told in alternation. Later on in the story a group of knights from Arthur's court set out to search for Walewein, who has disappeared. Then we are told, among other things, how Dodineel, Keye and Tristan are defeated by Lancelot, who fights incognito. Acglaval kills Gregorias, who stole Walewein's horse earlier on in the story. Thus a narrative thread from the Middle Dutch translation of Chrétien's *Perceval* is tied up (Oppenhuis de Jong 1996).

It will be clear that *Perchevael* is actually an incorrect title for the compiler's version. The romance's main character is not Perceval, but Walewein. While Perceval plays a modest role and is not associated with the Grail, Walewein is the undisputed hero of the work, which fits the context of the *Lancelot* Compilation.

Wrake van Ragisel

Walewein is also the main character in the *Wrake van Ragisel* ('The Avenging of Ragisel'), the Middle Dutch translation of *Vengeance Raguidel*. The Old French romance was rendered into Middle Dutch in the first decades of the thirteenth century on the border between Brabant and Flanders (Gysseling, *Corpus*, 352; van den Berg 1983, 207–8). About 1,000 lines of this work have been preserved (Besamusca 1985, 71–4; Kienhorst 1988, 224–7). If one compares the remains of this translation with the Old French original, the Middle Dutch poet appears to have been a creative adaptor (Gerritsen 1963, 85–151). For example, he increases the tension of certain situations by arranging events differently. Furthermore, he amplifies descriptions of duels, festive meals, and other topoi of Arthurian romance. The *Vengeance Raguidel*'s love scenes are rewritten in such a way that Walewein is a much more courtly lover than Gauvain in the Old French romance.

A radically abridged version of the Middle Dutch translation of the *Vengeance Raguidel* is part of the *Lancelot* Compilation. Here the text numbers 3,400 lines (Gerritsen 1963). The romance begins at Arthur's court, with the arrival of a ship richly fitted out and bearing Ragisel's corpse. Walewein is able to draw the broken lance point from the dead knight's chest, which means that he is the chosen knight to avenge Ragisel's death with the remainder of the weapon. He must be assisted by Ydier, the knight who drew the five golden rings from the dead man's hand. But when Walewein leaves the court, he forgets to take the lance point. On his way he defeats the Black Knight who harboured a deep hatred against him, and liberates his brother Gariet from the hands of the Damsel of Galestroet. Because Walewein had scorned her, she had planned to decapitate him with a sort of guillotine in a window. Against his brother's wishes Walewein next frees a damsel, Ydeine, with whom he immediately falls in love. The three of them travel to Arthur's court, where an ill-fitting magic cloak has revealed the infidelity of the queen and of Keye's beloved. Ydeine is not faithful to Walewein either. Disappointed, he gives her to Druidein, the knight who had claimed her as his beloved. While the Black Knight marries the Damsel of Galestroet, Walewein meets Ragisel's lady friend in Scotland. This time he has not forgotten to take the lance point. Assisted by Ydier, Walewein defeats Ragisel's murderer, Gygantioen. Ydier marries Gygantioen's daughter. When Ydier has become a knight of the Round Table and is on his way home, Lancelot forces him to a duel. Bohort manages to reconcile the two knights. A short while after, Lancelot and Bohort help Dodineel to save a damsel whose hair had been woven into the branches of a tree.

In the *Lancelot* Compilation, the *Wrake van Ragisel* is placed immediately after the *Queeste vanden Grale*. The two romances are linked by means of a reference ahead in the *Queeste vanden Grale* and by means of a passage in which the Damsel of Galestroet's love for Walewein is explained. She is said to have fallen in love with Arthur's nephew already in *Queeste vanden Grale* and to have captured Gariet to lure the object of her love to her castle (Gerritsen 1963, vv. 1–74). This passage is one of the compiler's many interpolations in the abridged Middle Dutch translation of *Vengeance Raguidel*. He inserted two chapters in his abridged part, and added two more (Gerritsen 1963, 193–261).

In the first inserted episode Walewein wants to know the thoughts of women (vv. 1475–894). His wish arises from his uncertainty concerning Ydeine's chastity. In a forest he meets a dwarf king who is able to transform people. The king's wife is forced to take her meals in a separate room as a punishment for her adultery with a servant. When Walewein wants to know more about the thoughts of women, he and the king go to Arthur's court together. In the guise of a dwarf Walewein effortlessly seduces Ydeine. In this way it becomes clear that women are essentially promiscuous. This anti-feminist episode is probably intended to disguise Walewein's shortcomings in the story. His impulsive and naive behaviour in love, one of Gauvain's traditional flaws in the Old French romances, is pardoned as it were because women are depraved creatures anyway.

The second chapter which was inserted in the Middle Dutch translation of *Vengeance Raguidel* is about the Black Knight and Gariet (vv. 2025–426). When the Damsel of Galestroet wants to burn her maid at the stake because of her assistance in the escape of Walewein and Gariet, the girl is saved by the Black Knight. Together with Gariet and Arthur's army, he besieges the Damsel of Galestroet's castle. In a duel the Black Knight defeats the damsel's champion, who turns out to be Keye. The Black Knight marries the damsel. The interpolation is clearly meant to provide a conclusion to the adventures of the Black Knight, Gariet, the Damsel of Galestroet and her maid.

The compiler added two episodes after the translation of *Vengeance Raguidel* (vv. 2977–3414). In these passages Lancelot again appears on the stage. He reacts to the test with the cloak (Besamusca 1996, 115–16). His beloved's loss of honour has infuriated him. When he meets Ydier with Ragisel's lady friend, he loses his self-control as soon as he sees her cloak. The knights engage in a fight, which is interrupted by Bohort, who reconciles the two parties. In reply to Lancelot's inquiry as to how the queen reacted to the test with the cloak, Bohort comments that there was far more commotion over Keye's friend, also that the arrival of Walewein and his brother Gariet (the latter had long been imprisoned) brought such joy that the cloak was not mentioned again (Gerritsen 1963, vv. 3159–70). Bohort's report eases Lancelot's mind, since the queen's shame was evidently hardly noticed. This concludes the compiler's account of the magic cloak.

Lanceloet en het hert met de witte voet

The shortest text in the *Lancelot* Compilation numbers about 850 lines. It is *Lanceloet en het hert met de witte voet* ('Lancelot and the Stag with the White Foot'), which begins with a powerful queen's announcement at Arthur's court that she will marry the knight who is able to bring her the white foot of a certain stag that is guarded by lions. With a small white dog for a guide, Keye is the first to set out, but he fails. Lancelot succeeds in his attempt. He kills the lions, but is cheated by a knight who leaves him behind severely wounded and who then claims the damsel with the aid of the white foot. Walewein sets out in search of Lancelot. He finds him and arrives just in time to prevent the impostor's marriage to the damsel. When Lancelot has recovered, he goes to the damsel's court together with Walewein, where Arthur's nephew announces Lancelot's wish to postpone the marriage until his family will be able to attend. When the damsel has consented to this, the two knights return to Arthur's court.

Lanceloet en het hert met de witte voet has been transmitted exclusively in the *Lancelot* Compilation. In all probability the compiler made use of a Middle Dutch text dating from the second half of the thirteenth century. This work is somehow related to the Old French *Lai de Tyolet*. It is possible that both texts go back to a common source, a tale reminiscent of the dragon tongue episode in the Tristan tradition. It is also conceivable that *Lanceloet en het hert met de witte voet* is a reworking of the second part of *Lai de Tyolet* (Zemel 1992).

If one compares the Old French text with the Middle Dutch work, the role of Keye is the first thing to attract attention. In *Lai de Tyolet* it is Lodoër who makes the first attempt. When he does not succeed in crossing the dangerous river, he returns to Arthur's court without lamenting his failure. In the Middle Dutch text Keye is portrayed as the traditional failure with a bad character. He does not dare to cross the river either. But, contrary to Lodoër, he worries about his reputation. He tries to kill the little dog in order to solve his problems. When he fails, he can only think of a silly excuse: he had suddenly fallen ill.

Whereas it is Tyolet who is successful in *Lai de Tyolet*, it is Lancelot who acquires the white foot in the Middle Dutch text. Unlike Tyolet, however, Lancelot is not a free man. In the context of the *Lancelot* Compilation he is the devoted lover of Arthur's wife. This has consequences for the end of the story. Whereas Tyolet marries the damsel, Lancelot's marriage is postponed, and the narrator comments that Lancelot is well pleased at this, since his love for the queen is the most important thing in the world for him, and because of this love he would not have taken the damsel to wife (*Lanceloet en het hert met de witte voet* vv. 823–31). So Lancelot had undertaken a quest that was not his. Because of his love for the queen, his pursuit of the stag is a foolish venture. The poet may have wished to ironize Lancelot by this, with the intention of creating a contrast with Walewein, who is the positive and successful hero of the text (Zemel 1992).

Torec

Like *Lanceloet en het hert met de witte voet*, *Torec* has been transmitted only in the *Lancelot* Compilation. This story of about 4,000 lines deals with Torec's quest for a precious diadem stolen from his grandmother. The object has by then passed into the hands of Miraude, who wants to marry only the knight who succeeds in defeating all the knights of the Round Table. During his search for Miraude Torec has several adventures. A magical ship, for example, takes him to a castle where he spends three days in the Chamber of Wisdom listening to conversations about virtues and love. Torec's narrative thread is interlaced with that of Melions, a knight who saves an abducted princess from the hands of a giant and is therefore granted the reward of her hand in marriage. At the castle of Miraude Torec defeats forty of King Arthur's knights. At Walewein's suggestion half of them fight with cut saddle girths to make it easier for Torec. At Arthur's court the same trick is used, so that Torec unseats all his opponents. Finally, he is himself defeated by Arthur, who surpasses everyone in strength. When Torec's mother, Tristoise, sees Miraude with the diadem, she smiles for the third time since her son's birth. Torec and Miraude are married.

The compiler almost certainly used an older version of the Torec story. His source was probably a romance written by Jacob van Maerlant around 1262. Maerlant's text has not come down to us, but in the prologue to his *Historie van Troyen*, written around 1264, he mentions that he has written a *Toerecke*. This text may have been intended as a mirror for princes. Together with some of Maerlant's other works, such as the *Historie van den Grale* and the *Boek van Merline*, *Torec* would have been meant to prepare a group of aristocratic youngsters on the island of Voorne, among them the later count, Floris V, for their future tasks. The romance would have functioned for this audience both as wish fulfilment and as a source of inspiration (Koekman 1988; van Oostrom 1996, 130–2).

In Old French literature a romance about Torec existed which is now lost: *Torrez, le Chevalier au cercle d'or*. The title unmistakably points to the same story that Maerlant tells, which makes it very likely that the Flemish poet reworked an Old French Arthurian romance. It is impossible to establish what Maerlant's source was like, what he did with it and how, in his turn, the compiler went about his work (van Oostrom 1979).

In the Chamber of Wisdom Torec listens to conversations on virtues, desirable behaviour and love. It has been suggested that this episode in *Torec* is of Maerlant's own invention, because the argument about the decline of the world, which is caused in particular by greed, matches Maerlant's tone (van

Oostrom 1996, 238–41). The Flemish poet may also be responsible for the striking portrait of Arthur as an invincible knight. Because Arthur surpasses everyone, he does not participate in tournaments, for he would always win. Moreover, he sets out incognito to fight against injustice in his realm. This characterization of the king accords so well with Maerlant's ideas about the ideal sovereign that it has been suggested that we owe this royal portrait in *Torec* to him (van Oostrom 1996, 249–50).

A remarkable aspect of *Torec* is the link with Chrétien's *Perceval*. When Torec has liberated the Damsel of Montesclaire, she tells him that she had provoked the siege of her castle by refusing to accept any knight as her lover. The siege formed part of her plan to find the ideal husband. She expected to get one of the best knights of the Round Table to protect her castle and to take him as her husband thereafter (*Torec* vv. 1270–80). This explanation leads to a reinterpretation of the events in *Perceval*. In the Old French romance the Loathly Lady announced that the knight who raised the siege of Montesclaire would receive the sword of the strange rings. According to the *Torec*, however, she appeared at Arthur's court to lure a suitable husband to Montesclaire. It is likely that this connection with Chrétien's *Perceval* was already present in the Old French *Torrez*, because in the compiler's *Perchevael* the damsel had previously been liberated by a group of Arthur's knights.

Ferguut

Unlike most Arthurian romances treated in this section, *Ferguut* has not come down to us in the *Lancelot* Compilation. The only extant manuscript is in Leiden University Library: MS Ltk. 191 (Deschamps 1972, 42–47; *Ferguut: A facsimile*). The codex was made between 1325 and 1350 in western Brabant (Kuiper 1989, 25–60; Klein, J. W. 1995, 10–11). The first folio of the manuscript contains a damaged historiated initial, depicting a knight standing upright and carrying a sword and a shield. This knight could be the patron of the manuscript or he could represent the protagonist of the romance (Meuwese 1996, 154).

A different, but contemporary hand made almost 250 corrections in the manuscript. This unknown corrector justifies his work in the colophon:

> Here, hier hebdi van Ferragute
> Van beghinne ten inde al ute
> Ghecorrigeert van miere hant
> Over al soe waer ict vant
> In rijm, in vers, in ward messcreven.   (*Ferguut* vv. 5597–601)

(*Lord, here you have the story about Ferguut, from beginning to end corrected by me wherever I found wrongly written rhymes, lines and words.*)

The corrector did not have another *Ferguut* manuscript at his disposal. For his interventions he based himself on the immediate context or he repeated the original text in other words. In this, he paid special attention to the formal aspect of the text, such as impure rhymes (Kuiper 1989, 71–215).

In the opening episode of *Ferguut* Perceval wins the golden cup which Arthur had promised to the knight who succeeded in killing the white stag. Ferguut meets Arthur's retinue and wants to become a knight as well. At the court he is mocked by Keye, who challenges him to defeat the Black Knight. On his way to the black rock Ferguut spends the night at the castle of Ydel, where Galiene, niece to the lord of the castle, declares her love for him. But Ferguut does not have time for love, he is under the spell of knighthood. When he has defeated the Black Knight on the next day and returns to Ydel, Galiene has disappeared. Ferguut realizes that he has behaved shamefully towards her. He decides to go and look for the damsel, with whom he has all of a sudden fallen in love. The knights whom he defeats during his search are sent to Arthur's court. A dwarf tells him he has to win the White Shield to be able to find Galiene. After searching far and wide he is able to secure the shield by defeating two giants. When he hears that Galiene's castle is under siege, he goes to her rescue without disclosing his identity. Galiene realizes that she cannot rule her territory on her own and therefore she asks Arthur to find her a husband. The king will organize a tournament, the prize being Galiene's hand in marriage. In this tournament Ferguut revenges himself on Keye by unseating him. Ferguut defeats all the knights of the Round Table, with the exception of Gawein. When he has been recognized and been declared the winner of the tournament, he marries Galiene.

Ferguut is based on Guillaume le Clerc's *Fergus*, which has come down to us in two manuscripts. The Middle Dutch romance, written in the first half of the thirteenth century, is closely related to the so-called A-redaction (MS Chantilly 472) of *Fergus*. There are places, however, where *Ferguut* is in agreement with the text of the P-redaction. This proves that the Middle Dutch poet did not use the Chantilly manuscript (Kuiper 1989, 60–3; Zemel 1991, 188–95).

In *Ferguut*, which runs to 5,604 lines, two parts can be distinguished. Up to v. 2592 the Middle Dutch romance is a translation of the Old French text. In the part that follows, the Middle Dutch poet shows greater independence. This difference has raised the question of how many authors have been at work here. *Ferguut* may have been composed by two authors: a translator who stopped at v. 2592, and a gifted poet, who, knowing Guillaume's text by heart, continued the work as a free adaptation of *Fergus* (Kuiper 1989, 217–301). It is also conceivable that a single poet set out to translate the Old French text, but had to rely on his memory at a later stage because a manuscript of *Fergus* was no longer available (Zemel 1991, 8–9).

The translated part of *Ferguut* is an abridged version in comparison to Guillaume's *Fergus*. Not only did the Flemish poet leave individual Old French lines untranslated or render them in a condensed fashion, but he also skipped lengthier passages. This has resulted in a different type of romance. *Ferguut* shows a much stronger emphasis on the narrative course of events than the Old French. In comparison to Guillaume's sophisticated romance, *Ferguut* is an obvious simplification (Zemel 1991, 203–340).

This simplification is also related to the literary game that Guillaume played with Chrétien's *Perceval*. *Fergus* is an answer to Chrétien's text, which introduced a knighthood inspired by religion. Guillaume corrected this new direction with a renewed treatment of the profane-love-and-chivalry model. His Fergus is presented as the new Perceval, transcending Chrétien's hero (Zemel 1994). This intertextual dimension of Guillaume's text was adopted in the Middle Dutch romance only in a reduced form. Because of the abridgements and changes, many of the parallels with Chrétien's text have disappeared. In contrast to *Fergus*, *Ferguut* was not designed as a literary criticism of Chrétien's *Perceval* (Zemel 1991, 115–22).

Another remarkable aspect of *Fergus* is its unique Scottish setting. Fergus does not travel through the vague landscape typical of Arthurian romance, but through southern Scotland. This realistic geographical setting is absent in *Ferguut*. The topography of the Middle Dutch romance is almost completely arbitrary, virtually all Scottish place names have disappeared. As to the setting, *Ferguut* does not differ from the average Arthurian romance (Zemel 1991, 169–77).

Yet *Ferguut* is more than a simplification, and this is especially apparent in the altered conclusion to the Middle Dutch romance. In the final episode of Guillaume's text both Arthur and Galiene are looking for Fergus. This is not the case in *Ferguut*. Arthur organizes a tournament to find Galiene another husband instead of Ferguut, who has disappeared. This situation reflects ironically on Ferguut, because he neglected to visit Galiene when the siege of her castle had been raised. If he had visited her, Galiene would then not have had to find a husband and Arthur would not have had to organize a tournament. That this error does not have fatal consequences for Ferguut, he owes to a dwarf who happens to tell him about Arthur's tournament. When Ferguut wins the tournament, Galiene unexpectedly gets the knight whom she had wanted for her lover earlier on in the story. With this humorous conclusion *Ferguut* ends (Zemel 1991, 65–7).

The name Walewein is a special problem in *Ferguut*. In Middle Dutch literature, Arthur's nephew Gauvain is called Walewein. However, contrary to this, he is called Gawein in *Ferguut*. Moreover, in a list of the knights of the Round Table we hear the names of Gawein, Ywein, Bohort and others, but also

of 'Walewein, een ridder van prise' (v. 4325, 'Walewein, a noble knight').
Apparently the author of this passage did not know that Walewein is the name
for Gauvain's Dutch counterpart. No acceptable explanation for his ignorance
has yet been given (Kuiper 1989, 59–60).

Indigenous Romances

Penninc and Pieter Vostaert, *Walewein*

We do not know for whom *Walewein* was composed, although it has been
suggested that the romance, like *Sir Gawain and the Green Knight*, first circulated in
an urban-noble culture (Riddy 1996). The Flemish authors, Penninc and Pieter
Vostaert, remain silent on this subject. The prologue makes it clear that *Walewein*
is not a translation, but an indigenous romance. Penninc would have translated the
story if it had existed in French (vv. 4–7). Penninc and Vostaert's text, written
around the middle of the thirteenth century (Besamusca 1993, 33–8; Janssens 1994,
125), was probably the first example of such an indigenous work. In the epilogue
Vostaert states that he completed Penninc's unfinished romance by composing
about 3,300 lines (vv. 11186f.). In all probability he continued Penninc's story from
v. 7844 onwards (Draak 1975, 204–6). The romance numbers 11,198 lines.

    Walewein is constructed around a threefold quest. Arthur's nephew Walewein
leaves the court after having promised the king to bring him the chess set that
had come floating into the castle only to disappear again shortly after. He finds
the Floating Chess Set at the castle of King Wonder, who is willing to give it to
Walewein in exchange for the remarkable Sword with the Two Rings, which is in
the possession of King Amoraen. Amoraen is willing to part with the sword, on
the condition that Walewein brings him King Assentijn's beautiful daughter
Ysabele, who lives in India. Assisted by the fox Roges, an enchanted young man,
the hero succeeds in abducting the damsel but, being in love with her, he is not
willing to hand her over to Amoraen. Fortunately, however, the latter has died
in the meantime, so that Walewein can return to King Wonder with the sword
and Ysabele. There the fox is restored to his human shape. After exchanging the
sword for the chess set, Walewein returns to Arthur. He gives an account of his
adventures and presents the king with the object of the quest.

    The underlying structure of *Walewein* is derived from a fairy tale, which, just
like Grimm's *Der goldene Vogel*, must have been a variant of Aarne-Thompson
550 (Draak 1975). This tale was turned into a romance by providing it with a
knightly and courtly setting. Whereas in the tale the hero achieves his goal after
a series of failures, Walewein remains blameless throughout his adventures. The
Middle Dutch authors seem to have balanced this loss of drama by the addition
of chivalric episodes taken from the Arthurian tradition (Haug 1995).

In the inserted episodes Walewein has to face threatening adventures. Entrapped in a dark mountain, he fights dragons. In a robber's castle he kills everybody, thus abolishing the custom of brutal toll. He defends a damsel against an evil knight, whom he wounds mortally and whose body he protects all night against devils. Together with Ysabele, he is imprisoned by a duke when it turns out that he has killed the duke's son, who had claimed Ysabele. He defeats an extremely strong knight, Lancelot's brother Estor, who had abducted Ysabele. In these inserted episodes Walewein appears as the ideal courtly knight, who is strong, courageous, generous, merciful, loyal etc. It has been suggested that in the course of these adventures he develops from a courtly knight into a courtly lover (Verhage-van den Berg 1983).

The love theme in *Walewein* is given form with the aid of two borrowings from the Old French *Perceval* Continuation by Gerbert. In Gerbert's text, Gauvain meets a beautiful damsel called Bloiesine. At her father's castle, the body of her dead brother starts to bleed in the presence of Gauvain, pointing to Arthur's nephew as the murderer. Bloiesine tells her father that she intends to torture the imprisoned Gauvain during the night, but instead they spend an enjoyable time together (Gerbert de Montreuil, *Perceval* vv. 12383–14073). In *Walewein* this adventure is used twice. In Penninc's part of the text, Ysabele uses Bloiesine's ruse to get Walewein into her room (vv. 7395–403); Vostaert borrowed the violation of hospitality and the motif of the bleeding corpse in his description of Walewein's imprisonment at the duke's castle (vv. 8531–9134). In both episodes the motifs borrowed from Gerbert's romance lead to a dungeon scene. This recurring imprisonment of Walewein and Ysabele is intended chiefly to demonstrate just how true their love is (Besamusca 1992; Janssens 1994, 119).

In two scenes Walewein is compared to Tristan in his role of lover. When Walewein and Ysabele are enjoying the pleasures of love in her room, they are betrayed and Assentijn surprises them. Walewein refuses to flee through a secret corridor (vv. 7965–8272). In the Tristan story, however, Tristan does flee when he and Isolde are caught in the orchard by King Mark. The comparison suggests that Walewein surpasses Tristan, which is confirmed in another episode. Walewein decides not to give up his beloved Ysabele to Amoraen, although this implies that he is going to fail in his quest, because then he will not obtain the Sword with the Two Rings (vv. 9399–468). This, too, reminds us of Tristan, who likewise set out to bring a princess from afar for a third person, but contrary to Walewein he is willing to give up his beloved Isolde to the king. Thus Walewein is portrayed not only as the perfect knight but also as the perfect lover (Haug 1995, 201–3).

The remarkably positive picture that Penninc and Vostaert paint of Walewein differs strongly from the portrayal of Gauvain in French literature. In contrast to his flawed French counterpart, Walewein is a character of chivalric and moral excellence (Lacy 1995, 310f.). This positive image of Walewein is supported by motifs drawn from the Grail quest. At the beginning of the romance a magic chess set floats into Arthur's court, just as the Grail does in the *Prose Lancelot*. At King Wonder's castle, Walewein takes a protecting seat, where neither lightning nor thunder can harm him; in the *Queste del Saint Graal*, Galahad sits down in the Perilous Seat of the Round Table. Whereas Galahad is predestined to receive the Sword of the Strange Rings, Walewein is the chosen bearer of the Sword with the Two Rings. The Middle Dutch audience is thus invited to compare three religious objects with their worldly counterparts and to compare Walewein with Galahad, the figurehead of celestial chivalry. In the *Queste del Saint Graal* celestial chivalry undermines the courtly ideal of chivalry inspired by profane love, which results in the decline of Gauvain. In *Walewein*, the destructive influence of religious chivalry on the Arthurian world is resented. Secular chivalry, personified by Walewein, is restored to its old glory in the Middle Dutch romance (Besamusca 1995; Lacy 1995, 316f.).

Walewein has come down to us in fragments dating from the second half of the fourteenth century and in one complete manuscript, kept at Leiden University Library: MS Ltk. 195 (Deschamps 1972, 39–42; Besamusca 1985, 45–9; Kienhorst 1988, 217f.). At the end of the codex, the scribe gives 1350 as the year in which he completed his work. This *Walewein* manuscript contains the best-known Middle Dutch Arthurian illustration, the full-page opening miniature of the romance which depicts Walewein on horseback pursuing the floating chess set. His arms (argent, a lion's head gules) are shown seven times on the armour. The chess set is depicted without the chess pieces and, erroneously, with seven horizontal rows on the board instead of eight. Although inserted on a single leaf of parchment, the miniature was intended for the present manuscript from the beginning (Meuwese 1996, 151–4).

Moriaen

At the beginning of *Moriaen*, a wounded robber knight, who has been defeated by Perceval, arrives at Arthur's court. When Arthur laments Perceval's absence, Walewein and Lancelot set out to find the famous knight. On their way they meet a Moorish knight, Moriaen, who is in search of his father, Perceval's brother Acglaval. At a crossroads the knights decide that each of them will follow one of the three possible directions. Walewein delivers a damsel and kills her ravisher, who later turns out to be the son of his host. Walewein is taken prisoner. At the same time nobody is willing to ferry Moriaen to Ireland out of fear for his black skin. He returns to the crossroads, arriving just in time to rescue Walewein, whose enemies had decided to kill him. Then Gariet brings bad news: Arthur has been kidnapped by the Saxons and the Irish, who have invaded the country. While

Walewein goes in search of Lancelot, Moriaen and Gariet will have to find Perceval and Acglaval. When the latter two are found with their uncle, a hermit, Perceval goes back to save Arthur's kingdom; the wounded Acglaval stays behind to recover. Walewein finds Lancelot, who had slain a dragon but was then betrayed by an evil knight who had taken advantage of the hero's injuries to obtain the monster's foot (for this course of events see also *Lanceloet en het hert met de witte voet*). Together the most important knights of the Round Table expel the invaders and rescue Arthur. Afterwards the knights travel with Acglaval, now recovered, to Moriaen's country, where Acglaval marries Moriaen's mother.

Outside the *Lancelot* Compilation, *Moriaen* has come down to us only in a fourteenth-century fragment (Besamusca 1985, 43f.; Kienhorst 1988, 144f.). In the compilation the romance runs to about 4,700 lines. The work is preceded by a prologue which is important for our knowledge of the textual history, because its author, the compiler of the *Lancelot* Compilation, provides us with valuable information about his source (vv. 1–22). In that text Perceval was Moriaen's father. As this did not fit in with the core of the compilation, in which both Perceval and Galaad are virgins, the compiler allotted Moriaen's paternity to Perceval's brother Acglaval. Moreover, he presents his rendering of *Moriaen* as a sequel to *Lanceloet*, in which Acglaval had been searching for Lancelot who was wandering around insane at that time. That the compiler did, indeed, replace Perceval by Acglaval appears from a number of inconsistencies in his reworking. For example, Walewein and Lancelot set out to search for Perceval, but they tell Moriaen that they want to find Perceval and Acglaval (Besamusca 1993, 87–93).

It is regrettable that the compiler blocks our view of the original *Moriaen*, for everything shows that the Flemish author of this romance created a highly individual work. Writing in the second half of the thirteenth century, he borrowed, for example, two episodes from *Walewein* by Penninc and Pieter Vostaert. The passages about the maltreated damsel (vv. 3676–4352) and the violation of hospitality (vv. 8713–9176) were reworked into one episode (vv. 1213–2340). The *Moriaen* poet deviates systematically and consistently from *Walewein*. In his adaptation he stresses the abuse of feudal power and the contrast between appearances and reality (Besamusca 1993, 100–10).

The link between *Moriaen* and Chrétien's *Perceval* is particularly interesting. In the Flemish romance Arthur declares that Perceval set out to search for the Grail and the Bleeding Lance and that he has since sent many defeated knights to the court (vv. 231–8). This reminds us of Chrétien's *Perceval*: during the five-year search which precedes the meeting with his uncle the hermit, Perceval sends more than sixty knights to Arthur's court. Later on in *Moriaen* Gariet tells his brother Walewein that Perceval has retreated to his uncle's hermitage because of his sins. Perceval realized that he would never be able to find the Lance and the Grail because he had left his mother behind in the woods and she then died of sorrow (vv. 3057–82). Because of this reference to Chrétien's romance the narrative events in *Moriaen* and *Perceval* take place simultaneously. Perceval's quest for the Grail and the Bleeding Lance is presented as a sub-plot in *Moriaen*, and Perceval's visit to his uncle functions as a point of synchronization.

A crucial difference between both romances concerns Perceval. In Chrétien's text it is suggested that the hero will continue his quest after the visit to his uncle and that he will then succeed. In *Moriaen*, however, Perceval realizes that he has failed, for he will never find the Grail and the Lance. He abandons his quest and retires from the world to live as a hermit. His role as the hero is taken over by his son Moriaen, who, in contrast, is successful, but in another field, i.e. as a courtly knight. This indicates that *Moriaen* was meant to be a literary reaction to Chrétien's romance. The negative view of secular knighthood and the religious orientation of the Old French romance were corrected by the poet of *Moriaen*. The successful son of the unsuccessful Grail seeker demonstrates that the ideals of secular knighthood are not outmoded after all (Zemel 1996).

Ridder metter mouwen

Like *Moriaen*, the *Ridder metter mouwen* ('The Knight with the Sleeve') has been preserved in the *Lancelot* Compilation. In this romance a nameless young man arrives at Arthur's court to become a knight. In the absence of the king and virtually all his knights – only Keye has remained behind because of an illness – the young man, by request of the queen, fights a knight who has maltreated a damsel. Walewein's niece Clarette gives him a white sleeve, which provides him with his nickname, and some good advice. When he has defeated the damsel's tormentor, he has it proclaimed at the court that he will revenge himself on Keye, who insulted him, and that he loves Clarette. Then he has a number of adventures. In the Forest without Mercy he puts an end to the terrors that rule there. He defeats Keye and wins a three-day tournament with Clarette's hand in marriage as the prize. Then his mother appears, who tells him his name: Miraudijs. After his marriage Keye's nephew Galyas accuses him of having maltreated his uncle and calls him a bastard. The Knight with the Sleeve sets out to find his father, who turns out to be in prison. The hero frees his father and rescues Arthur's realm by defeating the king of Ireland, who had invaded the country. Miraudijs wins the postponed duel against Galyas. When Arthur's knights have been ambushed and captured by the king of Ireland, Ywein frees them. When returning to Arthur's court they come past the castle of Miraudijs's mother who is being besieged. After Miraudijs's parents have married, the father defeats the besieger in a duel. Then all travel to Arthur's court.

The *Ridder metter mouwen* has been transmitted to us in two ways. An abridged but complete version of about 4,000 lines has been preserved as part of the *Lancelot* Compilation (*Die Riddere metter mouwen*). In addition, a fragment dating from *c.* 1360–70 contains 320 lines of the original, far more elaborate, version (Besamusca 1985, 59–61; Kienhorst 1988, 178f.). This Flemish romance, written in the second half of the thirteenth century, was abridged to a third of its length for the *Lancelot* Compilation. It is not clear whether the compiler altered the structure of the romance. It has been argued that in the original romance Miraudijs's search for his father preceded his marriage to Clarette, and that the compiler changed this order into a diptych, in which Miraudijs gets married halfway through the romance and effects his parents' marriage at the end of the text (Smith 1989). However, it is not clear what reasons the compiler may have had for this peculiar adaptation.

The *Ridder metter mouwen* shows strong similarities with the Old French romance *Richars li biaus*. In both texts, for example, the hero receives a white sleeve and giants besiege castles. In both romances a three-day tournament takes place and the hero is called a bastard. These parallels indicate that the Flemish poet made use of the Old French romance. But the *Ridder metter mouwen* is not a reworking of *Richars li biaus*. The Old French romance was one of the materials which the Flemish author used to create an indigenous romance (Smith 1988).

Two episodes indicate that the poet used Penninc and Vostaert's *Walewein* (Besamusca 1993, 151–5). In Miraudijs's first adventure, he defends a damsel against a knight who has maltreated her (*Roman van den Riddere metter Mouwen* vv. 123–445). This episode is borrowed from the passage about the maltreated damsel in *Walewein* (vv. 3676–4103), which was also used by the *Moriaen* poet. Later in *Ridder metter mouwen* Miraudijs finds a severely wounded knight in the forest. He takes the knight's confession and offers him Communion in the form of soil. That night he kills three robber knights, whom he sees riding on devils afterwards (vv. 2534–638, 3020–59). This adventure, too, is based on *Walewein* (vv. 4097–353, 4784–883).

Moriaen is the second Middle Dutch Arthurian romance which the poet of *Ridder metter mouwen* used (Besamusca 1993, 155–8). In the war against the Irish Arthur's kingdom is threatened with destruction. But Miraudijs prevents the king's defeat (vv. 2838–966, 3069–191). The poet took the episodes in question from *Moriaen*, in which Arthur has to fight against the Irish who invade his realm and the Saxons who abduct him (vv. 2851–3033, 4152–533). Contrary to the course of events in *Moriaen* the rescue of Arthur's kingdom in *Ridder metter mouwen* is the work of one knight, Miraudijs.

As well as drawing on *Walewein* and *Moriaen* to paint a positive picture of his hero, the poet of the *Ridder metter mouwen* also underlines Miraudijs's chivalric qualities by comparing him intertextually with other heroes from the (Old French) Arthurian romances. Like Perceval in Chrétien's *Conte du Graal* the

Knight with the Sleeve settles his score with Keye who had ridiculed him; like Lancelot, Miraudijs is so wrapped up in thoughts of love that he does not react to a knight who attacks him; and in the Forest without Mercy Miraudijs's actions remind us of Chrétien's *Yvain* (Smith 1991; Smith 1992; Besamusca 1993, 141–51).

As in Chrétien's romances, knighthood in the *Ridder metter mouwen* is closely connected with love. And just like Chrétien, the Flemish poet considers knighthood and marital love compatible. In the *Ridder metter mouwen* love gives Miraudijs the power to be a superior knight and his warm feelings towards Clarette lead to marriage. This conception of love is emphasized at the romance's opening. Arthur and his knights are absent, because they will be attending the funeral of Tristan and Isolde. This reference to the Tristan tradition is meant to stress the theme of love in the romance. In contrast to the adulterous love relationship between Tristan and Isolde, ending in death, the *Ridder metter mouwen* tells of a love that is crowned by marriage (Besamusca 1993, 136–41; Smith 1995, 45f.).

Walewein ende Keye

The last indigenous romance to be discussed has also been preserved in the *Lancelot* Compilation. The text comes after the *Ridder metter mouwen*. At the beginning of *Walewein ende Keye* Arthur appoints Walewein his deputy. Out of jealousy Keye falsely accuses Walewein of boasting that he could undertake more adventures in one year than all the other knights of the Round Table together. Walewein leaves the court. On his way he rescues a damsel from a well, defeats the lord of a castle and kills a dragon. In the meantime Keye and his companions have secretly left the court. Their adventure fails miserably. Walewein defeats an arrogant duke and also a knight who deemed himself invincible owing to a well with healing powers. Next, Walewein arrives in a country that is being destroyed by two giants. He defeats his two opponents and thereby liberates the 300 damsels they kept imprisoned. A short while later he participates in a tournament between the kings of Aragon and Portugal, and succeeds in reconciling them. On the appointed day all Walewein's defeated opponents appear before Arthur's castle. When Walewein arrives, he is welcomed with honour, and Keye and his companions are defeated by Walewein's opponents. While Keye flees to a hermit, his companions admit their lie. Arthur curses his seneschal.

Walewein ende Keye has been preserved exclusively in the *Lancelot* Compilation. It is a text of almost 3,700 lines (*Roman van Lancelot*, Book III, vv. 18603–22265). In all probability the compiler reworked an existing romance from the second half of the thirteenth century. The nature and extent of his adaptation, however, are largely hidden from our view. For example, it is still unclear whether he abridged his source, as happened in the case of other romances (Hogenbirk 1996a, 93).

The romance is built on the contrast between two Arthurian figures who invariably belong to the entourage of Arthur's court. Keye functions as a negative character. In *Walewein ende Keye* the seneschal is explicitly malicious and treacherous. Opposed to Keye is the exemplary character of Walewein. He is the ideal courtly knight, the personification of virtues such as courage, wisdom and helpfulness. The hero's modesty is stressed in particular in *Walewein ende Keye*. Not only does Walewein behave modestly; he also deals with arrogant opponents. The romance teaches us that one should imitate the modest knight, Walewein; Keye with his arrogance is a deterring example (Hogenbirk 1996a).

In order to paint as positive a picture of Walewein as possible, the poet of *Walewein ende Keye* makes abundant use of other Arthurian romances. Walewein's adventure with the two giants (vv. 21068–303) is reminiscent of the Pesme Aventure episode in Chrétien's *Yvain*. Just as Yvain fights two enormous devil's children, so Walewein takes up the fight against two giants. Through their respective victories both heroes liberate three hundred damsels from their wretched imprisonment (Hogenbirk 1994, 72–4).

The *Vengeance Raguidel* or its Middle Dutch translation is brought to mind in the episode in which Walewein defeats the lord of a castle (vv. 19107–369). This knight had promised to obtain Walewein's head for his lady. She refused to make love with the knight until Walewein's head had been put in a shrine that had been made for it. When the conquered knight informs Walewein of the situation, Arthur's nephew fulfils the promise by simply putting his head in the shrine. This is a humorous correction of Gauvain's adventure with Maduc and the Dame de Gautdestroit in the *Vengeance Raguidel*. In the Old French romance Maduc sees Gauvain as his rival, whom he must defeat in order to gain the love of the Dame de Gautdestroit. This lady is in love with Gauvain and wants to decapitate him, so that they can be buried together. In contrast to Walewein in *Walewein ende Keye*, Gauvain in the *Vengeance Raguidel* does not succeed in reconciling the couple (Hogenbirk 1996b, 265–8).

Walewein ende Keye also contains a variant of the story of the dragon-killer (vv. 19410–683). A country is being devastated by a dragon. He who kills the monster will receive the hand of the king's daughter in marriage. Walewein kills the dragon, but is severely wounded. Then the seneschal enters the scene. In accordance with, for instance, the story of Tristan, one expects him to deceive Walewein and to pretend at the court that he killed the dragon himself. However, he takes care of Arthur's nephew and honours him at the court as the best knight in the world. This variant of the story about the dragon-killer underlines Walewein's outstanding qualities (Hogenbirk 1994, 74f.).

In two places in *Walewein ende Keye* Walewein is called 'der aventuren vader' ('father of adventures', vv. 19229 and 21948). This epithet is also found in other Middle Dutch Arthurian romances, such as *Lantsloot vander Haghedochte*, *Arturs doet*, Velthem's *Merlijn* Continuation, *Wrake van Ragisel*, and the indigenous romances *Walewein* and *Moriaen* (Janssens 1982, 299–303). This laudatory description of Arthur's nephew does not occur, however, in the Arthurian romances outside the Low Countries. The epithet confirms the extremely favourable picture that Middle Dutch authors have of Walewein. In their eyes he was the prototype of ideal knighthood. *Walewein ende Keye* is the most pronounced representation of this tradition.

The Legacy

After the Middle Ages interest in Arthurian material in the Low Countries disappeared for centuries. It was not until the nineteenth century that people began to be interested again in the stories about King Arthur and his knights of the Round Table (Verbeke et al. 1987, 303–6; Lacy 1991, 123–4). Forerunners were the eighteenth-century linguists Balthazar Huydecoper (1695–1778) and Zacharias H. Alewijn (1742–88). Huydecoper was the owner of manuscripts of *Ferguut*, *Walewein* and *Wigalois*. At the auction of Huydecoper's library in 1779 the codices were bought by Alewijn, who bequeathed them in 1788 to the Maatschappij der Nederlandse Letterkunde (Society of Dutch Literature) in Leiden, founded in 1766. The manuscripts are now at Leiden University Library, bearing the signatures Ltk. 191, Ltk. 195 and Ltk. 537.

In the nineteenth century W. J. A. Jonckbloet (1817–85) initiated research into the Middle Dutch Arthurian romances. In his two literary histories, *Geschiedenis der Middennederlandsche Dichtkunst* ('History of Middle Dutch Poetry', 1851–5) and *Geschiedenis der Nederlandsche Letterkunde* ('History of Dutch Literature', 1868–72) he discussed the texts. Some years before, in 1846, he had published the first part of his *Walewein* edition (the second part appeared in 1848) and the first part of his edition of the *Lancelot* Compilation (the second part was published in 1849). He may justly be called the first Dutch Arthurian scholar.

Penninc and Pieter Vostaert's *Walewein* was reworked in modern Dutch in 1890 by M. C. H. Betz. The result was a text of 4,073 lines, written under the influence of Tennyson's *Idylls of the King*. If one compares the two texts, profound differences come to light. In Betz's *Walewein*, for instance, the hero does not find the flying chess set at King Wonder's castle, but at the castle of King Amoraen. Ysabele, whom Amoraen wants to have in exchange for the chess set, is in Betz's text the daughter of Tarquyn van den Foreeste (Tarquyn of the Forest), a name that has been borrowed, through Malory, from the prose *Lancelot*. While Walewein is travelling to Tarquyn's castle, a damsel called Joyeuse Garde falls in love with him. This passage does not occur in the Middle Dutch *Walewein*. These differences show that Betz's *Walewein* is an idiosyncratic adaptation of Penninc and Pieter Vostaert's romance (Verbeke et al. 1987, 307f.).

A few decades later, their work was adapted once more. From October 1917 until June 1918 *Het zwevende schaakbord* ('The Floating Chess Board') by Louis Couperus appeared in weekly instalments in *De Haagsche Post*. The text was published in book form in 1922. Couperus presents his novel as a sequel to the text by Penninc and Vostaert. The events take place ten years later, and in all those years nothing has happened at Arthur's court. People are bored. Merlin then provides another chess board, a technical masterpiece, as the magician is well versed in the new magic of electricity, the telephone and the aeroplane. Gawein (Couperus considered this a tougher name than Walewein, which is too weak in his opinion) then undertakes a new adventure, which is a repetition of his experiences in the Middle Dutch romance – but with differences, such as the female squire Amadijs, who falls in love with Gawein. Couperus's version of *Walewein* is ironic and melancholic in character (Verbeke et al. 1987, 308–9).

Dutch authors writing after Couperus have shown only slight interest in the Arthurian material (Verbeke et al. 1987, 308–10; Lacy et al. 1991, 124f., 219, 268). In his *Tristan en Isolde* (1920) Arthur van Schendel reworked the Tristan story by Gottfried von Strassburg. In the same year, Marie Koenen adapted the Perceval story in her *Parzival*. P. C. Boutens wrote *Liederen van Isoude* ('Songs of Isold', 1921) and Stijn Streuvels based his *Tristan en Isolde* (1924) on the German *Tristrant und Isalde* (1484). In later years, Hubert Lampo showed himself to have been inspired by the Grail theme in novels such as *De heks en de archeoloog* ('The Witch and the Archaeologist', 1967) and *Wijlen Sarah Silbermann* ('The Late Sarah Silbermann', 1980). Leon de Winter's *Zoeken naar Eileen W.* (1981) shows the influence of the Tristan matter. Finally, juvenile Arthurian fiction written by D. L. Daalder, H. de Bruijn, Jaap ter Haar and Frank Herzen (Verbeke et al. 1987, 308–10; Lacy et al. 1991, 124f.) shows that the world of Arthur which was first conveyed to audiences in the Middle Ages lives on in a modified form for young Dutch readers today.

Note

The Dutch version of this chapter was translated into English by Ans Bulles. Her work has been made possible by a subsidy of the Royal Netherlands Academy of Arts and Sciences (Vertaalfonds KNAW/Stichting Reprorecht). I would like to thank Frank Brandsma and Marjolein Hogenbirk for their comments on the first version of this chapter.

The bibliography was closed 1 September 1998.

Bibliography

Primary Sources

Ferguut. Ed. by E. Rombauts, N. de Paepe and M. J. M. de Haan, 1994 (Middelnederlandse tekstedities, 1). Hilversum.

Ferguut: A Facsimile of the Only Extant Middle Dutch Manuscript (Leiden, University Library, Ms. Letterkunde 191). Ed. by M. J. M. de Haan, 1974. Leiden.

Gerbert de Montreuil, *La Continuation de Perceval*. 3 vols. Ed. by M. Williams and M. Oswald, 1922–75 (CFMA, 28, 50, 101). Paris.

Gysseling, M., *Corpus van Middelnederlandse teksten (tot en met het jaar 1300)*. Series 2 (Literaire handschriften), 1 (Fragmenten), 1980. 's-Gravenhage.

Historie van Merlijn, in Kronenberg, M. E. 1929. 'Een onbekend volksboek van *Merlijn* (c. 1540)', *TNTL*, 48, 18–34.

Jacob van Maerlant, *Historie van den Grale und Boek van Merline*. Ed. by T. Sodmann, 1980. Cologne and Vienna.

Jacob van Maerlant, *Merlijn*. Ed. by J. van Vloten, 1880. Leiden.

Jacob van Maerlant, *Spiegel historiael*. 3 vols. Ed. by M. de Vries and E. Verwijs, 1863. Leiden.

Lanceloet. De Middelnederlandse vertaling van de Lancelot en prose overgeleverd in de Lancelot-compilatie. Part 1 (vv. 1–5530, preceded by the lines of the Brussels fragment). Ed. by B. Besamusca and A. Postma, 1997 (Middelnederlandse Lancelotromans, 4). Hilversum.

Lanceloet. De Middelnederlandse vertaling van de Lancelot en prose overgeleverd in de Lancelot-compilatie. Part 2 (vv. 5531–10740). Ed. by B. Besamusca, 1991 (Middelnederlandse Lancelot-romans, 5). Assen and Maastricht.

Lanceloet. De Middelnederlandse vertaling van de Lancelot en prose overgeleverd in de Lancelot-compilatie. Part 3 (vv. 10741–16263). Ed. by F. Brandsma, 1992 (Middelnederlandse Lancelot-romans, 6). Assen and Maastricht.

Lanceloet. De Middelnederlandse vertaling van de Lancelot en prose overgeleverd in de Lancelot-compilatie. Part 4 (vv. 16264–26636). Ed. by A. Postma, 1998 (Middelnederlandse Lancelot-romans, 7). Hilversum.

Lanceloet en het hert met de witte voet. Ed. by M. Draak, 1953 (Klassieken Nederlandse Letterkunde). Zwolle.

Lancelot. II Nach der Kölner Papierhandschrift W. f° 46 Blankenheim und der Heidelberger Pergamenthandschrift Pal. Germ. 147*. Ed. by R. Kluge, 1963 (Deutsche Texte des Mittelalters, 47). Berlin.

Lancelot. Roman en prose du XIIIe siècle. 9 vols. Ed. by A. Micha, 1978–83 (TLF, 247, 249, 262, 278, 283, 286, 288, 307, 315). Paris and Geneva.

Lantsloot vander Haghedochte. Fragmenten van een Middelnederlandse bewerking van de Lancelot en prose. Ed. by W. P. Gerritsen et al., 1987 (Middelnederlandse Lancelotromans, 2). Amsterdam.

Lodewijk van Velthem, *Voortzetting van den Spiegel historiael (1248–1316)*. 3 vols. Ed. by H. van der Linden et al., 1906–38. Brussels.

Moriaen. Ed. by H. Paardekooper-van Buuren and M. Gysseling, [1971] (Klassiek Letterkundig Pantheon, 183). Zutphen.

Penninc and Pieter Vostaert, *Roman van Walewein*. Ed. and transl. by D. F. Johnson, 1992 (Garland Library of Medieval Literature, Series A, 81). New York and London.

La Queste del Saint Graal. Roman du XIIIe siècle. Ed. by A. Pauphilet, 1949 (CFMA, 33). Paris.

Die Riddere metter mouwen. Ms. The Hague, Royal Library 129 A 10 fol. 167–177 verso and the fragment Brussels, Royal Library IV 818. Ed. by C. W. de Kruyter, 1975. Leiden.

Roman van den Riddere metter Mouwen. Ed. by M. J. M. de Haan et al., 1983 (Publikaties van de [Leidse] Vakgroep Nederlandse Taal- en Letterkunde, 11). Utrecht.

Roman van Lancelot (XIIIe eeuw). 2 vols. Ed. by W. J. A. Jonckbloet, 1846–49. 's-Gravenhage.

Torec. Ed. by M. and J. Hogenhout, 1978. Abcoude.

The Vulgate Version of the Arthurian Romances. 7 vols. Ed. by H. O. Sommer, 1979. New York.

Winkelman, J. H. 1988. 'Zu den Wiener *Tristant*-Fragmenten', in Tuczay C., Hirhager U. and Lichtblau K., eds., *Ir sult sprechen willekomen. Grenzenlose Mediävistik. Festschrift für Helmut Birkhan zum 60. Geburtstag.* Berne, 821–38.

Die Wrake van Ragisel. See Other Literature, Gerritsen 1963.

Other Literature

Berg, E. van den 1983. *Middelnederlandse versbouw en syntaxis. Ontwikkelingen in de versifikatie van verhalende poëzie ca. 1200–c. 1400,* Utrecht.

Berg, E. van den 1987. 'Genre en gewest. De geografische spreiding van de ridderepiek', *TNTL,* 103, 1–36.

Berg, E. van den 1995. 'Ridderepiek in Vlaanderen. Van centrum tot periferie', *TNTL,* 111, 206–24.

Berg, E. van den 1998. 'Stedelijke ridderepiek?' in Janssens et al. 1998, 247–60, 360–7.

Besamusca, B. 1985. *Repertorium van de Middelnederlandse Arturepiek. Een beknopte beschrijving van de handschriftelijke en gedrukte overlevering,* Utrecht.

Besamusca, B. 1991. 'De Vlaamse opdrachtgevers van Middelnederlandse literatuur. Een literair-historisch probleem', *NTg,* 84, 150–62.

Besamusca, B. 1992. 'Gauvain as lover in the Middle Dutch verse romance *Walewein', The Arthurian Yearbook,* 2, 3–12.

Besamusca, B. 1993. *Walewein, Moriaen en de Ridder metter mouwen. Intertekstualiteit in drie Middelnederlandse Arturromans,* Middeleeuwse studies en bronnen, 39, Hilversum.

Besamusca, B. 1994. 'Cyclification in Middle Dutch literature: the case of the *Lancelot* Compilation', in Besamusca 1994 (see Gen. Bibl.), 82–91.

Besamusca, B. 1995. '*Walewein*: a Middle Dutch antidote to the Prose *Lancelot', BBIAS,* 47, 301–10.

Besamusca, B. 1996. 'Lancelot and Guinevere in the Middle Dutch *Lancelot* Compilation', in Walters, L. J., ed., *Lancelot and Guinevere: A Casebook,* Garland Reference Library of the Humanities, 1513, New York and London, 105–24.

Besamusca, B. 1998. 'Het publiek van de Middelnederlandse Arturromans', in Janssens et al. 1988, 145–57, 327–9.

Besamusca, B. and Brandsma, F. 1994. 'Between audience and source: the first-person narrator in the Middle Dutch *Lanceloet*', in Busby, K. and Lacy, N. J., eds., *Conjunctures: Medieval Studies in Honor of Douglas Kelly,* Faux Titre, 83, Amsterdam, 15–29.

Besamusca, B. and Brandsma, F. 1998. 'Jacob de Maerlant, traducteur vigilant, et la valeur didactique de son *Graal-Merlijn*', in Faucon, J.-C., Labbé, A. and Quéruel, D., eds., *Miscellanea Mediaevalia. Mélanges offerts à Philippe Ménard,* Nouvelle Bibliothèque du Moyen Age, 46, Paris, 1, 121–31.

Besamusca, B. and Lie, O. S. H. 1994. 'The prologue to *Arturs doet*, the Middle Dutch translation of *La Mort le Roi Artu* in the *Lancelot* Compilation', in Kooper 1994, 96–112.

Biemans, J. A. A. M. 1995. '*Arturs Doet* op papier of perkament?' *Queeste,* 2, 72–3.

Biemans, J. A. A. M. 1998. *'Onsen Speghele Ystoriale in Vlaemsche'. Codicologisch onderzoek naar de overlevering van de 'Spiegel Historiael' van Jacob van Maerlant, Philip Utenbroeke en Lodewijk van Velthem,* Leuven.

Brandsma, F. 1995. 'Opening up the narrative: the insertion of new episodes in Arthurian cycles', *Queeste,* 2, 31–9.

Buuren, A. M. J. van 1994. 'Dirc Potter, a medieval Ovid', in Kooper 1994, 151–67.

Croenen, G. and Janssens, J. D. 1994. 'Een nieuw licht op de Lancelotcompilatie? De betekenis van het pas gevonden fragmentje van *Arturs Doet', Queeste,* 1, 3–11, 108–25.

Deschamps, J. 1972. *Middelnederlandse handschriften uit Europese en Amerikaanse bibliotheken*, 2nd revised edn, Leiden.

Draak, M. 1954. *De Middelnederlandse vertalingen van de proza-Lancelot*, Mededelingen der Koninklijke Nederlandse Akademie van Wetenschappen, afd. Letterkunde, Nieuwe Reeks, dl. 17, no. 7, Amsterdam.

Draak, M. 1975. *Onderzoekingen over de Roman van Walewein (Met aanvullend hoofdstuk over het Walewein onderzoek sinds 1936)* (rpr. Groningen and Amsterdam).

Draak, M. 1976. *Oude en nieuwe Lancelot-problemen, en de noodzakelijkheid van lezen*, Mededelingen der Koninklijke Nederlandse Akademie van Wetenschappen, afd. Letterkunde, Nieuwe Reeks dl. 39, no. 8, Amsterdam.

Frappier, J. 1959. 'The Vulgate Cycle', in Loomis 1959 (see Gen. Bibl.), 295–318.

Gerritsen, W. P. 1963. *Die wrake van Ragisel. Onderzoekingen over de Middelnederlandse bewerkingen van de Vengeance Raguidel, gevolgd door een uitgave van de Wrake-teksten*, 2 vols., Neerlandica Traiectina, 13, Assen.

Gerritsen, W. P. 1976. 'Corrections and indications for oral delivery in the Middle Dutch Lancelot manuscript The Hague KB 129 A 10', in Gumbert, J. P. and de Haan, M. J. M., eds., *Neerlandica manuscripta: Essays presented to G. I. Lieftinck*, Litterae Textuales, 3, Amsterdam, 39–59.

Gerritsen, W. P. 1981. 'Jacob van Maerlant and Geoffrey of Monmouth', in Varty, K., ed., *An Arthurian Tapestry: Essays in Memory of Lewis Thorpe*, Glasgow, 368–88.

Gerritsen, W. P. 1984. 'Walewein van Melle (anno 1118) en de Oudnederlandse Arturlitteratuur', *Naamkunde*, 16, 115–34.

Gerritsen, W. P. 1994. 'Een avond in Ardres. Over middeleeuwse verhaalkunst', in Oostrom, F. van et al., *Grote lijnen. Syntheses over Middelnederlandse letterkunde*, Nederlandse literatuur en cultuur in de Middeleeuwen, 11, Amsterdam, 157–72, 220–3.

Gerritsen, W. P. and Oostrom, F. P. van 1980. 'Les Adaptateurs néerlandais du *Lancelot (-Graal)* aux prises avec le procédé narratif des romans arthuriens en prose', in *Mélanges de langue et littérature françaises du Moyen Age et de la Renaissance offerts à Charles Foulon*, Rennes, 2, 105–14.

Groninger neerlandici 1983. *Hoe Artur sinen inde nam. Studie over de Middelnederlandse ridderroman Arturs doet*, 2nd edn, Groningen.

Haug, W. 1995. 'Kombinatorik und Originalität. Der *Roman van Walewein* als nachklassisches Experiment', *TNTL*, 111, 195–205.

Hoecke, W. van, Tournoy, G. and Verbeke, W., eds. 1991. *Arturus Rex, II: Acta Conventus Lovaniensis 1987*, Mediaevalia Lovaniensia, Ser. I, Studia, 17, Leuven.

Hogenbirk, M. 1994. '"Die coenste die ie werd geboren". Over *Walewein ende Keye*', *NTg*, 87, 57–75.

Hogenbirk, M. 1996a. '*Walewein ende Keye*: hoogmoed ten val gebracht', in Besamusca, B. and Brandsma, F., eds., *De kunst van het zoeken: studies over 'avontuur' en 'queeste' in de middeleeuwse literatuur*, Uitgaven Stichting Neerlandistiek VU, 21, Amsterdam and Münster, 89–111.

Hogenbirk, M. 1996b. 'Gauvain, the lady, and her lover: the Middle Dutch *Walewein ende Keye* and Old French romance', *BBIAS*, 48, 257–70.

Hogenhout-Mulder, M. 1984. *Proeven van tekstkritiek. Een onderzoek betreffende de tekstgeschiedenis van de Renout van Montalbaen en de Perceval*, Groningen.

Janssens, J. D. 1982. 'Oude en nieuwe wegen in "het woud zonder genade". (Terreinverkenning voor verder onderzoek van de Mnl. niet-historische Arturroman)', *NTg*, 75, 291–312.

Janssens, J. D. 1988. *Dichter en publiek in creatief samenspel. Over interpretatie van Middelnederlandse ridderromans*, Leuvense studiën en tekstuitgaven, Nieuwe Reeks, 7, Leuven and Amersfoort.

Janssens, J. D. 1994. 'The *Roman van Walewein*, an episodic Arthurian romance', in Kooper 1994, 113–28.

Janssens, J. D. et al. 1998. *Op avontuur. Middeleeuwse epiek in de Lage Landen*, Nederlandse literatuur en cultuur in de Middeleeuwen, 18, Amsterdam.

Janssens, J. and Meuwese, M. 1997. *Jacob van Maerlant, Spiegel Historiael. De miniaturen uit het handschrift Den Haag, Koninklijke Bibliotheek, KA XX*, Leuven.

Kienhorst, H. 1988. *De handschriften van de Middelnederlandse ridderepiek. Een codicologische beschrijving*, 2 vols., Deventer Studiën, 9, Deventer.

Klein, J. W. 1990. 'Codicologie en de Lancelotcompilatie: de invoeging van de *Perchevael* en de *Moriaen*', *NTg*, 83, 526–39.

Klein, J. W. 1995. '"Het getal zijner jaren is onnaspeurlijk". Een herijking van de dateringen van de handschriften en fragmenten met Middelnederlandse ridderepiek', *TNTL*, 111, 1–23.

Klein, J. W. 1998. 'De status van de *Lancelotcompilatie*. Handschrift, fragmenten en personen', *TNTL*, 114, 105–24.

Klein, Th. 1994. 'Zur Sprache des Münchener Prosa-Lancelot-Fragments', in Mehler, U. and Touber, A. H., eds., *Mittelalterliches Schauspiel. Festschrift für H. Linke zum 65. Geburtstag*, *ABäG* 38–9, Amsterdam, 223–40.

Koekman, J. 1988. '*Torec*, een vorstelijk verhaal. Zinvolle verbanden in een complexe tekst', *NTg*, 81, 111–24.

Koekman, J. 1991. 'A guiding thread through the textual labyrinth of the Middle Dutch *Lancelot en prose*', in van Hoecke et al. 1991, 361–6.

Kooper, E., ed. 1994. *Medieval Dutch Literature in its European Context*, Cambridge Studies in Medieval Literature, 21, Cambridge.

Kuiper, W. 1989. *Die riddere metten witten scilde. Oorsprong, overlevering en auteurschap van de Middelnederlandse Ferguut, gevolgd door een diplomatische editie en een diplomatisch glossarium*, Thesaurus, 2, Amsterdam.

Lacy, N. J. ed. 1991. *The New Arthurian Encyclopedia*, Garland Reference Library of the Humanities, 931, New York and London.

Lacy, N. J. 1995. 'Convention and innovation in the Middle Dutch *Walewein*', *TNTL*, 111, 310–22.

Lacy, N. J., ed. 1996. *Medieval Arthurian Literature: A Guide to Recent Research*, Garland Reference Library of the Humanities, 1955, New York and London.

Lie, O. S. H. 1987. *The Middle Dutch Prose Lancelot: A Study of the Rotterdam Fragments and their Place in the French, German and Dutch Lancelot en prose Tradition* (with an edition of the text), Middelnederlandse Lancelotromans, 3, Amsterdam.

Lie, O. S. H. 1991. 'The Flemish exemplar of MS W. f° 46* Blankenheim, a fifteenth-century German translation of the *Suite de la Charrette*', in van Hoecke et al. 1991, 404–18.

Loomis, R. S. 1953. 'Edward I, Arthurian enthusiast', *Spec*, 28, 114–27.

Loomis, R. S. 1959 (see Gen Bibl.).

Meuwese, M. 1995. 'Jacob van Maerlant's *Spiegel historiael*: iconography and workshop', in Smeyers, M. and Cardon, B., eds., *Flanders in a European Perspective: Manuscript Illumination around 1400 in Flanders and Abroad*, Leuven, 445–56.

Meuwese, M. 1996. 'Arthurian illuminations in Middle Dutch manuscripts', in Busby, K., ed., *Word and Image in Arthurian Literature*, New York and London, 151–73.

Oostrom, F. P. van 1979. 'De oorspronkelijkheid van de *Torec*, of: de vrije val van een detail door de Nederlandse litteratuurgeschiedenis', *Spiegel der Letteren*, 21, 197–201.

Oostrom, F. P. van 1981. *Lantsloot vander Haghedochte. Onderzoekingen over een Middelnederlandse bewerking van de Lancelot en prose*, Middelnederlandse Lancelotromans, 1, Amsterdam.

Oostrom, F. P. van 1996. *Maerlants wereld*, Amsterdam.

Oppenhuis de Jong, S. 1996. 'Agloval en de compilator. De geschiedenis van een verhaaldraad in de Lancelotcompilatie', *Nederlandse Letterkunde*, 1, 355–66.

Pesch, P. N. G. 1985. 'Het Nederlandse volksboek van *Merlijn*. Bron, drukker en datering', in Nave, F. de, ed., *Liber Amicorum Leon Voet*, Antwerpen, 303–28.

Prevenier, W. 1994. 'Court and city culture in the Low Countries from 1100 to 1530', in Kooper 1994, 11–29.

Prins-s'Jacob, J. C. 1980. 'The Middle Dutch version of *La Queste del Saint Graal*', *NTg*, 73, 120–32.

Riddy, F. 1996. 'Giving and receiving: exchange in the *Roman van Walewein* and *Sir Gawain and the Green Knight*', *TNTL*, 112, 18–29.

Smith, S. 1988. 'Richars en de Riddere metter Mouwen toch neven? Nieuwe aandacht voor een oude hypothese', *Voortgang*, 9, 91–116.

Smith, S. 1989. 'Van koning tot kroonprins. Over de structuur van de *Roman van den Riddere metter Mouwen*', in Bree, F. de and Zemel, R., eds., *'In onse scole'. Opstellen over Middeleeuwse letterkunde voor Prof. Dr Margaretha H. Schenkeveld*, Amsterdam, 109–41.

Smith, S. 1991. 'Dat begin van den Riddere metter Mouwen', *Voortgang*, 12, 151–79.

Smith, S. 1992. '"Der minnen cracht". Over de thematiek van de *Roman van den Riddere metter Mouwen*', *Voortgang*, 13, 37–63.

Smith, S. 1995. 'Intertekstualiteit in opmars', *Spektator*, 24, 32–54.

Summerfield, T. 1998. 'Simon de Montfort, Edward I en koning Arthur in Velthems *Voortzetting van de Spiegel historiael*', *TNTL*, 114, 1–16.

Tilvis, P. 1957. *Prosa-Lancelot-Studien I–II*, Annales Academiae Scientiarum Fennicae, B/110, Helsinki.

Vekeman, H. and Schröder, H. 1997. 'De vertaling van het eerste kapittel van Hugo van Saint-Victors *De modo orandi* in *Arturs Doet*', *Ons geestelijk erf*, 71, 108–44.

Verbeke, W., Janssens, J. and Smeyers, M., eds. 1987. *Arturus Rex*, I: *Catalogus Koning Artur en de Nederlanden. La matière de Bretagne et les anciens Pays-Bas*, Mediaevalia Lovaniensia, Ser. I, Studia, 16, Leuven.

Verhage-van den Berg, T. 1983. 'Het onderschatte belang van de neven-episoden in de *Walewein*', *NTg*, 76, 225–44.

Wells, D. A. 1971. 'Source and tradition in the *Moriaen*', in King, P. K. and Vincent, P. F., eds., *European Context: Studies in the History and Literature of the Netherlands. Presented to Theodore Weevers*, Cambridge, 30–51.

Winkel, J. te 1881. 'De Borron's *Joseph d'Arimathie* en *Merlin* in Maerlant's vertaling', *TNTL*, 1, 305–63.

Winkelman, J. H. 1986. 'Tristan en Isolde in de minnetuin. Over een versieringsmotief op laatmiddeleeuws schoeisel', *ABäG*, 24, 163–88.

Winkelman, J. H. 1995. 'Weshalb sprechen Tristan und Isolde eine deutsch-niederländische Mischsprache in Valkenisse (NL)? Über deutsch-niederländische Kulturbeziehungen im späten Mittelalter', *WB*, 41, 249–60.

Winkelman, J. H. 1998. 'Tristant in Gelderland. Een bijdrage tot de Oostmiddelnederlandse hofliteratuur uit het midden van de dertiende eeuw', in Janssens et al. 1998, 51–62, 293–5.

Zemel, R. M. T. 1991. *Op zoek naar Galiene. Over de Oudfranse Fergus en de Middelnederlandse Ferguut*, I, Thesaurus, 3, Amsterdam.

Zemel, R. 1992. '"Hoe Walewein Lanceloet bescudde ende enen camp vor hem vacht". Over *Lanceloet en het hert met de witte voet*', in Besamusca, B. and Brandsma, F., eds., *De ongevalliche Lanceloet. Studies over de Lancelotcompilatie*, Middeleeuwse studies en bronnen, 28, Hilversum, 77–97.

Zemel, R. 1994. 'The new and the old Perceval: Guillaume's *Fergus* and Chrétien's *Conte du Graal*', *BBIAS*, 46, 324–42.

Zemel, R. 1996. 'Moriaen en Perceval in "Waste Land"', *TNTL*, 112, 297–319.

Part Four

Other Literary, Pictorial and Social Manifestations of Arthurian Culture

13

ARTHURIAN ROMANCE AND GERMAN HEROIC POETRY

John L. Flood

Thirteenth-century Germany knew two principal cycles of heroic poetry: the Nibelungen material, featuring Sivrit (Siegfried), Kriemhild, Hagen, the Burgundian king Gunther and the Hun king Etzel (Attila); and the Dietrich poems, telling of various exploits of Dietrich von Bern (Theodoric of Verona).[1] The popularity of these two bodies of material in due course led to an attempt to link the two, with Sivrit being matched against Dietrich von Bern. (An association between the two was virtually inevitable, given that Etzel was common to both traditions.) In the *Rosengarten* complex of poems Dietrich is brought together with the characters who appear in the *Nibelungenlied*. Kriemhild or her father Gibich challenge Dietrich and his men to fight against the twelve warriors who guard Kriemhild's rose-garden at Worms. Dietrich has to fight Siegfried and overcomes him. There is also a fight between Dietrich and Siegfried in *Die Rabenschlacht*, and the motif is borrowed from the *Rosengarten* by *Biterolf*.

In a similar way it was almost inevitable that, given the proliferation and popularity of works focusing on the figure of King Arthur and his court, these would leave their mark on other contemporary narrative literature, and the 'cross-fertilization' of Arthurian romance and heroic poetry, especially the Dietrich cycle, is no surprise. At the lowest level, we find allusions in Arthurian romances to heroic material and vice versa. An extended example is found in Wolfram's *Parzival* where Liddamus, Duke of Galicia, says:

'For my part I will not be deluded by love of anyone into exposing myself unto undue harassment. Why should I play Wolfhart? My path to battle is moated, my keenness for prey hooded. Though you should never forgive me for it, I would rather do as Rumold did, who offered advice to King Gunther when he was leaving Worms for Hunland – he asked him to toast long slices and twirl them in the cauldron!'
    The bold Landgrave said, 'You speak as many of us have been accustomed to hear from you, all your days. You are advising me to do what I myself am set on, and you claim you would do what a cook advised the Nibelungs, who blithely set out for where vengeance was wreaked on them for what had been done to Sivrit. I shall teach Gawan direst revenge, else he must slay me!' (*Pz.* 420, 20–421, 12, transl. Hatto 1980, 215–16)

And a few lines later:

> 'Yet I am well received by the King as I am. Sibeche never drew sword and was always amongst those who sought flight; nevertheless people had to come to him cap in hand. Though he never hacked sword through helmet he received many great gifts and many fiefs from Ermenrich.' (*Pz.* 421, 22–28, transl. Hatto 1980, 216)

These passages show Wolfram's (and presumably his audience's) familiarity with the *Nibelungenlied* (the hot-head Wolfhart and the wise counsellor Rumold, King Gunther, Worms, Sivrit) and the historical Dietrich poems (Wolfhart again, the evil counsellor Sibeche and the usurper Ermenrich).[2] In *Willehalm* 439, 16 Wolfram refers to Hildebrant (Wolfhart's uncle) and his wife Uote (again from the Dietrich cycle). Similarly, Dietrich and Hildebrand are mentioned in Eilhart's *Tristrant* (v. 5976), while *Lorengel* mentions both Etzel (W 1, 2) and Dietrich ('her Ditereich / dem nie kein hellt auff erden mocht geleichen', W 7, 2–3).

An instance of the mention of Arthurian characters in heroic poetry is found in the Dresden Heldenbuch version of the *Eckenlied* (*Ecke d* 88, 2) where Gabein (= Gawein) is said to have been a former owner of Ecke's sword Eckesahs. Parzival is named in *Virginal* 1045, 12. Generally, however, it is Arthur himself who finds mention in heroic poems, though, whereas *Biterolf* and *Rosengarten* present trials between the heroes of different cycles, of Bern and of Worms, Arthur and Dietrich never meet in person: Arthur is simply used as a point of comparison. Thus in *Dietrichs Flucht* it is said of Dietrich's ancestor Dietwart that 'er lebte rehte als Artûs / mit rehter ritterschefte' ('he lived a life of perfect chivalry just like Arthur', 106f.) and that he 'lebte sô vürstlîche / als Artûs ie gelebete' ('he lived in a princely manner as Arthur had always done', 131f.). Explicit comparison is made between the court of Dietrich's protector, Etzel – Dietrich, as an exile, has no court he can call his own – and that of Arthur in the later Dietrich epics. *Wunderer B* even asserts not that Etzel was to be compared with Arthur, but Arthur was to be compared with Etzel:

> Künig Arthus was auch reiche
> zû der selben zeit
> künig Etzel was er gleiche.   (*Wunderer B*, 3, 1–3)

(King Arthur was also rich at that time; he was the equal of King Etzel.)

Virginal maintains that no one as courageous as Dietrich had ever appeared at Arthur's court:

> was man von helden ie gesach
> oder ie hat vernumen,
> das ist gen den von Pern entwicht;
> kunig Artus ist so kunes nicht
> an seinen hof ie kumen.   (*Virginal w* 482, 2–6)

(*What you have ever seen or heard of heroes was nothing compared with Dietrich von Bern; no one as courageous as he had ever visited Arthur's court.*)

A late echo of the comparison of Germanic heroes with Arthurian ones is to be found in the *Historia von dem Gehörnten Siegfried*, written in the mid-seventeenth century but of which no edition earlier than that of 1726 survives. The preface begins:

> Es wird in vielen Historien gelesen, wie, daß König Artus, aus Britannien, zu seiner Zeit, so eine herrliche Hoffhaltung mit den allerwerthesten Rittern, so zu der Zeit gelebt, gehalten habe, bey der Taffel-Runde; von demselben ist auch zum Ritter geschlagen der vortreffliche noch junge Herr Wigoleiß vom Rade. (*Historia von dem Gehörnten Siegfried*, 64)

> (*We read in many stories how King Arthur of Brittany once had such a splendid court with the most distinguished knights of his day at the Round Table. As a young man, the excellent Sir Wigoleis of the Wheel [of Fortune] was dubbed a knight by him.*)

The first chapter introduces Siegfried as having lived 'at the time when Sir Wigoleis lived'. The link between the two is not inappropriate since both Siegfried and (as the preface specifically recalls) Wigoleis are both dragon-slayers.

A number of works present a mixture of genres. In *Antelan*, a short piece in the *Hildebrandston* strophe – a form characteristic of heroic poems such as the *Jüngeres Hildebrandslied* and the *Lied vom hürnen Seyfrid* – three duchesses send out the dwarf king Antelan (described also as 'kunig anteloy ausz schotten lant', King Anteloy of Scotland (or Ireland)! – the name Anteloy appears to derive from Ulrich von Etzenbach's *Alexander*) on adventure to Arthur's court. Here the dwarf, who is modelled perhaps on Laurin, defeats Parzefal, Gawan and Galleman (perhaps a doublet of Walewan or Gawan; Chandler 1992, 304) in battle, and declines Parzefal's invitation to stay at the court, preferring to report back to the duchesses (who are reminiscent of the three queens who send out Ecke in the *Eckenlied*). Form and style of the poem are decidedly heroic – the first strophe distinctly echoes the opening of the *Nibelungenlied* – but some of the characters at least are Arthurian. A novel feature is the resounding defeat of the Arthurian knights – as the manuscript heading proclaims, Antelan 'stach si all ab und behiellt preis und er ob in allen'. Burlesque though this clearly is, Ebenbauer interprets the poem as fundamental criticism directed against de-generate Arthurian chivalry in which combatants do battle with men with whom they have no quarrel (Ebenbauer 1990, 72).

More striking, however, is the way in which, in *Wunderer*, Dietrich von Bern finds himself caught up as protagonist in an Arthurian-type plot. Here we find a distressed maiden seeking help at the court of a weak king (Etzel, not Arthur) where one of the knights (Dietrich) accepts the challenge and succeeds in the adventure. Dietrich, in fact, assumes the role not only of the Arthurian knight who rises to the challenge, his role is also that of protector from the Wild Hunt. The phenomenon of the Wild Hunt, indeed, provides another interesting link between King Arthur and Dietrich, for both figure as leaders of it. Gervase of Tilbury and Etienne de Bourbon both tell of Arthur in this role, and in several parts of France at least the belief was still current in the nineteenth century. Similar tales were told of Dietrich von Bern in various parts of Europe over an equally long period (Flood 1973 and 1999).

The story of Herbort of Denmark, a typical 'bride quest' story, provides an illuminating illustration of how, in different versions, the same character can get involved with different cycles. In *Biterolf* Herbort is one of Gunther's men, fighting Dietrich in the battle for the gates of Worms (v. 6227); we hear that Herbort has abducted Hildeburg of Ormanîe and defeated her father Ludwig and her brother Hartmuot (vv. 6452ff.); later he has taken Hildeburg to the Rhine, overcoming the opposition of Dietrich and Hildebrant. In *Rosengarten D* he is also associated with the Nibelungs, being one of Gibeche's men, opposing those of Dietrich at Worms. In the Norwegian *Thidrekssaga* (a prose compila-tion based on German sources), in contrast we find Thidrekr (= Dietrich) and Herburt involved with Arthur (Artus of Bertangaland, that is Brittany; Pfaff 1959, 36).[3] Here Herburt (brother of Tristram!) is a nephew of Thidrekr who sends him as his emissary to Arthur's court to win for him the hand of his daughter Hilldr. Herburt attracts the attention of the closely chaperoned princess while she is in church by letting two mice ornamented with gold and silver run around; later, by dint of drawing a hideous representation of Thidrekr on the wall, he persuades Hilldr to accept himself as a suitor instead of his uncle. He abducts her and kills the band of men Arthur sends in pursuit (Erichsen 1967, 272–9). On the strength of the detailed accounts in *Biterolf* and *Thidrekssaga*, Schneider and Wisniewski (1964, 87) postulate not merely a 'Herbortlied' but a full-blown 'Herbortepos' from shortly before 1250.

Arthurian romance and heroic poems may display many points of contact in respect of individual motifs, underlying structures, and narrative technique. Hugo Kuhn, for instance, drew attention to extensive parallels underlying Gottfried's *Tristan* and the *Nibelungenlied* (1973), while Jillings found it evident from 'far-reaching schematic and detailed similiarities' that Heinrich von dem Türlin's *Crône* had 'absorbed heroic structures' (1980, 54). More recently, Matthias Meyer has investigated the narrative structures in Stricker's *Daniel vom blühenden Tal*, Heinrich's *Crône*, the *Eckenlied*, and *Laurin* (1994). Some of the German heroic poems make use of stylistic features characteristic of Arthurian romance. Even the *Nibelungenlied* betrays the influence of the *roman courtois* and has been compared to 'a good hunk of boar's meat smothered in a delicious sauce from the French kitchen' (de Vries 1963, 63). There are striking similarities between the lavish descriptions of courtly finery in the Arthurian poems and the *Nibelungenlied*,[4] and French linguistic and literary influence is already apparent when the *Nibelungenlied* uses the phrases *riters namen gewinnen* (*Nl.* 31, 4) and *riter werden* (*Nl.* 33, 3) in connexion with the investiture of Sivrit and his 400 companions (Jackson 1994, 41–2, 71).

For all that they preserve many features of heroic poetry, the poems telling of Dietrich's encounters with dwarfs, giants and other non-human creatures (*Goldemar*, *Eckenlied*, *Herr Dietrich von Bern* (*Sigenot*), *Laurin*, *Virginal*, *Wunderer*) share many of the trappings of Arthurian romance. *Laurin*, for instance, which begins with a prologue clearly modelled on Arthurian prologues (Meyer 1994, 238–40), opens with an indirect but obvious allusion to Hartmann von Aue's *Erec* and *Iwein* when the poet praises Dietrich's aides:

> wie selten sie verlâgen
> êre unde frümekeit!   (*Laurin A*, 14–15)

(How rarely they failed to live up to what honour and valour demanded of them!)

But, whereas in Hartmann the maintenance of *êre* is the mainspring of the action, in *Laurin* honour is not thematized as a problem of knightly existence. Yet the poet was certainly well aware of the characteristics of Arthurian romance. *Laurin* has a double cursus structure, the hinge being provided by the first reconciliation between Dietrich and Laurin which turns out to be an illusory state of harmony. In *Laurin K* the analogy with Arthurian romance is even closer, with Laurin being baptized and integrated into society. Yet, against all this, *Laurin* also preserves distinctly heroic, non-Arthurian features, such as the battle in the hall (which figures in the *Nibelungenlied*), and, moreover, the second part of the action is driven not by the Arthurian motif of liberation or redemption but by a heroic thirsting for revenge, Laurin's desire for vengeance on Dietrich (Heinzle 1978, 23–6; Heinzle, *VL*, V, cols. 625–8; Meyer 1994, 237–70, especially 259).

The *Eckenlied* likewise has a double structure which appears to be modelled on the pattern of the classical double cursus, yet here, too, there is a significant difference from the Arthurian romance: in the first part of the poem Ecke is inevitably doomed to tragic failure in the heroic manner, but in the second Dietrich triumphs in the Arthurian mode (Meyer 1994, 187–236, especially 233–5). The hinge between the two halves is represented by Dietrich's typically Arthurian encounter with Frau Babehilt at a spring who heals his wounds (str. 151–60).[5] Another, more concise instance of a narrative parallel with an Arthurian work is the fight between Ecke and the *Meerwunder* (str. 52–4), a centaur-like beast ('das was halp ros und halbes man') with a horny skin. This shows remarkable similarities with the fight between Arthur and the Chevalier Poisson in the prose *Chevalier du Papegau*. Whereas Zink (1971) considered there might be a genetic link between the two, this has been denied by Heinzle (1978, 151), though the jury is still out. (For valid criticism of Heinzle's dogmatic view see Brévart 1986, 268 and 318–22; Meyer 1994, 235.)

One of the most obvious features that the poems about Dietrich's youthful exploits share with Arthurian romance is the happy ending, so very different from the scene of death and desolation at the end of the *Nibelungenlied*. In *Wunderer*, for example, Etzel runs a court which is very similar to Arthur's. (On the parallel between Arthur's court and that at Bern (Verona) see Wessels 1962, 258.) When the court is challenged by the distressed maiden – who turns out to be Lady Fortune (Frau Sælde), a familiar figure indeed both in Arthurian romance and in the Dietrich poems[6] – Dietrich rises to the occasion: he liberates the maiden, slays Wunderer, and presents the monster's head as a trophy to the court. Leaving aside the decapitation motif (Flood 1994), all this is very similar to Wirnt von Gravenberg's *Wigalois* where Nereja appears at Arthur's court, requesting on behalf of her mistress assistance in a perilous adventure that has already cost many knights their lives; Wigalois craves the king's permission to accept the challenge, which Arthur reluctantly grants (1717–1811). Inevitably, our hero eventually succeeds, slaying the monstrous Roaz and marrying Larie. A happy outcome is found, too, in Albrecht von Scharfenberg's *Seifrid de Ardemont*, where the hero – if indeed he may be identified with the Sivrit of the *Nibelungenlied*[7] – is linked now with Arthurian romance as a knight of the Round Table; after many adventures he marries the Princess Mundirosa to live happily ever after.

Returning to *Wunderer*, the image of Etzel in this poem was doubtless at least in part determined by the one given of him in all the Upper German epics, which have a tendency to show him fading silently into the background when a man of action is required. The *Nibelungenlied*, for instance, depicts him as a ruler who, for all his high renown, is overwhelmed by unstoppable events. But the figure of the weak king was widespread in medieval European literature: other examples are King Gunther in the *Nibelungenlied* and King Marke in Gottfried's *Tristan*, while King Arthur himself rarely has more than a passive role in the poems in which he appears. Even within the Arthurian poems themselves criticism of Arthur's court is not unknown (Schirok 1989).

Another manifestation of the influence of Arthurian romance on heroic poetry may perhaps be seen in the fact that some of the poems about Dietrich von Bern are composed in couplets rather than strophes. Whereas *Alpharts Tod*, *Die Rabenschlacht* and *Wunderer B* are composed in a strophic form similar to that of the *Nibelungenlied* and *Kudrun*, and *Goldemar*, *Ecke*, *Sigenot* and *Virginal* are written in the complex thirteen-line strophe of the 'Bernerton' (or 'Herzog Ernst-Ton'), *Dietrichs Flucht* and *Laurin* are composed in rhyming couplets. Schneider and Mohr (1961, 17; for another view Meyer 1994, 237f.) believed that use of couplets in heroic poetry was deliberately intended to associate it more closely with other genres such as the courtly romance and the verse chronicle.

From the foregoing it will have become clear that the medieval audience did not draw fine distinctions between courtly (Arthurian) romance and heroic poetry. These genres coexisted and overlapped. The close association between different narrative cycles is neatly exemplified in the magnificently embroidered cap sported by Helmbrecht, Wernher der Gartenaere's upstart peasant 'hero' (third quarter of the thirteenth century). Though the description does not specifically mention the Arthurian cycle, it might well have done, for in addition to depicting scenes from the stories of Aeneas and Helen of Troy, of Charlemagne, Roland, Turpin and Oliver, of Dietrich von Bern, Witege and the battle of Ravenna, we learn that 'nothing was omitted concerning knights and ladies' (*Helmbrecht*, vv. 91–3). Three manuscripts now in the Austrian National Library at Vienna well illustrate how Arthurian and heroic material may be transmitted side by side. The early fourteenth-century Cod. Vindob. 2779 contains sixteen texts, including not only Hartmann von Aue's *Iwein*, but also *Ortnit*, *Dietrichs Flucht*, *Die Rabenschlacht* and Heinrich von dem Türlin's *Crone*, a juxtaposition which indicates that at this time both genres appealed to the same kind of audience (Becker 1977, 63). 'Linhart Scheubels Heldenbuch' (Cod. Vindob. 15478), written *c.* 1480–90, contains *Virginal (w)*, *Antelan*, *Ortnit*, *Wolfdietrich*, the *Nibelungenlied* and *Lorengel* (Becker 1977, 156–8). With the exception of *Antelan*, all these poems are bride-quest stories. Similarly, the 'Ambraser Heldenbuch' (MS Ser. n. 2663), written in the Tyrol between 1504 and 1517, contains not only Hartmann's *Iwein* and *Erec*, but also *Dietrichs Flucht*, *Die Rabenschlacht*, the *Nibelungenlied*, the *Klage*, *Kudrun*, *Biterolf*, *Ortnit* and *Wolfdietrich*, together with various other works (Becker 1977, 52, 153–5).

Such manuscripts demonstrate that the audience for Arthurian romance and heroic epic was – or at least could be – substantially the same (Fechter 1935; Becker 1977, 194–221). But the purpose of such collections was not always primarily to serve the private pleasure of their owners. When Emperor

Maximilian I, known as 'the last of the knights', had the 'Ambraser Heldenbuch' compiled, not the least of his aims was to bring together accounts of the deeds of his glorious ancestors and thereby to add further lustre to the imperial dignity. Of all the many projects he planned to enhance the name of the House of Habsburg, his monumental tomb in the Hofkirche at Innsbruck was the grandest (Oberhammer 1935). Among the figures who stand watch at the tomb are Arthur and Dietrich von Bern, representing models of chivalry. Possibly designed at least in part by Albrecht Dürer as early as 1512, the statues were executed in bronze by Peter Vischer the Elder in 1513 (Oettinger 1966, plates 24–30); ironically, they both had to be pawned to the bishop of Augsburg to cover debts and were only transferred to Innsbruck in 1532, more than a decade after Maximilian's death (Oettinger 1966, 18–23). Of the eleven statues completed before Maximilian's death in 1519, these were the only two to represent ancient, half-legendary forebears, the remainder being of historical personages of the thirteenth to fifteenth centuries (Oettinger 1966, 1).

Maximilian, as a good Christian, will have died in the expectation of resurrection. What better guardians of his tomb could there have been than two figures from the past of whom, in the case of Arthur, it was confidently expected that he would return in the hour of need (Loomis 1959, 64–71) and, in the case of Theodoric-Dietrich, it was believed that (despite clerical propaganda to the contrary) he had been taken unto the bosom of God: *Thidrekssaga* asserts that it had been revealed to Germans in a dream that Thidrekr enjoyed the support of God and the Virgin and would return because he had remembered them in his final hour (Erichsen 1967, 459–60); and that great fifteenth-century compendium of heroic poems, the *Heldenbuch*, reports that when it was Dietrich's turn to quit this earthly scene a little dwarf, clearly echoing Christ's own words (John 18:36), had assured him that 'Thy kingdom is not of this world' (Kuhn 1961, 425).

Notes

[1] For a general account of German heroic poetry see Hoffmann 1974, and for the poems about Dietrich von Bern in particular Heinzle 1978, Wisniewski 1986 and Flood 1996.

[2] For these and other names mentioned in this chapter see Gillespie 1973, Chandler 1992 and Paff 1959.

[3] Arthur has two sons, Iron and Apollonius, who take refuge with Attila at Soest after they have been driven out of Brittany after their father's death (Erichsen 1967, 284).

[4] In the description of the fine clothes prepared for Sivrit's and Gunther's journey to Island in the *Nibelungenlied* there is mention of silks from such exotic locations as Zazamanc (*Nl.* 362, 2) and Marroch (*Nl.* 364, 1). Zazamanc is Belakane's land in *Parzival* 16, 2, and Marroch is also mentioned there (*Pz.* 15, 17). Azagouc (*Nl.* 439, 2) is

found in *Pz.* 30, 23. Since Wolfram clearly knew the *Nibelungenlied*, it seems likely that he borrowed these names from there, though Lachmann, Panzer, Werner Schröder and others have held that the borrowing was in the opposite direction.

[5] For discussion of this passage see Meyer 1994, 222, and the commentary in Brévart 1986, 285–6.

[6] Cf. *Crône*, vv. 15663 and 15823–48 (de Boor 1975); *Daniel von dem Blühenden Tal* v.541; *Ecke* 160, 11 (Brévart 1986, 287). Meyer 1994, 124–32.

[7] Both are dragon-fighters, but the link is problematic. See H. Brunner, 'Hürnen Seyfrid', in *VL*, IV, 317–26, here 320.

Bibliography

Primary Sources

'Ambraser Heldenbuch' = *Ambraser Heldenbuch. Vollständige Faksimileausgabe.* Ed. by F. Unterkircher, 1973 (Codices selecti, 43). Graz.

Antelan = W. Scherer, 'Antelan', *ZfdA*, 15, 1872, 140–9.

Biterolf. In *DHB*, I, 1–197.

Chevalier du Papegau = *Le Chevalier du Papegau.* Ed. by F. Heuckenkamp, 1896. Halle.

Crône = Heinrich von dem Türlin, *Diu Crône.* Ed. by G. H. F. Scholl, 1852 (BLVS, 27). Stuttgart (repr. Amsterdam 1966).

Daniel von dem Blühenden Tal = Der Stricker, *Daniel von dem Blühenden Tal.* Ed. by M. Resler, 1983 (ATB, 92). Tübingen.

DHB = *Deutsches Heldenbuch*, 5 vols. Ed. by O. Jänicke, E. Martin, A. Amelung and J. Zupitza, 1866–73. Berlin (repr. Berlin and Zurich 1963–8).

Dietrichs Flucht. In *DHB*, II, 55–215.

Eckenlied = *Das Eckenlied.* Middle High German and New High German. Edition, transl. and commentary by F. Brévart, 1986 (RUB, 8339). Stuttgart. Also *Das Eckenlied. Sämtliche Fassungen.* Ed. by F. Brévart, 1998 (ATB, 111). Tübingen; and in *DHB*, V, 217–64.

Erichsen = See *Thidrekssaga* [German translation].

Heldenbuch. Nach dem ältesten Druck in Abbildung, 2 vols. Ed. by J. Heinzle, 1981–7 (Litterae, 75/I and II). Göppingen.

Helmbrecht von Wernher dem Gartenaere. Ed. by H.-J. Ziegeler, 1993 (ATB, 11), 10th edn. Tübingen.

Historia von dem Gehörnten Siegfried. In *Hürnen Seyfrid*, 63–99.

Hürnen Seyfrid = *Das Lied vom hürnen Seyfrid.* Ed. by W. Golther, 1911 (Neudrucke deutscher Litteraturwerke des 16. u. 17. Jhs., 81/2), 2nd edn. Halle.

Laurin = *Laurin und Walberan.* In *DHB*, I, 199–257.

Lorengel. Ed. by D. Buschinger, 1979 (GAG, 253). Göppingen.

Nibelungenlied = *Das Nibelungenlied.* Ed. by K. Bartsch and H. de Boor, 1972 (Deutsche Klassiker des Mittelalters), 20th edn. Wiesbaden. [*Nl.*]

Parzival. In *Wolfram von Eschenbach.* Ed. by K. Lachmann, 1926, 6th edn. Berlin and Leipzig. [*Pz.*]

Rabenschlacht. In *DHB*, II, 217–326.

Rosengarten = *Die Gedichte vom Rosengarten zu Worms.* Ed. by G. Holz, 1893. Halle.

Seifrid de Ardemont = *Merlin und Seifrid de Ardemont von Albrecht von Scharfenberg in der Bearbeitung Ulrich Füetrers.* Ed. by F. Panzer, 1902 (BLVS, 227). Tübingen.

Thidrekssaga = *Saga Þiðreks af Bern.* 2 vols. Ed. by H. Bertelsen, 1905–11 (Samfund til udgivelse af gammel nordisk litteratur, 24). Copenhagen.

Thidrekssaga [German translation] = *Die Geschichte Thidreks von Bern.* Transl. by F. Erichsen and ed. by H. Voigt, 1967 (Thule, 22). Darmstadt. [Erichsen].

Tristrant = *Eilhart von Oberge*. Ed. by F. Lichtenstein, 1877 (Quellen und Forschungen zur Sprach- und Culturgeschichte der germanischen Völker, 19). Strasbourg.

Virginal [h version]. In *DHB*, V, 1–200.

Virginal w = *Dietrichs erste Ausfahrt*. Ed. by F. Stark, 1860 (BLVS, 52). Stuttgart.

Wigalois = Wirnt von Gravenberc, *Wigalois, der Ritter mit dem Rade*. Ed. by J. M. N. Kapteyn, 1926 (Rheinische Beiträge und Hülfsbücher zur germanischen Philologie und Völkerkunde, 9). Bonn.

Willehalm = Wolfram von Eschenbach, *Willehalm*. Ed. with translation and commentary by J. Heinzle, 1991 (Bibliothek des Mittelalters, 9). Frankfurt.

Wunderer (B) = *Le Wunderer. Fac-similé de l'édition de 1503*. Ed. by Georges Zink, 1949 (Bibliothèque de philologie germanique, 14). Paris.

Other Literature

Becker, P. J. 1977. *Handschriften und Frühdrucke mittelhochdeutscher Epen*. Wiesbaden.

Brévart, F. 1986. See Primary Sources, *Eckenlied*.

Chandler, F. W. 1992. *A Catalogue of Names of Persons in the German Court Epics*, ed. by M. H. Jones, King's College London Medieval Studies, 8, London.

de Boor, H. 1975. 'Fortuna in mittelhochdeutscher Dichtung, insbesondere in der *Crône* des Heinrich von dem Türlin', in Fromm, H., Harms, W. and Ruberg, U., eds., *Verbum et Signum*, Munich, II, 311–28.

de Vries, J. 1963. *Heroic Song and Heroic Legend*, transl. by B. J. Timmer, London.

Ebenbauer, A. 1990. 'Antelan – kurze Bemerkungen zu einem Zwergenkönig', in Reichert, H. and Zimmermann, G., eds., *Helden und Heldensage. Otto Gschwantler zum 60. Geburtstag*, Philologica Germanica, 11, Vienna, 65–73.

Erichsen, 1967. See Primary Sources, *Die Geschichte Thidreks von Bern*.

Fechter, W. 1935. *Das Publikum der mittelhochdeutschen Dichtung*, Frankfurt (repr. Darmstadt 1966).

Flood, J. L. 1973. 'Dietrich von Bern and the human hunt', *Nottingham Mediaeval Studies*, 17, 17–41.

Flood, J. L. 1994. 'The severed heads: on the deaths of Gunther and Hagen', in Honemann et al. 1994 (see Gen. Bibl.), 173–91.

Flood, J. L. 1996. 'Dietrich von Bern', in Müller, U. and Wunderlich, W., eds., *Mittelalter Mythen I: Herrscher, Helden, Heilige*, St Gallen, 287–304.

Flood, J. L. 1999. 'Die Wilde Jagd', in Müller, U. and Wunderlich, W., eds., *Mittelalter Mythen II: Dämonen, Monster, Fabelwesen*, St Gallen, 583–601.

Gillespie, G. T. 1973. *A Catalogue of Persons named in German Heroic Literature*, Oxford.

Hatto, A. T., transl. 1980. *Wolfram von Eschenbach, Parzival*, Harmondsworth.

Hauck, K. 1961. *Zur germanisch-deutschen Heldensage*, WdF, 14, Darmstadt.

Heinzle, Joachim. 1978. *Mittelhochdeutsche Dietrichepik. Untersuchungen zur Tradierungsweise, Überlieferungskritik und Gattungsgeschichte später Heldendichtung*, MTU, 62, Munich.

Hoffmann, W. 1974. *Mittelhochdeutsche Heldendichtung*, Grundlagen der Germanistik, 14, Berlin.

Jackson 1994. See Gen. Bibl.

Jillings, L. 1980. *Diu 'Crône' of Heinrich von dem Türlein: The Attempted Emancipation of Secular Narrative*, GAG, 258, Göppingen.

Kuhn, Hans. 1961. 'Heldensage und Christentum', in Hauck 1961, 416–26.

Kuhn, Hugo. 1973. 'Tristan, Nibelungenlied, Artusstruktur', *Sitzungsberichte der Bayerischen Akademie der Wissenschaften*, phil.-hist. Klasse, no. 5, Munich.

Loomis 1959. See Gen. Bibl.

Meyer 1994. See Gen. Bibl.

Oberhammer, V. 1935. *Die Bronzestandbilder des Maximiliansgrabmals in der Hofkirche zu Innsbruck*, Innsbruck.

Oettinger, K. 1966. *Die Bildhauer Maximilians am Innsbrucker Kaisergrabmal*, Erlanger Beiträge zur Sprach- und Kunstwissenschaft, 23, Nuremberg.

Paff, W. J. 1959. *The Geographical and Ethnic Names in the Þiðriks Saga*, The Hague.

Schirok, B. 1989. '*Artus der meienbære man*. Zum Stellenwert der "Artuskritik" im klassischen deutschen Artusroman', in Schnell, R., ed., *Gotes und der werlde hulde. Literatur in Mittelalter und Neuzeit. Festschrift für Heinz Rupp zum 70. Geburtstag*, Berne and Stuttgart, 58–81.

Schneider, H. and Mohr, W. 1961. 'Heldendichtung', in Hauck 1961, 1–30.

Schneider, H. and Wisniewski, R. 1964. *Deutsche Heldensage*, Sammlung Göschen, 32, 2nd edn, Berlin.

Scholz, M. G. 1978. '*Antelan (König Anteloy)*', in *VL*, I, 396–7.

Wessels, P. B. 1962. '*König Laurin*. Quelle und Struktur', *PBB* (Tübingen), 84, 245–65.

Wisniewski, R. 1986. *Mittelalterliche Dietrichdichtung*, Sammlung Metzler, 205, Stuttgart.

Zink, G. 1971. 'Eckes Kampf mit dem Meerwunder', in Hennig, U. and Kolb, H., eds., *Mediaevalia litteraria. Festschrift für Helmut de Boor*, Munich, 485–92.

14

ARTHURIAN ELEMENTS IN DRAMA AND *MEISTERLIEDER*

John E. Tailby

Drama

Medieval drama is an urban genre. Arthurian material with its noble and royal personages is, therefore, largely alien to it and makes the transition only where an episode has features which are also characteristic of drama. Though it is not correct to equate secular medieval German drama completely with *Fastnacht-spiele* ('Shrovetide plays' or 'Carnival comedies') these do constitute the great majority of secular plays from the medieval period. In recent decades we have been encouraged to believe that the genre is especially characteristic of Nuremberg, where records show that it was performed by groups of journey-men, members of trade guilds, who took their playlets around private houses and inns during the period preceding Lent. In the simplest *Reihenspiele* ('Revue plays') the performers speak only once each and the speeches are only loosely connected by a central theme, such as the outrageousness of their professed sexual exploits, or by reference to a central figure who has to choose between them. Plays with a real plot (*Handlungsspiele*) are considered a secondary development.

Recent work by Eckehard Simon (1993) has shown that Shrovetide plays were performed all over the German-speaking area, and that in some places such as Lübeck, and in Switzerland, the subject matter was serious and edifying. In Nuremberg the sub-literary tradition of telling 'tall stories' in turn in competitive fashion was taken over by Hans Rosenplüt and after him Hans Folz, and our attention has been drawn to it by the survival of a small number of manuscript compendia, compiled after the performances, which constitute the great majority of the surviving texts.

One of these, Munich codex cgm 714, contains in the middle of a group of *Fastnachtspiele* two Arthurian plays, numbered 80 and 81 in Keller's edition. Interestingly, they are preceded by two others plays, K 78 and K 79, which include kings and knights among their personnel. What is particularly striking from the point of view of Arthurian studies is the fact that the two Arthurian plays do not take up grand themes of chivalric activity, but the motif of the chastity test, which figures often in Arthurian literature from the twelfth century onward, but which was by no means restricted to an aristocratic court public and was, with its sexual humour and its reflections on marital behaviour, well able to command the interest of urban audiences.

Keller 81, *Der Luneten Mantel* ('Lunete's Mantle'), revolves around the revelation of a series of marital infidelities and thus is entirely appropriate material for a *Fastnachtspiel*. The mantle in the title will fit only the faithful wife of the king of Spain, the youngest wife of the oldest king; nothing is here made of their disparity in age. Typical of the genre is the drastic metaphorical language used to describe infidelities: 'She has admitted a strange shopkeeper into her store and has allowed another man to plough her field' (668, 7f.).

Though the subject matter and its treatment account for the importation into the genre of essentially alien material, the play is not a typical *Fastnachtspiel*. The king of Spain is delighted when the coat fits his wife; his reaction, 'happy is the man who has such a pure wife', sounds quite out of place in a Nuremberg *Fastnachtspiel*. The commonest character in the *Fastnachtspiel* is the peasant fool (the labels peasant and fool are almost interchangeable). Here we have the 'fool's wife' (*Nerrin*) being dissuaded by her husband from trying on the coat, since she will only be disgraced like the other women; his argument that 'wanting to have too much honour rarely leads to any good' makes him a wise fool, otherwise unknown in the genre.

The closing section of the play also reveals such juxtaposition of alien and typical features. The speech of the first herald includes a reference to 'freude und hohen mut' ('joy and high spirits') which echoes the jargon of courtly literature and is followed by two references to God and an 'amen'. By contrast, his last four lines are entirely typical including: 'Landlord, don't take our piece amiss', and 'Farewell now and goodnight.' Since the play is not comfortable in the genre, we have another herald as final speaker who, while still referring to the performers as kings and queens, works in the usual request for cash donations from the audience.

In K 80, *Das vasnachtspil mit der kron* ('The Shrovetide play with the Crown'), by contrast, the infidelities of the royal husbands are revealed. This play begins with the reinforcement of three heralds, who are necessary to launch the plot with the explanation that the king whom the crown best suits gets to keep it, and that any adulterous husband will be shown up. When the king of the Orient appears to have goat's horns when he tries it on a herald explains: 'He makes love secretly with the miller's wife from the foot of his castle; and none of his peasants' daughters is safe from him.' Despite the noble personnel, we are here in the basic territory of the genre. As in K 81, here too the deceived spouse complains: 'You have been taking my meagre nourishment elsewhere, which I had need of here at home.' Her husband produces the original excuse that he was sparing her so that she could look good longer; unusually there is here no counter-accusation of infidelity. The king of Cyprus tries to avoid wearing the crown; when he is found out he blames his wife for refusing him too often. Two heralds suggest getting rid of this crown as it only causes disharmony. At this point Arthur's sister Lanet launches into accusations against Arthur's queen, who has not spoken. No indication of the validity of these accusations is given; Arthur confiscates Lanet's lands and banishes her, and would have executed her, were she not his sister. Echoes of known Arthurian plots are evident here, but neither Arthur's wife nor her alleged lovers are named. While here Lanet is Arthur's sister, in K 81 the person called Lunete in the title and Luneta in the heading to her speech says to the king: 'I don't know your court at all.'

No location is suggested for K 81, but in K 80 Arthaus (*sic*!) is addressed as 'Noble King of England'.

In his *Nachlese* Keller includes as K 127 a play the substance of which is a variant on the material treated in K 80 and K 81. The manuscript title matches the length of the play: 'Here begins a very entertaining Shrovetide Play which tells of King Arthur, how he invited seven princes with their wives to his court and how they were disgraced by a horn, very entertaining to hear.' The play fills twenty-three pages, whereas the average play in the whole collection is only five or six pages long, the shortest only a couple of pages.

In this play Arthur invites to his festival the kings of Kriechenlandt, Engellandt, Kerlingen (possibly Caerleon, i.e. Wales), Franckenreich, Preyssen, Tenmark and Spanger landt. The queen, again unnamed, ensures that their wives are included in the invitations. Even when reminded by his queen, Arthur refuses to invite his sister, the queen of Zippern. All ranks of the court are invited, and Ayax will ensure that there is enough to eat and drink. As they sit down they say the *benedicite*, which is not usual in a *Fastnachtspiel*.

While they eat, the scene shifts to the queen of Zippern and her maid Hilla, whom she sends to Arthur's court with a drinking horn to stir up 'hatred and anger'. Any man whose wife is unreliable will pour the wine over himself when he attempts to drink from the horn. Hilla is to hide the identity of the donor, note which kings and queens are present, and report back. She sets off 'to Britain, King Arthur's land'. Weigion, a knight at Arthur's court, reads out what is written on the horn, and Hilla returns 'on horseback'. Each king in turn gets a soaking, even though his queen has just reasserted her virtue. It is not yet clear whether the horn is telling the truth or whether the queen of Zippern is using sorcery as well as malice, as the queen of Kerlingen suggests. The truth only becomes clear when the queen of Spangen's virtue is shown by her husband not getting wet. In encouraging him she states that they are less wealthy than anyone else present, but they have their honour. Arthur rewards the king of Spangen with a duchy as well as the horn.

In a new strand of the action Ayax tells Arthur that Weigion was the queen's (Arthur's wife's) lover. Weigion denies this and is prepared to fight a duel. He calls on Christ to support him to prove his virtue, and duly wins. Ayax is banished and Weigion is praised for defending the queen's honour. But Arthur did get wet! Arthur proposes more drinking and dancing; the king of Kriechenland replies for all, including the wish that God may protect Arthur, whose final speech also includes four references to God.

These details make clear the interrelationship of K 127 with K 80 and K 81. They also show how Arthurian figures and motifs are connected with typical *Fastnachtspiel* features: a fight on stage, enthusiasm for food and drink, a dance towards the end of the play and at the very end the herald addresses the host of the play directly, coupling this with a further reference to drinking.

Meisterlieder

The *Meistersinger* were townsmen who met in 'brotherhoods' or 'societies' from the fifteenth to the seventeenth century for the purpose of making and performing songs in competition with each other. Most were craftsmen or tradesmen, though some were from higher professions. They regarded themselves as the descendants of the great lyric poets of the High Middle Ages and revered the 'twelve old masters' going back to Walther von der Vogelweide. They had a technical, even mechanical, approach to composition, which became subject to increasingly codified rules in the sixteenth century. The survival (and publication) of their texts has been haphazard, and they have attracted modest scholarly attention.

A *Meisterlied* version of the story told in K 127, *Dis ist Frauw Tristerath Horn von Saphoien* ('This is Lady Tristerat of Saphoien's Horn') survives together with *Luneten Mantel* (*lanethen mantel* in the manuscript) in the Hamburg manuscript cod. germ. 6, known as MS Go of Wolfram's *Parzival*; and in cgm 4997, the Kolmarer Liederhandschrift (*c.* 1460); this version lacks the scene in which Weigion is accused of adultery with the queen. Recently, Gottzmann (1989, 219f.) and Walsh (1989) have tried to establish relationships between these surviving versions. Walsh's assertion (307) that the *Meisterlieder* – *Luneten* (or *Lanethen*) *Mantel* and *Frauw Tristerath Horn* – are the 'immediate sources' for the dramas K 81 and K 127 postulates a more direct relation between these works than can be proven. It is clear that the idea of tests of marital fidelity derives ultimately from French sources, notably Robert Biket's *Lai du cor* and the anonymous *Le mantel mautaillié*, with which is associated the German fragment *Der Mantel*. However, we cannot know just which German writers had access to which, if any, French versions. Regarding French sources, though the point is scarcely provable, there seems a distinct possibility that somewhere in the translation an error or confusion has arisen concerning, on the one hand, the (drinking) horn (OF *cor*) which causes the unfaithful husbands to drench themselves in K 127 and the associated *Meisterlied*, and, on the other hand, the crown (Latin *corona*) which causes the unfaithful husbands to grow horns in K 80.

Hans Sachs

Strikingly, of all the works of Hans Sachs in the sixteenth century, only one refers to Arthur: a *Spruch* entitled *König Artus mit der ehbrecher-brugk* ('King Arthur and the adulterers' bridge'). Arthur is presented here as king of 'Britania . . . das man auch nennet Engelland' ('Britain that is also called England'). His capital Trimoantem is located on the river Ramesis – apparently an error for Tamesis. This poem is thematically close to the three *Fastnachtspiele* discussed above. Arthur's queen, again unnamed, is suspected of infidelity. The magic bridge constructed by the nigromancer Virgilius (later referred to consistently as Filius) in fact proves her innocence, but demonstrates the infidelities of other members of the court and guests, who fall off it. The Conclusion, constituting about one-fifth of the whole text, is a diatribe against adultery, though the main thrust of the text up to that point has been the harmful nature of suspicion. Könneker (1971) argues plausibly that Sachs knew his medieval German literature through the filter of the *Gesta Romanorum* and the *Volksbücher* (chapbooks), and for that reason it is little wonder that almost nothing Arthurian comes through.

This filter doubtless also accounts for the nature of Sachs's one play about Tristan, which shows why his 'tragedies' and 'comedies' are generally held in much lower esteem than his *Fastnachtspiele*. These plays were composed for the *Meistersingerbühne* (mastersingers' theatre), a money-making undertaking put on in the then secularized church of St Martha in Nuremberg, to which the public were admitted on payment of an entry fee, in contrast to the private competitive performances of *Meisterlieder*. It is still unclear how these plays were staged. The striking features of the church today are its smallness and its popularity for concerts due to its excellent acoustics. Sachs's play is entitled *Tragedia mit 23 personen, von der strengen lieb herr Tristrant mit der schönen königin Isalden, unnd hat 7 actus* ('Tragedy with twenty-three persons, of the strong love of Sir Tristrant for the beautiful queen Isalde, and has seven acts'). These 'acts' have no dramatic significance and are best regarded as episodes from the story of Tristan and Isolde. The amount of material they contain varies greatly. Act 1 opens with a Herald who tells the story of the love potion, but then the action begins with the killing of Morholt by Tristrant, the patriot fighting 'for the fatherland' against Irish tyranny. Act 2 takes the action to the point where Tristrant kills the dragon. In Acts 3 and 4 Tristrant and Isalde take the potion and deceive King Marx. Act 5 is striking for the amount of action it covers. Marx again catches Tristrant and Isalde *in flagrante* after advice from barons and dwarf. Tristrant escapes from the chapel where he was confessing before execution. He frees Isalde from the executioner (how is not shown, only reported) and they decide to live in the forest in a hut he and Curnefal will make. Marx reports finding them sleeping with a sword between them, and we are told they have been in the woods for two years. At Isalde's suggestion they confess to Marx's confessor Ugrim and obtain forgiveness for her to return to court. Tristrant remains banished. The action from Tristrant being reported as having escaped from the chapel to this point takes only three and a half pages of text. At the start of Act 6 Tristrant has married 'another Isalde'. In Act 7 he has gained another poisoned wound in helping his brother-in-law Cainis in an amorous adventure concerning Gardelago, wife of king Nampeconis. The action ends with the black sail/white sail motif.

Sachs draws for his drama on the prose adaptation of Eilhart's romance which was first printed in 1484, with further editions following in the sixteenth century. The edition of 1484 already provided a moralizing conclusion (see Chinca, chapter 7 above), and Sachs typically develops this by having the Herald, in a closing speech, warn against the excesses of extra-marital love, thus integrating the story of Tristrant's and Isalde's great love into the experience of his sixteenth-century urban audience by presenting it as a moral example of the dangers of adultery. Indeed, perhaps the central common feature linking the reception of Arthurian and Tristan material in drama and *Meisterlieder* in the fifteenth and sixteenth centuries is the extremely selective way in which authors with an urban public in mind focus on themes and motifs that relate by way of humour or moral example to the question of marital fidelity.

Bibliography

Primary Sources

K = *Fastnachtspiele aus dem fünfzehnten Jahrhundert*, 2. Ed. by A. v. Keller, 1853 (BLV, 29). Stuttgart (K 80 *Vasnachtspil mit der kron*, 654–63; K 81 *Der Luneten Mantel*, 664–78); and *Nachlese* [separate pagination, but play numbering continuous], 1858 (BLV, 46). Stuttgart (K 127 *Ain hupsches vasnachspil*, 183–215).

Lanethen mantel and *Frau Tristerath Horn*, in C. Brentano, *Sämtliche Werke und Briefe*, 9/1. Ed. by H. Rölleke, 1975. Stuttgart etc., 647–55.
Hans Sachs, *Werke*. Ed. by A. v. Keller and E. Götze, vol. 2, 1870 (BLV, 103). Stuttgart (*König Artus mit der ehbrecher-brugk*, 262–7); and vol. 12, 1879 (BLV, 140). Tübingen (*Tragedia . . . von der strengen lieb herr Tristrant . . .*, 142–86).

Other Literature

Aylett, R. and Skrine, P., eds. 1995. *Hans Sachs and Folk Theatre in the Later Middle Ages*, Lampeter.

Catholy, E. 1966. *Fastnachtspiel*, Sammlung Metzler, 56, Stuttgart.

Gottzmann, C. 1989. *Artusdichtung*, Sammlung Metzler, 249, Stuttgart.

Könneker, B. 1971. *Hans Sachs*, Sammlung Metzler, 94, Stuttgart.

Linke, H. 1991. 'Germany and German-speaking central Europe', in Simon, E., ed., *The Theatre of Medieval Europe*, Cambridge, New York and Melbourne.

Schanze, F. 1980. '*Luneten Mantel*', *VL*, V, 1068f.

Simon, E. 1993. 'Organising and staging carnival plays in late medieval Lübeck: a new look at the archival records', *JEGP*, 92, 57–72.

Walsh, M. W. 1989. '*Arthur cocu*: comic abuse of the Round Table in fifteenth-century *Fastnachtspiele*', in *FCS*, 15, 305–21.

15

KING ARTHUR AND HIS ROUND TABLE IN THE CULTURE OF MEDIEVAL BOHEMIA AND IN MEDIEVAL CZECH LITERATURE

Alfred Thomas

When, in Heinrich von Freiberg's late thirteenth-century continuation of Gottfried's *Tristan*, a squire explains to the eponymous hero the meaning of the Round Table which Arthur has founded (vv. 1307–404), it is as if Heinrich himself were introducing something that was not completely familiar to all sections of his Bohemian audience. In order to understand the reasons for this apparently retarded and limited reception of Arthurian literature in the Bohemian Lands in the thirteenth and fourteenth centuries, it is important to consider the cultural, social and political conditions which prevailed there. The ethnic relations between the Germans and the Slavs are a major factor to be considered in assessing the literary culture of medieval Bohemia (Rádl 1928, Wiskemann 1938, Thomas 1989a). In the thirteenth century Bohemia and Moravia (corresponding to the present-day Czech Republic) were ruled by a native Slav dynasty, the Přemyslides. A century earlier the Czech kings had responded to the lack of skilled manpower in their territories by inviting Germans to come and settle there as farmers to cultivate the thickly wooded border regions and, with the subsequent rise of a money economy, as miners to excavate the kingdom's rich resources of gold, silver and copper. Large German communities were founded first in the border area and, later, within the heartland of the Bohemian Lands. By the thirteenth century, many German towns had been founded which enjoyed their own laws distinct from those affecting the indigenous Slav population. Prague itself became a predominantly German-speaking town, although by the mid-fourteenth century Czechs began to settle in the 'New Town' founded by Charles IV, king of Bohemia and Holy Roman emperor (1346–78).

The need to balance the ethnic interests of the German settlers and the Czech nobility was no easy task for the kings of Bohemia. Two thirteenth-century Bohemian rulers, Přemysl Ottokar I (1197–1230) and Přemysl Ottokar II (1253–78) bore Slavonic and German names with the obvious intention of satisfying both ethnic camps, and Přemysl Ottokar II even had two seals inscribed, one for his Czech-speaking lands with the name Přemysl and one for his German-speaking subjects with the name Ottokar (Bartlett 1993, 201). Although the nobility had been instrumental in carrying through the process of German settlement, there are signs by the late thirteenth and early fourteenth century that many members of the gentry at least were becoming resentful of the Germans' growing influence at the court and in the church. The anonymous author of *The Dalimil Chronicle* (*c.* 1308–10), speaking on behalf of the gentry, complains bitterly about the Přemyslide practice of favouring Germans and neglecting the welfare of the Czechs. Other works are less virulently xenophobic, but the pervasive sense of resentment is unmistakable.

The Czech nobility was probably justified in some of its concerns, since the late Přemyslide kings of Bohemia were intent on creating a strong German middle class in order to strengthen their own economic power at the expense of their regional magnates. Since their political orientation was towards the German lands in the west, it made sense for the kings of Bohemia to identify with German culture rather than with the language of their frequently hostile nobility. Consequently, a major centre of German literary activity developed at the courts of Wenceslas I (1230–53), Přemysl Ottokar II and Wenceslas II (1278–1305). Just as, a century later, King Edward III of England initiated an Arthurian cult at Windsor in order to add lustre to his martial ambitions in France, so did the thirteenth-century kings of Bohemia encourage the German guest poets at their court to legitimize their political prominence within the empire by comparing them with the heroes of antiquity, the Bible and Arthurian Britain (Behr 1989). The German poet Meister Sigeher, who resided at the Prague court between the 1250s and the 1270s, extols Wenceslas I for his generosity, his wisdom and his chivalry, comparing him (respectively) with King Fruot, King Solomon and King Arthur (*Meister Sigeher*, 93). Wenceslas's son, Přemysl Ottokar, was similarly compared with King Arthur, as well as with Alexander the Great, by the poet Friedrich von Sonnenburg.

In 1306 the native Přemyslide dynasty came to a sudden and violent end with the murder of Wenceslas III. A few years later John of Luxembourg, son of the Holy Roman Emperor Henry VII, was chosen by the Bohemian nobility to fill the empty throne (king 1310–46). According to Peter of Zittau, author of the fourteenth-century *Chronicon Aulae Regiae*, some young Bohemian noblemen requested the new king to establish a Round Table, with jousts and festivities, so that his reputation and fame should spread abroad. John duly invited princes and knights from all over Germany to come to Prague to attend a Round Table festivity in 1319. But no one responded to the invitation, causing Peter of Zittau to reflect in characteristic clerical fashion on the folly of such courtly enterprises when they are inadequately advertised abroad (*Chronicon*, 252).

Peter's clerical resistance to the Round Table probably reflects a larger antipathy towards secular courtliness within the Bohemian church and aristocracy at this time. King John's desire to establish a Round Table in Prague seems to have met with the partial hostility of the Bohemian nobility. When the king was unhorsed and dirtied during a second tournament held at Prague during Shrovetide two years after the first 'Artushof', several onlookers applauded the disaster which had befallen him (Barber and Barker 1989, 58). A similar tone of hostility is felt in the concluding chapter of *The Dalimil Chronicle* which warns the king to adhere to the advice of the Czech nobility or leave the realm in peace. The same author has little time for jousting, which he characterizes, along with gambling with dice, as a sign of moral decline among the nobility. Tournaments are frequently castigated as alien practices by medieval Czech writers (Thomas 1998, 64, 117, 130). Thus many of the Czech nobility retained a conservative, anti-courtly vision of knighthood based on the old-fashioned clerical ideal of the crusading *miles Dei*. The fashionable ideal of the courtier-knight cultivated by King John and encouraged by some of his subjects was, on the whole, alien and anathema to them.

John's son, Charles IV, was closer in temperament to the sober values of his Czech-speaking subjects. Dubbed *rex clericorum* by William of Ockham, this pious and pragmatic ruler appears to have disliked chivalric romances. Instead he commissioned religious works, especially saints' lives cast in a courtly-chivalric mould. A good example of this fusion of courtliness and lay piety is an anonymous *Life of Saint Catherine of Alexandria*, which dates from about 1360–75. The author was probably one of the many clerics who moved between the royal court and the University of Prague, which the emperor had founded in 1348 (Thomas, 1998). The Czech *Life of Saint Catherine* combines the moral purity of a virgin with the courage of a knight; and it is in this work that we find the first sustained allusion to the *matière de Bretagne* in medieval Czech literature. It comes in the scene where Catherine has just been cruelly whipped by the pagans and compares her love for her mystical bridegroom Christ with Isolde's love for Tristan, vv. 2385–90:

> Drahé Izaldy napitie
> Bieše jí dřieve zavdáno,
> Když ve snách by dokonáno
> jejie sl'úbenie s Tristranem
> jenž jest nade vší věcí pánem,
> mimoňž mocnějšieho nenie.

(The precious drink of Isolde had already been given to her in her visions after her betrothal to Tristan, who is lord over all things, none more powerful than he.)

The presence of this courtly eucharistic conceit in the *Life of St Catherine* suggests that the audience may have been familiar with Gottfried von

Strassburg's *Tristan* or even the pious, christological ending of Heinrich von Freiberg's continuation, which was composed in Bohemia for the nobleman Raimund von Lichtenburg in the late thirteenth century. All this is consistent with what we know of Charles IV's cosmopolitan court in which French, German, Czech and Latin cultures coexisted.

Charles IV's son and heir, Wenceslas IV (1378–1419), was as different from his father as Charles had been from his. Lacking his father's mystical inclinations, he was a great lover of books, including chivalric romances. Among the volumes which can be attributed to his library is a beautifully illuminated manuscript of Wolfram von Eschenbach's chivalric epic *Willehalm*. It is from these final two decades of the fourteenth century that we begin to find Czech verse and prose romances, all of which rely upon Austro-Bohemian sources in German and which survive in fifteenth-century codices postdating the destructive Hussite Wars (1420–36). These works inevitably reflect the changing political and cultural climate of the day. Their medial-style realism, and occasional lapse into burlesque, suggest that they were not intended for a court audience but for those increasingly influential Czech-speaking members of the gentry and the merchant class who wished to familiarize themselves with Arthurian literature without subscribing to its alien courtly ethic.

Tandariáš a Floribella

The first of two Arthurian romances to be adapted into Czech was *Tandareis und Flordibel* by the Austrian writer Der Pleier, working probably in Salzburg between 1240 and 1270. This lengthy tale deals with marginal members of the Arthurian world: Tandareis, King Arthur's nephew, and Flordibel, an orphaned Indian princess who arrives at court to seek the protection of the king, and to whom Arthur assigns Tandareis as her personal squire. The princess and her squire fall in love and elope from the court. After several years of separation, during which time Flordibel returns to court alone and Tandareis is sent into exile as punishment for his wrongdoing, the lovers are finally reunited and given the king's blessing to marry (Kern 1981). The Czech version of the story is much more vigorous and fast-moving than its German model. *Tandariáš a Floribella* dates from about 1380, although it is preserved in three fifteenth-century manuscripts dating from 1463, 1472 and 1483 (Bamborschke 1982). With 1,842 lines, it is only one-tenth the length of the original and is conceived in a quite different fashion from it (Brušák 1970). Reflecting the different taste of its late fourteenth-century Czech audience, the reworking places the emphasis throughout on action rather than reflection, on external detail rather than on inner meditation. In the early scenes where Tandariáš serves Floribella as her page, Pleier devotes long passages to reflecting on the significance of courtly love, whereas the Czech adaptor allows the relationship to speak for itself through concrete action. When Tandariáš cuts himself while carving, but does not seem to notice the wound because he is too busy looking at his lady, the Czech author omits all of Pleier's authorial interjections (Thomas 1985b). The author also focuses his attention on the three main protagonists (Tandariáš, Floribella and King Arthur) and omits many characters included by Der Pleier. The story thus becomes a simple, unvarnished tale of triumphant love which completely ignores the predicaments of courtly convention and the feudal obligation which binds Tandariáš to his royal uncle. In fact, the Czech author sometimes pushes Arthur so far into the background that he almost disappears completely. For example, Floribella defends herself at her trial, revealing her forceful personality; instead of sending the conquered knights to Arthur as in Der Pleier, Tandariáš sends them to Floribella who intercedes for them with the king. The tendency to place the spotlight firmly on the lovers – even at the expense of the king – recalls some of the popularizing tendencies in the later fifteenth-century prose versions of German romances. As Helmut Melzer has shown in his systematic study of these works (1972), the changes introduced are not merely generic but are integral to the tastes and expectations of the burgher audience for whom they were conceived and written. The same might be said of *Tandariáš* with its emphasis on the horizontal relationship between equal individuals rather than on the vertical feudal bond between the king and his vassals. This popularizing principle is consistent with the political changes in late fourteenth-century Bohemia, a time when power was slowly and gradually being wrested from the king and concentrated in the hands of the gentry and the middle classes. Allied to changes in the religious climate and the increasing clamour for reform in the church, these political changes would culminate in the momentous Hussite Wars in the next century.

Tristram a Izalda

The second Czech Arthurian romance is *Tristram a Izalda* (*c.* 1400). At 9,000 verses, it is a complete version of the Tristan story and the longest narrative poem in medieval Czech literature. *Tristram* combines three German sources: Eilhart von Oberg's twelfth-century version, Gottfried's courtly romance and Heinrich von Freiberg's continuation of Gottfried. The Czech adaptation is preserved in two fifteenth-century manuscripts, the Strahov MS (A, dated 1449) and the Brno MS (B, dated 1483). By contrast with the German sources, the Czech version alternates between medial-style realism and low-style burlesque. The former is more characteristic of the early part of the story based on Eilhart and Gottfried, the latter of the later part based on Heinrich von Freiberg.

In the scene from Eilhart where Tristram and Izalda mistakenly drink the love-potion intended for King Mark and his new bride, the Czech adaptor exploits the dramatic tension of the original by reducing the symbolic function of the drink and focusing on the purely human aspect of the relationship between the protagonists (Thomas 1985a, 1989b). Unlike Eilhart's heroes, whose strange behaviour reflects the magical power of the love-potion, Tristram and Izalda behave like real lovers: Tristram runs impulsively to greet Izalda like a love-sick youth whereas Tristrant moves slowly and with great difficulty. The Czech author intensifies the emotional turmoil of his protagonists by the effective use of one-line verbal exchanges and by omitting Isolde's conventional address to *Vrau Amur*. These realistic and popularizing tendencies are taken so far that the work almost ceases to be a romance in the accepted sense of the word.

In the scenes based on Heinrich von Freiberg, a more carefree mood seems to prevail. Just as Tandariáš indulges in horse-play during the tournament at Arthur's court by throwing his companions over his shoulder, so does Tristram's behaviour frequently deviate from the courtly code inscribed in the original German works. When Tandariáš is bathing and is subjected to a playful beating with a straw by the daughter of the queen, or Tristram throws stinking cheese across the hall and mistakenly hits a lady of the court in the face, it is no longer the courtly ethos of German romance which is at work but a slapstick spirit more characteristic of the other Czech chivalric romances of the time. In the late fourteenth-century Czech version of the Tyrolean epic *Laurin*, for example, the knights who invade the dwarf king's rose-garden act in a rather boorish way and make a bed for themselves in the rose bushes. Even at the royal court in Prague, the chivalric ideal had undergone a remarkable transformation since the days of John of Luxembourg. As in Ricardian England, the emphasis at the court of Wenceslas IV was now on the epicurean pleasures of peace rather than on the knightly prowess of warfare. This hedonistic climate may well have had a 'trickle-down' effect on the Czech verse romances of the time, attenuating the moral earnestness and knightly severity so characteristic of the epic *Alexandreida*.

It would be wrong to claim, therefore, as early critics of the Czech verse romances have done, that the author of *Tristram* misunderstands the spirit of the German models simply because he uses medial-style realism or even low-style burlesque rather than Eilhart's pre-courtly symbolism or Gottfried's courtly code (Nebeský 1846; Gebauer 1879). The point is that the author's style and ideology are part and parcel of each other. For example, the apparently premature formulaic reference to Tristram's devotion to his lady as the pretext for fighting against the Irish giant Morholt (vv. 387f.) does not mean that the author is ignorant of the feudal convention of the source but that he wishes to highlight – even at this early stage of the story – the prominence of the two protagonists at the expense of King Mark, a popularizing feature consistent with the narrative strategy followed by the author of *Tandariáš* and indicative of the complex, ambivalent political relations between the Czech nobility and their ruler Wenceslas IV (Thomas 1998, 121). This apparent simplification of a complex set of feudal relations inscribed in a source text is not merely the consequence of ignorance or crudity on the adaptor's part but a crucial example of what has been termed the 'acculturation' of late medieval adaptations of chivalric romances, that is to say, the microcosmic process whereby small, seemingly incidental departures from the original encode the ideological preconceptions and cultural values of the target audience (Taylor 1998).

Bibliography

Primary Sources

Dalimil Chronicle = Staročeská kronika takřečeného Dalimila. 2 vols. Ed. by J. Daňhelka, 1988. Prague.
Heinrich von Freiberg, *Tristan*. Ed. by R. Bechstein, 1877. Leipzig.
Meister Sigeher. Ed. by H. P. Brodt, 1913 (Germanistische Abhandlungen, 42). Breslau.
Life of Saint Catherine = Život svaté Kateřiny, in *Dvě legendy Karlovy doby*. Ed. by J. Hrabák, 1959. Prague, 93–259.
Peter of Zittau, *Chronicon Aulae Regiae*. Ed. by J. Emler, 1884 (Fontes Rerum Bohemicarum, 4). Prague.
Der Pleier, *Tandareis und Flordibel*. Ed. by Ferdinand Khull, 1885. Graz.
Tandariáš a Floribella = Der altčechische Tandariuš. Ed. by U. Bamborschke, 1982. Berlin.
Tristram a Izalda = Das altčechische Tristan-Epos. 2 vols. Ed. with Middle High German parallel texts and modern German translation by U. Bamborschke, 1968–9. Wiesbaden.

Other Literature

Bamborschke, U. 1982. See Primary Sources, *Tandariáš*.
Barber, R. and Barker, J. 1989. *Tournaments: Jousts, Chivalry and Pageantry in the Middle Ages*, Woodbridge.
Bartlett, R. 1993. *The Making of Europe: Conquest, Colonization and Cultural Change, 950–1350*, London.
Behr, H.-J. 1989. *Literatur als Machtlegitimation. Studien zur Funktion der deutschsprachigen Dichtung am böhmischen Königshof im 13. Jahrhundert*, Munich.
Brušák, K. 1970. 'Some notes on *Tandariáš a Floribella*, a Czech 14th century chivalrous romance', in Auty, R. et al., eds., *Gorski vijenac: A Garland of Essays Offered to Professor Elizabeth Mary Hill*, Cambridge, 44–56.
Gebauer, J. 1879. 'Tristram', *Listy filologické*, 6, 108–39.
Kern, P. 1981. *Die Artusromane des Pleier. Untersuchungen über den Zusammenhang von Dichtung und literarischer Situation*, Philologische Studien und Quellen, 100, Berlin.
Klassen, J. 1978. *The Nobility and the Making of the Hussite Revolution*, Boulder.
Lacy 1996. See Gen. Bibl.
Melzer, H. 1972. *Trivialisierungstendenzen im Volksbuch*, Hildesheim and New York.
Nebeský, V. 1846. 'Tristram welký rek', *Časopis Českého Muzeum*, 277–300.

Petrů, E. 1982. 'Specifičnost rytířské epiky ve slovanských literaturách', *Slavia*, 52/3–4, 250–8.

Rádl, E. 1928. *Válka Čechů s Němci,* Prague.

Taylor, J. H. M. 1998. 'The significance of the insignificant: reading reception in the Burgundian *Erec* and *Cligès*', *FCS,* 24, 183–97.

Thomas, A. 1985a. 'The treatment of the love theme in the Old Czech *Tristram*', *Die Welt der Slaven*, 30/2, 260–8.

Thomas, A. 1985b. 'The treatment of the love scenes in *Tandariáš a Floribella*,' *Wiener Slawistisches Jahrbuch*, 31, 99–104.

Thomas, A. 1989a. 'Czech-German relations as reflected in medieval Czech literature', in Bartlett, R. and Mackay, A., eds., *Medieval Frontier Societies*, Oxford, 199–215.

Thomas, A. 1989b. *The Czech Chivalric Romances Vévoda Arnošt and Lavryn in Their Literary Context*, GAG, 504, Göppingen.

Thomas, A. 1996. 'Czech Arthurian literature', in Lacy 1996 (see Gen. Bibl.), 106–8.

Thomas, A. 1998. *Anne's Bohemia: Czech Literature and Society, 1310–1420*, Medieval Cultures at Minnesota, 13, Minneapolis.

Wiskemann, E. 1938. *Czechs and Germans: A Study of the Struggle in the Historic Provinces of Bohemia and Moravia*, Oxford.

16

THE MEDIEVAL GERMAN PICTORIAL EVIDENCE

James Rushing

In addition to the widely varied reception of the Arthurian material in medieval German texts, the *matière de Bretagne* also manifested itself in a great variety of visual art works throughout the Middle Ages and throughout the German-speaking realms. Although much of this material has long been familiar to Arthurian scholars,[1] it is only in relatively recent times that scholars have begun to develop methodologies for studying the content and meaning of art works based on vernacular literature, and for understanding the complex relationships between texts and images, artists and audiences. The academic discipline of art history has traditionally tended to ignore or scoff at art works based on vernacular literary materials because of the frequently inferior quality of those works, and efforts to interpret images and analyse narrative structures have been hampered by the traditional emphasis on stylistic history and sources. Literary historians, for their part, have often regarded art works quite wrongly as evidence for the reception of the texts, as if an artist's response to a subject could be simplistically equated with the response of a typical reader/listener to a particular text. In reality, some pictorializations represent radical rethinkings of the material, while others follow the texts fairly closely, but each pictorialization is a fundamentally independent work of art. It can be assumed neither that an artist's response to a given story was that of the typical contemporary, nor that an artist's goal was the slavish 'translation' of a text into another medium. A complete catalogue of German Arthurian art would be beyond the scope of the following survey, which will, however, offer a general sense of the dimensions of the corpus and suggest some of the key issues involved in its interpretation and study. The diversity of artistic approaches and the issues of interpretation can aptly be demonstrated in an opening discussion of the pictorializations of Iwein.

Iwein as example

One of the most striking and fascinating Arthurian art works from anywhere in Europe is the cycle of large, colourful wall paintings at the castle of Rodenegg

Figure 1. Iwein fights the lord of the fountain, Ascalon, Rodenegg castle (photo: author)

near Brixen (Bressanone) in the South Tyrol (Bonnet 1986; Rushing 1995, 30–90; Schupp and Szklenar 1996; Curschmann 1997, esp. 12–19).[2] Probably painted in the 1220s (or 1230s), the eleven scenes of the Rodenegg cycle stretch around all four walls of a relatively small ground-floor room.[3] The narrative begins with the departure of the knight from a castle, over the door of the Iwein room, and proceeds along the north wall as Iwein encounters the wild herdsman, pours water from the magic fountain onto a stone, and fights the lord of the fountain, Ascalon (Fig. 1). After striking his opponent a serious blow to the head, Iwein pursues him around the corner onto the west wall, where Ascalon collapses and Iwein's horse is struck by the falling portcullis. In the centre of the west wall, in the first image to strike the viewer entering the room, Ascalon lies dead or dying in the arms of his wife, Laudine. Obviously derived from the Lamentation scene in Christian iconography, the image powerfully evokes Laudine's grief. Lunete gives Iwein a ring that makes him invisible, and the narrative then continues on the south wall, with Ascalon's funeral, the search for the invisible Iwein, and Lunete's presentation of Iwein to Laudine (Fig. 2). Here,

Figure 2. Lunete's presentation of Iwein to Laudine, Rodenegg castle (photo: Leonhard Graf von Wolkenstein)

Iwein kneels before the grief-stricken Laudine in an overwhelmingly negative image devoid of any suggestion that Iwein has 'won' Laudine or is about to marry her, though that is what happens next in the story as told by Hartmann von Aue and Chrétien de Troyes. This abrupt and unhappy ending casts the Iwein story in an entirely new light, calling the ethos of *âventiure* decidedly into question. This interpretation is supported by the carefully planned visual structure of the cycle, in which the scenes of knightly glory on the north wall are opposed to the scenes of grief, danger and lamentation on the south wall, with the Lamentation-inspired death scene in the middle of the cycle dominating the room. The Rodenegg narrative contrasts the glorious side of *âventiure* with the death and mourning that it causes and makes profound grief the very centre of the narrative.[4]

At Schmalkalden (Thuringia), on the other hand, in murals painted late in the first half of the thirteenth century, not more than a decade or two after the Rodenegg cycle, we find a completely different thematic emphasis (Loomis and Loomis 1938, 77f. and figs. 161–6; Bonnet 1986; Rushing 1995, 91–132). Here, the Iwein story is narrated in six registers of paintings, on the walls and vaulted ceiling of a modest ground-floor room (now a basement) in the medieval building known as the Hessenhof. Overall, the Schmalkalden cycle follows the structure of the Iwein story as we know it from Hartmann much more closely than the Rodenegg murals, even beginning with the scene in which Arthur and Guinevere have retired for a nap, leaving the other knights telling stories in another room. But the painter devotes an entire register in the middle of the cycle to a narrative segment which, though important, is narrated very cursorily by Hartmann: the wedding of Iwein and Laudine. Three scenes in a row depict preliminary conversations, followed by the wedding itself, and then by a depiction of Iwein and Laudine in bed – a logical conclusion to the wedding sequence, but a moment that is not mentioned by Hartmann. After the wedding, Iwein successfully defends the fountain against intruders (identifiable with reference to a text as Arthur, Kay and so on), then sets out again to seek further adventures. Iwein's rescue of a lion from a dragon is the last scene, though limited evidence suggests that additional paintings *may* originally have followed. But, in striking contrast to what happens in the texts, Iwein's second departure is not driven by anything more specific than the convention that knights go out for adventures. The nadir of the story as told by Chrétien and Hartmann – Iwein's estrangement from Laudine, which motivates his second, purgatorial series of adventures, beginning with the rescue of the lion – simply does not exist in the story as told at Schmalkalden. While the Rodenegg cycle stresses the negative side of knightly adventure, the Schmalkalden cycle ignores the negative entirely.

On the other hand, the Schmalkalden cycle seems to reflect a greater awareness of the story's status as literature. The story here is embedded in a frame of courtly leisure – the large feast scene on the end wall, the figure offering a toast near the entrance to the room, the opening scene of Arthur's nap, and the scene of conversation that precedes Iwein's departure. While the Rodenegg murals present events directly as a story, albeit a story very consciously accented and organized for specific thematic purposes, the Schmalkalden murals move towards presenting the events as framed narrative, drawing attention to the unreality of the events, to their status as a narrative related by courtly people.

The two non-narrative Iwein art works from the German realms demonstrate how a literary material can be detached from its original narrative context, adopted into a new thematic structure, and thus given a new life and a new meaning. The so-called Malterer embroidery, made in or for the convent of St Katherine in Freiburg in 1310–30, represents five stories or motives in the context of the Slaves of Love or Power of Women topos (Rushing 1995, 219–44; Smith 1995, 152–68). In three pairs of scenes, the stories of Aristotle and Phyllis, Virgil in the Basket, and Samson and Delilah are represented. In each case, the first image shows the man at the height of his powers; the second scene shows him humiliated by the love of a woman. All three men were well-established members of the catalogue of Slaves of Love or Power of Women as it developed from misogynist patristic and biblical souces in the Middle Ages. New in this

Figure 3. Parzival, Gawein and Iwein, from the Runkelstein series (photo: author)

context is the story of Iwein: the fourth pair of scenes shows first Iwein defeating Ascalon, then Iwein kneeling before Laudine. The final, unpaired medallion in the series depicts the surrender of the unicorn. Whether the overall point is a condemnation of erotic love, set against the divine love represented by the unicorn (Maurer 1953, esp. 230f.), an exaltation of married love (Smith 1995, 152–68), or a playful, general affirmation of the power of love (Rushing 1995, 238), the embroidery detaches Iwein almost completely from his story, making him into an exemplary figure.

At Runkelstein near Bozen (Bolzano) in South Tyrol, Iwein appears again as an exemplary figure, this time without any narrative context at all, in the vastly expanded Nine Worthies cycle known as the 'Triads' (Haug et al. 1982). The topos of the Nine Worthies originated in Jacques de Longuyon's Alexander romance, *Les Voeux du Paon* (*c*. 1312–13), and remained important in the verbal and visual arts for five centuries. The original list of 'nine best men' consisted of three classical heroes (Hector, Alexander and Julius Caesar), three Old Testament heroes (Joshua, David and Judas Maccabaeus) and three Christian rulers (Arthur, Charlemagne and Godfrey of Bouillon). In a unique expansion of the Nine Worthies, the Runkelstein series (*c*. 1400–5) adds six further triadic groupings, including the best or most famous heroes, giants, giantesses and dwarfs, as well as the three greatest knights of the Round Table – Parzival, Gawein and Iwein (Fig. 3) – and the three most famous pairs of lovers – Aglie and Wilhelm von Österreich, Isolde and Tristan, and Amelie and Willehalm von Orlens. Here, Iwein and the other figures are completely isolated from their narratives, reduced entirely to the role of exemplary characters (Rushing 1995, 245–56).

All these images and sets of images involving Iwein are fundamentally independent works of art, strikingly different from each other, and strikingly independent of Hartmann's text. In this respect, the Iwein images offer an excellent paradigm for the relationship of other works in the visual arts to the literary traditions that inspire them.

Arthur

A broader survey of Arthurian art in the German-speaking lands might reasonably begin with depictions of King Arthur himself. But in Germany, the story of Arthur's life and death did not achieve the immense popularity that it did in France, as reflected in the enormous number of manuscripts, many lavishly illuminated, of the vast prose compilation known as the Vulgate Cycle. The German prose *Lancelot* exists in a much more modest manuscript tradition than its French counterpart (see chapter 9), and none of the manuscripts contains illustrations. In the Low Countries, especially those areas that were part of the French sphere of direct political and cultural influence, the 'historical Arthur' and the 'Prose Lancelot' had a greater popularity (Janssens 1987b, 264), but few Dutch treatments of the Arthurian material were illustrated. A notable exception is Jacob van Maerlant's *Spiegel Historiael* (*c.* 1283–8), the lavish illuminations of which in one West Flemish manuscript from around 1330 include four miniatures illustrating the story of Arthur (The Hague, Koninklijke Bibliotheek, Bruikleen Koninklijke Nederlandse Akademie van Weten-schappen, XX; see Loomis and Loomis 1938, 125 and fig. 342; Meuwese 1996, 155–8 and figs. 6.3–6.6; chapter 12 above, p. 190).

As an exemplary figure, Arthur appears in a number of visual treatments of the Nine Worthies topos in the German-speaking world. The great expansion of the Nine Worthies at Runkelstein has been discussed above, and more than twenty German Worthies cycles can be catalogued – in wall painting, panel painting, stained glass, sculpture, textiles, and woodcuts (Schroeder 1971). A late medieval expansion of the Hall of Fame idea implicit in the Nine Worthies topos is the series of statues at the memorial to Emperor Maximilian I in Innsbruck, which includes a bronze statue of Arthur by Peter Vischer (Egg 1974, 32, figs. 525–3). The figure of Arthur appears, of course, as a supporting character in many of the art works centred on other Arthurian heroes. But, as a hero in his own right, Arthur's presence in the German visual arts is limited almost exclusively to his appearance as an exemplary king in representative works, above all in the context of the Nine Worthies.

Tristan

Of all the romance motives treated in the visual arts of the European Middle Ages, the Tristan material is the most popular, represented in some forty-five art works in the German-speaking region alone (on Tristan art generally, see Ott 1975 (the most complete catalogue); Ott 1982; Curschmann 1990; Walworth 1995). Beyond the sheer number of artefacts, two things distinguish the iconography of Tristan from that of other romance materials: the subject's immense popularity in non-book settings and non-cyclical works, and the thematic uniformity of Tristan pictorializations. While the number of illuminated German *Tristan* manuscripts is surprisingly small (four of Gottfried's text and one of Eilhart's, compared with, for example, eight illuminated manuscripts of *Parzival* and thirteen of *Willehalm*), the number and variety of Tristan images in wall paintings, textiles, ivory and wood carvings, decorated objects, and sculptures is enormous – around thirty in the German-language area, including seven or eight narrative cycles, as compared with five non-manuscript pictorializations of *Parzival* and four of *Iwein*.[5] Both the cyclical and the non-cyclical works display a strong tendency to regard Tristan as an exemplary knight and Tristan and Isolde as exemplary lovers.

Among the narrative works, the mural cycle at Runkelstein (Loomis and Loomis 1938, 48–51 and figs. 64–75; Ott 1982, 196–201) presents perhaps the strongest endorsement of Tristan and Isolde's love. The narrative begins with the battle with Morold, and then devotes several scenes to the deeds of Tristan as warrior and dragon-slayer (Fig. 4). The drinking of the potion appears as the turning-point of the narrative, and the second part of the cycle is devoted to the love of Tristan and Isolde. The narrative climaxes in the false oath and the test of the hot iron (Fig. 5), representing the ultimate triumph of Tristan and Isolde's love, which appears to have been not only accepted but even blessed by God.

The illustrated *Tristan* codices, though small in number, include one of the most famous illuminated German manuscripts – Munich, Bayerische Staatsbibliothek cgm 51 (Fig. 6), with its roughly 118 miniatures (Loomis and Loomis 1938, 132–4 and figs. 359–66; Falkenberg 1986; Curschmann 1990, 2–7; Walworth 1995, 265–70). The manuscript was written towards the end of the first half of the thirteenth century and illuminated soon after;[6] the miniatures cover both sides of fifteen surviving picture folios (at least two are lost), which were inserted into the text after its completion. The pictorial narrative is fairly episodic and somewhat uneven (a number of artists may have been involved),

Figure 4. Tristan as dragon-slayer, from the Runkelstein series (photo: Hubert Welder,
Landesdenkmalamt-Bozen)

but generally it seems to aim for a complete narration of the story of Tristan and
Isolde, beginning with the story of Tristan's parents, and continuing to the
burial of the lovers. The emphasis is clearly on the adventures of Tristan in the
early part and on the repeated triumph of the love of Tristan and Isolde in the
later parts.

The other illuminated manuscripts are all considerably later. The manuscript
dated 1323, now in Cologne (Historisches Archiv W 88*), illustrates Gottfried's
text with seven line drawings and Ulrich von Türheim's continuation with two
(Van D'Elden 1996, figs. 9.20–9.28). The Brussels manuscript, a product of the
Diebolt Lauber workshop (first third of fifteenth century), illustrates its three
Tristan texts with ninety-one large drawings – 79 for Gottfried's *Tristan*, 10 for

Figure 5. Tristan and Isolde and the test of the hot iron, from the Runkelstein series (photo: Hubert Welder, Landesdenkmalamt-Bozen)

Tristan als Mönch, and 2 for Ulrich's continuation (Gaspar and Lyna 1945). Accompanied by rubrics, which are also recorded in a massive table of contents at the beginning of the manuscript (Bibl. Royale 14697), the drawings introduce sections of the text (Schaefer 1996, 180). Eilhart's text is illustrated in a Swabian manuscript of 1465–70 (Heidelberg Universitätsbibliothek cpg 346) with ninety-one coloured pen drawings, which are closely related to the woodcuts in two printings of the prose version, *Tristran und Isalde* (Fouquet 1972). The Tristan story remained popular in the early print era, represented in at least four illustrated sixteenth-century printings, and finally became a part of Sigmund Feyerabend's 1587 *Buch der Liebe* (Heitz and Ritter 1924, 187f.). Overall, the Tristan cycles in the German-language area show a remarkable consistency in regarding Tristan as an exemplary knight and the love of Tristan and Isolde as an exemplary love.

In non-cyclical works, the most popular motive by far is the 'tryst beneath the tree' or 'orchard scene', which appears in a variety of media (Fouquet 1973).

Figure 6. Mark arranges for the burial of Tristan and Isolde (photo: Bayerische
Staatsblibliothek, Munich)

Tristan and Isolde stand or sit on either side of a fountain or other pool beneath a tree; Mark is visible both in the tree and in the water. The scene stands in a close relationship to Fall of Man iconography – male and female figures on either side of a tree, with the fountain analogous to the River of Paradise and the face in the tree analogous to the serpent – and the sacred model played an obvious role in establishing both the standard form of the orchard scene and its popularity. But the orchard scene is not likely to have been intended or read allegorically in any of its visual contexts (if not alone, usually with love scenes or *Minnesklaven*) or functional contexts, most often decorated objects such as boxes, combs, shoes etc. (Curschmann 1990, 7–16). More than thirty art works depicting the orchard scene in non-narrative settings, either alone or together with other scenes of lovers or courtly life, have been catalogued, at least seventeen made in the German-language region.

One of the less-known manifestations of the orchard scene is the group of fragments of leather slippers recently found in the Netherlands and in Belgium, all depicting Tristan and Isolde seated under a tree (Sarfatij 1984, with illustrations; Janssens 1987a, 134–7). Between them are a well, in which Mark's face is visible, and a chessboard. The accompanying texts refer in most cases to the general idea of suffering for love; on one, the text refers more directly to the Tristan story: 'Triestra[m] siedi niet d[a]t viselkiin [?]' ('Tristan, don't you see the little fish?'). The shoes were probably made for wedding gifts from groom to bride (Sarfatij 1984). While it might seem inappropriate to present one's bride with a depiction of a famous scene of adultery, the idea of adultery seems to have been subsumed in the general idea of Tristan and Isolde as famous and exemplary lovers. That is not only the case with the shoes, but also generally in depictions of the orchard scene.

In the end, despite all variation, the essential thematic uniformity of the Tristan images remains striking. Artists seem almost universally to have regarded Tristan as an exemplary knight, and the love of Tristan and Isolde as an ideal and exemplary love. This contrasts sharply with the great differences in attitude towards the story found among the Iwein artists, as we have seen, and the Parzival artists, as we will now see.

Parzival

The visual manifestations of Parzival reflect a considerable range of responses to the material. Two aspects of the visual response to Parzival, both of which contrast strikingly with the Tristan situation, are immediately obvious from a quick survey of the twelve works of art that can be catalogued for the German-language area. While the great majority of the Tristan images are non-cyclical

Figure 7. Parzival at the Grail Castle; his reunion with Condwiramurs, and the baptism of Feirefiz (photo: Bayerische Staatsblibliothek, Munich)

and only a few of the narrative cycles appear in books, ten of the twelve Parzival works are narrative, and seven of them are book illustrations. These are fascinating contrasts whose full implications remain to be studied.

In a thematic survey of the Parzival cycles (all illuminations in *Parzival* manuscripts are published in Schirok 1985), we may locate the well-known illuminations in Munich, Bayerische Staatsbibliothek, cgm 19, at one extreme (Fig. 7). This manuscript, which shares one of its several scribes with the Munich *Tristan*, was made in the Alemannic region not long before 1250 (Schneider 1987, 150–4; Klein 1988, 161–3).[7] It contains twelve miniatures on the two sides of a single bifolio, probably (although not provably) part of a larger lost or incomplete programme of illumination similar to that in cgm 51. The extant images represent the climaxes of both the Parzival and Gawain plots, culminating in a festive meal at the Grail Castle, Parzival's reunion with Condwiramurs, and Feirefiz's baptism and his destruction of heathen idols – a concluding image which suggests an equation of knighthood with salvation and a profound religious meaning for the work as a whole. Even the layout of the illuminations in three registers supports a religious interpretation, since this layout, rare in secular manuscripts, was traditionally reserved for Bible manuscripts and New Testament picture cycles in lectionaries. The iconography, with resonances of the Last Supper in the several feast scenes and the baptism of Constantine in Feirefiz's baptism, further strengthens the salvific reading (Saurma-Jeltsch 1992).

At the other end of the spectrum we might locate the illuminations of the *Parzival* manuscripts produced in the Alsatian workshop of Diebolt Lauber. Active from about 1426 to 1467, the Lauber workshop produced about fifty known manuscripts and might, in the context of the late pre-Gutenberg era, fairly be regarded as a manuscript factory (Kautzch 1895). The Lauber workshop produced three illustrated *Parzival* manuscripts between 1440 and 1450. Now in Vienna, Heidelberg and Dresden,[8] the three manuscripts all scatter a fairly large number of large coloured drawings through the text. All three picture cycles are relatively episodic: the drawings do not add up to independent pictorial narratives, but appear to have been intended for viewing by readers.[9] The Lauber picture cycles also tend to deproblematize the story and largely to strip it of transcendent significance. All three end with Parzival asking the question; there is nothing of Feirefiz's conversion, none of the weddings, no sense of the profound religious significance of the Grail (Saurma-Jeltsch 1992).

The Berne manuscript (Berne, Bürgerbibliothek, Cod. AA 91), however, dated 1479 and the most recent illuminated *Parzival*, offers a more symbolically charged pictorial narrative (Saurma-Jeltsch 1992, Curschmann 1992). The miniature cycle focuses on Parzival's development from a young fool into a great knight, climaxing in his battle with Feirefiz, which appears not only to represent

Parzival's greatest achievement as a warrior, but also to suggest a transcendence of pure worldly martiality, both in the reconciliation of the fighters (this is the first combat scene in which Parzival does not appear to have killed his opponent) and in the defeat of heathendom. The picture cycle may also suggest that Parzival must overcome the temptations of love – the assault on Jeschute, here depicted as a carnal act rather than an innocent mistake (Parzival grabs Jeschute's breast), and the episode of the blood drops in the snow. Parzival's career may also be contrasted with that of Gawain, whose entire story is reduced to a short sequence culminating in his embrace of Orgeluse, after which the pictorial narrative returns to Parzival for his climactic battle with Feirefiz. The implication is perhaps that Gawain, though a worthy knight, is limited to the winning of a lady, while Parzival, the purer warrior, achieves greater heights by virtue of his having escaped the snares of love and overcome his earlier carnality.

Two known cycles of Parzival wall paintings decorated the walls of patrician town houses. The mid-fourteenth-century murals discovered in Lübeck in 1929 were described and photographed but not preserved (Loomis and Loomis 1938, 75f. and figs. 150–4; Schirok 1992, 174–81 and figs. 35–6). The ten scenes in round medallions that survived in 1929 were clearly the beginning and the ending of the cycle, but how much is missing in between is unclear. The final three scenes were in poor condition when they were studied, and their identification is uncertain, but they appear to have represented Parzival's battle with Feirefiz, the half-brothers' reconciliation, and Parzival's presentation with the Grail. Running parallel under the Parzival paintings is an Ages of Man cycle, evidently depicting a life from baptism to death. The relationship between the cycles has apparently never been discussed, but if the Parzival narrative indeed does end with Parzival receiving the Grail, a typological parallel between his progress to the Grail and the progress of the paradigmatic Christian to salvation may have been fairly obvious.

The early fourteenth-century wall paintings in the Haus zur Kunkel in Constance (about twenty-two scenes in three registers) are so fragmentarily preserved that even the identification of the cycle as a Parzival narrative is somewhat tentative, though probable (on the cycle, Schirok 1988; Wunderlich 1996, 78–103 and photos on 8–9). The clearest Parzival references are the youth's assault on Jeschute and the scene in which Iwanet helps Parzival put on the Red Knight's armour. The cycle appears to narrate the youth of Parzival, from his birth to (perhaps) his first encounter with Sigune. But the poorly preserved paintings of the third register cannot be identified with any confidence at all.

The Haus zur Kunkel also contained a set of wall paintings of the Slaves of Love in round medallions (early fourteenth century), each accompanied by the appropriate verse from a poem formerly attributed to Frauenlob. The paintings are no longer extant, but are preserved in good twentieth-century copies. The probable Parzival medallion (identified by process of elimination, since its inscription is missing) simply depicted a man and woman embracing (photo in Wunderlich 1996, 155), presumably accompanied by the line 'Parcivâl grôzse sorge nam' ('Parzival had great worries'; see Frauenlob, 141, 19). Here, the figure of Parzival, much like that of Iwein on the Malterer embroidery, has been removed from its narrative context and placed in a new structure – the topos of the 'Minnesklaven' – which creates new meaning for the character. The same thing happens at Runkelstein, where Parzival and Gawain appear with Iwein as the three greatest knights of the Round Table in the Triads (see above).

Wigalois

To those accustomed to thinking of medieval literature in terms of the modern medievalist canon, it may be surprising to discover that after Tristan, Parzival and Arthur himself, the most commonly represented material from Arthurian romance in German art is the story of Wigalois. And yet Wirnt von Gravenberg's *Wigalois*, with over forty complete and fragmentary manuscripts (Dick 1994, 177) and a printed tradition that stretches well into the modern era, was one of the most popular German romances, and its popularity is well reflected in the visual arts.

Perhaps the grandest Wigalois pictorialization is the extensive, though fragmentarily preserved, mural cycle at Runkelstein (Loomis and Loomis 1938, 79–81 and figs. 171–83; Huschenbett 1982b). Though as much as half the cycle has been lost, the narrative appears to have been uncommonly extensive, probably consisting of over forty scenes and offering more or less the entire Wigalois story as told by Wirnt. Despite the great number of scenes, the narrative appears to have been largely episodic, with an emphasis on scenes of combat, and on dragons, dwarfs and other fantastic creatures. The cycle does not appear to provide a structure for understanding the adventures as having any overriding telos or symbolic value.

Two *Wigalois* manuscripts contain fairly extensive miniature cycles. The most impressive is a manuscript from 1372, made by the monk Jan von Brunswik for Duke Albrecht II von Braunschweig-Grubenhagen, and now in Leiden (Bibl. der Maatschappij der Nederlandsche Letterkunde no. 537; see Stammler 1962, 143; Loomis and Loomis 1938, 134f., figs. 367–74). The manuscript has forty-seven elaborate, colourful miniatures in an unusual style that may have been inspired by embroidery techniques. Most unusually, the scribe/illuminator has included at the end of the text a portrait of himself: a stylized monk standing at a writing desk, working on the book (Loomis and Loomis 1938, fig. 374). A somewhat less extensive miniature cycle accompanies the *Wigalois* text in a Lauber manuscript now in Donaueschingen (Fürstlich Fürstenbergische Bibliothek, Cod. 71), with twenty-five (another is clearly missing) large coloured pen drawings (illustrations in Dick 1994, 178 and 181). A manuscript of *Wigalois* and *Iwein*, made in Bavaria or Tyrol in 1468, now in the British Library, has on fol. 1v a full-page drawing of the scene in which a maiden appears to inform Wigalois of his mother's death (London, British Library MS Add. 19554; blank frames for fifty-four small miniatures are also scattered through the *Wigalois* text; Rushing 1988, 226).

Wigalois also made the leap into print with considerable success. The *Wigalois* 'Volksbuch' was illustrated with woodcuts from the beginning. The first printing, Augsburg 1493, has twenty-eight woodcuts; the Strasbourg printing of 1519 has thirty-five (Melzer 1973, 3). Roughly four additional sixteenth-century printings followed, all illustrated, and the *Wigalois* printed tradition culminated, in a way, in the *Buch der Liebe* (1587), in which *Wigalois*, *Tristan* and eleven other texts were brought together in an illustrated book by the Frankfurt printer Sigmund Feyerabend (Heitz and Ritter 1924, 208; chapter 18 below, p. 299f.).

Jüngerer Titurel

The so-called *Jüngerer Titurel* (*c.* 1272) is another text that has never quite made it into the modern canon, but that was immensely popular and important in the Middle Ages. Widely regarded as something like the Bible of chivalry, the work is preserved in some sixty complete and fragmentary manuscripts (Nyholm 1992, xx), two of which are extensively illustrated. The most remarkable is the Fernberger–Dietrichsteinische manuscript (Munich, Bayrische Staatsbibliothek, cgm 8470; see Fig. 8), made in South Tyrol in the first half of the fifteenth century (Becker 1977, 130), and illustrated with eighty-five full-colour miniatures with gold leaf (listed in Wolf 1968, xvii–xx): a luxury manuscript of a type more commonly associated with religious texts or with texts regarded as historical, such as *Willehalm*. The paintings reflect a strong Italian influence (or an Italian painter) and show a quality, polish and Renaissance modernity that constrasts sharply with most other German Arthurian illumination of the period (Kraus 1974, 82, illustrations on 80, 81, 82, 143–5 and frontispiece).

The quasi-historical, quasi-salvific status of the *Jüngerer Titurel* in the later Middle Ages is well illustrated by the full-page dedication picture at the beginning of a manuscript dated 1441 (Vienna, Österreichische Nationalbibliothek 3041). The painting is divided into two spheres. Above, God the Father crowns Mary, who sits next to him on a bench; a speech roll held by angels bears the words 'Gloria in excelsis et in terra pax'. Below, a knight and lady kneel,

Figure 8. Signe in a lime tree, from the Fernberger–Dierichsteinische *Jüngerer Titurel* (photo: Bayerische Staatsblibliothek, Munich)

both holding rosaries, unidentified arms between them – presumably the patron and his wife (described in Wolf 1955, lxxiii). The Berleburg manuscript (Fürstlich Sayn-Wittgensteinsche Schloßbibliothek, RT 2/1), dated 1479, has a full-page picture at the beginning of each chapter (Wolf 1955, lxvi–lxvii; one picture folio reproduced in Heinzle 1973, K. Lage VII, fol. [7v]). The illustration programme may be based on that in the incunable printed by Mentelin at Strasbourg in 1477, which leaves space for prints in the same places (Becker 1977, 129).

Other subjects

Some eight other German Arthurian romances find visual manifestation in one or more art works; in addition, two Dutch romances exist in illuminated manuscripts. Virtually all the 'minor' romances are pictorialized only in manuscripts, not in the monumental arts. A notable exception is the mural cycle at Runkelstein based on Der Pleier's *Garel* (Huschenbett 1982a). Of what were apparently twenty-two original scenes, ten survive, and seven more are known through nineteenth-century drawings. The cycle narrates Garel's career in a highly independent fashion, from his departure to seek adventure to his acceptance at the Round Table and his return home in glory. The 'classic', Hartmannesque double plot of the text is ignored, however: the hero experiences no obvious crisis, but moves rather simply through a series of adventures to his final success.

A number of romance texts beyond those that are best known today exist in illuminated manuscripts, mostly from the fifteenth century, many from locations of near mass production, such as the Lauber workshop, the Henneflin workshop in Stuttgart, and the 'Alsatian Workshop of 1418'. Though none are illuminated more than once or twice, the very existence of this diverse group of illustrated books suggests an important point about the literary culture of the later Middle Ages. Patrons and purchasers were not interested only in those works that were already established as classics – *Parzival*, *Tristan*, *Jüngerer Titurel*, and the like – but also in Der Stricker's *Daniel von dem blühenden Tal*, Konrad von Stoffeln's *Gauriel von Muntabel*, Ulrich von Zatzikhoven's *Lanzelet*, and in *Lohengrin*, *Wigamur* and *Anteloye*.[10]

The Arthurian material enjoyed an enormous popularity in the Low Countries, but the majority of the manuscripts that this popularity produced were in French. Only two Middle Dutch manuscripts contain illustrations of Arthurian romance in the narrow sense. A fourteenth-century manuscript of *Ferguut* (Leiden, University Library, MS Letterkunde 191) opens with a large initial D, in which a knight stands, holding shield and sword (Meuwese 1996,

154–5 and fig. 6.2). Much more striking is the large painting at the beginning of *Walwein* in a manuscript made about 1350 in West Flanders (Leiden, University Library, MS Letterkunde 195): Walwein mounted, with a flying chessboard in the air above him (Meuwese 1996, 151–3 and fig. 6.1; Janssens 1987b, 286–90; Verbeke et al. 1987, ill. 1). Another Dutch illumination is a depiction of the Tristan orchard scene in Dirc Potter's *Der Minnen Loep* (Leiden, University Library, MS Letterkunde 205, dated 1486; Meuwese 1996, 158–60 and fig. 6.7).

Conclusions

In concluding this chapter, it seems appropriate not to attempt a reduction of the diverse material to a few common denominators, but to consider briefly the status of research in this general field. Although a good deal of work has been undertaken, especially in recent years, so much remains to be done that the whole field of 'word and image' research may fairly be said to remain in its infancy, especially as far as Arthurian art and other visual manifestations of secular literary materials are concerned. Even in terms of gathering material, over sixty years after the monumental effort of Roger Sherman Loomis and Laura Hibbard Loomis (1938), we are little closer to possessing a truly comprehensive catalogue of Arthurian images in German art, let alone a more international catalogue (see also Stones 1991, 25). Recent discoveries are recorded in scattered, diverse, often relatively obscure publications and, despite works such as those of Whitaker (1990) and Stones (1991), no common reference work exists.

From a certain point of view, the battle for the methodological 'right' to view the pictures as relatively autonomous works of art, rather than as slavish servants of texts, has largely been won – though the acceptance of this point of view is by no means universal. And, if something of a methodological common ground for the study of images like those discussed here has been created, it has only begun to be cultivated. Relatively few studies even of major subject matters and picture cycles have appeared that fully respect the independence of the images.

Not only does much of the basic work of cataloguing and describing remain to be done, and not only do the majority of the art works remain to be studied in detail, but the effort to understand diachronically the role of images in the development of secular, vernacular literature, and in the transformation of society from oral to literate, has only begun. Highly suggestive potential frameworks for such study may be found in recent works by Kemp and Curschmann. Kemp 1987 finds, for example, that both early and late medieval narratives in stained glass narrate episodically, while late twelfth- and early thirteenth-century windows tend to narrate in more fully developed, more independent sequences. Curschmann 1997 traces an evolution from highly independent, active reception as represented by the Rodenegg paintings to book-orientated, readerly, passive reception as represented by the Sigenot murals at Wildenstein, which are based directly on the woodcuts in a printed book. Both theories explain the works they consider extremely well, but both need to be tested against larger bodies of images before they can be generalized as a framework for a broad history of image-text relations. Moreover, any diachronic theory of evolution will have to take into account synchronic variation, such as the relatively uniform pictorial response to Tristan, as opposed to the divergent responses to Parzival and Iwein, or the striking difference between the rather crude illustrations in the Lauber manuscripts and the elaborate, Renaissance-influenced paintings in the roughly contemporary Fernberger–Dietrichsteinische *Jüngerer Titurel*.

All in all, we are only beginning to write a history of the role of the visual arts in the dissemination and reception of medieval secular literature, including the Arthurian materials. More than forty years have passed since the publication of Loomis's *Arthurian Literature in the Middle Ages* – a work that, despite its editor's great knowledge of Arthurian art, did not include a systematic consideration of the pictorial materials. If the present volume is succeeded in its turn, the writer of a new chapter on Arthurian materials in the visual arts will no doubt survey the field from a more secure vantage point than I do today. But the most striking aspect of the visual evidence will surely remain its fascinating, sometimes bewildering diversity.

Notes

[1] Loomis and Loomis 1938 remains the most comprehensive catalogue of Arthurian art, although a number of works have been discovered since its publication. Whitaker 1990 is a survey (of rather mixed quality), not a comprehensive catalogue.

[2] On Iwein images generally, see Rushing 1995.

[3] On the date, Rushing 1995, 32–7, with further references. Schupp and Szklenar 1996 (109–12) attempt to renew older arguments for an earlier date; Curschmann 1997 (p.10) accepts the 1220s consensus.

[4] Persistent speculation about a lost ending – for which no real evidence exists – reflects a misunderstanding of the artistic process, in which the painter is assumed to have as his goal the reproduction of the text in pictures (for this speculation, see most recently Schupp and Szklenar 1996 (esp. 102–5); for the counter-argument, Curschmann 1997, 14; Rushing 1998).

[5] The statistics in this sentence do not take into account some nine illustrated early printed editions of *Tristan*.

[6] Cgm 51 is closely related to cgm 19 (see n. 7), which cannot have been written before 1243.

[7] The older dating of cgm 19 to 1228–36 and the localization in Strasbourg, which are still repeated in the scholarship (e.g. Whitaker 1990, 30 and 51), no longer appear tenable.

[8] Vienna, Österreichische Nationalbibliothek, Cod. 2914 (25 miniatures); Heidelberg, Universitätsbibliothek, cpg 339 (64 miniatures); Dresden, Sächsische Landesbibliothek, M 66 (46 miniatures).

[9] This is true despite the fact that the pictures themselves frequently do not follow the text in detail (Saurma-Jeltsch 1992, 147). The details of the individual pictures suggest how they were created (illustrator following rubrics); the narrative structure of the picture sequence suggests how they were used.

[10] Der Stricker's *Daniel*: Berlin MS Germ. quart. 1340 (now Cracow, Biblioteka Jagiellońska); Middle Rhine, *c.* 1410–30 (Resler 1990 reproduces 10 miniatures). Konrad von Stoffeln, *Gauriel von Muntabel*: Donaueschingen, Fürstlich Fürstenbergische Bibliothek, Cod. 86, 1 miniature at the beginning of the text (Jeitteles 1861, 385 and the woodcut on 389). *Lanzelet*: Heidelberg, Universitätsbibliothek, cpg 371, dated 1420, from the 'Alsatian workshop of 1418', 2 miniatures (Loomis and Loomis 1938, 136; Wegener 1927, 18). *Lohengrin*: Heidelberg, Universitäts-bibliothek, cpg 345, *c.* 1457, Henneflin workshop, Stuttgart, 98 illuminations (see Wegener, 1927, 83–5, Abb. 74–6, Taf. III). *Wigamur*: Wolfenbüttel, Herzog-August Bibliothek, 51.2.Aug.4°, fifteenth century, 67 coloured pen drawings (Henderson 1989; Buschinger 1987, with 11 reproductions). *Anteloye:* Vienna, Österreichische Nationalbibliothek, Cod. 15 478, mid-fifteenth century, 1 miniature (Stammler 1962, 146).

Bibliography

Becker, P. J. 1977. *Handschriften und Frühdrucke mittelhochdeutscher Epen*, Wiesbaden.

Bonnet, A. M. 1986. *Rodenegg und Schmalkalden: Untersuchungen zur Illustration einer ritterlich-höfischen Erzählung und zur Entstehung profaner Epenillustration in den ersten Jahrzehnten des 13. Jahrhunderts*, tuduv-Studien: Reihe Kunstgeschichte, 22, Munich.

Busby, K. ed. 1996. *Word and Image in Arthurian Literature*, New York.

Buschinger, D. 1987. *Wigamur. Edité avec Introduction et Index*, GAG , 320, Göppingen.

Curschmann, M. 1990. 'Images of Tristan', in Stevens and Wisbey 1990 (see Gen. Bibl.), 1–17.

Curschmann, M. 1992. 'Der Berner *Parzival* und seine Bilder', WSt 12, 153–71.

Curschmann, M. 1997. *Vom Wandel im bildlichen Umgang mit literarischen Gegenständen. Rodenegg, Wildenstein, und das Flaarsche Haus in Stein am Rhein*, Wolfgang Stammler Gastprofessur für germanische Philologie: Vorträge, 6, Freiburg (Switzerland).

Dick, E. S. 1994. 'Wirnt von Grafenberg', in Hardin, J. and Hasty, W., eds., *German Writers and Works of the High Middle Ages: 1170–1280*, Dictionary of Literary Biography, 138, Detroit, 177–84.

Egg, E. 1974. *Die Hofkirche in Innsbruck: Das Grabdenkmal Kaiser Maximilians I. und die silberne Kapelle*, Innsbruck.

Falkenberg, B. 1986. *Die Bilder der Münchener Tristan-Handschrift*, Europäische Hochschul-schriften, Reihe 28: Kunstgeschichte, 67, Frankfurt.

Fouquet, D. 1972. 'Spätmittelalterliche Tristan-Illustrationen in Handschrift und Druck', *Guten-berg-Jahrbuch*, 292–309.

Fouquet, D. 1973. 'Die Baumgartenszene des Tristan in der mittelalterlichen Kunst und Literatur', *ZfdPh*, 92, 360–70.

Frauenlob (Heinrich von Meissen), *Leiche, Sprüche, Streitgespräche und Lieder*. Ed. by L. Ettmüller, 1843. Quedlinburg.

Gaspar, C., and Lyna, F. 1945. *Les principaux manuscrits à peintures de la bibliothèque royale de Belgique*, 2nd part, Paris.

Haug, W., et al. 1982. *Runkelstein: Die Wandmalereien des Sommerhauses*, Wiesbaden.

Heinzle, J., ed. 1973. *Wolfram von Eschenbach: 'Titurel'. Abbildung sämtlicher Handschriften mit einem Anhang zur Überlieferung des Textes im 'Jüngeren Titurel'*, Litterae, 26, Göppingen.

Heitz, P. and Ritter, F. 1924. *Versuch einer Zusammenstellung der deutschen Volksbücher des 15. und 16. Jahrhunderts nebst deren späteren Ausgaben und Literatur*, Strasbourg.

Henderson, I. 1989. 'Illustrationsprogramm und Text der Wolfenbütteler *Wigamur*-Handschrift', in McConnell W., ed., *in hôhem prîse: A Festschrift in Honor of Ernst S. Dick*, GAG, 480, Göppingen, 163–81.

Hoecke, W. van, Tournoy, G. and Verbeke, W., eds. 1991. *Arturus Rex*, II: *Acta Conventus Lovaniensis 1987*, Mediaevalia Lovaniensia, Ser. I, Studia, 17, Leuven.

Huschenbett, D. 1982a. 'Beschreibung der Bilder des *Garel*-Zyklus', in Haug et al. 1982, 129–39.

Huschenbett, D. 1982b. 'Beschreibung der Bilder des *Wigalois*-Zyklus', in Haug et al. 1982, 170–7.

Janssens, J. 1987a. 'Arturstof in de Nederlanden', in Verbeke et al. 1987, 105–43 (English summary, 140–3).

Janssens, J. 1987b. 'De middelnederlandse Arturroman', in Verbeke et al., 1987, 263–300 (English summary, 297–300).

Jeitteles, A. 1861. 'Gauriel von Montavel von Konrad von Stoffeln. Im Auszuge bearbeitet', *Germania*, 6, 385–411.

Kautzch, R. 1895. 'Diebolt Lauber und seine Werkstatt in Hagenau', *Centralblatt für Bibliothekwesen*, 12, 1–113.

Kemp. W. 1987. *Sermo Corporeus. Die Erzählung der mittelalterlichen Glasfenster*, Munich.

Klein, T. 1988. 'Ermittlung, Darstellung und Deutung von Verbreitungstypen in der Handschriftenüberlieferung mittelhochdeutscher Epik', in Honemann and Palmer 1988 (see Gen. Bibl.), 110–67.

Kraus, H. P. [firm]. 1974. *Monumenta codicum manu scriptorum: An Exhibition Catalogue of Manuscripts from the 6th to the 17th Centuries*, New York.

Loomis, R. S., ed. 1959. *Arthurian Literature in the Middle Ages*, Oxford.

Loomis, R. S. and Loomis, L. H. 1938. *Arthurian Legends in Medieval Art*, MLA Monograph Series, New York.

Maurer, F. 1953. 'Der Topos von den "Minnesklaven". Zur Geschichte einer thematischen Gemeinschaft zwischen bildender Kunst und Dichtung im Mittelalter', *DVj*, 27, 182–206.

Melzer, H., ed. 1973. *Wigalois*. Deutsche Volksbücher in Faksimiledrucken, A, 10, Hildesheim.

Meuwese, M. 1996. 'Arthurian illumination in Middle Dutch manuscripts', in Busby 1996, 151–73.

Nyholm, K. 1992. 'Einleitung', in Nyholm, ed., *Albrechts von Scharfenberg 'Jüngerer Titurel'*, III/2, Deutsche Texte des Mittelalters, 77, Berlin, viii–xxiv.

Ott, N. H. 1975. 'Katalog der Tristan-Bildzeugnisse', in Frühmorgen-Voss, H., *Text und Illustration im Mittelalter. Aufsätze zu den Wechselbeziehungen zwischen Literatur und bildender Kunst*, ed. N. H. Ott, Munich, 140–71.

Ott, N. H. 1982. '*Tristan* auf Runkelstein und die übrigen zyklischen Darstellungen des Tristanstoffes. Textrezeption oder medieninterne Eigengesetzlichkeit der Bildprogramme?' in Haug et al. 1982, 194–239.

Resler, M., trans. 1990. *Daniel of the Blossoming Valley (Daniel von dem blühenden Tal)*, by Der Stricker, New York.

Rushing, J. A., Jr. 1988. 'Adventures beyond the Text: Ywain in the Visual Arts', diss., Princeton University.

Rushing, J. A., Jr. 1995. *Images of Adventure: Ywain in the Visual Arts*, Philadelphia.

Rushing, J. A., Jr. 1998. Review of Schupp and Szklenar 1996, *Spec*, 73, 592–3.

Sarfatij, H. 1984. 'Tristan op vrijersvoeten? Een bijzonder versieringsmotief op Laat-Middeleeuws schoeisel uit de Lage Landen', in Cappon, C. M. et al., eds., *Ad fontes*, Amsterdam, 371–400.

Saurma-Jeltsch, L. E. 1992. 'Zum Wandel der Erzählweise am Beispiel der illustrierten deutschen *Parzival*-Handschriften', WSt, 12, 124–52.

Schaefer, J. T. 1996. 'The discourse of the figural narrative in the illuminated manuscripts of *Tristan* (*c*. 1250–1475)', in Busby 1996, 174–93.

Schirok, B. 1985. *Wolfram von Eschenbach: Parzival. Die Bilder der illustrierten Handschriften*, Göppingen.

Schirok, B. 1988. 'Parzival in Konstanz. Wandmalereien zum Roman Wolframs von Eschenbach im "Haus zur Kunkel"', *Schriften des Vereins für Geschichte des Bodensees und seiner Umgebung*, 106, 113–30.

Schirok, B. 1992. 'Die Parzivaldarstellungen in (ehemals) Lübeck, Braunschweig und Konstanz', WSt, 12, 172–90.

Schneider, K. 1987. *Gotische Schriften in deutscher Sprache. I. Vom späten 12. Jahrhundert bis um 1300*, Wiesbaden.

Schroeder, H. 1971. *Der Topos der Nine Worthies in Literatur und bildender Kunst*, Göttingen.

Schupp, V. and Szklenar, H. 1996. *Ywain auf Schloß Rodenegg. Eine Bildergeschichte nach dem 'Iwein' Hartmanns von Aue*, Sigmaringen.

Smith, S. L. 1995. *The Power of Women: A Topos in Medieval Art and Literature*, Philadelphia.

Stammler, W. 1962. 'Bebilderte Epenhandschriften', in Stammler, *Wort und Bild. Studien zu den Wechselbeziehungen zwischen Schriftum und Bildkunst im Mittelalter*, Berlin, 136–60.

Stones, A. 1991. 'Arthurian art since Loomis', in van Hoecke et al. 1991, 21–78.

Van D'Elden, S. C. 1996. 'Discursive illustrations in three Tristan manuscripts', in Busby 1996, 284–319.

Verbeke, W., Janssens, J. and Smeyers, M., eds. 1987. *Arturus Rex*, I: *Catalogus Koning Artur en de Nederlanden. La matière de Bretagne et les anciens Pays-Bas*, Mediaevalia Lovaniensia, Ser. I, Studia 16, Leuven.

Walworth, J. 1995. 'Tristan in medieval art', in Grimbert, J. T., ed., 1995, *Tristan and Isolde: A Casebook*, New York, 255–99.

Wegener, H. 1927. *Beschreibendes Verzeichnis der deutschen Bilderhandschriften des späten Mittelalters in der Heidelberger Universitätsbibliothek*, Leipzig.

Whitaker, M. 1990. *The Legends of King Arthur in Art*, Arthurian Studies, 22, Cambridge.

Wolf, W., ed. 1959. *Albrechts von Scharfenberg 'Jüngerer Titurel'*, Deutsche Texte des Mittelalters, 45, Berlin, I, xliv–cviii (Einleitung II).

Wolf, W., ed. 1968. *Albrechts von Scharfenberg 'Jüngerer Titurel'*, Deutsche Texte des Mittelalters, 61, Berlin, II/2, vii–xxvii (Einleitung).

Wunderlich, W. 1996. *Weibsbilder al Fresco. Kulturgeschichtlicher Hintergrund und literarische Tradition der Wandbilder im Konstanzer Haus 'zur Kunkel'*, Constance.

17

THE ARTHURIAN MATERIAL AND GERMAN SOCIETY IN THE MIDDLE AGES

W. H. Jackson

The Arthurian legend did not, in Germany, have the national-political significance that it possessed in England, and German Arthurian romance often has a strongly fictional, self-consciously literary thrust. However, German Arthurian literature was also meshed into broader social life, especially that of the aristocracy, in the Middle Ages. The spread of Arthurian literature in the German empire was part of a broader reception and appropriation of French aristocratic culture which included material goods, styles of dress, forms of speech and new practices in military sports (Bumke 1986, 83–136). The rapid spread of Arthurian story material on the Continent testifies to its social relevance; indeed the very lack of historiographical encumbrance helped Arthurian literature to express imaginatively the contemporary concerns of authors, patrons and public, and thus makes this literature into a valuable source for the study of aristocratic mentality and ideology (Störmer 1972).

Arthurian romance itself has a place in social as well as in literary history, not least because it expressed and shaped the values of chivalry and courtliness, which were major factors in the cultural identity of the upper levels of German society from the twelfth century through to the end of the Middle Ages. Consequently, the contributions on literary works in this volume already throw light on the social role of Arthurian material. Moreover, Arthurian themes and figures also spread out from literature into other spheres of life, throwing further light on the social relevance of this material. The present chapter will treat the social appropriation of Arthurian matters in medieval German life by considering the giving of Arthurian names, the use of Arthurian motifs in military sports and festivities, the social institution of 'Arthur's Court', the continuing relevance of an Arthurian framework of reference for the aristocracy in the fifteenth century, and the fading of this framework in the sixteenth century.

Arthurian names

The percolation of Arthurian motifs into everyday life is perhaps most amply documented in the widespread evidence of the giving of names drawn from

Arthurian literature to sons and daughters in the Middle Ages. The adoption of literary names (including Arthurian names) in real life has been studied regionally for the Tyrol by Zingerle (1856), for Carinthia by Müller (1895), for Bavaria by Panzer (1896), for the Upper Rhine by Socin (1903), for the Central and Low German areas by Kegel (1905), for the early Middle Dutch area by de Smet (1989), and Schirok lists names drawn from *Parzival* throughout the German areas (1982, 158–71). Arthurian names of one kind or another occur in all German areas during the Middle Ages, and the frequency and the chronological, social and geographical spread of individual names throws up some interesting features.

A few Arthurian names appear in the twelfth century, then the numbers rise in the thirteenth century and increase further in the fourteenth and especially the fifteenth centuries. The occurrences are predominantly in noble families, with the lesser nobility, the *ministeriales*, adopting literary names more often than the old, free nobility (Panzer 1896, 219; Kegel 1905, 133), while burgher families figure increasingly from the thirteenth century onward, especially in central and north German towns (Fechter 1935, 79).

The comment that daughters were named after literary models more often than sons (Bumke 1986, 712) is not borne out by the Arthurian evidence, which shows a frequent use of masculine names. Parzival is the most widespread Arthurian name in real life in Germany: Schirok lists 106 occurrences from the thirteenth to the sixteenth century, and in all regions from Styria to the Baltic coast (1982, 159–68). Some other names show more regional concentration. Artus is widely documented in west central and Low German (northern) sources (twenty-four times as a personal name before 1400) but is far less frequent elsewhere (Kegel 1905, 23–38). Iwein, Iwan and similar forms (actual spelling varies with all names in the documentary sources) present difficulties of interpretation because the Slavonic name Ivan is a possible source as well as the Arthurian strand. Kegel (1905, 44–52) lists no fewer than seventy-three occurrences of Iwan in the central and Low German areas before 1500, with a clustering around Cologne, and with the earliest instances in the twelfth century, well before a possible reception of the works of Hartmann von Aue. The forms Gawan and Walwan and the like have a regional distribution, with Wa- forms in central and Low German documents, and Ga- forms further south (Kegel 1905, 114–16; Panzer 1896, 213). Iwein and Walwein name forms occur in Dutch even earlier than in German, and this may indicate the reception in the Netherlands of Arthurian material in the early twelfth century, even before Geoffrey of Monmouth's work (de Smet 1989). Wigelais and variants (from Wirnt's *Wigalois*) is comparable to Parzival in popularity in Bavaria, with twenty occurrences in the fourteenth and fifteenth centuries (Panzer 1896, 210), and is known but less frequent elsewhere (Kegel 1905, 102–5). Tristan is documented in various forms (especially Tristram and similar) across the German areas and from the thirteenth to the sixteenth century (Panzer 1896, 217f.; Kegel 1905, 108–11, 119–24). Other masculine names from Arthurian literature appear sporadically in real life: Genteflor, Schionatulander, Gramoflanz, Segremors, Lanzelet (see index of names in Kegel 1905, 139f.). Erec may derive from Hartmann's romance in two occurrences in Carinthia in 1293 and 1314, but the name is not recorded by scholars elsewhere in the southern areas, and further north it probably links up to Scandinavian usage (Kegel 1905, 41f.). The relation of the historical name Gamaret and similar to Wolfram's Gahmuret is a matter of dispute (Panzer 1896, 211f.; Kegel 1905, 74–6; Chandler 1992, 93).

Of the women's names drawn from Arthurian literature, Sigune appears most frequently (usually as Sigaun or similar): Schirok lists forty-two occurrences, with a heavy predominance in Bavaria and Austria (1982, 164–70). Forms of Herzeloyde appear in Bavaria and further west and north. Isolde, whilst less frequent than Tristan (Panzer 1896, 218), appears in Bavaria and (usually as Isalda) in central and Low German sources from the thirteenth to the fifteenth century; Enide appears in Styria, the Upper Rhine and further north, but infrequently; Lunete appears more frequently, in Styria, Bavaria, Meissen and Saxony; also recorded sporadically are Amphalisa, Laudina, Secundilla, Orgeluse.

It is a matter of conjecture just how direct a literary influence underlies individual cases of naming, but a general influence is clear. It is striking that the use of names in real life corresponds in broad outline to the numbers of known manuscripts and early printed books to indicate a widespread reception (in whatever detail) of Wolfram's *Parzival*, which seems to have been followed by *Wigalois* (especially in south Germany), the Tristan story and Hartmann's romances. By the fifteenth century clusters of literary names are recorded in individual families. An extreme instance is that of the Bavarian free noble (*Freiherr*) Bernhardin von Stauff, who married Catharina von Törring in 1486, and named four children after characters from *Parzival*: 'Gramoflantz', 'Ferafis', 'Argula' (Wolfram's Orgeluse) and 'Secundilla' (Bastert 1993, 139). Argula links medieval and Reformation culture in her own life, for while she was born of a family that drew on the past in its literary naming, she herself went on to become a noted and controversial writer of Reformation pamphlets (see John Flood on early printed editions, chapter 18 below).

Round Tables and Arthur's Courts

Arthurian characters and motifs also made an important contribution to military sports and festivities in the upper levels of society. In Germany this imitation of Arthurian material in real life received large-scale expression in the practice of 'Round Tables' and the social institution of 'Arthur's Court'.

Arthurian romances provided various motifs for real tournaments, and role-playing according to Arthurian models was particularly closely associated with the chivalric gatherings known as Round Tables (Cline 1945; Loomis 1959; Barker 1986, 88–95; Barber and Barker 1989, *passim*). The term Round Table was taken from Arthurian romance. In real life, Round Tables were festive gatherings at which knights undertook single jousts with blunt lances, at times explicitly adopting the names of knights of the literary Round Table. Round Tables are recorded in various parts of Europe, including Germany, from 1223 through to the fourteenth century and occasionally later. Despite their festive nature they involved sufficient danger for Pope Clement V around 1310 to include them under the ban that had for long applied to the more warlike tournaments (Hirsch 1864, 16).

One of the earliest and most remarkable examples of Round Table role-playing is the Styrian noble Ulrich von Liechtenstein's poetic account of a jousting journey undertaken in 1240, from Styria to Vienna (Peters 1971, 173ff.). Ulrich journeyed in the role of King Arthur, who had returned from paradise (*Frauendienst* 466, 9–11), and to the knights who successfully broke three spears in jousting against him he gave membership of his Round Table and Arthurian names, Parcifal, Gawan, Yban, Tristram, Ither, Lanzilet, Ereck, Segramurs (*Frauendienst* 487, 32–488, 26). There is surely political comedy in Ulrich's account of how he, as 'King Arthur' graciously offered to take Frederick, Duke of Austria, into his retinue and grant him all that he wished in the way of castles and lands; for in reality Frederick was Ulrich's lord, and the role-reversal causes laughter among the attendant nobles (*Frauendienst* 466, 25–467, 10). Indeed, details in Ulrich's Arthurian journey point to its having a political as well as a ludic dimension, with the Round Table forming an association to represent the interests of the Styrian nobility and to demonstrate (especially to the duke) Ulrich's prestige and influence (Höfler 1950, 145; Störmer 1972, 956f.).

The motif of the Grail was also taken up in festivals in north German towns from the thirteenth to the fifteenth century. The earliest and fullest account of a Grail festivity relates to an event held around 1280 in Magdeburg and recorded in the Magdeburg *Schöppenchronik* (*ChrdSt* VII, 168f.; see Wolff 1927; Schirok 1982, 155–8; Zotz 1991, 202–6). The festivity was a jousting match, with no reference in the accounts to a spiritual dimension. The Grail itself was some kind of construction or arena equipped with tents and a tree on which champions hung their shields for challenge; and 'merchants who wished to practise chivalry there' were invited by 'courtly letters' which were sent to Goslar, Hildesheim, Brunswick, Quedlinburg, Halberstadt 'and other towns'. Young men (*jungelinge*) came from all these towns to take part in the jousts. Whilst the account of this event suggests that it may have been something out of the ordinary in its details, it is also described in the Magdeburg chronicle as one of a variety of such games, including Round Tables, which were customarily held at Whitsun. The Grail joust was arranged by the *kunstabelen*, the sons of the wealthy burghers who evidently formed some kind of chivalric community, and planned by one of their number, Brun von Schönebeck, who is also known as an author. Even the Magdeburg event seems at best tenuously connected to Wolfram's *Parzival*, and later 'Grail' festivities show no such connections (Schirok 1982, 157).

Although no other text provides as much detail as does Ulrich von Liechtenstein, references to Round Tables are found in several other German historical and literary sources from *c.* 1300 onward. In 1319 young sons of the baronage asked King John of Bohemia to hold a 'tabula rotunda' for the exercise of arms and the increase of glory; the king had stands built for spectators in Prague and invited participants from the whole of Germany, but none of the nobles from elsewhere turned up (*Königsaaler Geschichtsquellen* 404f.; see also Alfred Thomas, chapter 15, above). Strasbourg sources of the fourteenth century speak of the period four weeks after Easter as the customary time for a Round Table; in this case the event is mentioned only because of a quarrel that arose between hostile groups in 1332 (*ChrdSt* VIII, 122; IX, 776, 933). In Cologne a civic decree of 1345 spells out the duties of those involved in organizing Round Table jousts in the market place; the participants include lords, knights and esquires from the countryside ('vanme lande') and the burghers ('burgere') of Cologne, and the duties of the hosts include physical preparation of the jousting strip (*QuGeschStK*, 300). Round Tables as military sports are also mentioned in literary works from about 1300 onwards (*Reinfried von Braunschweig* vv. 190, 284; Heinrich von Neustadt, *Apollonius von Tyrland* v. 18427; Ulrich Boner, *Edelstein* no. 75, v. 9; *Herzog Ernst* 77, 8).

Clearly, Round Tables were well known in historical reality in the German empire in the later Middle Ages. They were mentioned in historical sources, usually when some special circumstance arose such as a disturbance or the need to establish regulations. Round Tables were concentrated in towns where, together with other chivalric practices, they were a customary form of aristocratic self-definition, especially for the younger members of the urban patriciate (Zotz 1985, 491–3). Moreover, the Round Tables in towns in western and northern Germany (Strasbourg, Cologne, Magdeburg) show sociological and chronological similarities with the civic *festes* with a chivalric flavour (including the adoption of Arthurian motifs) that were widely practised in the late thirteenth and fourteenth centuries in the neighbouring areas of northern France and the Low Countries (Vale 1982, 25–41).

An urban and northern focus is evident also in the social institution of 'Arthur's Court' (Hirsch 1864; Simson 1900; Keyser 1932; Schlauch 1959;

Keyser 1971; Störmer 1972, 962ff.). During the first half of the fourteenth century, associations of the upper levels of urban society crystallized in the manner of guilds or brotherhoods in the main towns of Prussia, along or near the Baltic coast, where the German influence had been growing with eastward settlement and the conduct of crusading warfare on the eastern frontier. These associations were linked with the patron saint of chivalry, St George, and with King Arthur, whence they drew their designation as *Artushöfe*. The term first appears, as *curia regis Arthus* in Elbing sources of 1319/20 in connection with the Brotherhood of St George, then in Danzig (Gdansk) in 1350 and Braunsberg in 1353. Similar institutions also appear in Thorn (Torun), Kulm and Königsberg (Kaliningrad), with parallels in Riga and Stralsund. Scholars have looked mainly to England and the Low Countries for possible models for the Prussian *Artushöfe*, but their origins are still unexplained (Paravicini 1990, 168–70). The Prussian towns, for example Thorn (Semrau 1930, 46–50), had trading connections with these areas, and from the beginning of the fourteenth century onwards western knights travelled to Prussia in increasing numbers to take part in the crusading campaigns of the Teutonic Knights (Paravicini 1989, 21–44). The lay chivalric Order of the Garter, founded by Edward III in England in 1344/9, also combines Arthurian elements with the patronage of St George (Boulton 1987, 101–66), but the possible relationship of this to the Prussian institutions is obscure, as is much in the early history of the Prussian associations of St George and the *Artushöfe*.

What is clear is that the emergence of Arthur's Courts in Prussia extends the spread of chivalric culture in towns even further northwards and eastwards. Danzig is the best documented of the courts and exhibits their main characteristic features (see especially Simson 1900; Keyser 1932). From an early stage, the term 'Arthur's Court' indicated in the Baltic towns both an association of men and the building in which they met. Originally, it was only the oldest, most powerful and wealthy families who were members, including those who had fought in the Northern Crusade in the thirteenth century. These were elite families who combined long-distance trade (for instance by sea with England, France and Flanders) with traditions of military chivalry. With the passage of time the chivalric element in the court at Danzig declined, and entry was granted to wider circles. By 1421 lesser merchants were granted entry, but craftsmen, beersellers and those who worked for wages were still excluded. In the sixteenth century the numbers gaining entry rose in some years to several hundred, including many guests from elsewhere in Germany and Europe, and some representatives of the more respected crafts. The ordinances governing entry to the court (e.g. that of 1421) also excluded any man who had acted dishonourably, and they stated that no one was to bring a woman of ill repute to the dancing there (Simson 1900, 311). This combination of hierarchical and moral criteria for participation shows a remarkable similarity between the Prussian 'Arthur's Courts' and the south German noble tournaments of the fifteenth century, with the difference that the Prussian courts served the corporate identity of an increasingly prosperous urban society, whilst the southern tournaments sought to maintain the status of an old nobility by setting it, against the economic tide, apart from urban, mercantile pursuits (Jackson 1986, 56f.).

There is little direct evidence of the detailed activities of Arthur's Courts in the fourteenth century, but surviving ordinances and accounts of meetings provide a fuller picture for Danzig from the early fifteenth century onwards. From their beginnings the courts were centres of social interaction where the urban elite met to drink, amuse themselves, entertain visitors and discuss business. They were normally open daily, and the ordinances of the Danzig court provide details about the permitted hours of drinking, the guests who were allowed, the election and tenure of officers, the avoidance of quarrels, the payment of fines for offences, and other matters necessary for the orderly running of a social club. The court was host to many foreign merchants on trading visits, and it was a port of call for nobles travelling to join the campaigns of the Teutonic Order: Henry of Derby, later King Henry IV of England, while on a Prussian venture (Du Boulay 1971) visited the Danzig Arthur's Court in 1390 (Keyser 1932, 49).

Despite the lack of direct evidence, there can be no doubt that military sports were an important part of the festivities of Arthur's Courts from the earliest stages and, once records begin, jousting is well documented at the Danzig court. Records include a Round Table (*tabelrunde*) held at Shrovetide in 1494 (Hirsch 1864, 28). The social prestige of jousting is reflected in the ordinance of 1527, which grants a special place in the court to those who have taken parts in jousts, but this practice became less frequent during the course of the century, and the last record of a joust at the court was one arranged to take place in 1580 (Simson 1900, 138–41). The history of the joust, whilst characterizing a diminution of the chivalric element in King Arthur's Court in Danzig, by no means signalled a general decline in the institution. On the contrary, the sixteenth century was a time of great material wealth for Danzig, and the *Artushof*, as the chief focal point of public sociability and display in the city, flourished in this period too, only now the emphasis was on peaceful festivities, ceremonial triumphs and artistic contributions to the building itself, which made it into a leading expression of civic and private patronage. The Danzig *Artushof* never recovered its pre-eminence after a time of warfare and plague in the early seventeenth century. However, the building continued to be used for civic, social, cultural and mercantile purposes into the twentieth century. It was badly damaged in the Second World War but has been restored, has kept its name and is now a major tourist attraction.[1]

The Fifteenth and Sixteenth Centuries

As well as influencing chivalric sports and festivities, the Arthurian material made an important contribution, in the form of visual images, to the decor of aristocratic life in medieval Germany. Pictorial representations of Arthurian subjects are treated in a separate chapter of the present volume. Suffice it to point out here that, like other forms of cultural display, the visual arts show the exploitation of Arthurian figures as a mark of social prestige in the German areas from the thirteenth century onwards, first for the feudal knightly nobility and then also in urban patrician contexts, as has been shown with regard to visual images of Ywain (Rushing 1995, 219–23) and of King Arthur as one of the Nine Worthies (Schroeder 1971, 104–8).

Arthurian motifs preserved their importance in noble circles, too, in the fifteenth century. Jakob Püterich III von Reichertshausen and Wilwolt von Schaumburg testify to Arthurian and more broadly chivalric interests in the lesser nobility at this time. The Reichertshausen family was of Munich patrician stock and had grown wealthy through trade and the granting of credit. The knightly line of the family was probably founded in the fourteenth century by Püterich's grandfather. Püterich himself was born *c.* 1400 and married three times, each time to a woman from the higher nobility. He cultivated a traditional knightly lifestyle by participating in noble tourneys, he encouraged the promotion of chivalric literature, and himself produced, in his *Ehrenbrief* (completed 1462), a remarkable document of aristocratic culture. He collected literary manuscripts, including Arthurian works, and he tells of searching for the grave of Wolfram von Eschenbach (*Ehrenbrief* sts. 127f.). He also named at least two of his children after figures in Wolfram's *Parzival*: a son Gamureth and a daughter Orgeluse are recorded (Bastert 1993, 138f.). In the biography of the knight Wilwolt von Schaumburg (completed 1507), Wilwolt is placed in an Arthurian perspective when the author likens him to 'the men of the Round Table who in times past rode out alone in search of adventure' and claims that, were King Arthur still alive, he would welcome Wilwolt as a member of the Round Table (*GuT* 66f., 202).

At a higher noble level, Count Gerhard von Sayn recommended in his testament (1491) that his sons should read and follow the advice of the 'Tyterel vnd Brackenseil', that is the *Jüngerer Titurel*. This work, Gerhard goes on to say, is good for his sons and other nobles ('Adell') to read, for it is the godliest teaching ('die gotlichste Lere') that can be found in German books, and contains all the virtues and honour ('Doegent vnd Ere') according to which princes and lords should act and rule, and if his sons follow the teachings of this book they will want for nothing (text in Meier 1889, 218 and Becker 1977, 235). This testament is a remarkable personal, family document of the continuing relevance of chivalric literature in the self-understanding of the nobility at the end of the fifteenth century. More especially, the *Jüngerer Titurel* was valued in the late Middle Ages not merely as entertainment, but as a repository of divine and human wisdom and as an all-embracing guide to good and virtuous living for the nobility (Becker 1977, 235f.).

At the level of German rulers, Arthur's court appears as an almost proverbial image of aristocratic pastimes in the late fifteenth century. The court of Duke Bogislaw X of Pommerania is described around 1480 as rivalling 'Khoning Arthus Hoff' in the fame of its chivalric sports (*Chronik von Pommern* 334) and, in a letter of 18 January 1480, Kurfürst Albrecht of Brandenburg tells his son, Markgraf Johann, of the family's relaxation: 'and we have Arthur's court here with hunting, falconry, jousting and all kinds of pastime' (*Privatbriefe* 212). Finally, at the peak of the social hierarchy and in the transition from the medieval to the early modern world, Arthurian material figures in the cultural projects of Emperor Maximilian I. During a banquet at the imperial diet of Worms in 1494, Maximilian had princes and lesser nobles assume the names of Round Table Knights and prepare for combat 'as in King Arthur's times' (*GuT* 158; Zotz 1985, 460f.); this echoes the more frequent association of the king with Arthurian role-playing and the Round Table in England (Barker 1986, 90–4). King Arthur himself appears twice in the works by which Maximilian sought to perpetuate his memory for all time, in a place of honour in the *Triumphzug* (no. 108) and, most impressively, as one of the twenty-eight larger-than-life bronze statues which still form part of Maximilian's tomb in the Hofkirche in Innsbruck (the statue of Arthur is illustrated in Scheicher 1986, 377). This programme of statues (which was originally intended to number forty) combines figures from recent history with real and half-legendary ancestors so as to shed glory on the house of Habsburg by connecting it with the great ruling families of Europe. King Arthur has a place in this scheme as the embodiment of chivalric kingship and as the most celebrated ancestor of Maximilian's English relatives (on the relevance of Arthur to Maximilian's genealogical projects see also Jackson on the *Spruch von den Tafelrundern* in this volume). The statue of Arthur has affinites with that of Theoderick (Dietrich von Bern) which also guards the tomb. Both were cast in bronze by Peter Vischer the Elder in 1513, and although the carver of the models is unknown, the statues are thought to have been designed by Albrecht Dürer (Scheicher 1986, 377, 380; see also Flood, chapter 13, above).

Given the patchiness of some of the evidence reviewed in this chapter and the lack of detailed descriptions of events which contemporaries took for granted, caution is appropriate in drawing general conclusions. However, some patterns do emerge in the spread of Arthurian material in medieval German society.

In terms of chronology, it is in the thirteenth century that evidence builds up of Arthurian material having an impact on 'real life' in a variety of ways: the attribution of moral effects to Arthurian literature, Arthurian elements in name-giving and in various forms of socializing. Arthurian elements of one kind or another continue to appear in real life down to the fifteenth century, perhaps even gaining ground in the 'chivalric renaissance' of the second half of the fifteenth century. Regionally, Arthurian material figures, with some variations, from the far south to the far north. Arthurian interests have to be seen in the medieval German areas as part of the larger field of chivalric and courtly culture, which was particularly strong in the southern areas. The chivalric renaissance and the great supra-regional tournaments of the late fifteenth century, for instance, had a southern focus. However, the Round Table jousts in northern towns and the Prussian *Artushöfe* also show Arthurian motifs precisely in northern contexts (see also Paravicini 1990). German Arthurian literature was largely a product of the south, and the diffusion of Arthurian motifs in German society was closely connected with this literature, but parallels between north Germany and the Low Countries also suggest that cultural practices may have spread along an eastward axis in the north, becoming independent of literary origins. In terms of social function, Arthurian material formed an important focus for the expression of group mentalities in the upper reaches of German society. Whilst the Arthurian world acted as a cultural rallying point for the whole of the aristocracy, from rulers downwards, it seems at times to have held a particular ideological attractiveness for the lesser nobility, and from the late thirteenth century onwards Arthurian forms were also cultivated in urban society (Störmer 1972). Indeed, the social exploitation of Arthurian motifs indicates that chivalry and urban life, far from being completely separate phenomena, met at many points in a complex relationship of such regional, chronological and cultural diversity as to escape easy generalization.

Some Arthurian elements which were taken up in German life during the Middle Ages were still discernible in the sixteenth century, but they were rapidly diminishing in importance and met with decreased understanding and interest in all the social circles in which they had earlier been cultivated. The burghers of Nuremberg built a fountain in 1365–96 which was decorated with statues of the Nine Worthies, including King Arthur, but in two poems describing the fountain in the fifteenth and sixteenth centuries this figure appears as 'King Eckhart of France' (Schroeder 1971, 162–4). By the sixteenth century all memory of the true origins of the *Artushof* in Danzig had been lost. In 1569 the town clerk of Danzig, himself a frequent visitor in the Court, wrote in his rhymed chronicle that it had been founded by King Arthur, but in 1596 the city council energetically dismissed this view and insisted that the Court had been built by the burghers themselves (Simson 1900, 13). The sixteenth century was a period of cultural flowering for the

Artushof in Danzig. However, the many new works of art that were produced at this time to decorate its interior included biblical and other religious subjects, Roman imperial history and classical mythology, recent history and contemporary rulers, but there is no reference to Arthurian subjects (Simson 1900, 148–202).

The iconography of the Danzig *Artushof* is typical of a broader tendency in that it indicates a reduced status of Arthurian decor and ethos in the cultural world of Renaissance humanism. Princely tournaments and festivals of the sixteenth and early seventeenth centuries had some echoes of the Arthurian world, for instance when the marshal at the court of Dresden adopted the name Tristrand in running at the ring in 1588 (Gurlitt 1888, 518). However, motifs and characters from classical history and mythology, mediated by Renaissance learning, played a far more important part in these events (Watanabe-O'Kelly 1992, 29–63). Finally, in May 1570 Tyrolean government officials sent a memorandum to Archduke Ferdinand about the bronze statues commissioned for Emperor Maximilian's grave, proposing (amongst other things) that the legendary statues of Arthur and Dietrich von Bern might be renamed, with King Arthur altered to Leopold, Duke of Swabia (*JbkSaK* CXXIII, Reg. 10226). The intention of this proposal was to cut the legendary element out of the programme and replace it with a stronger focus on the genealogical sequence (Scheicher 1986, 365), and a side effect would have been to remove the ideal of the chivalric King Arthur. The plan was not put into effect. But its tendency remains significant. The Arthurian world, which for centuries had acted as a cultural ideal for the upper levels of German society, was fading in the sixteenth century to give way to new forms of display at court and in town that were more dynastically local or, with the reception of classical learning, more humanistically universal in range.

Note

[1] On the *Artushöfe* in Prussian towns see now the illuminating study by Selzer (1996). Selzer discusses the *Artushöfe* afresh in the light of the early sources and with regard to their social function. On the important matter of origins, Selzer convincingly sees parallels and models for the Prussian institutions in the urban culture of northern France and Flanders and in the Arthurian jousts and festivities in other north German towns rather than in England (88–90).

Bibliography

Primary Sources

Boner, Ulrich, *Der Edelstein*. Ed. by F. Pfeiffer, 1844. Leipzig.
ChrdSt = *Die Chroniken der deutschen Städte vom 14. bis ins 16. Jahrhundert*, VII, 1869; VIII, 1870; IX, 1871. Leipzig.
Chronik von Pommern = *Des Thomas Kantzow Chronik von Pommern in hochdeutscher Mundart*. Ed. by G. Gaebel, 1897. Stettin.
GuT = *Die Geschichten und Taten Wilwolts von Schaumburg*. Ed. by A. von Keller, 1859 (BLV, 50). Stuttgart.

Heinrich von Neustadt, *Apollonius von Tyrland*. Ed. by S. Singer, 1906 (Deutsche Texte des Mittelalters, 7). Berlin.

Herzog Ernst = Das Lied vom Herzog Ernst. Ed. by K. C. King, 1959 (Texte des späten Mittelalters, 11). Berlin.

JbkSaK= Jahrbuch der kunsthistorischen Sammlungen des allerhöchsten Kaiserhauses, 14, 1893. Vienna.

Die Königsaaler Geschichtsquellen. Ed. by J. Loserth, 1875 (Fontes rerum Austriacarum, Scriptores, 8). Vienna.

Privatbriefe = Deutsche Privatbriefe des Mittelalters, 1: Fürsten und Magnaten, Edle und Ritter. Ed. by G. Steinhausen, 1899 (Denkmäler der deutschen Kulturgeschichte, 1/1). Berlin.

Püterich von Reichertshausen, Jakob, *Der Ehrenbrief*. In M. Mueller, 1985. *Der 'Ehrenbrief' Jakob Pütrichs von Reichertshausen, die 'Turnierreime' Johann Hollands, der 'Namenkatalog' Ulrich Fuetrers. Texte mit Einleitung und Kommentar*. Diss. City University of New York, 67–117.

QuGeschStK = Quellen zur Geschichte der Stadt Köln, IV. Ed. by L. Ennen, 1870. Cologne.

Reinfried von Braunschweig. Ed. by K. Bartsch, 1871 (BLV, 109). Stuttgart.

Triumphzug = Der Triumphzug Kaiser Maximilians I. 1516–1518. Ed. by H. Appuhn, 1979 (Die bibliophilen Taschenbücher). Dortmund.

Ulrich von Liechtenstein, *Frauendienst*. Ed. by R. Bechstein, 1888 (Deutsche Dichtungen des Mittelalters 6, 7). Leipzig.

Other Literature

Barber, R. and Barker, J. R. V. 1989. *Tournaments, Jousts, Chivalry and Pageantry in the Middle Ages*, Woodbridge.

Barker, J. R. V. 1986. *The Tournament in England 1100–1400*, Woodbridge.

Bastert, B. 1993. *Der Münchener Hof und Fuetrers 'Buch der Abenteuer'. Literarische Kontinuität im Spätmittelalter*, Mikrokosmos, 33, Frankfurt, Berlin etc.

Becker, P. J. 1977. *Handschriften und Frühdrucke mittelhochdeutscher Epen*, Wiesbaden.

Boulton, D'A. J. D. 1987. *The Knights of the Crown: The Monarchical Orders of Knighthood in Later Medieval Europe 1325–1520*, Woodbridge.

Bumke, J. 1986. *Höfische Kultur. Literatur und Gesellschaft im hohen Mittelalter*, 2 vols., Munich.

Chandler, F. 1992. *A Catalogue of Names of Persons in the German Court Epic*. Ed. by M. Jones, King's College London Medieval Studies, 8, London.

Cline, R. H. 1945. 'The influence of romances on tournaments of the Middle Ages', *Spec*, 20, 204–11.

Du Boulay, F. R. H. 1971. 'Henry of Derby's expeditions to Prussia 1390–91 and 1392', in Du Boulay and Barron, C. M., eds., *The Reign of Richard II*, London, 153–72.

Fechter, W. 1935. *Das Publikum der mittelhochdeutschen Dichtung*, Deutsche Forschungen, 28, Frankfurt (repr. Darmstadt 1966).

Gurlitt, C. 1888. 'Das deutsche Turnierwesen in der zweiten Hälfte des 16. Jahrhunderts', *Zeitschrift für Politik und Geschichte*, 5, 500–19.

Hirsch, T. 1864. 'Über den Ursprung der preußischen Artushöfe', *Zeitschrift für preußische Geschichte und Landeskunde*, 1, 1–32.

Höfler, O. 1950. 'Ulrichs von Liechtenstein Venusfahrt und Artusfahrt', in Kienast, R., ed., *Studien zur deutschen Philologie des Mittelalters. Friedrich Panzer zum 80. Geburtstag am 4. September 1950 dargebracht*, Heidelberg, 131–52.

Jackson, W. H. 1986. 'The tournament and chivalry in tournament books of the sixteenth century and in the literary works of Emperor Maximilian I', in Harper Bill, C. and Harvey, R. eds., *The Ideals and Practice of Medieval Knighthood: Papers from the First and Second Strawberry Hill Conferences*, Woodbridge, 49–73.

Kegel, E. 1905. *Die Verbreitung der mittelhochdeutschen erzählenden Literatur in Mittel- und Niederdeutschland, nachgewiesen auf Grund der Personennamen*, Hermaea, 3, Halle.

Keyser, E. 1932. 'Der Artushof und der "Gemeine Kaufmann" in Danzig', *Mitteilungen des westpreußischen Geschichtsvereins*, 31, 37–54.

Keyser, E. 1971. 'Artushöfe', in Erler A. and Kaufmann, E., eds., *Handwörterbuch zur deutschen Rechtsgeschichte*, I. Berlin, 235–7.

Loomis, R. S. 1959. 'Arthurian influence on sport and spectacle', in Loomis, R. S., ed., *Arthurian Literature in the Middle Ages: A Collaborative History*, Oxford, 553–9.

Meier, J. 1889. 'Mhd. Miscellen, 1. Zum Titurel', *AfdA*, 15, 217f.

Müller, R. 1895. 'Beiträge zur Geschichte der höfischen Epik in den österreichischen Landen, mit besonderer Rücksicht auf Kärnten', *Carinthia I. Mitteilungen des Geschichtsvereins für Kärnten*, 85, 33–51.

Panzer, F. 1896. 'Personennamen aus dem höfischen Epos in Baiern', in *Philologische Studien. Festgabe für Eduard Sievers*, Halle, 205–20.

Paravicini, W. 1989. *Die Preußenreisen des europäischen Adels*, Teil I, Beihefte der Francia, 17/1, Sigmaringen.

Paravicini, W. 1990. 'Rittertum im Norden des Reichs', in Paravicini, W., ed., *Nord und Süd in der deutschen Geschichte des Mittelalters*, Kieler Historische Studien, 34, Sigmaringen, 147–91.

Peters, U. 1971. *Frauendienst. Untersuchungen zu Ulrich von Lichtenstein und zum Wirklichkeitsgehalt der Minnedichtung*, GAG, 46, Göppingen.

Rushing, J. A., Jr. 1995. *Images of Adventure: Ywain in the Visual Arts*, Philadelphia.

Scheicher, E. 1986. 'Das Grabmal Kaiser Maximilians I. in der Hofkirche', in Felmayer, J. et al., eds., *Die Kunstdenkmäler der Stadt Innsbruck, Die Hofbauten*, Österreichische Kunsttopographie, 47, Vienna, 357–426.

Schirok, B. 1982. *Parzivalrezeption im Mittelalter*, Erträge der Forschung, 174, Darmstadt.

Schlauch, M. 1959. 'King Arthur in the Baltic towns', *BBIAS*, 11, 75–80.

Schroeder, H. 1971. *Der Topos der Nine Worthies in Literatur und bildender Kunst*, Göttingen.

Selzer, S. 1996. *Artushöfe im Ostseeraum. Ritterlich-höfische Kultur in den Städten des Preußenlandes im 14. und 15. Jahrhundert*, Kieler Werkstüke, Reihe D, 8, Frankfurt.

Semrau, A. 1930. 'Thorn im 13. Jahrhundert', *Mitteilungen des Copernicus-Vereins für Wissenschaft und Kunst zu Thorn*, 38, 1–64.

Simson, P. 1900. *Der Artushof in Danzig und seine Brüderschaften, die Banken*, Danzig.

Smet, G. A. R. de 1989. 'Namenprobleme aus der frühmittelniederländischen Dichtung', in Debus, F. and Pütz, H., eds., *Namen in deutschen literarischen Texten des Mittelalters*, Kieler Beiträge zur deutschen Sprachgeschichte, 12, Neumünster, 161–71.

Socin, A. 1903. *Mittelhochdeutsches Namenbuch. Nach oberrheinischen Quellen des zwölften und dreizehnten Jahrhunderts*, Basle (repr. Hildesheim 1966).

Störmer, W. 1972. 'König Artus als aristokratisches Leitbild während des späteren Mittelalters, gezeigt an Beispielen der Ministerialität und des Patriziats', *Zeitschrift für bayerische Landesgeschichte*, 35, 946–71.

Vale, J. 1982. *Edward III and Chivalry: Chivalric Society and its Context 1270–1350*, Woodbridge.

Watanabe-O'Kelly, H. 1992. *Triumphall Shews: Tournaments at German-Speaking Courts in their European Context 1560–1730*, Berlin.

Wolff, L. 1927. 'Das Magdeburger Gralsfest Bruns von Schönebeck', *Niederdeutsche Zeitschrift für Volkskunde*, 5, 202–16.

Zingerle, I. V. 1856. 'Die Personennamen Tirols in Beziehung auf deutsche Sage und Literaturgeschichte', *Germania*, 1, 290–5.

Zotz, T. 1985. 'Adel, Bürgertum und Turniere in deutschen Städten vom 13. bis 15. Jahrhundert', in Fleckenstein, J., ed., *Das ritterliche Turnier im Mittelalter*, Veröffentlichungen des Max-Planck-Instituts für Geschichte, 80, Göttingen, 450–95.

Zotz, T. 1991. 'Die Stadtgesellschaft und ihre Feste', in Altenburg, D. et al., eds., *Feste und Feiern im Mittelalter. Paderborner Symposion des Mediävistenverbandes*, Sigmaringen, 201–13.

Part Five

The Legacy

18

EARLY PRINTED EDITIONS
OF ARTHURIAN ROMANCES

John L. Flood

For all the wealth of their manuscript tradition in late medieval Germany, the Arthurian poems barely succeeded in making the leap into print. Indeed, it is conceivable that, had printing been invented a hundred or even only fifty years later than in fact it was, none of them might have found their way into the new medium at all until they were rediscovered by eighteenth- and nineteenth-century antiquarians and scholars. After all, this was the fate of Gottfried's *Tristan*, of Hartmann's *Iwein*, and various others: it was Johann Christoph Myller (1740–1807) who, in his three-volume *Samlung deutscher Gedichte aus dem XII., XIII. und XIV. Jahrhundert* (Berlin 1784–5), first made accessible to the modern age such works as Heinrich von Veldeke's *Eneit*, Hartmann's *Der arme Heinrich*, Wolfram's *Parzival*, Gottfried's *Tristan* with Heinrich von Freiberg's continuation, and Hartmann's *Iwein* (though consistently misspelling the name as *Twein*!), together with various other pieces. This collection, together with Myller's edition of the *Nibelungenlied* (1782), represented the bulk of what medieval literature was accessible in printed form to inquiring antiquaries at the end of the eighteenth century.

As good fortune would have it, however, four German Arthurian works did make the transition into print in the fifteenth century. These were Wolfram's *Parzival*, Albrecht's *Jüngerer Titurel* (but ascribed to Wolfram at the time), Eilhart's *Tristrant* and Wirnt's *Wigalois*.

Though texts in the German language figured among the products of the early printers from the start – the so-called *Fragment vom Weltgericht*, part of a poem based on Sibylline prophecies, appears to be one of the earliest surviving pieces from Gutenberg's experimental period at Strasbourg in the early 1440s (Kapr 1995, 92–9; but see now Schanze 2000), and Albrecht Pfister was printing Ulrich Boner's *Edelstein* and the *Ackermann aus Böhmen* at Bamberg soon after 1460 – the printing of vernacular texts developed above all in the 1470s at major printing centres like Strasbourg (Chrisman 1982) and Augsburg (Künast 1997).

Strasbourg was initially perhaps not a place that one associates particularly strongly with books in the vernacular, though its output in this field certainly expanded around 1500 and especially in the early sixteenth century when printers like Johann Grüninger, Hans Knobloch and Bartholomäus Kistler established a reputation for illustrated works. Nevertheless, there were some notable books printed there in the German language between 1466 and 1480: they included the first printed German Bible, published by Johann Mentelin in 1466, the editions of *Parzival* and the *Jüngerer Titurel*, both printed by Mentelin in 1477, and that famous compendium of German heroic poems, the *Heldenbuch*, printed by Johann Prüss in 1479 or shortly thereafter.

The editions of *Parzival* and the *Jüngerer Titurel*, which were the last books Mentelin printed (he died in December 1478), are remarkable productions in many ways. Why he decided to print them at all is not clear; it has been suggested that he may have done so at the suggestion, or even at the behest, of his patron and former employer Ruprecht von Pfalz-Simmern (1420–78), bishop of Strasbourg, though this cannot be proved (Flood 1989). Very few (if any) of the numerous surviving copies[1] of the two works show signs of having been read, and even though spaces were left at various points in the text for illustrations to be painted in, in not a single case has this been done. It seems that the fledgling market for printed books in the vernacular was misjudged. If they were designed to appeal to an aristocratic public, they were evidently not yet ready for them,[2] and it is unlikely that a humanist public would have had a taste for the medieval vernacular romances. Though there is no proof that Mentelin made a loss on the enterprise, it is at least clear that his pioneering endeavours on behalf of Arthurian literature did not find any imitators. *Parzival* was not printed again until it was rediscovered three centuries later, and with the *Jüngerer Titurel* things took even longer.

One of the reasons why *Parzival* and the *Jüngerer Titurel* found little interest may have been that they were in verse. It is evident that at the end of the fifteenth century the literary public was developing a taste for prose romances, and this explains why Eilhart's *Tristrant* and Wirnt's *Wigalois* were so much more successful when they were issued in print. The first edition of the prose redaction of Eilhart's poem was issued by Anton Sorg at Augsburg in 1484 and the prose version of Wirnt's *Wigalois* was likewise published at Augsburg, by Johann Schönsperger, in 1493. Whereas *Parzival* and *Titurel* had both been bulky folio volumes (of 320 and 614 pages respectively) still requiring the expensive attention of an illuminator before they could be regarded as finished products, *Tristrant* and *Wigoleis* were much slimmer books of a handier size, illustrated with simple but adequate woodcuts. Sorg was already playing a particularly significant role in the provision of popular prose reading matter: he had, for instance, earlier published three editions of a prose version of *Herzog Ernst* (in the mid-1470s) as well as one of Johann von Würzburg's *Wilhelm von Österreich* (1481). What Sorg did, Schönsperger also did: his 1493 *Wigoleis* was followed by *Tristrant* in 1498. There is no reason to think that these Augsburg printers regarded the Arthurian works as constituting a particular genre: like the other works mentioned, they were simply further titles on a heterogeneous list of books of adventure, of the fabulous, of travel.

The emergence of the prose narrative as a literary form at this time is an event of particular importance. The 1484 *Tristrant* specifically states that it was intended for readers who did not feel comfortable with verse, for people 'die söllicher gereymter bücher nit genad haben, auch etlich die die kunst der reymen nit aigentlich versteen kündent' ('who do not like such rhymed books and for those who are not able to appreciate the art of rhyming' (Brandstetter, 1966, 197–8)), and it may be assumed that similar thinking lay behind the commission for *Wigalois* to be turned into prose. It is tempting to think that the readership for such books lay amongst the patrician and merchant classes in the free imperial cities – the people who developed a taste for prose novels like *Melusine* (Augsburg 1474), *Herzog Ernst* (F version) (Augsburg *c.* 1475) or *Fortunatus* (Augsburg 1509) – yet it would seem likely that they were also appreciated by members of the aristocracy. After all, the prose version of *Wigalois* was made at the request of 'etlich edel und auch ander personen' ('various persons of nobility and others'), and in the 1470s we find people like Mechthild Countess Palatine and other members of court circles in south-west Germany being introduced to German literary prose by Niklas von Wyle, and somewhat later, in the 1530s, Johann von Simmern, Count Palatine, is producing German prose narratives like *Fierrabras*, a story based on the exploits of the heroes of the Carolingian age. This was a period of experimentation in literary form – in the mid-sixteenth century, for instance, we find Hans Sachs reusing the same material in a whole variety of different forms (Flood 1995). As yet it was far from settled that prose would become the normal medium for narrative works. Ulrich Füetrer recast Wirnt's *Wigalois* (a romance in couplets) in strophic form in the 1480s, and verse was to remain the dominant medium for heroic poetry right down to the later seventeenth century.[3] As late as 1587 or 1588 even the story of Faust, the prose *Historia von D. Johann Fausten*, is being retold in rhyming couplets 'dann zweiffels ohn dieser stylus von menniglichen mehr gelobet wirt' ('for without doubt many people praise this form more highly'), as the versifier, Johannes Feinaug, assures us in his preface (Mahal 1977, fol. A4ᵛ).

Who made the prose versions of *Tristrant* and *Wigoleis* is not known. In both cases the author deliberately refers to himself as anonymous, 'ich Vngenant'. The title of the 1484 *Tristrant* includes the curious remark

> weliche histori einer vorrede wol würdige wäre / vnd doch vnnutz / dann die lesenden vnnd zuhörenden / in langen vorreden verdriessen nemend Darumb sag ich die histori auff das kürtzt (Brandstetter 1966, 1)

(which story well deserves a preface, but this would be pointless because readers and listeners get bored by long prefaces, wherefore I will tell the story as briefly as possible).

It would be nice to think that since this comment is part of the preliminaries to the book, which are normally prepared by the publisher, the 'ich' ('I') might be Anton Sorg himself, but corroborative evidence pointing to his authorship of the whole is lacking. The fear of boring the public surfaces also in the prose *Wigoleis*, though here one has the impression that the redactor was chiefly giving vent to his own lack of enthusiasm for having been entrusted with the task. The preface and afterword spell this out at some length – he tells how he was asked to take on the commission in 1472 but procrastinated until eventually in 1483 his patrons insisted that the work be put in hand at last – but his distaste for the job also reveals itself at various points, as for instance when he writes:

> das laß ich durch kürcz vnderwegen . dann söllich groß kost vnnd reychtumb bey vns gancz vngeleüblich sind . auch an söllicher sag nit mer vil ligt denn daz die hystori dardurch gelengert würde

> *(I will omit this for the sake of brevity, for such great luxury and wealth are quite inconceivable to us, and such an account serves no real purpose other than that of making the story longer)*

and

> dann solt ich künig . fürsten vnd herren so zů dem brautlauff kumen . vnd vnder den gezelten hof hielten alle besunder nennen war mir zů vil zů sagen . vnd zů hören vnnücze (Flood 2000)

> *(for if I were to mention by name all the kings, princes and lords who came to the wedding and held court in these pavilions it would take me too long and would be pointless to listen to).*

Seeing that the manuscript was completed in 1483, a decade before Schönsperger's edition appeared, it is not impossible that a printed edition appeared during the 1480s, published perhaps even by Anton Sorg, which has simply not survived – after all, even Sorg's *Tristrant* edition is known only from a single copy in Berlin. If, on the other hand, Schönsperger's edition really was the *editio princeps*, we have to ask why he chose to print it. Matthey (1959) suggested that Emperor Maximilian I himself may have been instrumental in encouraging Schönsperger to print German heroic poems but, even if this was the case, the emperor's acknowledged delight in Arthurian romance is unlikely to have motivated him to encourage Schönsperger to publish this rather bald prose version of Wirnt's fine poem (Brandstetter 1971, Melzer 1972). All we can say is that Wirnt's story seems to have enjoyed some popularity in southern Germany at this time: quite apart from the evidence for fifteenth-century manuscripts of the original poem, at approximately the same time as the prose version was made Ulrich Füetrer in nearby Munich was recasting the story in strophes in his *Buch der Abenteuer*. Whether Füetrer himself knew the prose version is uncertain (Flood 1977).

Undeniably, the Arthurian stories are rather meagrely represented among popular narratives of the sixteenth century. *Parzival* and *Titurel* being already forgotten, it was left to *Tristrant* and *Wigoleis* to represent the Arthurian tradition on the German book market. But by now there was considerable competition from other stories old and new, of French, Italian and indeed native German origin, all vying for the attention of the growing reading public. When medieval poems did make a successful leap into print it was not the Arthurian romances but poems about the exploits of Germanic heroes of old, Siegfried but above all Dietrich von Bern, that appealed to the public (Flood 1967, Koppitz 1980, Flood 1982).[4] Unlike the Arthurian poems which had been composed predominantly in rhyming couplets, heroic poems like the *Lied vom Hürnen Seyfrid*, the *Eckenlied* and *Herr Dietrich von Bern* (*Sigenot*) – the last being frequently printed between *c.* 1487 and 1661 – or even *Herzog Ernst* (G version) had the distinct advantage of being in a more memorable, indeed singable, strophic form (Kornrumpf 1984).[5]

Nevertheless, the 1550s saw editions of *Tristrant* appearing at Worms, Augsburg, Frankfurt and Strasbourg, with further ones at Frankfurt in 1565 and 1570. *Wigoleis* was reissued at Strasbourg in 1519, at least three times at Frankfurt between about 1558 and 1586, and at Augsburg in 1580; there may have been further editions which have not survived (Gotzkowsky 1991–4). From this period we have some comparative sales figures for these books. At the Frankfurt Lenten and Autumn fairs in 1568 and the Lenten fair of 1569 combined, one publisher sold 328 copies of *Tristrant* and 188 of *Wigoleis*, compared with 818 copies of *Till Eulenspiegel*, 580 of *Fortunatus* and 460 of *Melusine* (Schmidt 1996, 289), and the bookseller Simon Hüter supplied thirty copies of *Tristrant*, twenty of *Wigoleis*, but 115 of *Eulenspiegel*, fifty of *Fortunatus* and twenty of *Melusine* for sale at the Leipzig fair in 1568 (Pallmann 1881, 161). We also have evidence at least of *Tristrant* being read by people as far afield as the mining communities of the Tyrol and the more sophisticated environment of Dresden in the same period (Flood 1990, 199 and 208).

In 1587 the Frankfurt publisher Sigmund Feyerabend brought out his *Buch der Liebe*, a large compendium of romances illustrating 'was recht ehrlich, dargegen auch was vnordentliche, Bulerische Lieb sey' ('what honourable and in contrast what dishonourable, licentious love is'). This comprised thirteen narratives – the number was deliberately chosen to match the thirteen books of

Amadis von Gaula that were then available in Germany – and among them were
Tristrant and *Wigoleis* (Flood 1987, Veitschegger 1991). The title page of the
Buch der Liebe clearly indicates the type of reader envisaged by the publisher:
'Allen hohen Standes personen / Ehrliebenden vom Adel / züchtigen Frauen vnd
Jungfrauen / Auch jederman in gemein' ('For all persons of high rank, nobles
who love honour, virtuous ladies and maidens, and everybody in general').

The *Buch der Liebe* was printed only once. After 1587 *Tristrant* and *Wigoleis*
continued to appear at well-spaced intervals during the sixteenth and early
seventeenth centuries, though by the time of the Thirty Years War their life-
force was spent. The last known editions of *Tristrant* appeared at Frankfurt in
1594, Erfurt 1619, and Nuremberg in 1644, 1653, and 1664. *Wigoleis* was issued
at Hamburg in 1611, at Nuremberg in 1643, 1653 and 1664, and once more at
Erfurt in 1664, while the text of the Frankfurt edition of 1564 was reprinted by
Heinrich August Ottokar Reichard in volume 2 of his *Bibliothek der Romane*,
Berlin 1778, 2nd edn Riga 1783, pp. 11–128. Thereafter the Arthurian stories
had to wait for the antiquaries and scholars of the Romantic age to rediscover
and breathe fresh life into them. Arthur would return after all!

Notes

[1] Precisely how many copies still survive is uncertain. Becker (1977, 245) lists 36 copies of
Parzival and 43 of *Titurel*, but while the British Library's *Incunabula Short Title Catalogue* (*ISTC*)
database (in June 2000) records only 27 copies of Parzival and 33 of *Titurel* these include several of
each title not known to Becker.

[2] Nevertheless, it is worth noting that Argula von Stauff (*c*. 1492–*c*. 1554), a lady of noble birth
who later, under her married name Argula von Grumbach, achieved some fame as a writer of
Reformation pamphlets, had three brothers and a sister who all bore names taken from *Parzival*:
Parzival, Feirafis, Gramaflanz and Secundilla (see Matheson, P., *Argula von Grumbach: A
Woman's Voice in the Reformation*, Edinburgh, 1995, 5 and 9; other scholars also derive the name
Argula from Wolfram's Orgeluse but do not mention a Parzival amongst Argula's brothers; see
Jackson's chapter on Arthurian material in German society in this volume). Yet, even though all
these persons may have been born after 1477, their parents could of course still have picked up
these names from reading a manuscript, rather than Mentelin's edition, of the work.

[3] Only in the third quarter of the seventeenth century was the story of Siegfried's dragon-fight,
well known in the strophic *Lied vom Hürnen Seyfrid*, turned into prose, to remain popular as the
Wunderschöne Historia von dem gehörnten Siegfried for some two centuries.

[4] See also the remarks on *Wunderer* in chapter 13, 'Arthurian Romance and German Heroic
Poetry', in the present volume.

[5] Despite its structural complexity, the 'Herzog Ernst-Ton' (or 'Bernerton'), to which the
Eckenlied and *Herr Dietrich von Bern* could also be sung, enjoyed huge popularity as a vehicle for
both secular and religious songs. Another of the poems about Dietrich von Bern, *Laurin*, also
achieved some success in print even though it was composed in rhyming couplets.

Bibliography

Primary Sources

There are no modern editions of the fifteenth-century printed versions of *Parzival* or the *Jüngerer Titurel*, the standard editions of these works being based on manuscript sources.

Tristrant

Tristrant und Isalde. Prosaroman. Ed. by A. Brandstetter, 1966 (ATB, Ergänzungsreihe, 3). Tübingen.

Tristrant und Isalde. Augsburg 1484. Ed. by H. Elsner, 1989 (Deutsche Volksbücher in Faksimiledrucken, A, 16). Hildesheim.

Wigoleis vom Rade

The text of the 1493 edition, based on the defective Munich copy of the original, is printed in Brandstetter 1971, 190–235 (see Other Literature).

For the revised text of the 1519 edition see *Wigalois. Straßburg: Johannes Knobloch, 1519.* Ed. by H. Melzer, 1973 (Deutsche Volksbücher in Faksimiledrucken, A, 10). Hildesheim.

Ulrich Füetrer, *Wigoleis.* Ed. by H. A. Hilgers, 1975 (ATB, 79). Tübingen.

Other Literature

Becker, P. J. 1977. *Handschriften und Frühdrucke mittelhochdeutscher Epen*, Wiesbaden.

Brandstetter, A. 1966. See Primary Sources, *Tristrant und Isalde. Prosaroman.*

Brandstetter, A. 1971. *Prosaauflösung. Studien zur Rezeption der höfischen Epik im frühneuhochdeutschen Prosaroman*, Frankfurt am Main.

Chrisman, M. U. 1982. *Lay Culture, Learned Culture, Books and Social Change in Strasbourg, 1480–1599*, New Haven and London.

Flood, J. L. 1967. 'Some notes on German heroic poems in print', *The Library*, 5th ser., 22, 228–42.

Flood, J. L. 1977. Review of Hilgers 1975, in *AfdA*, 88, 170–3.

Flood, J. L. 1982. Review of Koppitz 1980, *MLR*, 77, 753–6.

Flood, J. L. 1987. 'Sigmund Feyerabends *Buch der Liebe* (1587)', in Ashcroft, J., Huschenbett, D. and Jackson, W. H., eds., *Liebe in der deutschen Literatur des Mittelalters. St. Andrews-Colloquium 1985*, Tübingen, 204–20.

Flood, J. L. 1989. 'Johann Mentelin und Ruprecht von Pfalz-Simmern. Zur Entstehung der Straßburger *Parzival*-Ausgabe vom Jahre 1477', in Heinzle and Gärtner (see Gen. Bibl.), 197–209.

Flood, J. L. 1990. 'Subversion in the Alps: books and readers in the Austrian Counter-Reformation', *The Library*, 6th ser., 12, 185–211.

Flood, J. L. 1995. 'Hans Sachs and Boccaccio', in Aylett, R. and Skrine, P., eds., *Hans Sachs and Folk Theatre in the Late Middle Ages: Studies in the History of Popular Culture*, Lewiston, Queenston and Lampeter, 139–65.

Flood, J. L. 2000. 'Die schwere Geburt des Herrn Wigoleis vom Rade. Zur Entstehung und Formfindung eines frühneuzeitlichen Prosaromans', in Becker, P. J. et al., eds., *Scrinium Berolinense. Tilo Brandis zum 65. Geburtstag*, Berlin, 768–78.

Gotzkowsky, B. 1991–94. *'Volksbücher'. Prosaromane, Renaissancenovellen, Versdichtungen und Schwankbücher. Bibliographie der deutschen Drucke*. 2 vols., Bibliotheca Bibliographica Aureliana, 125 and 142, Baden-Baden.

Kapr, A. 1995. *Johann Gutenberg. The Man and His Invention*, Aldershot.

Knape, J. 1995. 'Augsburger Prosaroman-Drucke des 15. Jahrhunderts', in Janota, J. and

Williams-Krapp, W., eds., *Literarisches Leben in Augsburg während des 15. Jahrhunderts*, Studia Augustana, 7, Tübingen, 330–57.

Koppitz, H.-J. 1980. *Studien zur Tradierung der weltlichen mittelhochdeutschen Epik im 15. und beginnenden 16. Jahrhundert*, Munich.

Kornrumpf, G. 1984. 'Strophik im Zeitalter der Prosa. Deutsche Heldendichtung im ausgehenden Mittelalter', in Grenzmann, L. and Stackmann, K., eds., *Literatur und Laienbildung im Spätmittelalter und in der Reformationszeit*, Stuttgart, 316–43.

Künast, H.-J. 1997. *'Getruckt zu Augspurg'. Buchdruck und Buchhandel in Augsburg zwischen 1468 und 1555*, Studia Augustana, 8, Tübingen.

Mahal, G. ed. 1977. *Der Tübinger Reim-Faust von 1587/88*, Kirchheim/Teck.

Matthey, W. 1959. 'Der älteste Wiegendruck des Sigenot. Datierung, Bildschmuck, Nachwirkung', *Anzeiger des Germanischen Nationalmuseums 1954–59*, 68–90.

Melzer, H. 1972. *Trivialisierungstendenzen im Volksbuch. Ein Vergleich der Volksbücher 'Tristrant und Isalde', 'Wigoleis' und 'Wilhelm von Österreich' mit den mittelhochdeutschen Epen*, Hildesheim.

Müller, J.-D. 1985. 'Volksbuch – Prosaroman im 15./16. Jahrhundert. Perspektiven der Forschung', *Internationales Archiv für Sozialgeschichte der deutschen Literatur*, Sonderheft Forschungsreferate 1, 1–128.

Müller, J.-D. 1997. 'Augsburger Drucke von Prosaromanen im 15. und 16. Jahrhundert', in Gier, H. and Janota, J., eds., *Augsburger Buchdruck und Verlagswesen. Von den Anfängen bis zur Gegenwart*, Wiesbaden, 337–52.

Pallmann, H. 1881. *Sigmund Feyerabend, sein Leben und seine geschäftlichen Verbindungen*, Archiv für Frankfurts Geschichte und Kunst, Neue Folge 7, Frankfurt.

Schanze, F. 2000. 'Wieder einmal das *Fragment vom Weltgericht*. Bemerkungen und Materialien zur *Sybillenweissagung*', *Gutenberg-Jahrbuch*, 75, 42–63.

Schmidt, I. 1996. *Die Bücher aus der Frankfurter Offizin Gülfferich–Han–Weigand Han-Erben*, Wolfenbütteler Schriften zur Geschichte des Buchwesens, 26, Wiesbaden.

Veitschegger, Th. 1991. *Das 'Buch der Liebe' (1587). Ein Beitrag zur Buch- und Verlagsgeschichte des 16. Jahrhunderts*, Hamburg.

19

THE MODERN RECEPTION OF THE ARTHURIAN LEGEND

Ulrich Müller and Werner Wunderlich

The post-medieval appearance of the Arthurian legends in literature and art of the German-speaking world[1] is part of a new interest in the Middle Ages in general and medieval German culture in particular that began in the mid-eighteenth century. The Romantic movement, its scholars and poets, went on to idealize medieval German history and culture, which became a source for concepts of national identity and national unification, and a model for poetic vitality and a romantic view of life and the world (Gentry and Müller 1991). However, in contrast to the reception of the Nibelung sagas, the German reception of the Arthurian legend does not often draw parallels between Arthur's world and German history and German political ideology. This sets it apart from the English and American tradition of the genre, which had a national significance for several centuries, especially in the British Isles. Arthurian figures and stories occur in the German-speaking countries more as metaphors for the failure of utopianism and for history's inability to achieve lasting peace, freedom and progress, and as lasting patterns for the demonic power of love and sexuality.

The German reception of the Arthurian legends is also characterized by the relatively modest role of King Arthur himself, a 'reception of King Arthur without King Arthur' (Müller in Gamerschlag 1991). Since the revival of interest in Arthurian material in the late eighteenth century, German-speaking artists and authors have concentrated mainly on the stories of Parzival and the Grail, Tristan and Isolde, and the magician Merlin. The tales of King Arthur, Guinevere, Lancelot and the other knights of the Round Table have been, since Sir Walter Scott and Alfred Lord Tennyson, as popular in the English-speaking world as the fairy tales of the Grimm brothers have been in the German-speaking countries. But the Arthurian tales have never reached the same level of popularity in these countries, not even today, despite the influence of English and American translations and films, and still less in the nineteenth century. There are three different but closely related reasons for this pattern: the difficulty of 'exporting' the British understanding of King Arthur as a figure of national myth; the Germans' specific fixation on other myths or legends of the

Middle Ages (above all the Nibelungs); and the dominating influence of Richard Wagner on the reception of medieval myths, which highlighted the stories of Parzival, the Holy Grail and of Tristan and Isolde, and led, at least for a long time, to an almost complete neglect of the other knights of the Round Table such as Erec, Iwein, Gawain, Lancelot and Galahad.

Late Eighteenth and Nineteenth Century

Enlightenment and Romanticism

It is characteristic of many, perhaps all, cultural and political communities to create an individual identity by 'separating' themselves from others. Epic myths which embody religion and history play an important role in this respect. The European countries which had increasingly come to see themselves as nation states since the late eighteenth century were also trying to define their identity through their history and epic myths. The search for an identity rooted in a national past was particularly pronounced in those nationalities which, unlike France, England or Russia, did not have the political identity for which they strove: the Balkans, the non-German peoples of the Danubian monarchy, divided Poland, Italy and Greece, as well as German-speaking central Europe. Around and after 1800 the Germans, politically disunited and powerless, sought refuge in the past: their own history, especially the glorious time of the Hohenstaufen dynasty, was used to legitimate longings for national unity and national power which obviously could not be realized in the present. The story of Siegfried, the Nibelungs and Burgundians (published in full in 1782 for the first time), gradually became something like a German national myth; the *Nibelungenlied* acquired a significance it never had during the Middle Ages and became the German national epic with a claim to rank on a par with, if not even above, Homer, Virgil, Dante and the French *Chanson de Roland*. There was little room beside these works for material based on the Round Table, the Grail quest, or the Tristan legend.

However, the stories of Arthur, Parzival and the Grail, and Tristan and Isolde were not unknown to educated Germans at the end of the eighteenth and the beginning of the nineteenth century, albeit mostly through French and English versions. Late medieval printings of Wolfram's *Parzival* and the *Jüngerer Titurel* (published by Johann Mentelin in Strasbourg in 1477), as well as of a German prose adaptation of the Tristan story, were also available in several libraries.

The first modern printings of German Arthurian narratives were edited by the Swiss Christoph Heinrich Myller (*Samlung* [!] *deutscher Gedichte aus dem XII. XIII. und XIV. Jahrhundert*. 3 volumes, 1782–5, including also the *Nibelungenlied*).[2] Myller was a disciple of the writer and critic Johann Jacob Bodmer, living in Zurich, who had been the first to publish, between 1753 and 1781, some fragmentary translations from Wolfram's epics into modern German. He also published the first modern transcriptions of Middle High German lyrics from the manuscript which he called 'Codex Manesse'. Bodmer, like others, wished to show that there had been, centuries ago, German poetry of high quality, comparable with the classic works of Greek and Latin antiquity, and of the French.

However, there was generally little interest in these publications: King Frederick II ('the Great') of Prussia, to whom Myller dedicated a copy of his edition, responded politely, but stressed that these old poems had no value for him. It was the editions by Eberhard von Groote, Friedrich Heinrich von der Hagen and Hans Ferdinand Massmann (*Tristan*, 1821, 1823, 1843), Georg Friedrich Benecke/Karl Lachmann (*Iwein*, 1827), Karl Lachmann (*Parzival*, 1833), and Moriz Haupt (*Erec*, 1839), and particularly the translations of Alfred Schulz under the pen-name San-Marte (*Parzival*, 1836; *Titurel* and *Willehalm* 1841), Karl Simrock (*Parzival* and *Titurel*, 1842; *Tristan*, 1855) and Hermann Kurtz (*Tristan*, 1844) that first stimulated interest in the Arthurian legends.

The magician Merlin was rediscovered for German literature by the poet Christoph Martin Wieland (1733–1813). Probably around 1775 he read the medieval story of Merlin, Uther, Arthur and Viviane in the famous *Bibliothèque universelle des romans*, and in 1777 he published a brief retelling in prose with a commentary, *Merlin der Zauberer*, in his widely read journal *Der Teutsche Merkur* (founded 1784). Translations and retellings of the Merlin legend achieved some importance for the German tradition at the beginning of the nineteenth century. In 1804 Friedrich Schlegel published a translation from a French Arthurian manuscript in prose (the exact manuscript is not known): *Geschichte des Zauberers Merlin*. This first, only slightly abridged, translation of a full-length late medieval version was written by Schlegel's wife Caroline and her friend Helmina von Chézy in Paris, but was printed under Schlegel's name; he even incorporated it later into his collected works (vol.VII, 1827 – an odd suppression of authorship for this educated and progressive man). Further contributions to Merlin's fame were Ludwig Tieck's unstaged translation (1829) of William Rowley's grotesque drama *Birth of Merlin or The Child Hath Found Its Father* (published 1662), later used by Immermann and Dorst, and the translations from several medieval literatures in the collection *Die Sagen von Merlin* by San-Marte (1853). During the nineteenth century Merlin was used in several German lyrics as a symbol of erotic fixation and 'Naturliebe'.

Richard Wagner (1813–1883)

It is no exaggeration to say that the only medieval epic legends that played an important role for the modern reception in the German-speaking world, at least until recently, have been those Richard Wagner (1813–83) converted into his operas: the stories of Tannhäuser and the 'Sängerkrieg auf der Wartburg' (*Tannhäuser*, first performed 1845); the Grail, Lohengrin and Parsifal (*Lohengrin*, *Parsifal*, 1850 and 1882); Tristan and Isolde (1865); Siegfried, Brünnhilde and Hagen (*Der Ring des Nibelungen*, 1869, 1870, 1876). All the operas and music dramas which Wagner completed are bound up with the Middle Ages. This is true, in the widest sense, even of *Die Feen* (written 1833/4), *Rienzi* (1842) and *Der fliegende Holländer* (1843), as well as of the world of Hans Sachs and the Mastersingers (*Die Meistersinger von Nürnberg*, 1868), a world which belongs very much to the Middle Ages. Wagner's influence on the reception of Arthurian stories in the German-speaking area was strong and permanent. He influenced the canon of medieval works that were received and their interpretation by the educated German public in a way that is hard to overestimate.

Among the most recent writers to have dealt in detail with the subject of Wagner as 'mediator of the Middle Ages' are Peter Wapnewski (1978) and Volker Mertens (in Müller and Wapnewski 1992; see also Haymes in Grimm and Hermand 1991). Wagner himself claimed that he had, so to speak, distilled and depicted the essential meaning of each of the medieval tales which form the basis of his music dramas about Tristan and Isolde and about Parsifal.[3] However, this is more a statement of the composer's subjective view than an objectively valid judgement.

With regard to the treatment of his sources Wagner evolved in the direction of an increasingly drastic reduction of the relevant material. Initially, in his so-called 'Romantic operas' and even in the *Ring des Nibelungen* (using Nordic tradition as a main source, not the Middle High German *Nibelungenlied*), he mostly expanded the medieval source in various ways. In later works he left out more and more, concentrating instead upon individual sections of the action. In the case of the later music dramas *Tristan und Isolde* (first performed Munich, 1865) and *Parsifal* (Bayreuth, 1882) Wagner's primary sources were the romances of Gottfried von Strassburg and Wolfram von Eschenbach, both of them available to him in extensively annotated translations (by San-Marte, 1836; Karl Simrock, 1842; and Hermann Kurtz, 1844). On both occasions Wagner cut the action decisively, especially in the case of *Parsifal*.

The medieval love story of Tristan and Isolde was reduced by Wagner to three main events: the drinking of the love potion (Act 1), the protagonists' night of love and their detection by Marke (Act 2), the death of the severely wounded Tristan and Isolde's 'Liebestod' (Act 3). He also changed the meaning of the story: whereas the medieval couple is in conflict with feudal society and its morals, Wagner stresses that love is not possible at all in this life, but only in the otherworld of the Nirvana. Wagner's concept of love in *Tristan* was strongly influenced by the philosophy of Arthur Schopenhauer and by Buddhist ideas, and the same influences are found in his *Parsifal*.

Of his main source, Wolfram's *Parzival*, Wagner retains in his *Parsifal* only the protagonist (Parzival) and (in the form of a retrospective) his mother Herzeloyde, the wounded Grail King and the Castle of the Grail, Parzival's failure to ask after the cause of the king's suffering, and the final act of redemption. Wagner uses names from Wolfram's romance in his music drama (Gurnemanz and Klingsor), but both figures have been extensively modified, while the character and history of Wagner's Kundry are largely new. Only a few basic structures and key motifs, together with the names of the characters, have been retained by Wagner, although Wolfram's poem is still clearly recognizable as the source of the action in the opera. Wagner transforms Wolfram's all-embracing and world-affirming fairy-tale romance into a philosophical drama which, enlisting the persuasive art of music, proclaims an ideology of asceticism and propagates the irenic victory of world-denial over an unsettling affirmation of, and attachment to, the world, the triumph of the principle of conservatism over progress. Wagner again combines here a medieval legend with ideas from Buddhism and the philosophy of Arthur Schopenhauer (see Müller 1980, Wynn 1983).

In the second volume of San-Marte's translation, Wagner also found a lengthy excursus summarizing the current state of knowledge about the 'legend of the Holy Grail'. It was presumably from here that Wagner took the idea that the Grail (to quote from the Grail Narration of his *Lohengrin*) was 'a vessel of miraculous blessings', rather than Wolfram's stone, that is to say, according to the French tradition, a chalice used at the Last Supper and by Joseph of Arimathea to catch the Saviour's blood.

Regarding Wagner's approach to Wolfram's romance, a long letter which Wagner wrote on 29/30 May 1859 to his confidante Mathilde Wesendonck in Zurich is of particular importance. Here, he criticizes Wolfram's poem from a decidedly personal standpoint and draws a contrast between the universal medieval romance and his own concept of a three-part (i.e. three-act) philosophical drama:

> Wolfram is a thoroughly immature phenomenon, although it must be said that his barbaric and utterly confused age is largely to blame for this, fluctuating as it did between early Christianity and a more modern political economy. Nothing could ever come to fruition at such a period; poetic profundity was immediately submerged in insubstantial caprice. I almost agree with Frederick the Great who, on being presented with a copy of Wolfram, told the publisher not to bother him with such stuff! . . .
>
> Wolfram hadn't the first idea of what he was doing: his (scil. Parzival's) despair in God is stupid and unmotivated, and his conversion is even more unsatisfactory. The thing about the 'question' is that it is *so* utterly preposterous and totally meaningless.

I should simply have to invent everything here . . . I cannot choose to work on such a broad scale as Wolfram was able to do: I have to compress everything into *three* climactic situations of violent intensity, so that the work's profound and ramified content emerges clearly and distinctly; for *my* art consists in working and representing things in *this* way. And – am I to undertake such a task? God forbid! Today I take my leave of this insane project . . . (*Selected Letters of Richard Wagner*, trans. Stewart Spencer (London, 1987), 458–60)

In the same letter Wagner also comments dismissively on Gottfried von Strassburg's treatment of the Tristan legend. Indeed Wagner's letter to Mathilde Wesendonck shows clearly that, in the case of *Tristan* and especially *Parsifal*, Wagner's intention was not to follow the medieval poets, but to provide a different, and in his view, truer interpretation of the stories.

Parallel to the increasing tendentiousness of Wagner's later works, arguments as to how they should be interpreted have become sharper over the years, increasing in the bitterness with which they are conducted and threatening to develop into an absurd confrontation between Wagnerians on the one hand and anti-Wagnerians on the other. *Tristan, Parsifal* and parts of the *Ring* affect their listeners' lives deeply and challenge them to adopt a philosophical or even a religious stance towards the works. This tendency is particularly marked in the responses evoked by *Parsifal*, which Wagner himself already described as a 'dramatic festival of consecration' ('Bühnenweihfestspiel') and which claims to embody a message that almost amounts to an ersatz religion.

Accusations were made after the Second World War that *Parsifal*, in particular, contained anti-Semitic tendencies. Scholars such as Theodor W. Adorno, Hartmut Zelinsky, Robert Gutman and Marc A. Weiner (1995) voiced these claims and provoked heated discussions. Despite intensive and committed efforts, no convincing evidence has been found in the libretto or music to back up these accusations (Katz 1986, Kühnel 1991). On the other hand, it is undeniable that Wagner's subjective and emotionally charged anti-Semitism, as expressed in his notorious essay *Das Judentum in der Musik* (1850, 1869) and in many, and at times even contradictory, statements, played at least an underlying and often an important role in later interpretations of *Parsifal* by fanatical and conservative Wagnerians.

Fouqué and Immermann

Only two further German adaptations of Arthurian themes during the nineteenth century are of some importance, although one of them, a poetic retelling of *Parzival* by Fouqué, was not published until 1997, and the other, a Merlin drama by Immermann, was never produced in its own day.

Literary scholars were well aware that the Prussian officer and writer Friedrich Baron de la Motte Fouqué (1777–1843) descendant of Huguenot emigrants from France, was not only a best-selling Romantic author for several years, with *Der Held des Nordens* (1808–10), *Undine* (1811) and *Der Zauberring* (1813), but also later wrote *Der Parcival. Rittergedicht* (1831/2), the first and only retelling of Wolfram's *Parzival* in the nineteenth century. But hardly anyone knew this first Parzival version in modern German, simply because Fouqué, who had become totally out of date, could not find a publisher for his manuscript of roughly 500 pages. Fouqué's *Parcival* was at last edited in 1997 by Tilman Spreckelsen, Peter Henning Hischer, Frank Rainer Max and Ursula Rautenberg (Hildesheim etc.)

Fouqué follows Wolfram's storyline rather closely, but he uses an entirely different literary technique, combining elements of epic, dramatic and lyric poetry, using mostly verse of different metres, with and without rhyme, but also sometimes plain prose. The whole work is conservative in its message, antiquated in its highly stylized language, and subjective and emotional in its narration, but it might be fascinating for postmodern readers of the nineties. Indeed, Arno Schmidt, the eccentric author of *Zettels Traum* (1970) and well-known rediscoverer of many interesting but forgotten pieces of German literature, valued Fouqué's *Parcival* highly and praised it in his Fouqué biography of 1958. The modern German reception of Wolfram's *Parzival* thus began with a book that was inaccessible to readers for 150 years, a hidden treasure, something like a veiled Grail.

Karl Leberecht Immermann (1796–1840), legal clerk, writer and for five years owner of a private theatre in Düsseldorf, was occupied with the Merlin legend for many years. In 1831–2, he wrote his drama *Merlin. Eine Mythe* under the influence of Goethe, yet was trying to find his own new style.

Immermann never intended his *Merlin* to be produced on stage, although as director of a theatre he would have had the opportunity to do so. Consequently, he subtitled it 'A Myth'. It was not until 1918 that the drama was staged, at the Berlin Volksbühne, by Friedrich Kayssler – for the first and still today the only time. *Merlin* is more of a philosophical drama than a stage play, but is admired by literary scholars and has been praised as 'one of the most noteworthy philosophical productions in the field of German literature' (Weiss 1933, 111), although most Germans have never read or even heard of it.

Immermann's Merlin is a new Messiah and Anti-Christ as well. The main part of the drama is entitled *Der Gral*. Merlin, suspected and threatened on account of his unknown father, has to flee to Britain. He reveals to the hermit and chronicler Placidus (Blaise in French and English romance), that it will be his duty to extricate the Holy Grail, the blood of Christ, from the clan of Titurel and Parzifal, and as the new Messiah to give it into the custody of King Arthur and the knights of the Round Table. Satan (Merlin's father) realizes that he has no power over his son. Merlin appoints Arthur King of the Holy Grail, and leads the king, Ginevra and the knights to Montsalvatsch, which is according to Wolfram's *Parzival* the castle of the Grail, usually translated 'Mount of Salvation'. But, meanwhile, Parzival's father (!) Titurel was warned that the Anti-Christ will approach, and he orders the Grail to be removed to India (a motif first found in Albrecht's *Jüngerer Titurel* and since then familiar to German Grail tradition). In the forest of Briogne Merlin meets the beautiful Niniane and forgets his mission, and Niniane unintentionally imprisons him for eternity, not knowing that the spell cannot be undone. He cannot hear Arthur and his knights crying to the Holy Grail for help and guidance on their search, so all of them die on their quest in a hot desert. In the 'Nachspiel: Merlin der Dulder' ('Epilogue: Merlin, the Sufferer') Satan tempts his son by accusing him of having led Arthur and the knights not to the Grail, but to Hades, and by promising to liberate him. But Merlin turns to God, and dies praying the Pater Noster in repentance.

The rather symbolic, even allegorical, drama portrays the fate of Man who struggles for ambitious plans and unobtainable salvation, and is finally ruined by his own nature. Immermann took the German tradition (Wolfram von Eschenbach, Grail and India, Faust) as his starting point, but changed the legend considerably, for example with the otherwise unheard-of death of the 'Arthurian' Merlin. He also applied Gnostic doctrines, for example, by emphasizing an absolute and un-Christian dualism of God and the Devil fighting against each other. Many scholars praise Immermann's *Merlin* as an oustanding achievement in German poetry, comparing it with Goethe's *Faust* or Wagner's *Parsifal*. Although this high evaluation is not shared by all, there is no doubt that Immermann underlined the Germans' approach to the Merlin legend, their special handling of the person and his myth. He had a great influence on all future treatments of the Merlin legend.

1900 to 1945

Wagner and Wagnerism have dominated the reception of the Arthurian legends in the German-speaking world, with Parzival and the Grail quest as the main focus of attention. Here, Parzival became akin to a medieval brother of Faust, the prototype of a searcher spending his life on a quest. This tradition is found not only in literature (for example in Albrecht Schaeffer's neo-romantic *Parzival* of 1922, a novel in verse), but also in Rudolf Steiner's anthroposophy and in the depth psychology of the C. G. Jung school. But it was not until 1960 that Jung's wife Emma and Marie-Louise von Franz published a comprehensive inter-pretation based on Jung's ideas and presenting the Grail story as a symbolic-mystical 'experience of God'. The Grail itself is related to the alchemist's mystical vessel and therefore to the 'anima', which, in Jung's teachings, is the feminine component contained in every human soul. This interpretation of the Grail myth in terms of Jungian psychology has exercised considerable influence on the creative reception of the Grail material.

Given Wagner's dominance, it is hardly surprising that there have been few German modifications of the Parzival/Parsifal material (Hermand 1962), at least until well into the 1970s. Of course, there were – after San-Marte and Simrock – more modern translations of Wolfram's poem, and there was also a growing number of adaptations of the Parzival/Grail story for young readers (for example by Gerhart Hauptmann 1914), but most of these were of modest quality. Only two Arthurian authors writing in German in the early twentieth century are important enough to be mentioned here: Eduard von Stucken and Wilhelm Kubie.

Eduard von Stucken (1865–1936), born in Moscow as the son of an American-German businessman, was one of the neo-romantic poets, and he composed several poems, epics and dramas, including eight Grail dramas written between 1901 and 1924 and collected under the title *Der Gral. Ein dramatisches Epos* (1924). This Grail cycle was a great success in its day and comprises *Gawan* (1901), *Lanval* (1903), *Lanzelot* (1909), *Merlins Geburt* (1913, later entitled *Lucifer*), *Tristram und Ysolt* (1916), *Das verlorene Ich* ('The Lost Self', 1922, later entitled *Uther Pendragon*), *Zauberer Merlin* (1924) and *Vortigern* (1924). All these plays are full of neo-romantic colouring and often feverish sensuality, but they lack real dramatic impact; they are nowadays more or less forgotten (see Schulze in Kühnel et al. 1982, Schulze in Wapnewski 1986).

Under the pseudonym Wilhelm Kubie, the Austrian writer Willy Ortmann (1890–1948) composed one of the most fascinating German novels on Arthurian themes, *Mummenschanz auf Tintagel* ('Masquerade at Tintagel', first abridged publication 1937, unabridged publication 1947, reprinted in Schmidt 1989). The story is told by the knight Bedivir who presents a sombre view of the downfall of the Arthurian world. There is a strong element of farce in the style, and like many writers of his time Kubie takes a somewhat sarcastic view of ancient myths and visionary ideas. The novel, forgotten for nearly four decades and re-discovered by Schmidt and examined in her dissertation (1989), merits attention as an interesting modern contribution to the Arthurian tradition beside British and American retellings.

The reception of Tristan material in German was slightly different in that authors tried to avoid the influence of Wagner's music drama which, nevertheless, remained dominant (Poletti 1989; for the nineteenth century see Grill 1997). The German translation of Joseph Bédier's *Roman de Tristan et Yseult* (1900; German translation by R. G. Binding 1911) was important in this context. Bédier attempted to reconstruct the 'original' medieval Tristan tradition, retelling and combining all the romances of the twelfth and thirteenth centuries; his book is still popular today, both the French original and the German translation. The Swiss composer Frank Martin took three episodes from Bédier's work for his oratorio *Le Vin herbé* (1938–42; French and German versions). Although *Le Vin herbé* seems to be as far away from Wagner as possible, a close reading of this oratorio reveals that Frank Martin, too, was influenced by Wagner's music drama, probably against his explicit intention.

Beside Stucken's *Tristram und Ysolt* (1916), which was heavily influenced by Wagner, there was one more neo-romantic play that became a success in its day: *Tantris der Narr* by Ernst Hardt (1907), which focuses on the question of Tristan's guilt. Several years later, in the drama *König Hahnrei* ('King Cuckold', 1913), Georg Kaiser presented the story from the point of view of Marke, who is depicted as a self-deceiving fanatic. In the novel *Isolde Weißhand* by Emil Lucka (1909) it is the second Isolde who narrates the story. Thomas Mann used the Tristan legend and Wagner's music drama not for a retelling of the story but as metaphors in his novella *Tristan* (1903). A detailed comparison of the various medieval and modern Tristan versions, with reference to the lovers' confessing their love to each other, has been undertaken by Alexander Schwarz (1984).

Denis de Rougemont's treatise *L'Amour et l'occident* (1939) drew on the story of Tristan's and Isolde's love to illustrate the thesis that European mentality has been dominated by a 'myth of passion' and a longing for self-destruction. Although not translated into German until 1960 (*Die Liebe und das Abendland*), this work by the Swiss author has strongly influenced the German reception of the Tristan legend.

1945 to the Present

Following a period of only modest interest in Arthurian topics in the decades immediately after the Second World War, the Arthurian legends have attracted ever more attention in the German-speaking world since the end of the 1970s. The recent 'comeback' of King Arthur in German is largely due to the socio-political climate in the last decades of the century, which has brought a new recognition of the relevance of the Arthurian myth and a literary reassessment of its related legends (Wunderlich 1991). Distrust of the effects of nuclear power, concerns about the deterioration of the environment, natural catastrophes, fear of war itself, the collapse of powerful ideological and political systems, all these have influenced personal and public belief so that nightmarish visions of a tormented future exist beside a deep-rooted desire for a solution in which hope, peace, idyllic nature and brotherhood are united. Attempts to articulate these concerns can find a fruitful source of inspiration in the world of King Arthur and the Holy Grail and in the world of the wizard and magician Merlin. At the same time, the often fragmented interactions of past and present, myth and history, fiction and 'reality' which characterize recent reinterpretations of Arthurian material are also key features of postmodernism as a broader phenomenon in contemporary European and American culture.

The recent growth of German interest indeed owes much to America. The 'medievalism' of the Kennedy era brought a reinforcement and adaptation of the Arthurian myth. Moreover, the myth is open to radically different interpretations: on the one hand, an optimistic, confident view of the future, a vision of Utopia, and, on the other hand, its converse, the pessimism of dystopia, which denies any hope of perfection. Modern Arthurian writers have incorporated these two basic views in their works.

There is a considerable revival of 'classical' Anglo-American Arthurian literature in new German translations and editions: Thomas Malory, Alfred Tennyson, T. H. White, Mark Twain, John Steinbeck. Tennyson's *Idylls of the King* is a convincing example of the impact of this revival on German writers. Arno Schmidt's *magnum opus*, the voluminous novel *Zettels Traum* ('Bottom's Dream', 1970), uses many quotations from the fable of Merlin and Viviane. There are also translations of recent novels by Walker Percy (*Lancelot*), David Lodge (*Small World*; German title *Schnitzeljagd*) and Robert Ludlum (*The Parsifal Syndrome*) which transpose Arthurian figures, motifs and themes into contemporary plots and literary genres. During the past few years German translations of popular foreign books on Arthurian themes have enjoyed some favour, such as those by Geoffrey Ashe, Nikolai Tolstoy, Graham Phillips and Martin Keatman, or Norma Lorre Goodrich, which have influenced similar works in German by, for example, Wilfried Westphal (*'Einst wird kommen ein König. . .' Artus – Wahrheit und Legende*, 1989), Franz Baumer (*König Artus und sein Zauberreich. Eine Reise zu den Ursprüngen*, 1991) and Heinz Ohff (*Artus. Biographie einer Legende*, 1993). These works show not only a common interest in historical subjects in general, but also the impact of modern esoteric and feminist ideas on the interpretation of Arthurian topics.

But, above all, translations of works of fantasy imported from the USA and the UK have had an unbroken record of success in Germany (Wunderlich 1986, Müller in Kühnel et al. 1988). This remarkable success has been supported by films like *The Knights of the Round Table, Ivanhoe, Camelot* (the film, not the musical of 1960), the satirical *Monty Python and the Holy Grail*, John Boorman's *Excalibur*, George Lucas and Steven Spielberg's *Indiana Jones and the Last Crusade* and William Nicholson's *First Knight*, which attracted a remarkable response in Germany, much stronger than for other Arthurian films from Hollywood, France or even Germany (for 'Arthurian cinema' see Harty 1991).

In addition, role-playing games and computer games with Arthurian themes can be found in German software shops. British and American novelists who have treated Arthurian subjects at a variety of levels, such as Thomas Berger, Gillian Bradshaw, Vera Chapman, Hannah Closs, Park Godwin, Stephen R. Lawhead, Rob MacGregor, Naomi Mitchison, Richard Monaco, Sharan Newman, Anthony Price, Susan Shwartz, Mary Stewart, Harold Warner Munn and Marion Zimmer Bradley (most of them translated into German) have no real home-based competitors on the German market.

Similarly, juvenile Arthurian books by Susan Cooper and Rosemary Sutcliff are more popular in Germany than Arthurian tales by Käthe Recheis, W. J. M. Wippersberg, Auguste Lechner, Ulla Leipe, Erika Dühnfort and F. Hofbauer. Above all, Harold Foster's *Prince Valiant* series has enjoyed a long run of success in comics and paperbacks since the fifties (German title *Prinz Eisenherz*).

Arthurian Dramas

By far the most successful German dramatic version of the Arthurian legends was written by Tankred Dorst and Ursula Ehler: *Merlin oder Das wüste Land* ('Merlin or The Waste Land'), first produced in 1981. The literary sources are Malory's *Morte D'Arthur* (1485) and Wolfram's *Parzival*, William Rowley's *The Birth of Merlin* (1662), Karl Immermann's *Merlin* (1832), T. H. White's *The Once and Future King* (1939–58) and T. S. Eliot's *The Waste Land* (1922). In addition, there are quotations from Mark Twain's *A Connecticut Yankee in King Arthur's Court* (1889), San-Marte's collection of stories of Merlin (1853) and Alfred Tennyson's poem 'The Holy Grail' (1869).

The ninety-seven scenes of the drama tell the story from Merlin's birth to the end of the Arthurian world. An unabridged performance of this play, which combines dramatic, epic and lyric elements, would take about twelve hours or even longer. Its partly revue-like style is due to initial plans to stage an Arthurian production (directed by Peter Zadek) in a huge hall in Hamburg, which had been used hitherto for commercial purposes ('Fisch-Halle'). After this plan had failed the two authors developed their *Merlin* into a drama of monumental dimensions.

Merlin, the son of the Devil, disobeys his father's command that he should lead mankind astray. Instead, he offers the idea of the Round Table as a Utopian vision of peace and justice which will be brought into being by Arthur. Merlin's plan, however, is doomed from the beginning: it can only disintegrate because it focuses on the pragmatic solving of conflicts, ignoring the imperative to fulfil elementary and essential needs. Power, ruthless ambition, treachery and erotic entanglement prevent the realization of Merlin's Utopia. Even the quest for the Grail – a compensation for deficiencies in Arthur's world – fails. It becomes manifest that the Utopias have no realistic chance of surviving; they are sure to be destroyed by those who participate in them (see Krohn 1984, Knapp 1988).

The authors' use of the Arthurian myth reveals its relevance as a parable of how present-day desires for an ordered society and a secure future are disrupted by conflict. They pinpoint the confrontation between rebellious sons and pragmatic fathers that has been a feature of the socio-political scene since the late sixties. Indeed, recent history shows that Utopian ideals crumble away when they are beset by growing fears of war or environmental catastrophe and replaced by a desire to flee into some kind of alternative world.

Dorst and Ehler's *Merlin* has been a theatrical success, and there are still new productions of this monumental play. It also influenced new adaptations: a parody written by Wolfgang Buhl; a 'jazz oratorio' for television, *The Holy Grail of Jazz and Joy* by George Gruntz in 1985 (who composed the music for the performance of *Merlin* in Zurich in 1983); and alternative stage-productions, for example in West Berlin *Artus Suchbild* ('Wanted: King Arthur', 1986), and in Hanover *König Artus oder Aufstieg und Fall des Abendlandes* ('King Arthur or the Rise and Fall of the West', 1992). The Arthurian legend has even received treatment in ballet form with, for example, a highly praised production by John Neumeier (*Arthur,* Hamburg State Opera 1982, revised in 1986), and *Warlock* by Lothar Höffgen (Hanover State Theatre 1984). Earlier German dramas about Arthur have been quickly forgotten, for example plays by Rudolf Fahrner (*Launcelot*, 1971), Käthe Wolf-Feuer (*Parcival-Spiel*, 1974, with music) and Ernst von Cramer (*Einst und in alle Zukunft König* = 'The Once and Future King', 1982).

It is in keeping with German tradition that Parzival is the central character in many dramas, for example Hermann Schwemmer's *Parzival. Ein geistliches Spiel zur Vergegenwärtigung der mittelalterlichen Dichtung des Wolfram von Eschenbach* ('A Spiritual Play to Represent the Medieval Poem of Wolfram von Eschenbach', 1948); Arthur Maximilian Miller's *Der Gral* (1976); *Flechtungen. Der Fall Partzifall* ('Weavings: The Partzifall Case', 1978), an impressive and successful production by the German experimental theatrical group Werkhaus Moosach near Munich, which transposes Wolfram's hero into a schizophrenic character and which was also presented at the LaMama Theatre in New York; Nathalie Harder's puppet play *Recht Mitten Hindurch: Parzival, eine Miniature nach Wolfram von Eschenbach. Ein Traum aus dem Mittelalter* (Berlin, 1979; see Wagemann 1998); Beda Percht's enigmatic 'performance' *Performing Parzival* (Salzburg, 1993; see Eder 1994); Walter Müller's retelling of the story of Parzival for a juvenile audience (*Ein Parzival*, Salzburg, 1994; see Müller and Westreicher 1995); and *Parzival,* an 'opéra de chambre' conceived by Adriana Hölszky and Simon Wehrle (Gießen, 1999).

However, the most successful adaptions of the Parzival story were again written by Tankred Dorst and Ursula Ehler. Parzival disappears from the scene two-thirds of the way through the drama *Merlin*, because the Grail legend as told by Malory is incompatible with Wolfram's version. But Dorst and Ehler focus on Parzival in later works: *Der Wilde*, a scenario for a Parzival film (which has not yet been produced); *Der nackte Mann* (1986), a story originally intended as an interlude for *Merlin* (Blank 1989); and – above all – a highly successful staging by Robert Wilson at the Hamburg Thalia Theatre: *Parzival. Auf der anderen Seite des Sees* ('Parzival: On the Other Side of the Lake', 1987). The two authors and Robert Wilson have here used the medieval legend to express modern scepticism.

Parzival has thus remained a favourite symbolic figure for the German reception of Arthurian material. But he is no longer a saviour and redeemer. In Peter Handke's parable play *Das Spiel vom Fragen oder Die Reise zum sonoren Land* ('The Play of Questioning, or the Voyage to the Sonorous Land', 1989), Parzival is a nihilist, whose 'action' resides in fragmented and disordered conversations. The Austrian writer Handke treats the themes of communication breakdown and the crisis of language. His protagonist is the prototypical seeker and questioner. He makes his journey with seven companions, and their quest is for the 'Grail of Meaning'. But at the end Handke's Parzival is disillusioned and demoralized: all the questions he has put have elicited only wrong answers.

Unlike Dorst/Ehler and Handke, Christoph Hein had no intention of stressing the contemporary relevance of the myths of Parzival and Arthur. Instead, he presented, also in 1989, socio-political criticism disguised as an Arthurian masquerade. His comedy *Die Ritter der Tafelrunde* ('The Knights of the Round Table') concentrates on several figures of the Arthurian legend: Arthur, Parzival, Lancelot, Orilus, Kay, Mordred, Guinevere and Cunneware. Almost all of them have grown old and become a group of geriatric blockheads who have not yet realized that the quest for their Holy Grail must inevitably be fruitless. All that Parzival can do is to comment, as the publisher of an Arthurian journal, on the economic and political bankruptcy of the outdated ideal of the Round Table. Only Mordred, the rebellious and angry young man, offers some hope for the future. Hein's comedy, written and staged in the German Democratic Republic (Leipzig, April 1989), aroused special interest because it was understood as an only slightly hidden analysis and critique of the ruling class in the GDR (see Müller and Joschko in Burg et al. 1991). The comedy may be called '*the* drama of the "Wende"', but it can also be read as a sardonic commentary on geriatric societies in general, an interpretation which was later confirmed by Hein's play *In Acht und Bann* ('Outlawed', or 'Condemned', 1999), which presents the Arthurian knights as prisoners 'playing' politics in jail.

Several years later the Austrian writer Julian Schutting published *Gralslicht. Ein Theater-Libretto* ('Grail's Light: A Theatre-Libretto', 1994), combining medieval motifs and Wagner. In a railway compartment in the late nineteenth century, three persons called P(arsifal), G (Don Giovanni), and K(undry) discuss the problems of love; their controversial talk finally ends in modern fascism. At the same time, the Austrian artist Konrad Becker wrote and directed *Parzival*, describing the play as 'A Ritualistic Opera after Wolfram von Eschenbach' (Vienna 1994); it belongs to the esoteric branch of the modern Arthurian tradition, which flourishes especially in the UK and Ireland (see below for German examples).

Arthurian novels and poetry

Parzival is also a symbolic figure and a leading character in German Arthurian novels of the period since the Second World War. The authors adopt extremely different approaches to the Arthurian material. Lily Hohenstein's *Ich, Wolfram von Eschenbach* (1958) transposes the romance to a medieval setting and depicts Wolfram as a secularized Parzival who portrays himself in the protagonist of his work. Werner Heiduczek presents a highly modernized retelling of Wolfram's romance in *Die seltsamen Abenteuer des Parzival* (1974), which is this GDR novelist's most successful book. *Die Kinder des Grals* ('The Grail's Children', 1991), by Peter Berling, is a mixture of fantasy and historical novel about events in the year 1244. Heinz Ritter-Schaumburg's *Der Traum vom Gralsfelsen* ('The Dream of the Grail Rock', 1982) tells of a journey to Mount Ararat, here identified with Camelot; the novel is marred by pseudo-philosophical effusions about Progress and the Past. *Professor Parsifal* (1985), by Frido Mann (grandson of Thomas Mann), uses the narrative structure of the Grail quest to treat autobiographical issues. The story is presented as the protagonist's passionate search to find himself. Elements of Arthur's story (not Parzival's) were used by the feminist writer Incape (i.e. Petra) Künkel; her book *auf der reise nach avalun* ('On the Way to Avalon', 1982) is a montage of poems and prose texts which depict the attempt of a group of women to find a better, matriarchal world in 'avalun'.

The most important, impressive and successful narratives and novels using the character of Parzival and the Arthurian tradition have been produced in this period by Dieter Kühn, Adolf Muschg and Alois Brandstetter, authors from Germany, Switzerland and Austria.

Dieter Kühn's *Der Parzival des Wolfram von Eschenbach* (1986) combines the imaginative and the academic to create a new genre of literary biography – Kühn has published similar books about the medieval authors Oswald von Wolkenstein (1977) and Neidhart (1981). His *Parzival* begins with the author's own intensely personal quest for the medieval poet. The book deals with the epoch, life and work of Wolfram, mixing narrative fiction and historical facts into 'faction'. The second part of the book provides an extremely fine modern version of Wolfram's epic, using unrhymed verse, elegant in form and scrupulous in vocabulary. Kühn cuts about 5,000 lines of the original text, an excision which has Gawan as its primary casualty. A complete Parzival translation by Kühn was later published in a bilingual edition prepared by Eberhard Nellmann (1994).

In 1993, an excellent prose translation of *Parzival*, worthy of comparison with Wolfram's Middle High German verse, was published by Peter Knecht, while Wolfgang Mohr (one of the leading Wolfram scholars of his day) received much acclaim for his translation into rhyming verse – his translation of 1977 was used for a TV production of *Parzival* by Richard Blank (1980) and a radio series conceived by Peter Wapnewski (Berlin 1995), which was also published in CD form (1997).

An ingenious retelling of Wolfram's *Parzival* was delivered by the Swiss author and professor of German literature Adolf Muschg in 1993: *Der Rote Ritter. Eine Geschichte von Parzival* ('The Red Knight. A Story of Parzival'). He tells the story of Parzival and Gawan, which comprises three generations, with a technique similar to that which Wolfram used for his retelling of Chrétien's romance. Muschg follows his source closely but, nevertheless, makes omissions, additions (sometimes anachronistic and witty) and alterations, and his narrator, like Wolfram's, frequently comments ironically on the events, and addresses the reader and some of the characters. Following a medieval pattern, Muschg's novel is divided into four books of altogether 100 chapters. The table of contents announces that in chapter 100 the mystery of the Grail will be revealed – but no such chapter appears in the actual book. The modern author no longer believes in successful searches. We are not at all sure that Gawan will live 'happily ever after', and the Grail Castle which is finally found by Parzival is a world full of cruelty, injustice and unfeeling coldness.

Alois Brandstetter's *Die Burg* ('The Castle', 1986) does not simply use motifs, but rather employs structures of Arthurian romances in a way comparable to David Lodge's academic novel *Small World* (1984). The hero of the narrative is a teaching assistant of Middle High German who pursues an unsuccessful quest for an academic career, and who comes to realize that his research activities are analogous to the quest of an Arthurian knight. The author, a professor of medieval German literature (University of Klagenfurt, Austria), uses the medieval world as an ironic reflection of an academic career.

Poets as well as prose writers and dramatists have drawn on the Arthurian world in Germany. Eckart Klessmann's 'Botschaften Merlins an Viviane' ('Merlin's Messages for Viviane', 1974) is a poem of seven stanzas about Merlin's bewitching by Viviane. Wolfgang Uhlig uses the Grail symbol in a similar way; in his poem *Gralslicht* ('Grail's Light', 1986) the Grail is stylized into a supernatural object of desire and a shining light, a source of secret knowledge, which only a chosen few can achieve by virtue of self-denial.

Tristan

Post-war literary adaptations of Tristan in German are few and not always of high literary quality. Hans Erich Nossack employs motifs from Gottfried's *Tristan* in his novel *Spätestens im November* ('Wait for November', 1955) where the unconsummated love between a writer and a rich industrialist's wife leads to death. Leo Stettner's play *Tristan und Isôt. Ein Spiel nach einem alten Wandteppich* ('Tristan and Isôt. A Play According to an Old Tapestry', 1964) has the characters step out from a medieval tapestry and perform their love story in the forest. In 1976 the East German historian Bruno Gloger published the novel *Dietrich. Vermutungen um Gottfried von Strassburg* ('Dietrich: Speculations about Gottfried von Strassburg'), adroitly placing Gottfried's fragmentary romance in the frame of a fictional biography of the medieval poet. In 1991 the Swiss writer Hanno Helbling published *Tristans Liebe. Abendstücke* ('Tristan's Love: Evening Serenade'), a postmodern novel which combines fragments of the medieval Tristan legend, Wagner and some contemporary events to reflect on meaningful departures and arrivals.

A particularly amusing and impressive Tristan adaptation is a radio dialogue which was written by Ingomar von Kieseritzky and Karin Bellingkroth, broadcast several times, printed in 1987, and staged as a play: *Tristan und Isolde im Wald von Morois oder Der Zerstreute Diskurs* ('Tristan and Isolde in the Forest of Morois, or The Diffuse Discourse'). The ironic and witty piece depicts the couple in their pseudo-idyllic environment, suggesting that love in isolation, even if paradisal, is impossible.

Interest in the love story of Tristan and Isolde is demonstrated in the surprising number of German retellings (Ruth Schirmer 1969, Günter de Bruyn 1975), and translations (Günter Cramer 1966, Wolfgang Mohr, after Hermann Kurtz, 1980, Xenja von Ertzdorff, Doris Schulz and Carola Volkel 1980, Rüdiger Krohn 1980, Dieter Kühn 1991, Wolfgang Spiewok 1991).

Beside Frank Martin's Tristan oratorio *Le Vin herbé* (see above), which had its first stage performance at the Salzburg Festival in 1948, two other modern compositions have used Tristan material. In *Tristan, Prelude für Klavier, Tonbänder und Orchester* ('Tristan, Prelude for Piano, Tapes and Orchestra', 1973), the German composer Hans Werner Henze quotes the fourteenth-century Italian instrumental dance *Lamento di Tristano*, music by Brahms, Chopin and Wagner, and verses about Isolde's death from Thomas's *Tristan* to evoke the desolation of humanity (Müller 1982); and the Swiss composer Armin Schibler produced *La Folie de Tristan* (1978) as, in his own words, an oratorio-like 'mystère musical'.

Arthurian films

Numerous American and British cinema and television films dealing with Arthurian topics are well known to German audiences (for Arthurian films in general see Harty 1991); and at least film enthusiasts also know the French Arthurian films of Robert Bresson (*Lancelot du Lac*, 1974) and Eric Rohmer (*Perceval le Gallois*, 1978). The only two Arthurian fantasy films made in Germany also deal with the myth of Tristan and Isolde. *Feuer und Schwert* by Veith von Fürstenberg ('Fire and Sword', 1981/2) was produced in Ireland, overlapping in time with John Boorman's *Excalibur* (1981), but unlike Boorman's Arthurian fantasy it was neither an artistic nor a financial success. A recent TV mini-series about this 'eternal love story' (*Tristan und Isolde*, 1998) has received only mixed response.

Parzival is the main character of two acclaimed German movies, both of which use impressive, but different methods of unrealistic stylization (see Müller in Harty 1991). Richard Blank, in his highly stylized TV play *Parzival* (1980), uses the medieval legend to reflect on contemporary problems. And in 1982 Hans Jürgen Syberberg produced Wagner's *Parsifal*, one of the most interesting and exciting opera films ever made. Unlike other opera films, Syberberg's *Parsifal* uses no stage or stage-like scenario, but a gigantic death-mask of Wagner made of concrete, on which the action takes place.

Syberberg's film again emphasized the importance of Wagner's influence on the German reception of the Arthurian legends, which has been characterized by a strong focus on Parzival and his quest. However, the past twenty years have also brought re-evaluations of Wolfram's romance and a growth in popularity of Arthur and the Round Table, inspired by both films and books from Britain and the United States, and by the overwhelming home-bred success of Dorst and Ehler's *Merlin*. The closing years of the millennium were a time of change and diversity in the German-speaking world (and not here alone) when old, powerful ideologies were being questioned, and this situation is reflected in the variety of Arthurian subject matter and its treatment in recent years.

Notes

[1] The adjective 'German' (= 'deutsch') can mean either 'German as a language' or 'belonging to the nation or state of Germany' (or until 1990 the two states of Germany, i.e. the Federal Republic and the German Democratic Republic). For example, although Max Frisch and Peter Handke write in German, they are not 'Germans', but Swiss and Austrian. It would be misleading to call them 'German writers'. It must also be kept in mind that until 1871 there existed no German 'state' according to the modern understanding of the term. We use 'German' in this article mostly to mean the German language; any political meaning will be indicated.

[2] The works in Myller's *Samlung* appeared at separate dates from 1782 (*Nibelungenlied*) onwards. The individual works were then published together as vol. 1 of the *Samlung*, which appeared as a whole in 1784 (the title-page states that the volume was 'Geendiget im Anfang des Februars 1784'), and vol. 2, which appeared in 1785. The Arthurian narratives published by Myller appear (alongside other works) in these two volumes: Wolfram's *Parzival* in vol. 1, Gottfried's *Tristan* with Heinrich von Freiberg's continuation, and Hartmann's *Iwein* (as *Twein*) in vol. 2. Vol. 3 remained incomplete. It contains only the one section, Konrad von Würzburg's *Trojanerkrieg*, vv. 1–25245), which is not dated but which generally appears in catalogues as *c.* 1785. Erduin Julius Koch was to have completed the collection but he never did so (see V. Mertens, 'Bodmer und die Folgen', in G. Althoff, ed., *Die Deutschen und ihr Mittelalter*, Darmstadt, 1992, 50–80, 186–93, here 64f.). The complicated and incomplete nature of Myller's *Samlung* as a publication accounts for the various ways it appears in bibliographical references, as either a two- or three-volume work, and with starting dates ranging from 1782 to 1784.

[3] The different spellings of this name (Perceval, Perzival, Parsifal) have often led to confusion. Wolfram's source, *Li contes del graal* by Chrétien de Troyes, uses the name 'Perceval' (in the MSS also spelled and named 'Percheval', 'Perchevax' etc.), and so do Chrétien's French continuators and the later French Grail tradition. The hero's name in the manuscripts of Wolfram's poem is 'Parzival', written with c/s and f/v, and it should be pronounced /Partsifal/. Wagner mentions 'Parzival' as King of the Grail and Lohengrin's father in his romantic opera *Lohengrin*. In creating his music drama *Parsifal* he calls him first also 'Parzival', but decides later to use the spelling 'Parsifal'. Wagner used an etymology (Arabic *fal parsi* = 'pure fool') conceived by the German historian and journalist Joseph Görres, which was at first widely accepted, but later proved incorrect; when Wagner was informed by Judith Gautier about the new state of knowledge, he decided to leave everything as it was, and explained that there would probably be no Arabic philology specialists in his future audience.

Bibliography

Primary Sources

The year of first publication or performance of primary works is provided in the text. Further bibliographical information on most of the works mentioned in this survey can be found in Lacy 1996.

Other Literature

Blank, W. 1989. 'Schuld im *Nackten Mann*. Hoffnung wider alle Erwartung? Zu Tankred Dorsts *Parzival*-Geschichte', *Euph*, 83, 28–48.
Burg, I. von et al., eds. 1991. *Mittelalter-Rezeption IV: Medien, Politik, Ideologie, Ökonomie*, GAG, 550, Göppingen.
Eder, A. 1994. '"Performing Parzival". Dokumentation eines Versuches an der Universität Salzburg', in Bader, A. et al., eds., *Sprachspiel und Lachkultur. Rolf Bräuer zum 60. Geburtstag*, Stuttgarter Arbeiten zur Germanistik, 300, Stuttgart.
Gamerschlag, K., ed. 1991. *Moderne Artus-Rezeption 18.–20. Jahrhundert*, GAG, 548, Göppingen.
Gentry, F. G. and Müller, U. 1991. 'The Reception of the Middle Ages in Germany: An Overview', *StMed*, 3, 399–422.
Golther, W. 1907. *Tristan und Isolde in den Dichtungen des Mittelalters und der neuen Zeit*, Leipzig.

Golther, W. 1925. *Parzival und der Gral in der Dichtung des Mittelalters und der Neuzeit*, Stuttgart.

Grill, D. 1997. *Tristan-Dramen des 19. Jahrhunderts*, GAG, 642, Göppingen.

Grimm, G. and Hermand, J., eds. 1991. *Re-reading Wagner*, Madison.

Grosse, S. and Rautenberg, U. 1989. *Die Rezeption mittelalterlicher deutscher Dichtung. Eine Bibliographie ihrer Übersetzungen und Bearbeitungen seit der Mitte des 18. Jahrhunderts*, Tübingen.

Harty, K. J., ed. 1991. *Cinema Arthuriana: Essays on Arthurian Film*, Garland Reference Library of the Humanities, 1, New York, London.

Harty, K. J. 1999. *The Reel Middle Ages: American, Western and Eastern European, Middle Eastern and Asian Films about Medieval Europe*, Jefferson, NC.

Hasty, W., ed. 1999. *A Companion to Wolfram's 'Parzival'*, Rochester, NY and Woodbridge.

Hermand, J. 1962. 'Gralsmotive um die Jahrhundertwende', *DVj*, 36, 521–43.

Joschko, D. 1991. 'Christoph Heins *Die Ritter der Tafelrunde*: oder: Grals-Suche zwischen Auf- und Abbruch', in Burg et al. 1991, 525–41.

Katz, J. 1986. *The Darker Side of Genius: Richard Wagner's Antisemitism*, Hanover and London.

Kimpel, R. W. 1996. 'German Arthurian Literature (Modern)', in Lacy 1996, 188–94.

Knapp, G. R. 1988. 'Grenzgang zwischen Mythos, Utopie und Geschichte. Tankred Dorsts *Merlin* und sein Verhältnis zur literarischen Tradition', *ABäG*, 24, 225–60.

Krohn, R. 1984. 'Die Geschichte widerlegt die Utopie? Zur Aktualität von Tankred Dorsts Bühnenspektakel *Merlin oder Das wüste Land*', *Euph*, 78, 160–79.

Krohn, R., ed. 1986. *Forum. Materialien und Beiträge zur Mittelalter-Rezeption 1*, GAG, 360, Göppingen.

Krohn, R., ed. 1992. *Forum. Materialien und Beiträge zur Mittelalter-Rezeption 3*, GAG, 540, Göppingen.

Kühnel, J. 1991. 'Wagners *Parsifal* – ein antisemitisches Werk?' *Parsifal* programme Vienna State Opera, 49–55.

Kühnel, J. et al., eds. 1979. *Mittelalter-Rezeption [I]. Die Rezeption mittelalterlicher Dichter und ihrer Werke in Literatur, bildender Kunst und Musik des 19. und 20. Jahrhunderts*, GAG, 286, Göppingen.

Kühnel, J. et al., eds. 1982. *Mittelalter-Rezeption II. Die Rezeption des Mittelalters in Literatur, bildender Kunst und Musik des 19. und 20. Jahrhunderts*, GAG, 358, Göppingen.

Kühnel, J. et al., eds., 1988. *Mittelalter-Rezeption III. Mittelalter, Massenmedien, Neue Mythen*, GAG, 479, Göppingen.

Lacy, N. J., ed. 1996. *The New Arthurian Encyclopedia*, updated edn, Garland Reference Library of the Humanities, 931, New York and London.

Müller, U. 1980. 'Parzival und Parsifal. Vom Roman Wolframs von Eschenbach und vom Musikdrama Richard Wagners', in Stein, P. K., ed., *Sprache–Text–Geschichte*, GAG, 304, Göppingen, 479–502.

Müller, U. 1982. 'Mittelalterliche Dichtungen in der Musik des 20. Jahrhunderts III. Das Tristan und Isolde-Oratorium von Frank Martin (nach Joseph Bédier). Mit einem Ausblick auf die Tristan-Komposition von Hans-Werner Henze', in Bauer, W. M. et al., eds., *Tradition und Entwicklung. Festschrift für Eugen Thurnher zum 60. Geburtstag*, Innsbruck.

Müller, U. 1999. 'Wolfram, Wagner, and the Germans', in Hasty 1999, 245–58.

Müller, U. and Verduin, K., eds. 1996. *Mittelalter-Rezeption V / The Year's Work in Medievalism 5*, GAG, 630, Göppingen.

Müller, U. and Wapnewski, P., eds. 1992. *Wagner Handbook*, transl. ed. by J. Deathridge, Cambridge, Mass. and London.

Müller, U. und Westreicher, M. 1995. '"Am Anfang war Gewalt". *Ein Parzival* von Walter Müller (1994)', in Lindemann, D. et al., eds., *'bickelwort' und 'wildiu maere'. Festschrift für Eberhard Nellmann zum 65. Geburtstag*, GAG, 618, Göppingen, 167–83.

Poletti, E. 1989. *Love, Honour and Artifice: Attitudes to the Tristan Material in the Medieval Epic Poems and in Selected Plays from 1853–1919*, GAG, 509, Göppingen.

Schmidt, S. 1989. *Mittelhochdeutsche Epenstoffe in der deutschsprachigen Literatur nach 1945. Beobachtungen zur Aufarbeitung des Artus und Parzival-Stoffes in erzählender Literatur für Jugendliche und Erwachsene mit einer Bibliographie der Adaptationen der Stoffkreise Artus, Parzival, Tristan, Gudrun und Nibelungen 1945–1981*, I, GAG, 495, I, Göppingen.

Schwarz, A. 1984. *Sprechaktgeschichte. Studien zu den Liebeserklärungen in mittelalterlichen und modernen Tristandichtungen*, GAG, 398, Göppingen.

Wagemann, A. 1998. *Wolframs von Eschenbach 'Parzival' im 20. Jahrhundert. Untersuchungen zu Wandel und Funktion in Literatur, Theater und Film*, GAG, 646, Göppingen.

Wapnewski, P. 1978. *Der traurige Gott. Richard Wagner in seinen Helden*, Munich.

Wapnewski, P., ed. 1986. *Mittelalter-Rezeption: Ein Symposion*, Germanistische Symposien, 6, Stuttgart.

Weiner, M. A. 1995. *Richard Wagner and the Anti-Semitic Imagination*, Lincoln, Nebr. and London.

Weiss, A. M. 1933. *Merlin in German Literature: A Study of the Merlin Legend in German Literature from Medieval Beginnings to the End of Romanticism*, The Catholic University of America Studies in German, 3, Washington (repr. New York 1970).

Wunderlich, W. 1986. 'Mythen, Märchen und Magie. Ein Streifzug durch die Welt der Fantasyliteratur', *Wirkendes Wort*, 36, 26–34.

Wunderlich, W. 1991. '"Zuviel Durcheinander hier . . ." Literaturkritische Anmerkungen zur Mittelalter-Rezeption 1989', in Burg et al. 1991, 487–94.

Wunderlich, W. 1991. 'The Arthurian Legend in German Literature of the Nineteen-Eighties', *StMed*, 3, 423–42.

Wunderlich, W. and Papendorf, D. C. 1992. 'Bibliographie zur literarischen Rezeption der Artus-Legende im deutschsprachigen Raum 1980–1990', in Krohn 1992, 91–116.

Wynn, M. 1983. 'Medieval Literature in Reception: Richard Wagner and Wolfram's *Parzival*', *London German Studies*, 2, 94–114.

GENERAL BIBLIOGRAPHY

The General Bibliography lists chiefly work relating to medieval German Arthurian literature. General works on Dutch Arthurian literature are listed by B. Besamusca in the bibliography to chapter 12 in this volume. For individual German authors see *Die deutsche Literatur des Mittelalters. Verfasserlexikon*, 2nd edition, ed. K Ruh, B. Wachinger et al., Berlin and New York, 1978ff., and *Germanistik. Internationales Referatenorgan mit bibliographischen Hinweisen*, Tübingen 1960ff. For Arthurian literature in general, further guidance can be found in N. J. Lacy, ed., *Medieval Arthurian Literature: A Guide to Recent Research* (1996, see below), and information on current research is provided by the *Bibliographical Bulletin of the International Arthurian Society* (*Bulletin bibliographique de la Société Internationale Arthurienne*), 1949ff.

Bastert, B. 1993. *Der Münchner Hof und Füetrers 'Buch der Abenteuer'. Literarische Kontinuität im Spätmittelalter*, Mikrokosmos, 33, Frankfurt.

Becker, P. J. 1977. *Handschriften und Frühdrucke mittelhochdeutscher Epen. 'Eneide', 'Tristrant', 'Erec', 'Iwein', 'Parzival', 'Willehalm', 'Jüngerer Titurel', 'Nibelungenlied' und ihre Reproduktion und Rezeption im späteren Mittelalter und in der frühen Neuzeit*, Wiesbaden.

Besamusca, B. et al., eds. 1994. *Cyclification: The Development of Narrative Cycles in the Chansons de Geste and the Arthurian Romances*, Koninklijke Nederlandse Akademie van Wetenschappen Verhandelingen, Afd. Letterkunde, Nieuwe Reeks, 159, Amsterdam.

Brunner, H., ed. 1993. *Mittelhochdeutsche Romane und Heldenepen*, Stuttgart.

Bumke, J. 1979. *Mäzene im Mittelalter. Die Gönner und Auftraggeber der höfischen Literatur in Deutschland 1150–1300*, Munich.

Bumke, J. 1986. *Höfische Kultur. Literatur und Gesellschaft im hohen Mittelalter*, 2 vols., Munich. Transl. by T. Dunlop under the title *Courtly Culture and Society in the High Middle Ages*, Berkeley and Los Angeles 1991.

Buschinger, D., ed. 1984. *Lancelot. Actes du Colloque des 14 et 15 janvier 1984*, GAG, 415, Göppingen.

Buschinger, D., ed. 1987. *Tristan et Iseut, mythe européen et mondial. Actes du Colloque des 10, 11 et 12 janvier 1986*, GAG, 474, Göppingen.

Buschinger, D. and Spiewok, W., eds. 1994a. *König Artus und der Heilige Graal*, Wodan, 32, Greifswald.

Buschinger, D. and Spiewok, W., eds. 1994b. *Perceval-Parzival. Hier et aujourd'hui et autres essais sur la littérature allemande du Moyen Age et de la Renaissance. Recueil d'articles assemblés par D. Buschinger und W. Spiewok pour fêter les 95 ans de Jean Fourquet*, Wodan, 48, Greifswald.

Buschinger, D. and Zink, M., eds. 1995. *Lancelot – Lancelet. Hier et aujourd'hui. Recueil d'articles assemblés par Danielle Buschinger et Michel Zink pour fêter les 90 ans d'Alexandre Micha*, Wodan, 51, Greifswald.

Cormeau, Ch. 1977. *'Wigalois' und 'Diu Crône'. Zwei Kapitel zur Gattungsgeschichte des nachklassischen Aventiureromans*, MTU, 57, Munich.

Fleckenstein. J., ed. 1990. *Curialitas. Studien zu Grundfragen der höfisch-ritterlichen Kultur*, Veröffentlichungen des Max-Planck-Instituts für Geschichte, 100, Göttingen.

Gärtner, K. and Heinzle, J., eds. 1989. *Studien zu Wolfram von Eschenbach. Festschrift für Werner Schröder zum 75. Geburtstag*, Tübingen.

Gottzmann, C. L. 1986. *Deutsche Artusdichtung. I. Rittertum, Minne, Ehe, Herrschertum. Die Artuepik der hochhöfischen Zeit*, Information und Interpretation, 2, Frankfurt.

Gottzmann, C. L. 1989. *Artusdichtung*, Sammlung Metzler, 249, Stuttgart.

Green, D. H. 1979. *Irony in the Medieval Romance*, Cambridge.

Grubmüller, K. 1991. 'Der Artusroman und sein König. Beobachtungen zur Artusfigur am Beispiel von Ginovers Entführung', in Haug and Wachinger 1991, 1–20.

Grünkorn, G. 1994. *Die Fiktionalität des höfischen Romans um 1200*, Philologische Studien und Quellen, 129, Berlin.

Gürttler, K. R. 1976. *'künec Artûs der guote'. Das Artusbild in der höfischen Epik des 12. und 13. Jahrhunderts*, Studien zur Germanistik, Anglistik und Komparatistik, 52, Bonn.

Haferland, H. 1988. *Höfische Interaktion. Interpretationen zur höfischen Epik und Didaktik um 1200*, Forschungen zur Geschichte der älteren deutschen Literatur, 10, Munich.

Hasty, W. 1990. *Adventure as Social Performance: A Study of the German Court Epics*, Tübingen.

Haug, W. 1990. *Strukturen als Schlüssel zur Welt. Kleine Schriften zur Erzählliteratur des Mittelalters*, Tübingen.

Haug, W. 1992. *Literaturtheorie im deutschen Mittelalter. Von den Anfängen bis zum Ende des 13. Jahrhunderts*, 2nd edn, Darmstadt.

Haug, W. 1995. *Brechungen auf dem Weg zur Individualität. Kleine Schriften zur Literatur des Mittelalters*, Tübingen.

Haug, W., Heinzle, J., Huschenbett, D. and Ott, N. H. 1982. *Runkelstein. Die Wandmalereien des Sommerhauses*, Wiesbaden.

Haug, W. and Wachinger, B., eds. 1991. *Positionen des Romans im späten Mittelalter*, Fortuna vitrea, 1, Tübingen.

Hoecke, W. van, Tournoy, G. and Verbeke, W., eds. 1991. *Arturus Rex*, II, Mediaevalia Lovaniensia, Ser. I, Studia, 17, Leuven.

Honemann, V., Jones, M. H., Stevens, A. and Wells, D., eds. 1994. *German Narrative Literature of the Twelfth and Thirteenth Centuries: Studies Presented to Roy Wisbey on his Sixty-Fifth Birthday*, Tübingen.

Honemann, V. and Palmer, N. F., eds. 1988. *Deutsche Handschriften 1100–1400. Oxforder Kolloquium 1985*, Tübingen.

Jackson, W. H. 1994. *Chivalry in Twelfth-Century Germany: The Works of Hartmann von Aue*, Arthurian Studies, 34, Cambridge.

Jaeger, C. S. 1985. *The Origins of Courtliness: Civilizing Trends and the Formation of Courtly Ideals, 939–1210*, Philadelphia.

Jones, M. H. and Wisbey, R., eds. 1993. *Chrétien de Troyes and the German Middle Ages: Papers from an International Symposium*, Arthurian Studies, 26 / Publications of the Institute of Germanic Studies, 53, Cambridge and London.

Kaiser, G. and Müller, J.-D., eds. 1986. *Höfische Literatur, Hofgesellschaft, höfische Lebensformen um 1200. Kolloquium am Zentrum für Interdisziplinäre Forschung der Universität Bielefeld (3. bis 5. November 1983)*, Düsseldorf.

Kooper, E., ed. 1994. *Medieval Dutch Literature in its European Context*, Cambridge Studies in Medieval Literature, 21, Cambridge.

Kuhn, H. and Cormeau, Ch., eds. 1973. *Hartmann von Aue*, Wege der Forschung, 359, Darmstadt.

Lacy, N. J. 1996a. *The New Arthurian Encyclopedia*, updated edn, Garland Reference Library of the Humanities, 931, New York and London.

Lacy, N. J., ed. 1996b. *Medieval Arthurian Literature: A Guide to Recent Research*, Garland Reference Library of the Humanities, 1955, New York and London.

Lacy, N. J. and Ashe, G. 1988. 'Modern Arthurian Literature: German Literature', in *The Arthurian Handbook*, New York, London, 162–8.

Loomis, R. S., ed. 1959. *Arthurian Literature in the Middle Ages: A Collaborative History*, Oxford.

Loomis, R. S. and Loomis, L. H. 1938. *Arthurian Legends in Medieval Art*, MLA Monograph Series, New York.

McFarland, T. and Ranawake, S. 1988. *Hartmann von Aue: Changing Perspectives: London Hartmann Symposium 1985*, GAG, 486, Göppingen.

Mertens, V. 1998. *Der deutsche Artusroman*, RUB, 17609, Stuttgart.

Mertens, V. and Wolfzettel, F., eds. 1993. *Fiktionalität im Artusroman. 3. Tagung der deutschen Sektion der Internationalen Artusgesellschaft in Berlin vom 13.–15. Februar 1992*, Tübingen.

Meyer, M. 1994. *Die Verfügbarkeit der Fiktion. Interpretationen und poetologische Untersuchungen zum Artusroman und zur aventiurehaften Dietrichepik des 13. Jahrhunderts*, Beihefte zur *GRM*, 12, 2–19, 271–90.

Mohr, W. 1979. *Wolfram von Eschenbach. Aufsätze*, GAG, 275, Göppingen.

Paravicini, W. 1994. *Die ritterlich-höfische Kultur des Mittelalters*, Enzyklopädie deutscher Geschichte, 32, Munich.

Pérennec, R. 1984. *Recherches sur le roman arthurien en vers en Allemagne aux XIIe et XIIIe siècles*, GAG, 393, 2 vols., Göppingen.

Ruh, K. 1967. *Höfische Epik des deutschen Mittelalters. I. Von den Anfängen bis zu Hartmann von Aue*, Berlin.

Ruh, K. 1980. *Höfische Epik des deutschen Mittelalters. II. 'Reinhart Fuchs', 'Lanzelet', Wolfram von Eschenbach, Gottfried von Straßburg*, Berlin.

Schiewer, H.-J. 1988. '"Ein ris ich dar vmbe brach Von sinem wunder bovme". Beobachtungen zur Überlieferung des nachklassischen Artusromans im 13. und 14. Jahrhundert', in Honemann and Palmer 1988, 222–78.

Schirok, B. 1982. *Parzivalrezeption im Mittelalter*, Erträge der Forschung, 174, Darmstadt.

Schirok, B. 1989. '"Artus der meienbaere man". Zum Stellenwert der "Artuskritik" im klassischen deutschen Artusroman', in Schnell, R., ed., *Gotes und der werlde hulde. Festschrift für Heinz Rupp*, 58–81.

Schultz, J. A. 1983. *The Shape of the Round Table: Structures of Middle High German Arthurian Romance*, Toronto.

Schulze-Belli, P. and Dallapiazza, M., eds. 1990. *Liebe und Aventiure im Artusroman des Mittelalters. Beiträge der Triester Tagung 1988*, Göppingen.

Stevens, A. and Wisbey, R., eds. 1990. *Gottfried von Strassburg and the Medieval Tristan Legend: Papers from an Anglo-North American Colloquium,* Arthurian Studies, 23 / Publications of the Institute of Germanic Studies, 44, Cambridge and London.

Störmer, W. 1972. 'König Artus als aristokratisches Leitbild während des späteren Mittelalters, gezeigt an Beispielen der Ministerialität und des Patriziats', *Zeitschrift für bayerische Landesgeschichte*, 35, 946–71.

Thomas, N. 1989. *The Medieval German Arthuriad: Some Contemporary Revaluations of the Canon*, Berne.

Thomas, N. 1992. *The Defence of Camelot: Ideology and Intertextuality in the 'Post-classical' German Romances of the Matter of Britain Cycle,* Deutsche Literatur von den Anfängen bis 1700, 14, Berne.

Verbeke, W., Janssens, J. and Smeyers, M., eds. 1987. *Arturus Rex*, I: *Catalogus Koning Artur en de Nederlanden. La matière de Bretagne et les anciens Pays-Bas*, Mediaevalia Lovaniensia, Ser. 1, Studia, 16, Leuven.

Wais, K., ed. 1970. *Der Arthurische Roman,*WdF, 157, Darmstadt.

Whitaker, M. 1990. *The Legends of King Arthur in Art*, Arthurian Studies, 22, Cambridge.

Wolfzettel, F., ed. 1984. *Artusrittertum im späten Mittelalter. Vorträge des Symposiums der deutschen Sektion der Internationalen Artusgesellschaft vom 10.–13. Nov. 1983 im Schloß Rauischholzhausen*, Beiträge zur deutschen Philologie, 57, Giessen.

Wolfzettel, F., ed. 1990. *Artusroman und Intertextualität*, Beiträge zur deutschen Philologie, N.S., 67, Giessen.

Wolfzettel, F., ed. 1999. *Erzählstrukturen der Artusliteratur, Forschungsgeschichte und neue Ansätze*, Tübingen.

INDEX